Our Gigantic Zoo

Our Gigantic Zoo

A German Quest to Save the Serengeti

THOMAS M. LEKAN

OXFORD
UNIVERSITY PRESS

OXFORD
UNIVERSITY PRESS

Oxford University Press is a department of the University of Oxford. It furthers
the University's objective of excellence in research, scholarship, and education
by publishing worldwide. Oxford is a registered trade mark of Oxford University
Press in the UK and certain other countries.

Published in the United States of America by Oxford University Press
198 Madison Avenue, New York, NY 10016, United States of America.

© Oxford University Press 2020

CIP data is on file at the Library of Congress
ISBN 978–0–19–984367–1

3 5 7 9 8 6 4 2

Printed by Integrated Books International, United States of America

CONTENTS

PREFACE

This book brings together reflections on nature conservation and the entangled fates of humans and our non-human companions that have been simmering for decades. *Our Gigantic Zoo: A German Quest to Save the Serengeti* focuses on the environmental-historical significance of the former Frankfurt Zoological Society director Bernhard Grzimek, who was arguably Europe's most important wildlife conservationist of the twentieth century. Germans from both sides of the wall remember him primarily for his Sunday night television program *A Place for Animals*, the longest running show in German history (1956–1987), and the documentary *Serengeti Shall Not Die* (1959) produced with his son Michael. The film prompted Western audiences to send donations to protect the Serengeti and other national parks in Africa, but this book shows that the real sacrifice came from East Africans, particularly the pastoralist groups who had to leave their homelands to make room for tourists or the urbanites who paid the taxes that subsidized the park system's roads, lodges, and staff salaries. Grzimek's "troubles with wilderness" were not the same as those of more celebrated preservationists such as John Muir or Julian Huxley. As a veterinarian and former agricultural minister, Grzimek understood better than most the connections between ecological protection at home and abroad; he fought just as hard to save chickens from industrialized slaughter in Europe as he did to preserve endangered black rhinos in the Ngorongoro Crater in Tanzania.

Our Gigantic Zoo is a product of deep ambivalence about my own fascination with "celebrity conservationists" and media images of creatures great and small during roughly the same years that Grzimek was at the height of his influence. Viewing long-forgotten episodes of *A Place for Animals*, I'm reminded of my favorite television program of the 1970s: Mutual of Omaha's *Wild Kingdom*, hosted by Marlin Perkins of the St. Louis Zoo. My parents thought the show would satisfy my scientific curiosity, and the safe and harmonious animal scenes appeared resolutely apolitical during a time when they worried about the violent images of the war in Vietnam appearing on the nightly news. Perkins always left his sidekick Jim Fowler to do all the dangerous work with animals, and Jim's antics served as the perfect segue to selling life insurance (*Jim may not escape the jaws of the Upper Nile crocodile, but you can protect YOUR family by contacting Mutual of Omaha about a life insurance policy . . .*).

I did not know Grzimek the celebrity as a child; few North Americans did, though many German historians credit him with transforming the straitlaced boys and girls of the Adenauer years into the firebrand Green activists of the 1970s. Indeed, as he developed the show over the late 1960s and 1970s, Grzimek became much more activist, calling on his fellow West Germans to "risk more democracy" in ways that Perkins's corporate-sponsored *Wild Kingdom* would never dare. Yet I recognize now that *A Place for Animals* and *Serengeti Shall Not Die* confined scenes of danger and death to the "natural" give-and-take between predator and prey in the African savannas. The human-on-human violence triggered by the legacies of European colonialism, anti-imperialist struggles, Cold War proxy wars, and the land alienations needed to create national parks in sub-Saharan Africa and elsewhere never made it to the screen. *That* violence came from the realm of politics, and I accepted that the ecological crisis facing humanity was above these fleeting concerns. All I knew as a teenager was that beloved charismatic mammals were endangered, and that was enough for me to send small donations to the World Wildlife Fund, to study marine ecology and anthropology in Australia, and to work in environmental policy in Washington, DC, in the early 1990s. For various reasons, I became disillusioned with the quantitative quagmire of policy work and turned toward humanities perspectives. Projects about "managing" hazardous wastes or "mitigating" wetland destruction largely involved trying to determine an acceptable number of cancer deaths or putting a price tag on aesthetic experiences for cost-benefit analyses— a prelude to the "ecosystem services" approach that now dominates conservation in the neoliberal era. As I show in the pages that follow, this approach had its origins in the early 1960s as former imperial conservationists tried to sell African leaders on the benefits of wildlife for their newly independent countries.

As I began to fashion a second monograph, I imagined it initially as a kind of sequel to my first one on landscape preservation and national and regional identities in Germany. I had not dealt sufficiently with the issue of tourism in the first book, especially given Germans' well-known penchant for seeking out nature and wilderness abroad (a real glimpse of this came on a trip to Bryce Canyon National Park in June 2007, where the gift shop's checkout counter had another sign affixed to it: *Kasse*). Inspired by Samuel Hays's insights about the relationship between white-collar consumerism and the post-material values that spurred modern environmentalism, I wanted to know how the dialectic between consumption and conservation in so-called soft or green tourism informed twentieth-century German environmentalism. And so, with Hasso Spode's help, I began to look into the huge array of tourist guidebooks and tourist ephemera about German landscapes found at the Historical Archive of Tourism in Berlin and put together a first draft of a monograph during a generous leave made possible by an American Council of Learned Societies fellowship in 2006–2007.

While reading hiking guides to the Black Forest, I was drawn to the shelves of German-language guidebooks about foreign destinations and how these guidebooks framed places such as Africa, South America, and Asia for German-speaking visitors—a project for another time, I thought. I knew that Grzimek was a critical figure in postwar German environmentalism and tourism promotion, famous for encouraging tourists to save Africa's precious wildlife by booking package tours to the Serengeti, but I imagined that he would take up a chapter of the book—nothing more. In 2008–2009, I had done talks on Grzimek and his role in developing East African tourism at the American Society for Environmental History in Tallahassee, Florida, the "Chasing Eden" workshop at the University of Exeter, the Harvard German Studies Seminar, and as the Dante Lecturer at Manhattan College. The feedback at those venues was encouraging: many thanks to Timothy Cooper and Gregg Mitman for their comments on media and environmental activism and to Chris Conte, Gregory Maddox, Roderick Neumann, Jamie Monson, and Thaddeus Sunseri for underscoring Grzimek's importance to environmental historians of Tanzania. Thaddeus remained unbelievably generous with his advice thereafter, critiquing and serving as referee for grant applications and reading chapters of the draft manuscript. His deep knowledge of East African social history, forest reserves, disease impacts, and cattle cultures have informed this book; any mistakes in connecting the dots remain my own.

When I took up a fellowship at Princeton's Davis Center for Historical Studies in 2009, I decided to focus on the Grzimek chapters first, since his story fit the Center's theme of "Cultures and Institutions in Motion." I soon realized that Grzimek's engagement in the Serengeti revealed a much deeper story about Germany's colonial past in East Africa and the German-German rivalry during the Cold War that made tourism history especially exciting and provocative. My fellow scholars and mentors at the Davis Center, including Dan Rodgers, Jolie Olcott, Mary Nolan, and Pamela Smith, came to the same conclusion that my mentor and friend at the German Historical Institute in Washington, DC, Christof Mauch, had observed when I started the project: "You really should make Grzimek and East Africa the center of the story."

I loved the idea of engaging this material through a transnational lens, but I knew that writing a book of that scope would encompass unfamiliar histories and historiographies of African landscapes and decolonization that were not part of my toolkit in 2009. Luckily enough, new opportunities and new synergies emerged that made me more confident I could meet some of these challenges. A year at the National Humanities Center (NHC) on a Delta Delta Delta fellowship brought me into a reading group of fellow fellows that helped to launch this book with keen insights and fantastic writing advice, including Mia Bay, Jared Farmer, David Schoenbrun, and Ellen Stroud. Thanks to the efforts of former co-director Kent Mullikin to promote the environmental humanities, the Center arranged visits from former NHC fellows Stuart Marks and Shepard Krech III, both of whose works have been foundational for studies of indigenous peoples and environmental history. Professors Marks and Krech encouraged my thinking about the relationship between German imperial conservation, pastoralism, and national parks. Without the assistance of Jean Houston and the library staff at the NHC, I could never have made rapid progress on what became an intensive reading year.

In the summer of 2010, during a seminar on German sustainability strategies in Berlin, I happened to meet the renowned historian of German development studies Hubertus Büschel, who alerted me to a large cache of documents at the Political Archive of the German Foreign Office (Auswärtiges Amts) focused on West Germany's evolving Cold War relationship to the former "German East Africa" (Tanganyika) and Grzimek's activities there from 1959 onward. The documents at the Foreign Office archive were far more extensive that I could have imagined or hoped for: many thanks to Hubertus and to the University of South Carolina's Walker Institute for supporting my archival investigations in Berlin. These files detailed the "wildlife diplomacy" that Grzimek practiced in the early 1960s as Honorary Curator of Tanganyika National Parks, just as the Federal Republic was seeking to expand its influence and legitimacy through "technical assistance" to former British colonial territories in the developing world. It was clear from these documents that Grzimek's work had a diplomatic and environmental import far beyond Germany's borders, an impression amplified by my investigation of the international outreach of the Frankfurt Zoological Society housed at the Frankfurt Institut für Stadtgeschichte (Institute for the History of Frankfurt). Many thanks to archivist Frau Ute Schumacher in Frankfurt, who was initially alarmed at the high number of digital copies I ordered from the city archive's fantastic collection. These documents, along with those from the political archive in Berlin, form the backbone of chapters 6 and 7's discussions of Grzimek as a broker for the rights of animals during the first decade of independence in Tanganyika/Tanzania.

The summer of 2010 also brought me into contact with the Frankfurt Zoological Society staff and archives. Many thanks to Dr. Dagmar Andres-Brümmer, the communications director for the Frankfurt Zoological Society, who shared her insights about Grzimek's work and allowed me access to the Society's then not-yet-registered basement of documents. For those interested in the Society's work beyond 1970 and in Grzimek's activities in Sudan, Uganda, and in the former Zaïre, there is much to be gained from these folios. Though I spent many weeks with these materials, I did not incorporate them into the narrative or citations in this book.

A University of South Carolina Provost Humanities Grant enabled me to travel to Tanzania in 2011 and 2012 to follow Grzimek's story outside his "homeland" and assess its impact on communities, landscapes, and animals in the German–African contact zone of the 1960s. I used the rich repositories found in the Secretariat files of the Serengeti Board of Trustees at the Tanzanian National Archive; the tourist guidebook collection at the Tanzanian National Library; and the newspapers, pamphlets, government documents, and consultancy reports found in the East Africana Collection at the University of Dar es Salaam Library, particularly the special collection of papers from rural sociologist Henry E. Fosbrooke, the former Head Conservator of the Ngorongoro Conservation Area. These documents form the backbone of chapter 5 on the Serengeti controversies of 1951–1960 and the relationship between national park expansion and villagization mentioned in chapter 7. Thank you, Bernhard Gissibl and Thaddeus Sunseri, for helping me to navigate the Tanzanian collections.

I wish to acknowledge Mr. Mashuhuri Mwinyihamis and the Tanzania Commission for Science and Technology (COSTECH) for granting me permission to conduct research in Tanzania. Heartfelt thanks to Dr. Adalgot Komba, the former director of the University of Dar es Salaam's Development Studies Institute, for his willingness to serve as sponsor for my work there and for sharing his insights about traditional ecological knowledge and development. Many thanks also to Dr. Samuel Mhajida, now a lecturer in history at the University of Dar es Salaam, who assisted me in the National Archives. During my stays in Arusha, many individuals took the time to share with me in conversation their perspectives on Grzimek and the controversial legacies of national park development: Dr. Markus Borner, the former director of the Frankfurt Zoological Society's Africa Programme; Dr. Dennis Rentsch, a technical advisor for an EU-funded Serengeti Ecosystem Management Program; Mr. Navaya ole Ndaskoi, Mr. William Tate Olenasha, and the late Mr. Lazaro Moringe Parkipuny, all associated at the time with the Pastoralists Indigenous Non-Governmental Organizations (PINGO's) Forum. The divergent perspectives in these conversations reminded me that histories of conservation in East Africa are always what my friend Michel Pimbert has called "histories of the present." So many traces of German colonialism and development assistance written on the landscapes and in the memories of the people I met, so many different views of Bernhard Grzimek himself and the controversies over the Serengeti, as if they had happened a few years ago, rather than decades hence.

A fellowship from the Rachel Carson Center for Environment and Society (RCC) in Munich in 2013, the directorship of the University of South Carolina's College of Arts and Sciences History Center (theme: Transnational Histories), and a University of South Carolina semester-long sabbatical leave and Associate Development Award in 2015–2016 allowed me to synthesize these dispersed archival collections and draft the book's core chapters. Many thanks to co-director Helmuth Trischler and associate director Rob Emmett for allowing me to present and receive feedback on my work and for the advice and encouragement of fellow fellows Ellen Arnold, Lawrence Culver, John Meyer, Karen Oslund, Chris Pastore, Sabine Wilke, and, especially, longtime friend Thomas Zeller, who subsequently read and critiqued several chapters. The RCC helped my History Center to co-sponsor a week-long visit by Dipesh Chakrabarty and to publish a short volume on his "Four Theses of Climate History": many thanks to Prof. Chakrabarty for helping me to stay on target when it came to thinking about the different scales, ontologies, and political investments of the "planetary" versus the "global." A summer fellowship at the Max Planck Institute for the History of Science in Berlin, made possible by Senior Research Scholar Wilko Graf von Hardenberg and the Head of Department III, Dagmar Schäfer, allowed me time to introduce "baseline" thinking into chapter 5. The summer fellowship also allowed me to respond to the generous comments of the manuscript reviewers, whose sage advice on cutting the fat, integrating indigenous histories, and developing the park as a voice has improved the manuscript. Gaps unfortunately still remain—particularly on the textures of African social histories of the environment—but the specific references to additional secondary work were invaluable.

I would also like to thank a number of friends who took time out to read and critique individual chapters: Sandra Chaney, Kay Edwards, Laura Foxworth, Matt Melvin-Koushki, and especially Josh Grace, who shared his immense knowledge of Tanzanian histories of technology and sustainable development with me. Chapter 7 would not have been possible without Josh's "new materialist" perspectives. Heartfelt thanks go to my editor at Oxford University Press, Susan Ferber, who provided great insights in her comments, generously hand-editing several chapters, and helping me to keep the narrative focused on Grzimek even as I felt pulled by competing historiographies and readerships: German history, international environmental history, African history, and tourism studies.

Many thanks to John Lane for sharing "the Serengeti experience", being there for the down times, and reading every word of *Our Gigantic Zoo*. This book is dedicated to him.

A NOTE ON SOURCES

Given the geographically and disciplinarily diverse array of sources for this project, I have elected not to include a full bibliography but instead cite each source in full the first time it is used in a chapter. A full biography of Grzimek would include the dozens of books, short essays, newspaper columns, letters to the editor, and letters to friends and family he wrote over the course of over sixty adult years. For a solid start to understanding Grzimek's life and work, readers should refer to his autobiography *Auf den Mensch gekommen: Erfahrungen mit Leuten* (1974) and Claudia Sewig's *Der Mann, der die Tiere Liebte* (2009). Sewig hews closely to the chronological format of Grzimek's memoirs and includes rich details gleaned from archives and print sources as well as interviews with Grzimek's circles of colleagues and family.

Much has been published on Grzimek's significance for German domestic environmentalism, as documented in works such as Jens-Ivo Engels's *Naturpolitik in der Bundesrepublik* (2006) and Sandra Chaney's *Nature of the Miracle Years* (2008). Much more remains to be said about numerous topics on this front, ranging from the gendered depiction of consumerism in Grzimek's anti-fur industry campaigns to the relationship between Grzimek, the 1960s generation, and coming to terms with the colonial past in his reaction to the 1966 film *Africa Addio (Africa Blood and Guts)*. In this book, I have focused mostly on the often-unintended ecological and social impact of environmental visions beyond Germany and through conservationist and developmentalist interventions in the Congo and Tanzania. Future scholars will want to investigate this home-and-abroad theme more deeply and branch out as well; Grzimek's infamous efforts to court Idi Amin and Mobutu Sese Seko's favor are well known, but what Frankfurt Zoological Society funds and recognition meant for Tanzania's neighbors remain unexplored. Correspondence, reports, and essays available in the Institute for the History of Frankfurt archives and at the Frankfurt Zoological Society itself offer rich possibilities in this regard.

I have cited the English translations of Grzimek's most famous books—*No Room for Wild Animals* (1955), *Serengeti Shall Not Die* (1961), and *Rhinos Belong to Everybody* (1962)—in the hopes of making his work more available to scholars and students of East African and global conservation. I have found it advantageous in my own class on global conservation to pair the widely available English-dubbed DVD versions of *No Room* and *Serengeti* with Grzimek's writings to adumbrate the world of midcentury global conservation and the geopolitical concerns about decolonization, the Cold War, and the "population bomb" that animate seemingly apolitical wildlife documentaries. In some cases, I have relied on the German version where the translation seemed out-of-date, off the mark, or lacking in linguistic texture; I have noted these cases in the endnotes.

ABBREVIATIONS

AA	Auswärtiges Amt (West German Foreign Office)
AWF	African Wildlife Foundation
AWLF	African Wildlife Leadership Foundation
CDU	Christian Democratic Union
CDWA	Colonial Development and Welfare Act
DFG	Deutsche Forschungsgemeinschaft (German Research Foundation)
EATTA	East Africa Tourist Travel Association
EARC	East Africana Research Collection, University of Dar es Salaam
EEC	European Economic Community
FAO	Food and Agriculture Organization of the United Nations
FBW	Filmbewertungstelle (West German Film Evaluation Office)
FPS	Fauna Preservation Society
FSA	Frankfurt Stadtarchiv (Institute für Stadtgeschichte, Frankfurt Municipal Archive)
FRG	Federal Republic of Germany (West Germany)
FZS	Frankfurt Zoological Society
GAWI	Garantieabwicklungsgesellschaft, renamed Deutsche Förderungsgesellschaft für Entwicklungsländer in the early 1960s (German Agency for Promoting Developing Countries)
GDR	German Democratic Republic (East Germany)
HAT	Historisches Archiv zum Tourismus (Historical Archive for Tourism, Berlin)
HFC	Henry A. Fosbrooke Collection, University of Dar es Salaam Library
IUCN	International Union for the Conservation of Nature and Natural Resources

IUPN	International Union for the Protection of Nature
KdF	Kraft durch Freude (National Socialist Strength through Joy Program)
NCA	Ngorongoro Conservation Area
NCAA	Ngorongoro Conservation Area Authority
NGO	Non-Governmental Organization
NSDAP	Nationalsozialistische Deutsche Arbeiterpartei (Nazi Party)
NYZS	New York Zoological Society
PAAA	Politisches Archiv des Auswärtigen Amts (Political Archive of the Federal Foreign Office)
RNG	Reichsnaturschutzgesetz (Nazi Reich Nature Protection Law)
SPFE	Society for the Protection of the Fauna of the Empire
SRI	Serengeti Research Institute
TANU	Tanganyika African National Union
TNA	Tanzania National Archive
TNL	Tanzania National Library
TTC	Tanzania Tourism Corporation
VNP	Verein Naturschutzpark (Nature Protection Park Society)
UN	United Nations
UNESCO	United Nations Educational, Scientific and Cultural Organization
WWF	World Wildlife Fund

Our Gigantic Zoo

Introduction

Mission to Africa

> I see animals and human beings as parts of one great whole . . . which man, it is to be hoped, will not finally destroy. That is the paradise in which by associating with all animals, regardless of whether they are domestic animals, animals in a zoo, or animals in the nature reserves of Europe or distant parts of the globe, we can share.
> —Bernhard Grzimek, *Visions of Paradise*, 1978

> I personally am not very interested in animals. I do not want to spend my holidays watching crocodiles. Nevertheless, I am entirely in favour of their survival. I believe that after diamonds and sisal, wild animals will provide Tanganyika with its greatest source of income. Thousands of Americans and Europeans have the strange urge to see these animals.
> —Julius Nyerere, Leader of the Tanganyika African National Union and future President of Tanzania, 1961

During a 1960 broadcast of his popular television program *A Place for Animals*, the Frankfurt Zoo director Bernhard Grzimek pulled off the greatest bluff in German media history. Convinced that tourist money could provide the financial incentive that newly independent African nations needed to protect their wildlife, Grzimek requested that his thirty-five million viewers book three-week package tours to Tanganyika for a mere twenty-one hundred Deutsche marks (about $506 at the time), so that they could view up close the magnificent lions, rhinos, elephants, and zebras that often appeared on his program. Grzimek knew that no German tour operator offered such moderately priced packages; indeed, the price was the result of a quick calculation before the show. As he predicted, however, travel agencies were so flooded with inquiries that several companies scrambled to meet the unprecedented demand for "photo safaris" in the East African bush at just about the price he suggested.[1]

Grzimek's drive to convert armchair travelers into live safari tourists transformed the "all-inclusive package trip" associated with sun and sand on the Mediterranean coast into an instrument of conservation.[2] With jet airline

Our Gigantic Zoo. Thomas M. Lekan, Oxford University Press (2020). © Oxford University Press.
DOI: 10.1093/oso/9780199843671.001.0001

service connecting the globe like never before, he proposed that ordinary people could save nature by consuming it.[3] Tourist brochures and the popular press still referred to Tanganyika in the late 1950s as the "former German East Africa," but the imperial interlude that ended at Versailles in 1919 dislimned behind the splashy images of elephants and giraffes silhouetted against a sunset over the savannas.[4] Unencumbered by the decolonization crises that faced fellow Brits, Frenchmen, and Belgians, affluent West Germans could step confidently into a new role as cosmopolitan nature lovers, much like the intrepid zookeeper himself. Even when they decided to stay home and send donations to the Frankfurt Zoological Society's fundraising arm, "Help for the Threatened Animal World," television viewers could still feel themselves part of a grand quest to rescue Africa's wild creatures from extinction. With European imperial hegemony in Africa under assault and the Berlin Crisis in full swing, Grzimek and his compatriots galvanized audiences with a vision of wildlife conservation as a noble, apolitical cause above the ideological and Cold War anxieties that dominated Europe in the aftermath of the Third Reich.[5]

Grzimek did not see his quest solely as a German or even European duty but a global mission that depended on his unique skills in forging alliances between Western conservationist advocates and Africans who stood on the brink of decolonization.[6] His television bluff came on the heels of his first meeting with Julius Nyerere, the highly respected leader of the Tanganyika African National Union (TANU), who had mobilized popular grievances against the British colonial government, many of them centered on land rights and dubious conservation measures, into a fight for independence.[7] Grzimek's meeting with Nyerere occurred around the same time that the Belgian Congo's independence struggle had turned into a bloody civil war and forced mass evacuation of Europeans. These events stoked conservationists' fears that newly emancipated Africans might slaughter wildlife and dismantle game reserves as hated symbols of the imperial era, as was widely reported in the press. Emerging nations needed foreign investment, quickly, to demonstrate the value of wildlife.[8] Grzimek told Nyerere that East Africa could become a prime destination for novelty-seeking globetrotters if the young country made the bold decision to retain and expand its national parks. "Italy, Spain, and Switzerland are able to create a favorable balance of trade through tourism," Grzimek remarked bluntly. "But let's be clear, Dr. Nyerere: your country is actually not pretty enough to attract a stream of tourists—except maybe for Kilimanjaro . . . . What the animal-hungry mass tourists want to see are simply giraffes, elephants, lions, zebras, and rhinos!"[9]

In particular, Grzimek hoped to steer these "animal-hungry mass tourists" to Tanganyika's Serengeti National Park, the site of the earth's last remaining migrations of wildebeest, zebra, and gazelle.[10] The park was the subject of Bernhard

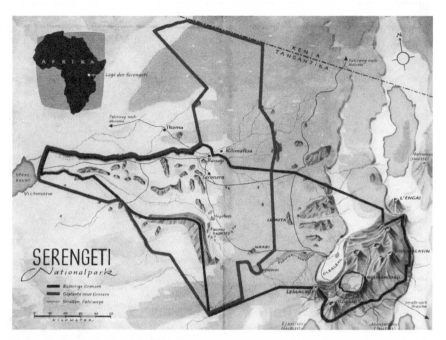

Figure I.1 Contested Borders: The Serengeti in 1957. Borders of the Serengeti National Park in 1957 (dark) and proposed new boundaries (paler). The British plan severed the Ngorongoro Crater region and Eastern Serengeti Plains (envisioned as a "mixed-use" area for cattle and wildlife) and added a new northern extension. The decision to divide the park came after almost a decade of debate over whether Maasai pastoralism was compatible with the goals of the National Park. Okapia, Ltd.

and his son Michael's Oscar-winning 1959 film *Serengeti Shall Not Die*, an epic of wildlife documentary that had been screened across British East Africa and dubbed into Swahili by the time of Grzimek and Nyerere's meeting. Bernhard and Michael had come to Tanganyika in 1957 shortly after the British colonial government had decided to reduce the park by a third in size and shift its borders northward and eastward. The British goal was to create a permanent homeland for Maasai herders in and around the massive Ngorongoro Crater, a caldera teeming with giraffes, elephants, African buffalo, and rare rhinoceroses. The decision came after years of wrangling over whether local Maasai pastoralists, whom the colonial government had guaranteed rights of occupancy under its 1948 charter for the park, were truly "full-blooded" indigenes who deserved to stay.[11] Yet Grzimek, along with cadres of international conservationists in the United States and Europe, was outraged by this "appeasement" of the Maasai "tribe" that many viewed as having no legitimate claim on this territory. For the Grzimeks, the Serengeti herds were a "cultural heritage of all mankind" more precious than the Acropolis or St. Paul's Cathedral.

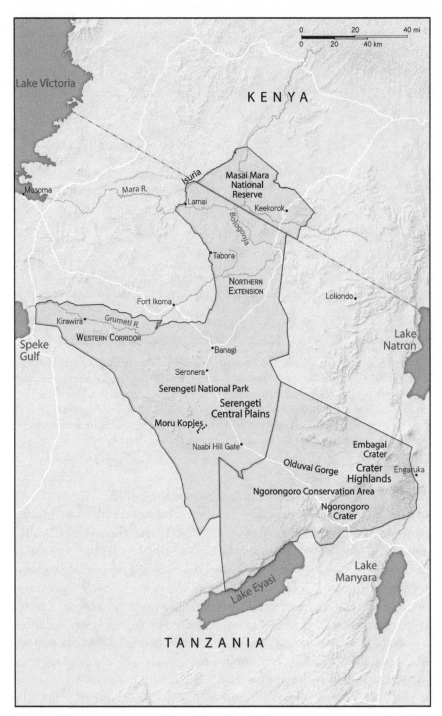

Figure I.2 The Serengeti Park and the Ngorongoro Conservation Area as they appeared in 1980. Note that by the time that Bernhard Grzimek died in 1987, the Ngorongoro Conservation Area had become its own self-administered mixed-use conservation area. The Lamai area listed here became another battleground over local people's customary access to the parklands in 1969. Created for the author by Mapping Specialists, Inc.

Figure I.3 Film Poster for *Serengeti Shall Not Die*, 1959. The Grzimeks' quest presented scientific research as a moral duty to save the Serengeti as a "cultural heritage of all mankind" that no single "nation" or "tribe" owned. But this form of globalism rendered African aspirations for environmental sovereignty secondary. Getty Images.

The Grzimeks captured in print and on film their aerial surveys of "our gigantic zoo," including an arduous journey from Frankfurt to Arusha in a zebra-striped, twin-engine Dornier DO-27; dangerous animal tagging experiments; and dramatic anti-poaching raids.[12] Using cameras carefully propped on airplane wings, the Grzimeks presented the Serengeti as an otherworldly terrain where national borders and anticolonial disputes on the ground dissolved into the curvature of the earth's distant horizon. The film admonished the British colonial government to establish the park's boundaries based on scientific study of the animals' natural migration routes, not political expediencies. A landmark documentary, *Serengeti Shall Not Die* was shown in over seventy countries across Europe, North America, and Africa during the 1960s and 1970s. In a tragedy that drew widespread sympathy for the conservationist cause, Michael Grzimek died in the latter stages of filming when the Dornier crashed into a griffon vulture. "He gave all he possessed for the wild animals of Africa," notes the epitaph at the end of *Serengeti Shall Not Die*.[13] Subsequent press releases and nature conservation campaigns drew on this image of Michael's martyrdom to assure donors that saving Africa's wildlife heritage was an unequivocal good, even a moral duty for the developed world. Yet the film leaves viewers with a disturbing conclusion: The Serengeti could only be saved by removing Africans from this paradise. "A national park must remain a piece of primordial wilderness to be effective," Grzimek wrote. "No men, not even native ones, should live inside its borders."[14]

Our Gigantic Zoo examines the misalliance between Grzimek's mission to create a vast open space for Africa's remaining large mammals and the rights of rural Africans and their livestock to inhabit the landscape on their own terms during the rapid expansion of wildlife conservation and national parks in East Africa during the late colonial and first postcolonial decades (1950–1975).[15] It advances three key arguments about Grzimek's contributions to the development and globalization of German environmentalism in these decades.

First, the success of Grzimek's books, films, TV series, and fundraising for Africa reflected West Germans' unsettled confrontations with their Nazi past rather than an effort to grapple with the imperialist legacies of wildlife control, epizootic diseases, and economic exploitation that had endangered wild animals in the first place. As a veterinarian and agricultural minister in the Third Reich, Grzimek wrote a series of popular stories that portrayed all humans as members of the same family of higher primates—albeit an especially aggressive and increasingly "degenerate" group therein. When he became director of the Frankfurt Zoo in 1945, he created a sanctuary from human brutality out of bombed-out paddocks and leftover rubble. He used the latest insights about animal behavior and territoriality to create this sanctuary. In subsequent journeys to the Ivory Coast in 1951 and the Belgian Congo in 1954, Grzimek and his son projected a zookeeper's ideal of sanctuaries free from marauding humans onto Africa. They offered a grim portrait of giant cities exploding out of the "bush," cheap consumer entertainments, and the "dangers" of intermarriage between ethnic groups as a foil for West Germans' own anxieties about the Americanization of cultural norms and the status of black Germans after the fall of the Nazi racial state.[16] Nature protection appeared as an inherent moral good for post-Hitler West Germans seeking to redeem themselves in the world community by saving life rather than destroying it.

Second, heroic descriptions of Grzimek as a harbinger of ecological consciousness in West Germany have largely overlooked the questionable environmental, social, and political impacts of his zookeeper vision abroad. Bernhard survived his son by almost three decades, a period in which he assembled their nearly complete scientific work into a series of academic articles; hosted West Germany's longest-running television series, *A Place for Animals*; and campaigned to stop the cruel hunting of arctic baby seals and end the killing of leopards and jaguars for fur coats.[17] West Germans who grew up between the 1950s and 1980s remember Grzimek fondly as the avuncular "animal whisperer" whose extemporaneous, professorial style spurred a passion for animal protection.[18] Much like Marlin Perkins's *Wild Kingdom,* Jacques Cousteau's *Undersea World,* or David Attenborough's *Life* series, *A Place for Animals* used animals in the studio alongside innovative time-lapse filmography in the field to present viewers, especially children, with an intimate view of animal behavior and exotic habitats unavailable through casual observation in a zoo or on a hike. Such programs became conduits for a soft conservationist message suited to a postindustrial society focused on white-collar leisure rather than agricultural labor, "renaturing" animals on screen even as their habitats abroad dwindled.[19] As one scholar has noted, "It is simply unimaginable, that anyone in Germany would not know the Frankfurt Professor. Television stars come and go, but Bernhard Grzimek was always a fixture."[20]

By the mid-1960s, Grzimek's program became much more ecological and alarmist. He transferred his earlier warnings of impending ecological collapse in Africa's grasslands and forests to the contamination of soil, water, and air that had fueled the postwar "economic miracle" in West Germany. Grzimek called on his viewers to "have civil courage" by petitioning officials to ban the use of DDT; end the cruel practice of keeping chickens in filthy, high-density cages; and support the establishment of West Germany's first national park in the Bavarian forest.[21] Often compared to Rachel Carson in German media for stimulating ecological consciousness in West Germany, Grzimek was a harbinger of the changes in European environmental politics that transformed conservation from a domain of expert planners into a democratic concern of ordinary citizens.[22] But behind his avuncular television image was a "strange German," as his chronicler Harold T. P. Hayes referred to him, whose notoriously cantankerous personality, long-denied Nazi past, and grand obsession to save the world's animals often resulted in disdain toward his fellow human beings.[23] Such a single-minded pursuit of animal protection rendered Africans' quest for self-determination—including reclaiming environmental sovereignty over forests, rivers, and wild animals usurped by the colonial powers—as trivial in comparison to humanity's ongoing "war against nature."[24]

Such trivialization of African aspiration created a gross asymmetry between the "greening" of West German and East African political cultures during the 1960s. Grzimek has rightly been called the "Father of African conservation" who, as the Swiss zoologist Heini Hediger noted in the 1970s "did more to save the African fauna than any other person."[25] As the Honorary Curator of Tanganyika National Parks (after the 1964 union with Zanzibar, the United Republic of Tanzania), Grzimek used the donations from the fundraising arm of the Frankfurt Zoological Society (FZS), the "Help for the Threatened Animal World," to funnel hundreds of thousands of Deutsche marks into East Africa to launch long-term ecological surveys, train African game scouts, create

Figure I.4 On set at *A Place for Animals*. Grzimek's television remains the longest running in German television history. The "professor" and zoo director perfected an intimate, off-the-cuff style that used a single camera to present animals from the zoological garden as "guests" interspersed with footage of Frankfurt Zoological Society conservation efforts in East Africa—much of it funded by television viewers' donations. Getty Images.

outreach materials to build national pride in the parks, develop tourist facilities, and arm anti-poaching brigades. As critics of Grzimek's legacy in Africa have noted, in his thirty-year career Grzimek "probably raised more money for conservation, educated more people about nature, and twisted more arms of more African bureaucrats than any man in history" using tactics that ranged from a "soft line" to "outright blackmail."[26] Among those who succumbed to Grzimek's arm-twisting were not only Nyerere but also Uganda's Milton Obote, Zaïre's Mobutu Sese Seko, and even Idi Amin. Grzimek flew to Kampala during Amin's reign of terror to warn the dictator about scaring off tourists. "I would sit down to dinner with either Hitler or Stalin if it made any difference for my animals," he once remarked.[27] In a world where overpopulation and habitat destruction had brought the environment to the point of collapse, Grzimek thought there was no time to quibble about the human rights records of current or former dictators.

Lastly, Grzimek's campaigns represent a critical chapter in the history of the "green network" of international conservation in their own right. Grzimek's story links the FZS to the International Union for the Conservation of Nature and Natural Resources (IUCN), the World Wildlife Fund (WWF), and other European and North American conservation NGOs that emerged shortly after independence.[28] As decolonization accelerated around 1960, Grzimek and a handful of others—former UNESCO and IUCN leader Sir Julian Huxley, for example, as well as World Wildlife Fund chair Prince Bernhard Lippe-Biesterfeld—feared that Africa's charismatic animals might "go the way of the buffalo." In a series of campaigns that some have called a new "Scramble for Eden," European conservationists called on UNESCO to spearhead an international rescue mission for wild animals that matched the funding and determination of the organization's effort to rescue the artifacts of Nubian civilization at Abu Simbel in Egypt from the rising waters of the Nile behind the Aswan Dam. Africa needed Westerners' continued help, they argued—a plea that barely masked their doubt that Africans could serve as effective caretakers of their own natural heritage after independence. Such efforts merged fears of animal extinction and political decolonization around 1960 in ways that made it difficult for independent African communities to articulate their own visions for using—and even abusing—the non-human denizens of their homelands.

Such attitudes were evident at the landmark Pan African Symposium on the Conservation of Nature and Natural Resources in Modern African States, which met in Arusha in September 1961 (hereafter Arusha Conference). Grzimek and Huxley were among those who encouraged Nyerere to declare Tanganyika's intent to protect its wildlife inheritance as a sign of entry into the family of "civilized nations" emerging out of the old imperial order.[29] Indeed, by obscuring Germany's former imperial ambitions, Grzimek envisioned himself as an apolitical "honest broker" working outside traditional diplomatic channels—a confidant of both "blacks and whites, communists and capitalists."[30] In his memoirs, Grzimek underscored how grateful he was that Germany had lost her colonies; had she retained them, he remarked, the Zoological Society could never have assumed its nongovernmental role in East African conservation.[31] He saw himself as a broker for bilateral aid and grants solicited from his own FZS and the West German Foreign Office, development agencies, and scientific foundations as "technical assistance." The FZS became the most important financial supporter of the Serengeti National Park administration and German development agencies and NGOs remain major stakeholders in protected areas throughout Tanzania today.[32]

Grzimek's story thus takes us beyond the more familiar Anglo-American story of international conservation to illuminate how West Germany—an inheritor state of the empire that lost its African colonies at Versailles in 1919—came to reoccupy a pivotal role in East African conservation during the period of decolonization. To press on with the conservationist mission after Michael's death and the division of the Serengeti, Grzimek depended on strategic alliances with West German organizations as well as with British expatriates such as Myles Turner, the chief game warden of the Serengeti, and John Owen, the director of the national parks department.[33] He distinguished himself from his Anglo-American colleagues by his willingness to fund the mundane tasks of park management—maintaining roads, concessions, and viewing platforms and paying game scout salaries. But he also knew how to sell nature. As a zoo-keeper, he had long understood the appeal of animals to the "masses" and made sure that FZS monies flowed to youth hostels and school trips that promoted Tanganyikan national pride in wild animals. Nonetheless, the fortress conservation model that emerged at Arusha, which insisted on a strict separation of humans from wildlife and other natural resources, has made Grzimek's legacies a flashpoint between nature conservationists and human rights advocates in Tanzania ever since.[34]

Grzimek's tireless advocacy for wildlife exemplifies the perils of "thinking locally and acting globally": that is, formulating scientific and moral claims about nature from one situated space of knowledge, power, and material relations and then universalizing them to encompass other places of encounter.[35] Grzimek epitomizes the "charismatic megascientist," a telegenic, white, and male conservationist whose personal affect and cosmopolitan connections enabled him to speak for Global Nature outside normal diplomatic channels and democratic participation.[36] During the Cold War and decolonization eras under investigation in this book, international conservationists like Grzimek found the "global" an especially appealing way to depoliticize explosive questions over aboriginal land rights and environmental sovereignty.[37] It signaled impartiality in ostensibly "local" political affairs and a higher, more scientific, more "whole earth" argument for setting aside land in the face of outdated, "tribal" prerogatives.[38] Part of the reason that most transnational histories of conservation erase the contingent origins of the global environment around 1960 is that they posit this topography of the imagination as an ontological given that acts upon other scales, rather than a subject of investigation in its own right.[39] In such global histories, impersonal non-human factors beyond human control (overpopulation, diseases, insects, or climate) often overshadow the textures of culture, landscape, and power.[40]

Like the ethnographer Anna Tsing, I find it useful instead to think of Grzimek and other celebrity conservations at mid-century as "conjuring" Global Nature to mobilize European audiences, donor communities, and political leaders.[41] Neither the global nor the local are fixed terrains in her formulation but emerge dialogically, "charged and enacted in the sticky materiality of practical encounters."[42] In the environmental arena, the global—whether in the guise of "overpopulation," a rinderpest epidemic, or capitalist expansion, does not simply diffuse its effects onto the local; nor is the local always a site of vulnerability or resistance to external forces. In the case of the Serengeti, Western conservationists conjured the image of a global heritage of mankind to supersede imperial authority over troublesome landscapes. At the same time, the Serengeti controversies and the British decision to divide the park started as a local conflict over customary land rights that mushroomed into a global controversy and reshaped the history of world heritage sites. The result is what Tsing calls "congeries of local/global interaction" that move across space and time in unpredictable ways.[43] What knots the trans-local exchanges and multiscalar encounters in this story is Grzimek himself: the ecological protagonist in an intimate portrait of the global marked by decolonization, Cold War conflict, mass media and tourism, and the accelerating loss of biodiversity.[44]

Our Gigantic Zoo illustrates the frictions that emerged between these realms of global ambition, national interest, and local place making with chapters that zoom out to illustrate transnational configurations of conservation activism and then zoom in on local places of encounter. I draw on an array of sources— from the Grzimeks' popular writings and films to Tanganyikan district officers' reports and memoranda—to illustrate the paradoxes of German and European conservation and nature tourism in the developing world. The frictions that emerge in this narrative illuminate the book's key themes: Grzimek's use of Africa as a "projection screen" for West German modernization anxieties, the gap between claims of global heritage and African national and local priorities, and the reemergence of Germany as a postcolonial player in East African conservation. Despite strong evidence of ideological and institutional continuity in wildlife protection and nature conservation between the late colonial and early postcolonial eras, I conclude that Grzimek and his compatriots never fully transformed Tanzania into the "beacon of hope" for international conservation that the Arusha Conference had assigned the young country. Instead, Grzimek and the FZS were forced to navigate a shifting and uncertain political terrain after 1961, hamstrung by chronic shortages of funding, a lack of inherited tourist infrastructure, and the resurgence of African demands for environmental sovereignty. By the time that Nyerere's government "Africanized" the national parks in the early 1970s, Grzimek and other conservationists feared that the Serengeti might be lost for good.

The story begins in Europe, where Grzimek's interest in nature reserves developed out of a desire to enhance animal welfare in zoological gardens based on the principles of ethology, the study of animal behavior so well developed in Central Europe.[45] Grzimek viewed with alarm the hopeful "expectations of modernity" that accompanied the rhetoric of West German business lobbyists and developmental experts, who applauded the wave of Africans "leaving the bush" for urban centers and industrial employment in the 1950s.[46] Based on his experiences of war, reconstruction, and Americanization in Europe, Grzimek and his son could only see in these trends an unwelcome repetition of Europe's ecological missteps.[47] Echoing the 1948 UN Universal Declaration of Human Rights, the Grzimeks eschewed Nazi and colonialist racism in making the case for conservation during their journeys to the Ivory Coast and the Belgian Congo. No longer was Africans' "savage hunting" blamed for wildlife extinction; instead colonial expansion, misguided vaccination campaigns, and big game trophy hunting were believed to have unleashed the process.

Yet eugenic worries inherited from the interwar era never lay far behind the pair's depictions of "primitive" Africans.[48] They fixated on intermarriage between different "tribes" in Central Africa as a sign of "degeneration," rein-forcing a dubious belief in "racial purity" as a condition for primitive peoples to inhabit national parks and game reserves.[49] In this vision, racial and ecologi-cal purity reinforced and supported each other—a logic that left no room for the British government's effort to compromise with the ethnically mixed Maasai "tribes" the Grzimeks encountered in the Serengeti region in 1957.[50] They lacked a deeper understanding of the relations of marriage, family, culture, and the exchange of livestock and staple crops between Maasai pastoralists and their Arusha and Meru agricultural neighbors. As such, the Grzimeks declared that there were no "full-blooded Maasai" left in the Serengeti who could claim cus-tomary rights to the land.[51] Such depictions of racial deterioration also made it easier to dispossess the Maasai and other rural Africans of traditional grazing lands, increasing the precarity of their sustenance and culture in an unforgiv-ing, semi-arid environment. The Grzimeks envisioned Africans in the 1950s as immature Europeans who were climbing up earlier "stages" of European development—and, thus, recapitulating the same environmental tragedy that had killed off large mammals to make room for farms, cities, and highways.[52] The quest for purity—of races, of spaces, of ecological integrity—also led the pair to discount the site-specific co-evolution of domesticated and wild animals on the African plains and the resilient capacity of the grasslands to bounce back from droughts, intensive grazing, and fire.[53]

The frictions between colonial cartographies and hybrid localities also meant that the Grzimeks could not envision the Serengeti itself as a cultural landscape forged by the interaction and mutual adaptation between pastoralists, domesti-cated livestock, and wild animals over centuries.[54] Maasai elders and a handful of sympathetic British ethnographers in the 1950s pointed to the critical role of livestock herders in maintaining the vitality of the savannas through controlled fire and the growth of shade trees atop the rich soils left on former homesteads— many abandoned in haste due to the rinderpest epidemics that devastated East Africa in the 1890s.[55] They warned that the dried-out Serengeti of 1960 was a temporary condition: a product of wide variations in seasonal weather patterns and an always shifting mosaic of grasslands and acacia bush mediated by fire and other "disturbances." Not until the 1980s, when a new school of rangeland ecologists began to study the longer-term impact of cattle herding in the mixed-use Ngorongoro Conservation Area (NCA), did conservationists realize how little the Serengeti region matched the Grzimeks' vision of a self-equilibrating island of plants and animals best segregated from human activities.[56] By channeling a diverse mosaic of cultural landscapes and species histories into a universal story of environmental degradation and overpopulation, wildlife conservation left no "middle ground" between sustainable use and wildness. Indeed, the insistence that zones of nature protection had to be strictly separated from zones of human settlement accelerated the very modernizing processes that Bernhard and Michael despised.

In the early 1960s, the gap between global extinction fears and local priorities became apparent as Grzimek advocated for expanding national parks in Tanganyika after independence without the consent of rural populations. Grzimek's ability to mobilize viewer donations, foundation support, and package tours did convince Nyerere and some of his ministers to see the national parks as potential wellsprings of foreign currency and patriotic pride. A united Tanzania established almost a dozen new national parks between 1960 and 1980—a sure sign that Bernhard and Michael's quest had succeeded: the last natural zoos were protected for all time.[57] Yet throughout the 1960s, Grzimek and John Owen insisted that the new national parks were the product of African sacrifice and not European initiative—flattery, to be sure, but also a commentary that held a deep grain of truth. Behind the scenes, both observers recognized that Europeans had failed to deliver on the Arusha Conference's bloated promises of aid and technical assistance.[58] Owen complained to Grzimek regularly that the big foundations tended to "cherry pick" flashy projects that appealed to donors, leaving him to go cap in hand, again and again, to Tanganyikan officials to make up for the park department's deficits. African political leaders, rangers, and especially displaced rural people found themselves responsible for this "world heritage" long after donor communities found new causes and globetrotting tourists discovered novel places for adventure.[59] Beyond a well-funded ecological research institute and a wildlife training college, the emergency development aid on the scale of Abu Simbel to rescue Tanzania's wildlife never materialized, leaving the young nation saddled with the costs of maintaining a vast network of national parks it could ill afford. Neither colonial nor postcolonial Europeans ever invested enough in Tanganyika to impose their desires on its emerging leaders, leaving both the national parks and the game departments to get by on a shoestring.[60]

The divide between global ambition and national development became apparent, too, when nature tourism failed to deliver on Grzimek's promises of an environmentally benign pathway to modernity. IUCN and FZS representatives insisted that nature tourism would save Africa's wildlife by steering European visitors away from trophy hunting and providing Africans an alternative income on ecologically marginal lands. Yet neither the number of overnight stays nor the aid funds available for tourism development could make up for the infrastructural deficits of British colonialism in Tanganyika Territory or compete with Kenya's more extensive road, hotel, and airport infrastructure. Such deficits were readily apparent to British expats and African bureaucrats before 1967, when Tanzania launched its ill-fated experiment in self-reliant African socialism and—a few years later—declared villagization as a national priority. Development scholars of the 1980s blamed this political experiment for destroying the country's infant tourism industry and channeling visitors to capitalist Kenya.[61] But the promoters of "structural adjustment programs" and private investment forgot the many failures of this earlier liberal phase of postcolonial development. It was not until the 1990s that Tanzanians could complain of great tourist migrations in the country's "Northern Circuit" of national parks.[62]

Despite the spotty record of conservation and development in the 1960s, West Germany's promises of bilateral aid and desire for diplomatic ties with the "former German East Africa" enabled the country to reemerge as a pivotal player in East African conservation: it was Tanganyika's third largest donor by 1964. Germany's status as Europe's first postcolonial nation resulted in a unique form of green internationalism that underpinned German organizations' reentry into global conservation networks they had been excluded from after 1919. Wild animals provided symbolic and diplomatic resources in the exchanges between West Germany and Tanganyika. The Federal Republic of Germany's (FRG) ministers—many of them big game hunters—saw wildlife conservation as a way for their country to spread goodwill in the region. They even sponsored innovative projects—such as game ranching initiatives—which sought to "make wildlife pay for itself" through the sustainable production, management, and distribution of animals as meat products in Africa and Europe. Such colonial nostalgia transformed West Germans from the "good colonizers" of 1900 into the globally minded conservationists of 1960 without confronting the imperialist legacies that had shaped their longings for wild Africa in the first place.

Despite this important West German presence in Tanganyika, most accounts of international conservation focus on the globalization of the US Yellowstone model of de-humanized parks during the late 1950s "conservation boom" in British Africa.[63] Grzimek certainly shared many of the assumptions and anxieties of the Anglo-American wing of the global conservation community. Yet the

German-inflected globalism that informed his mission in the 1950s continued to shape his activities in the postcolony, offering new insights on the early independence period. For one, Bernhard and Michael favored the Belgian model of the "integral nature reserve" set aside for scientific research rather than the Yellowstone or Yosemite models.[64] Grzimek's donor base also gave him unique opportunities for pursuing "wildlife diplomacy" outside the usual channels. Grzimek's "Help for the Threatened Animal World," which amassed donations from television viewers, wealthy Frankfurt bankers, and estate gifts, enabled the zookeeper to offer Congolese and Tanganyikan leaders direct assistance with everyday tasks and supplies.

Grzimek's initiatives in Tanganyika depended on alliances with West German diplomats, scientific institutes, development agencies, and corporate foundations that sought to expand their sphere of influence in East Africa. The West German agencies saw technical assistance for wildlife utilization as a form of soft power useful for rebuffing the German Democratic Republic's influence in postcolonial Africa.[65] Indeed, both West and East Germany saw the non-aligned nations of sub-Saharan Africa as proving grounds for competing liberal-capitalist and Marxist-socialist visions of modernity and asserted their interests diplomatically through foreign aid.[66] With Tanganyika's "historic ties" to Germany, the West German Foreign Office placed great hopes in the Nyerere regime to foster trade and cultural ties with the Federal Republic. But those hopes faded in 1964, when Zanzibari leader and Tanzanian vice president Abeid Karume invited East German technical advisors to the island after the revolution and they remained in place after unification with the mainland. This abrogation of the Hallstein Doctrine, which refused diplomatic recognition to any state that also recognized the GDR, eventually led Nyerere to cut off diplomatic ties to the Federal Republic in 1965. Relations between the two countries never fully recovered, and Grzimek shifted his focus to Uganda and domestic issues. The German-German Cold War rivalries are woven into the global history of conservation in East Africa.[67]

Such geopolitical shifts signaled that conservationists could not simply impose wilderness ideals onto powerless African statesmen. Instead, wildlife advocates had to face the shifting winds of the post-independence era that left the conservation mission unfinished and the long-term status of the parks vulnerable. Nyerere's Arusha Manifesto of 1961 described wild animals as a "wonder and inspiration," but the leader increasingly rebuffed Grzimek's calls for stricter conservation measures in the NCA and balked when the zookeeper meddled too much in state decisions to open up border regions of the Western Serengeti to limited grazing. Amidst the international outcry that ensued, Nyerere angrily reminded Grzimek that the parks were Tanzanian national

parks, not just world heritage. At the heart of these negotiations were competing claims to environmental sovereignty that gestures toward "world heritage"
could neither resolve nor justify.[68]

——

Such negotiations over environmental control foreground the improvisational
quality of postcolonial encounters. The Serengeti became a "contact zone" in
this period, a "space and time where subjects previously separated by geography
and history" were, for a short period, "co-present."[69] In the landscapes of the
Serengeti as depicted in films and television, both West Germany and Tanzania
sought to forge new partnerships and project positive national images abroad
amid Cold War rivalries that threatened the sovereignty of both. The contact
zone enmeshed West German scientists, television viewers, tourists, and zoological animals and Tanzanian statesmen, pastoralists, farmers, and wild game in
networks of interaction across vast distances. The most important symbol of this
new space of encounter was the Grzimeks' airplane, the D-Ente, which conveyed
the father and son back and forth between Frankfurt and the Serengeti before
Michael's premature death and then became an icon of their quest in posters,
memoirs, and photographs. A replica of the plane now hangs above exhibits in
both the Frankfurt Zoo and the Serengeti Visitor Center in Seronera—a powerful depiction of the role that the Grzimeks still play in the story of the Serengeti's
survival. Yet the Serengeti contact zone also engendered competing visions of
landscape and wildlife conservation on the brink of independence that reflected
the ecological history and volition of British, international, African, and non-
human actors, each of whom had their own stakes in this landscape. The
Grzimeks' quest converged and clashed with these other stakeholders, mold-
ing the park and its inhabitants and challenging the Grzimeks' effort to present
the Serengeti as a cultural heritage of humanity above political partisanship and
material struggles.

The first encounters that shaped the Grzimeks' mission to Africa reflected
Bernhard Grzimek's "zookeeper's ecology," the subject of chapter 1. Focusing on
the transition in Grzimek's career from agricultural minister in the Third Reich
to postwar director of the Frankfurt Zoo, I explore his interest in animal behavior, or ethology, and how practical questions about animal care in zoo settings
spurred his first journeys to Africa. Yet there is a more disturbing side to this narrative of animal care: one of wartime displacement and unfinished processes of
coming to terms with Nazism, articulated through fears of Americanization and
human degeneracy that explain the urgency of Grzimek's quest to save animals
from destruction. Grzimek envisioned all human beings—black or white—as
rogue primates bent on environmental destruction and unmoored from natural

Figure I.5 Replicas of the Grzimeks' D-Ente hover above both the Serengeti Visitor Center and the Grzimek House at the Frankfurt Zoo, a symbol of the presumed synchronization of conservation priorities within the German–East African contact zone. Photograph by the author.

laws of selection and population control. The only solution to the plague of human "scurvy" afflicting the planet was animal refuges set apart from human brutality.

As chapters 2 and 3 show, the Grzimeks' 1954–1955 journeys to the Belgian Congo, which resulted in their bestselling book and eponymous prize-winning film *No Room for Wild Animals*, projected this dark vision of degeneracy and Americanization onto Central Africa, with dubious consequences for understanding the colonial origins of wildlife conservation and the stark choices that the Congolese and other Africans faced on the brink of independence. Grzimek

Figure I.6 A replica of D-Ente above the House of Grzimek at the Frankfurt Zoo, 2014. Photograph by the author.

and his son envisioned a continent under siege by the forces of modernization and needing immediate intervention to save its charismatic wildlife from extinction. Yet the Grzimeks' encounters prompted deeper reflection on the homeland as well, spurring efforts to "rewild" the country's densely populated landscapes with wild animals in safari parks and a proposed national park.[70] The Grzimeks eschewed European colonial powers' racism, which blamed Africans for the endangerment of animals. They targeted European trophy hunters for perpetuating the belief that national parks were playgrounds for white men rather than resources for a global future. Thus began an extended battle with West German hunters over the contours of wildlife conservation in a postcolonial future that revealed the power of environmental globalism in a post-Hitler society.

The Grzimeks' mission soon merged and sparked frictions with new colonial actors and novel ecologies as they set off to stop the British plan to divide the Serengeti National Park, detailed in chapters 4 and 5. Fresh from their advocacy for national parks in the Congo, the Grzimeks were invited to the Serengeti at a moment of intense reappraisal of and conflict over the United Kingdom's approach to wildlife conservation and aboriginal rights. The Grzimeks arrived on the scene amid ongoing struggles within the colonial state between district officers sympathetic to "native" rights and skeptical about claims of wildlife extinction and preservationists in London. The preservationists insisted that national parks were necessary to protect precious habitat and stop Africans' "indiscriminate" hunting and pastoralist "overgrazing."[71] Britain also stood accused of mismanaging its trusteeship territory, destroying drylands soils through dubious cropland development, and fueling anticolonial movements through unjust land alienations and white settlement schemes. Commissioned to count the animals and document their movements using aerial ecological surveys, the Grzimeks provided new modes of aesthetic appreciation that tried to disentangle the Serengeti from its ugly imperial past and contemporary land-use struggles. The aerial view heralded the shift from elite steamship travel to jet airline service to Africa, mobilizing "camera hunters" interested in snapshots for their albums rather than trophies for their walls. From their carefully propped cameras, the park emerged as a "common property" erased of all territorial boundaries. This vision enabled them and several NGOs to take over the mantle of conservation from the British at independence but without resolving the environmental questions and dubious assumptions about aboriginal land use that had fueled conflicts in the first place.

The second group that entered the Serengeti contact zone between 1959 and 1961 was the international conservation community, which advocated for protecting Africa's wildlife as a global resource. As chapters 5 and 6 show, the IUCN and American NGOs pilloried British concessions to the Maasai in the Serengeti. Indeed, many US-based groups called on the United Nations to take over management of the region and were determined not to let indigenous rights thwart the global expansion of national parks. Bernhard yoked his conservation quest to these global ambitions in the wake of the Serengeti's division but charted his own course for the FZS as the decade of development unfolded. He abandoned his fear of decolonization in 1960 and embraced national independence as an opportunity to court African leaders, with tourism as the carrot used to divert them from export agriculture. As chapter 6 emphasizes, the Serengeti battles and the Congo Crisis paved the way for the Arusha Conference, which met just months before independence. Nyerere declared his commitment to wildlife protection—greatly relieving Western conservationists who feared that decolonization might lead to the mass slaughter of animals.[72] Grzimek proved himself an adept broker between international NGOs, West German interests, and Nyerere's fledgling regime, but the question of "whose landscape" was represented in Tanganyika's new national parks remained unresolved. At the heart of the Arusha compromise was an implicit bargain that left Grzimek and his British allies scrambling to secure funding and tourists before the inevitable Africanization of the park administration.

Between 1961 and 1964, African players entered the debate on the future of the Serengeti more forcefully, a third set of actors in the contact zone that proved more independent than Grzimek or other Western conservationists had expected. Nyerere pledged at Arusha to expand the country's network of national parks with Western assistance, resulting in over a dozen new parks by the late 1970s. Yet Grzimek and his allies needed to make good on the terms of the Arusha Bargain, cultivating strategic and unstable alliances with African statesmen who sought to secure their legitimacy through development and control.[73] As chapter 7 shows, support for German and European conservation measures was always contingent on the expansion of tourism—whose revenues proved small in comparison to the country's health, educational, and infrastructural needs. The constant meddling by Western sightseers who opposed commercial development, and, more ominously, the escalating number of poachers created increasingly militarized countermeasures. Park development did buttress the aims of the "developmentalist vanguard" of the nascent postcolonial state—especially by bringing marginal lands and "unruly" pastoralists into state development schemes. Nonetheless, Grzimek faced cascading challenges to the integrity of the Serengeti and other parks during the late 1960s and early 1970s, as local land users flouted park boundaries and reclaimed grazing lands and hunting territories as part of their own understanding of self-sufficiency and local autonomy. Nyerere, increasingly frustrated by the bleeding of tourists to Kenya and conservationist outcry over concessions to African communities on the park borders, rebuffed Grzimek's appeals to the "world community" and global heritage—closing the border with Kenya in 1977 and evicting tourists from the country.

In their own way, even the Serengeti ecosystem and its animals resisted the imposition of wilderness onto a landscape once shared with herders and hunters, as chapters 6 and 7 show. The Serengeti's unruly environment, with its inexplicable fluctuations in animal populations and wide seasonal weather swings, was not ready to submit to management schemes, scientific surveys, and tourist expectations of a timeless refuge from modern society. Despite Michael Grzimek's pioneering work and the models of carrying capacity and ecosystem equilibrium being developed by Berkeley ecologist Lee Talbot and others in the early 1960s, animal populations fluctuated wildly and unpredictably after the Maasai were excluded from the park. Wildebeest populations exploded, threatening Maasai cattle in Ngorongoro with catarrhal fever. Conservationists were not sure if the higher numbers of wildebeest and buffalo were the result of higher rainfall in 1963–1964 or the exclusion of competition from cattle and sheep. Populations of other species, including gazelle and other small browsers— appeared to be on the decline.[74] As Grzimek and an emerging cadre of scientists struggled to explain these differential outcomes, Henry Fosbrooke—the head of the Ngorongoro Conservation Area Authority (NCAA)—asked whether the mixed-use NCA provided a more sustainable model for conservation, with the non-hunting Maasai providing better anti-poaching forces than European-equipped ones. The Serengeti was the contact zone in which the Grzimeks' quest faltered on the environmental inequalities left by European imperialism, the unrealizable hopes for wildlife conservation as economic development, and African demands for environmental sovereignty.[75]

1

A Zookeeper's Ecology

> How often I've heard: I'm jealous of your job! Animals have no ideologies, no nationalist feelings, and no political parties. You've definitely chosen the right thing!
> —Bernhard Grzimek, *Being Down with People*

Bernhard Grzimek never considered himself a great explorer of Africa. He took his first trip to the continent in 1951, when he was already forty-one years old with an established career as a veterinarian and zoo director, famous for illustrated serials, radio broadcasts, and books about encounters with captive animals. "Not long ago, I found the place where I was to speak plastered with great placards," he wrote in his memoir of his journey to the Ivory Coast.

> Really a most embarrassing sight. Men like Livingstone, Stanley and Emin Pasha . . . will turn in their graves! All I had done was to wander round Africa for a few months, taking good care to keep my eyes and ears open. That I should write a book about it at all is audacious . . . and do not, I beg of you, run away with the idea that I am attempting a voluminous and exhaustive treatise on the Dark Continent![1]

As Grzimek liked to point out, these explorers' long, arduous journeys by sea and perilous treks across deserts and jungles infested with tropical diseases and populated by hostile "natives" were a thing of the past in the era of modern jet airline service. The landscapes that had lured nineteenth-century German-speaking explorers such as Gustav Nachtigal to the Kingdom of the Bornu in West Africa, Heinrich Barth to Timbuktu, Friedrich Gerhard Rohlfs, the "German Dr. Livingstone," to the Valley of the Nile, and Georg Schweinfurth to the rainforests of Central Africa were quickly disappearing.[2] During the interwar era, after Germany had lost her colonies, revanchists dreamed about Germans exploring (and perhaps seizing) those last "blank spaces" on the map.[3] Such dreams animated the "jungle fantasies" of hunters, writers, and filmmakers such

Our Gigantic Zoo. Thomas M. Lekan, Oxford University Press (2020). © Oxford University Press.
DOI: 10.1093/oso/9780199843671.001.0001

as Hans Schomburgk, Colin Ross, and John Hagenbeck, all of whom restaged the glory of the masculine German hunter as a pretext for discrediting the Allied injustice.[4]

Grzimek, by contrast, presented his readers with a sobering portrait of a continent under siege by forces of modernization. Previous zookeepers had rarely gone overseas due to the months-long treks into the interior to locate specimens. But with the new European airline hub at Frankfurt, Grzimek made it to the Ivory Coast in under fifteen hours.[5] "The wonderful expeditions which one sees in so many films are undertaken with the sole purpose of making a film," Grzimek wrote in *Dr. Jimek, I Presume,* "and to make it more exciting for the audience the film is dubbed 'The Great Trapping Expedition to Darkest Africa.'"[6] Whereas the opening passages of Schomburgk's *Mein Afrika* (1928) catalogue the shotguns he needed for felling an elephant, Grzimek fretted about customs formalities, which exposure of film to bring for his camera, and—most vexingly—where to find a lightweight linen suit in Frankfurt in December.[7] Within a few years, he would be followed by scores of Europeans "spending their summer holidays in the Congo or even flying over just for the weekend," while the slopes of Kilimanjaro would soon be dotted with hotels and sanatoria. "Even today the trip can be accomplished with more speed and less fuss than was required fifteen years ago for a journey to Venice," he remarked.[8] Discriminating European "travelers" had long considered Africa off the beaten path from the "hordes" who rushed from site to site, but Grzimek's writings presented a continent slowly being integrated into mass tourism's pleasure periphery.[9]

This chapter argues that Grzimek's fears about the spread of Western consumerism and "degeneracy" to the "Dark Continent" explains the urgency of his quest to save animals and their habitats—and the indifference he often displayed toward local and indigenous peoples who stood in the way of his pursuit. Investigating Grzimek's early biography, particularly his unexpected career transition from agricultural minister to zoo director in the 1940s, I explain Grzimek's skepticism toward human aspiration and fixation on animal suffering as consequences of his scientific interests in animal psychology, wartime displacement, and his unfinished process of coming to terms with Nazism. In a series of musings about animal behavior published in newspaper serials, popular science articles, and animal stories directed at youth, Grzimek piqued his audience's attention with hyped-up tales of marauding wolves or aggressive chimpanzees, only to turn the tables on the reader by exposing the human animal as the real brute. Behind his carefully crafted public image as the savior of Frankfurt's zoo animals, Grzimek revealed in his memoirs a much darker self, haunted by the "great dying out" (*grosses Sterben*) that had accompanied the rise of the industrialized slaughterhouse in Europe and the parasitic expansion of European colonialism abroad. In his grim natural history of the "ubiquitous biped," human beings appear as

rogue primates whose technological prosthetics desensitized them to the terrible fate of their fellow creatures and unhinged them from the sociobiological
mechanisms that restrained aggression among other mammals. Dislocation,
starvation, alienation, and extreme violence were inevitable results.[10]

Grzimek's gloomy portrait of our species emerges most clearly in his autobiography *Auf den Mensch gekommen* (*Being Down with People*) whose title
underscores his perception of humans' unjust disparagement of non-human animals. The book was published in 1974, just after Grzimek had stepped down as
West Germany's first federal minister for nature protection and in the wake of
bruising, failed battles to establish the country's first national park and merge
the ministries of nature conservation and environmental protection under one
umbrella agency.[11] It takes an anthropological view of the curious "bipeds" he
had to associate with over the course of his life, a perspective that he transferred
from the war-ravaged cities of Europe to the decolonizing territories of Africa.[12]
Evident in the autobiography, too, are the practical questions about the care and
breeding of animals in Frankfurt that first prompted Grzimek to study and protect their habitats abroad. Such a zookeeper's ecology was a logical extension of
Grzimek's abiding interest in ethology, the study of animal behavior, which had
animated his engagement with the works of Konrad Lorenz and Basel zoo director Heini Hediger. Hediger's investigation of the physiological and psychological requirements of captive animals spurred Grzimek's growing awareness of the
critical relationship between animals and their ecological niches in the wild.[13]
This was a first step toward the Frankfurt Zoo becoming a leader in zoological
gardens' transition from sites of entertainment into conservationist institutions.

By focusing his autobiographical reflections on the unrestrained aggressiveness of the human animal, Grzimek sidestepped any deeper reckoning with
National Socialism—including the careerism that led ordinary conservationists
like himself to join the regime's ranks as bureaucrats and embrace its "biological"
approach to social problems. Such a starkly organic understanding of human history has led some scholars to label Germany's greatest nature conservationist
an "avocado" environmentalist: green on the outside, but brown (fascist) in the
middle.[14] There are no doubt striking continuities between National Socialist
depictions of nature and society and Grzimek's postwar writings—apocalyptic
warnings about American "materialism," a fear that colonial tutelage had resulted
in an "unnatural" mixing of races, and a eugenicist belief in the necessity of managing human evolution. We now know that Grzimek was a National Socialist
party member—a charge he had denied throughout his life—though the timing of his party application in 1937 suggests the professional motives of a Third
Reich bureaucrat rather than an enthusiastic Nazi.[15]

Despite such affinities, Grzimek insisted that Nazi anti-Semitism and other
forms of racism were fanatical and unscientific—and gestured toward the

possibilities of racial tolerance in a post-fascist age. Like other West Germans at the time, Grzimek shifted the discussion of "race" in the 1950s from Jews to persons of African descent to prove his cosmopolitan bona fides, recounting friendly encounters with African American soldiers among the Allied occupiers who shared the German nation's victimhood. Grzimek also sympathized with the plight of the children some of these soldiers had with German women—the so-called occupation children (*Besatzungskinder*)—he and his wife Hildegard even adopted one.[16] As he began traveling to Africa in 1951, a zoological vision of *Homo sapiens* emerged that insisted on the biological equality of all "races": any ruminations about foibles, superstitions, or oddities of the "bipeds" in Africa applied just as equally to smug Europeans.[17] Yet such cosmopolitanism bypassed any reckoning with Germany's colonial encounters with Africans or the fate of black Germans in the national community.[18] Indeed, Grzimek's universal paradigm envisioned all societies moving through fixed stages of evolution—and eventual dissolution—rendering Africans' aspirations for political autonomy and economic modernity especially dangerous.[19] In his eyes, they had begun to "degenerate," just like the "savage Europeans" who had waged two world wars, dropped an atomic bomb, and banished wild animals to the margins of their homeland.[20]

A Barnyard Heimat

Grzimek's belief that popular misunderstandings about animals reflected modern alienation from nature emerged long before he became a zookeeper and conservationist. Born into a comfortably bourgeois, Catholic, and Center Party–leaning family in the mixed Polish-German speaking town of Neisse, about 250 miles southeast of Berlin, Grzimek spent his childhood focused on the practical care and breeding of domestic livestock—particularly chickens. This led him to veterinary school in the 1920s and sparked a lifelong scientific interest in animal psychology. After his father's untimely death in 1912, the family moved to the outskirts of the city, which Grzimek described as a paradise for animal lovers like himself. Teachers invited him to bring frogs, salamanders, mice, and even a hedgehog (the animal that became his personal mascot) to natural history classes. Grzimek also bred chickens—particularly Antwerp bearded hens—and as a teenager founded a local club dedicated to boosting the quality and number of their eggs.[21] Indeed, Grzimek was once awarded a kitschy coffee service as a prize for his hens at a local fair, a reward for which he claimed he was just as proud as receiving the Oscar in 1960 for *Serengeti Shall Not Die*. "I was only concerned with agricultural livestock at that time, rarely with wild animals . . . . I loved animals very much, but much in the way of a farmer."[22] This focus on caring for the barnyard menagerie diverged significantly from romantic ideals of *Heimat* (or homeland) that extolled hiking across picturesque landscapes and taking in panoramic views.[23]

In Grzimek's analysis, modern alienation stemmed first and foremost from the loss of daily contact with work animals. It pained Grzimek that West Germans of the 1970s spent their holidays building sand castles on the beaches of the Adriatic or southern Spain. In his day, nearly everyone spent a few weeks with their country cousins on a *Sommerfrische*, helping to milk cows, gather eggs, harvest vegetables, ride horses, or bail hay. "To our parents and grandparents," Grzimek recalled in 1978, "animals were as self-evident as the four walls of their houses. They lived with them, horses drew their carriages, they waited on them in the streets, pigeons pecked in their backyards, and girls collected fresh eggs from their own chicken houses. Now animals have become rare. Our children get to know them now only in films, at the zoo, and perhaps during the holidays. What has been lost gives food for thought, and its value recognized only later."[24]

Early interest in domestic livestock led Grzimek to envision nature and human beings' place within it in ways that diverged from the concerns about landscape aesthetics so characteristic of the prewar *Naturschutz* movement with which Grzimek is sometimes associated. Many of Germany's leading nature conservationists in the 1920s and 1930s had belonged, like Grzimek, to local *Wandervogel* movements, avoiding alcohol and smoking or experimenting with vegetarianism as they took to the countryside and wrote poetry, sang songs, and camped under the stars.[25] Such young men later filled the provincial nature conservation offices of the Weimar and Nazi periods, where they lobbied to protect the country's regional *Heimat* landscapes as a bulwark against the vicissitudes of modern society: mass migration to industrial cities, transnational commerce, and fluid social class boundaries. Such romantic conservationists referred to forests as magnificent "cathedrals" that no human hand could ever repeat and that all people, regardless of status, would appreciate in the same way.[26]

The belief in the power of landscape to shape German identity spurred the country's first attempts at environmental reform. In the wake of rapid industrialization and urbanization, conservationists called on provincial officials to set aside geologically or ecologically significant "natural monuments," promulgate regulations that might stem unbridled stream regulation, or curb the rapid replacement of hardwood forests with conifer plantations.[27] In 1904, the music professor Ernst Rudorff founded the German Association for Heimat Protection, an organization dedicated to protecting natural and historic monuments and promoting regionally distinct architectural styles and folklife. At the behest of the Prussian Assembly, the botanist Hugo Conwentz established the State Office for Natural Monument Preservation (*Staatliche Stelle für Naturdenkmalpflege*) within the Prussian Ministry of Culture in 1906.[28] The use of the term *Naturdenkmalpflege* marked this "care of natural monuments" as the "youngest child" of *Denkmalfplege*, or heritage preservation, which linked nature conservation to the celebration of regional landscapes and provincial German identities.

Grzimek, on the other hand, eschewed descriptions of persons as members of a region, nation, religion, or political party. Instead, he emphasized their shared evolutionary inheritance with other mammals among the millions of species that populated the planet. "This ball had been spinning around hundreds and hundreds of millions of years with only non-humans on it," he noted in 1943. Starlings still saw the world as a beautiful, colorful "starling earth," he thought, while wolves perceived it as the wolf's world.[29] Humans' social affiliations, in Grzimek's view, obscured their deeper biological kinship and commonalities with companionate species suffering the ills of modernization.

Not surprisingly, Grzimek chose a career path in veterinary science, completing university degrees at Leipzig and Berlin, where he defended a dissertation on chicken anatomy in January 1933, just days before the National Socialists seized power. During his education, Grzimek took a steamship journey to the United States that would shape his views of American consumer culture—and the failed promises of economic development—for decades to come. Under the auspices of the Prussian agricultural ministry's small livestock division, Grzimek set off for America in 1930 to study industrialized poultry farms, which at the time were considered far more advanced than those in Europe. As the ship entered New York Harbor, Grzimek saw a giant billboard for Wrigley's Chewing Gum— a foretaste of the false commercial blandishments of the big city. He was then swindled out of a fifty-dollar bill at a street fair ball toss stand, the beginning of a distaste for American culture he would hold for the rest of his life.[30]

The skyscrapers that appeared impressive in bird's-eye postcards were alien and unattractive at street level, he wrote, while the Hudson, much like the Rhine at home, was narrower and less impressive than it appeared in landscape paintings. Grzimek marvelled at the thousands of automobiles parked on New York's crowded streets, a symbol of a people on the move with no time for Sunday hobbies or family gatherings.[31] Grzimek was disappointed, too, by the spread of agribusiness across the Midwest, symbolized by acres of rotting apples atop small, abandoned farms. "It was clear to me then what would eventually come to Germany," he noted. "We studiously copy American developments that over there they've already recognized as mistakes," particularly the barbaric crowding of chickens in battery cages or the reconstructed modernist city center in Frankfurt that he detested. Germans' imitation of failed American experiments led Grzimek to reflect on the inevitable—and pathological—stages of development that would soon infect Africa as well.[32] "Where a hundred years ago Winnetou and Old Shatterhand still wandered among the endless herds of buffalo," he remarked, "within a few short decades the limitless grain fields of North America began to sway in the breeze, and today those same breezes are transforming vast tracts of territory which have been robbed of their binding grasses once more into dusty desert. Africa, too, will go the same way—and much more quickly than many might imagine."[33] For Grzimek, both Germany and Africa were being "colonized" by American consumerism—a stance that deflected Germany's own former colonial engagements by wallowing in his country's victimhood.

During the Third Reich, Grzimek was hired as a deputy minister in the live-stock division that had sponsored his trip to the United States. Later, he worked as an egg inspector in Richard Walther Darré's Reich Food Estate, where he specialized in bolstering the size and quantity of domestic egg production in line with the regime's autarkical goals.[34] This period coincided with his growing scientific interest in the study of animal behavior, including that of a chimpan-zee, Ulla, and a wolf cub, Genghis, which he brought into his family's home to observe their habits and publish weekly accounts of their antics in the *Illustrierte Zeitung* in Berlin and the *Illustriertes Blatt* in Frankfurt.[35] During the course of the 1940s, Grzimek also published a number of scientific pieces in the *Zeitschrift für Tierpsychologie* (*Journal of Animal Psychology*), a publication he helped to develop along with scientific luminaries Oskar Heinroth, Jakob von Uexküll, and Konrad Lorenz. Well into the 1950s his goal remained an academic scien-tific career, even though his 1936 postdoctoral study (*Habilitation*) on egg pro-cessing at the University of Berlin's veterinary science department—a critical step to securing a professorship—was rejected for insufficient scientific merit.[36]

The war produced the unexpected circumstances by which the "egg baron" became Germany's most important caretaker of wild animals. In the early 1940s, Grzimek's veterinary background earned him a relatively comfortable posting training horses on the Eastern Front. He moved his family to a small country house in southern Germany, where they survived the war without injury.[37] Yet before he fled Berlin, Grzimek accommodated the entreaties of his friend Lutz Heck, the director of the Berlin Zoo, to save an adult chimpanzee pair—Owa and Bambo—from their bomb-damaged paddock by placing them in the fam-ily's Berlin apartment.[38] It was Grzimek's first extended contact with exotic ani-mals from abroad and he used the opportunity to explore the chimps' reactions to domestic life—including the injuries he sustained from Owa while integrat-ing the pair into his home as the Allies drew nearer to the city.[39]

Grzimek shared Lorenz's view that animal behavior—much like animal morphology—could be traced back to instinctual drives, selected over millen-nia, which fostered species preservation. Domestication short-circuited this process of natural selection, leading to a proliferation of behavioral irregularities that matched, in Lorenz's view, the grotesque array of forms created by artificial breeding. Irregularities eliminated by natural selection in the wild among canines, for example, might be "prized for their novelty or cuteness" by human dog own- ers but led to the biological degeneration of the species.[40] Lorenz equated the harmful effects of domestication with the unnatural conditions found in human civilization. In his 1940 article "Disturbance of Characteristic Behaviors through Domestication," Lorenz argued that prehistoric clans moving across vast territo- ries had developed noble qualities in their efforts to "combat hunger, cold, pred- ators, and barbarians"; maladapted clan members faced extinction.[41] To remedy such decline, Lorenz advocated a eugenic solution: regulating human reproduc- tion in an effort to overcome the deleterious effects of the modern welfare state's "unnatural" selection of weak or infirm individuals.[42]

Grzimek shared Lorenz's fears of degeneration but was never as reductionist as Lorenz in his assessment of animal perception. He investigated instead how animals responded to their external environment through trial-and-error pro- cesses of learning, memory, and cognition. Like Karl von Frisch, who viewed the "dance of the bees" as a form of complex animal communication, Grzimek explored the variable expression of "instinct" as animals learned to adapt, largely through self-propelled choices that were not simply a product of innate drives.[43] Without a Habilitation in hand, Grzimek had to investigate theories of animal behavior while working as a veterinary doctor, maintaining his bureaucratic post, and raising a family in Berlin. To make extra money, Grzimek published his ruminations on humans' alienation from nature in popular serial columns, stories, and books in the 1940s. Grzimek used these writings to dispel myths about various "beasts" and present their real existing status in the conditions of modernity—marginalized, brutalized, and increasingly endangered. Their human persecutors, meanwhile, appeared in his work as degenerate primates whose "self-domestication" led to explosions of aggression and destruction.

Genghis the Wolf

Grzimek was fascinated especially by a "primitive" animal whose behavior within a home setting could be compared to its modern, canine cousin: *Dschingis*, or Genghis the Wolf. In a 1943 book about Genghis, Grzimek recounted how he tamed this animal, which many considered incapable of living in captivity.[44] Through trial-and-error methods that led to many bitten fingers, Grzimek con- vinces Genghis to accept him as the leader of the pack. At one point, Grzimek even teaches Genghis to use the typewriter, and the book's preface claims that the animals thereby "co-authored" the text: this claim was confirmed by the pawprint of Katja, another of Grzimek's wolves, on the cover.[45] Following Lorenz's work on animal behavior, Grzimek used the human family to channel

Figure 1.1 At Home with the Chimps, 1953. Grzimek's stories about the behavior of large mammals in the home with his first wife Hildegard first appeared in illustrated weeklies and popular books during the early 1940s, long before he went to Africa to study the animals' habitat. Getty Images.

innate characteristics into an animal suitable for domestication. But the story also served to teach humans about their own captivity in artificial urban environments that disrupted natural curbs on antisocial behavior.

Grzimek traced the persecution of the wolf to familiar tales such as "Little Red Riding Hood" or the legends of Remus and Romulus, which had justified wolves' mass killing throughout Central Europe. Such ferocious images stood in sharp contrast to photographs of Genghis being led on a leash throughout Berlin, including one in which the he waits patiently with Grzimek's wife Hildegard to board the tram. "Certainly wolves do not live on grass and hay,"

Grzimek notes, "but the statistics always have two sides."[46] Tens of thousands of Germans died each year through accidents caused by domesticated horses, cows, and pigs, he wrote, while at their worst wolves had killed only twenty-eight persons during the turmoil of the Napoleonic Wars. Far more horrifying for Grzimek was humans' brutalization of work animals. Ever-rising consumption of milk and butter, he noted, had led to the overcrowding and half-starvation of dairy cows during long winters, after which many did not have the strength to make it back to the spring meadows on their own volition.[47] Such "bait and switch" techniques soon became a hallmark of Grzimek's style, which tended to recount familiar legends, myths, or assumptions about animals as a pretext for jarring the reader into new forms of ecological insight and self-awareness. In this case, readers could see the wolf through new eyes: as a relatively harmless creature unnecessarily persecuted by a society mired in outdated myths and indifferent toward the suffering of fellow mammals.

Grzimek no doubt understood the enormous significance of wolves in the Third Reich. Hitler admired their strength, fighting spirit, and supposed "merciless" cunning and was fond of signing his private correspondence "Dein Wolf." The lower Saxon town of Wolfsburg—headquarters of Volkswagen—was founded in 1938 as a tribute to Hitler.[48] Grzimek's work with wolves brought him closer to the regime's inner circles when Leni Riefenstahl approached him with a starring role for Genghis in the film opera *Tiefland* (*Lowlands*).[49] The film, which was shot in the Dolomites in 1940–1941, has become notorious for its recruitment of Sinti and Roma detainees from a nearby "Gypsy camp" in Salzburg as extras to play "dark-skinned" Catalan villagers. Most of these detainees were murdered shortly thereafter in Nazi death camps with Riefenstahl's tacit knowledge.[50] According to Grzimek's account, the director's most pressing concern in 1941 was finding the right animal for a fight scene with a herder. Riefenstahl steadfastly refused to use a shepherd dog as a stand in, which she believed looked too fake, but an attempt to use a wolf from a nearby circus had resulted in the death of a production assistant.[51] She and her associate supposedly discovered Genghis and Grzimek on one of their walks in Berlin, and soon they were off to the mountains for filming. To convince Genghis to simulate stalking sheep by creeping toward the camera, Grzimek relied on a squeaky toy to get the wolf's attention, while in the fight scene, the actor used padded clothing to roughhouse with the wolf, much as Grzimek had done at home.[52] Whether Grzimek knew about the fate of the film's "extras" is unclear; but working with Riefenstahl proved critical to the development of his own operatic documentary style.

Grzimek's relationship to Riefenstahl developed at a time when he learned of Hermann Göring's efforts to pass animal and nature protection legislation designed to strengthen the ties between "blood and soil."[53] On April 21, 1933, three months after Hitler's seizure of power, the Nazi regime passed the first of dozens of animal protection laws that targeted Jewish kosher slaughter and then expanded to include the ethical treatment of animals in labs, on hunting expeditions, and as pets.[54] In a radio address of August 1933, Hermann Göring announced that "The German people particularly have always shown their greatest love of animals and the question of animal protection was always near their hearts. . . . To the German, animals are not merely creatures in the organic sense, but creatures who lead their own lives and who are endowed with perceptive facilities, who feel pain and experience joy and prove to be faithful and attached."[55] The mishandling of animals, Göring averred, was a product of "foreign conceptions of justice" that viewed animals as inert and subject entirely to human will.[56] Being an animal lover did not make one a good person, as Grzimek noted repeatedly in connection with Hitler's well-known passion for pets and wildlife.

Nature conservation was one arena where Grzimek found affinities with National Socialism. He lauded the National Socialist regime for passing the world's most comprehensive and stringent piece of nature protection legislation, known as the Reich Nature Protection Law. The statute realized decades-long hopes among Germany's nature conservationists for nationwide nature protection.[57] The law also owed its swift promulgation to Göring, who among his many ministerial roles was the head of German forestry. Göring argued that saving noble species such as the European bison went hand in hand with protecting imperiled "Nordic" peoples from "Jewish-materialist" civilization, though the text of the law was surprisingly free of Nazi ideology.[58] Both the animal and nature protection laws lacked any real punch in practice. *Heimatschutz* and *Naturschutz* advocates who hoped that the law would end environmentally destructive liberal property regimes quickly found themselves on the margins of power as the regime destroyed wetlands, cut down forests, and paved autobahns through the countryside as they prepared for their assault on Eastern Europe.[59] Meanwhile, animal experimentation continued apace in the Third Reich, and a host of exceptions allowed for medical researchers to use animals as controls in drug trials.[60] Nonetheless, Grzimek saw Göring's animal and nature conservation laws as a "model for the world" at the time.[61]

Grzimek was also familiar with Lutz Heck and his brother Heinz's bizarre animal breeding experiments designed to restore large mammal breeds back to the German Reich.[62] Heck first served Nazi leaders by "saving" (stealing) animals from the bombed-out Warsaw Zoo after the Nazi invasion and shipping them to zoos and game reserves inside Germany. As the Germans drove deeper into Polish territory, Heck arranged for the resettlement of European bison (*żubr*) and the rare wild species of horse known as the tarpan from the Białowieża forest in eastern Poland to Göring's imperial nature reserve in Pomerania.[63] Göring declared himself "Reich Hunting Master" and promulgated a series of laws that prohibited hunters from using traps and buckshot and outlawed the hunting of endangered species.[64] In a series of breeding trials that paralleled Nazi efforts to locate and replenish "Aryan racial stock" throughout Europe, Heck and his brother Heinz, the director of the Munich Zoo, tried to back-breed the *żubr* in the hopes of re-creating the extinct European aurochs, a type of semi-wild cow, by using bulls from Spain, Hungary, Corsica, and France.[65]

Grzimek, like most zoologists at the time, found such experiments dubious, though the strength and musculature of Heck's "Aryan cows" served Nazi propaganda purposes well.[66] Grzimek saw no reason to disavow Heck on this basis; at war's end, the zookeeper was welcomed in Frankfurt without reservation. "I never held it against Professor Lutz Heck that he had such close ties to Hermann Göring and other Nazi party leaders," Grzimek wrote, "because in the end he was able to expand the Berlin Zoo into the Tiergarten city park."[67] After he reached Frankfurt and settled into his role as zoo director, Grzimek told visiting British and American colleagues that zookeepers should focus on their gardens and avoid political advocacy. "If I were the leader of the Berlin Zoo and the Russians would occupy Germany, I would likely be happy if Stalin invited me to dinner. Because in this way I could perhaps achieve something for my animal garden and for the larger animal world."[68] For Grzimek, nature conservation was above partisanship; it mattered little if a government were a democracy or dictatorship so long as wild animals were well protected. The specific crimes of Nazism—and the merger of racial biology and governmentality that had propelled its growth—faded into obscurity. Small wonder, then, that interwar fears of European cultural decline and racial "degeneracy" resurfaced in Grzimek's postwar writings, masquerading as maladies affecting all *Homo sapiens*.

An Apolitical Conservationist

Grzimek's relationship to Riefenstahl and readiness to look past Heck's crimes have understandably heightened suspicion about deeper ideological ties to the Hitler regime.[69] Despite numerous incidents in his memoir of Gestapo suspicion and harassment, recent biographies have shown that he joined a Stormtrooper driving club in the early 1930s and the National Socialist Party in 1937, a year in which countless government bureaucrats formerly from different political stripes joined the party seeking to demonstrate their loyalty to the regime.[70] In 1948 Grzimek almost lost his position at the Frankfurt Zoo after Allied investigators arrested him for falsifying his questionnaire about former Nazi Party membership based on tips from disgruntled associates. The Allied Commission rightly determined that Grzimek had been a careerist *Mitläufer*—a fellow traveler, or bystander—rather than an ardent Nazi, but for a time in the late 1940s his career and reputation hung in the balance.[71] In traveling to Africa in the early to mid-1950s to observe chimpanzees in their wild habitat, Grzimek was also seeking refuge from lingering questions about his Nazi sympathies.[72]

Not surprisingly, Grzimek used his autobiography to portray himself and his fellow citizens as "good Germans" untainted by the Third Reich's crimes. In line with broader tendencies for West Germans to "blame everyone but themselves," Grzimek painted Germans as the real victims of the Third Reich—of Hitler-inspired terror, of Allied fire bombings and broken promises, and of ethnic cleansing and the loss of homeland.[73] Hitler appeared as a savior to ordinary Germans looking for a way out of the economic calamity of the Depression, Grzimek asserted, repeating Riefenstahl's tired claim that she was seduced by Hitler's promise of national awakening.[74] Grzimek associated anti-Semitism with the religious fanaticism that had led to persecution of heretics, as a form of self-righteous anger against those who did not share the faith.[75] Grzimek also found the rhetoric of "blood and soil" absurd from a biological standpoint. In one of the autobiography's more dubious claims, Grzimek recounted a casual meeting with the sadistic Martin Bormann, the head of the chancellery and Hitler's right-hand man. Grzimek could not fathom why Hitler had invaded the East for German settlers. "The Germans are now a people tired of the countryside," he told Bormann sardonically, "despite all of the propaganda . . . the daughter of a family farmer would much rather marry a postal clerk than a farmer" because she knew just how backbreaking and thankless the work was.[76] Keenly aware of the Polish origins of his own name, Grzimek illustrated for Bormann how nearly every German "east of Magdeburg" had Slavic origins. Europe was such a melting pot that it was impossible to distinguish different racial lines from each other, and the Poles were so hardworking they would "become good German nationalists in 200 years."[77]

The association of Nazi racism with fanaticism nonetheless allowed other dimensions of the Third Reich's social policy to linger on in Grzimek's postwar imagination, fueled by a eugenicist logic that equated modernization with a society's biological decline. Grzimek recounts long conversations with Riefenstahl about the regime's social policies that took place during the filming of *Tiefland*. According to Grzimek, Riefenstahl opposed the Nazis' forced sterilization and euthanasia policies, whereas Grzimek shared the regime's argument that "hereditarily ill and disadvantaged children" would have perished in pre-industrial times. Grzimek argued in favor of a "releasing injection" for the severely injured or mentally ill and echoed Nazi eugenicists' widely disseminated view that the share of the population made up of "asocials" and the "feeble minded" was increasing exponentially over the more valuable educated middle classes.[78] Grzimek regretted that Nazi "fanaticism" had made it impossible for enlightened scientists to help societies toward thinking "not only philosophically, but also biologically" about such moral and political questions.[79]

Grzimek accentuated this divide between "biological thinking" and racist "fanaticism" by recalling stories of his and his family's generosity and kindness toward persons of African descent. Seemingly unaware of the plight of Afro-Germans who had already lived in Germany for decades, Grzimek shifted the discussion of blackness to the family's encounters with the North African soldiers who served among the French occupying troops in southern Germany. Grzimek recalled Hildegard's invitation to Moroccan soldiers—ordered by their white French commander to sleep in the Grzimeks' barn in the last days of the war—to lay their mattresses on the floor of the house. This act was a symbolic repudiation of the 1929 "black horror" on the Rhine that had vilified an earlier Allied occupation with lurid images of the threat that French North African soldiers posed to white women's sexuality.[80] The soldiers ask Hildegard for the key to the kitchen cupboards, which they fill with coveted food rations from their own allocation in gratitude for her kindness.

Grzimek and Hildegard also befriended African American servicemen who came to Germany with Allied forces in 1945. After witnessing the treatment of these soldiers in the US Army, Grzimek and most other Germans shielded the young black servicemen from their white officers. They were "much loved by us," he reported, and in return for their protection, the soldiers gave the Germans extra rations from their own stores according to the principle: "We are slaves, you are also slaves!"[81] This integration of African Americans into a shared community of German suffering, coming just twelve years after the Third Reich had sterilized the "Rhineland bastards" as the first step toward "racial hygiene," served as another striking symbol of post-fascist tolerance in Grzimek's account. Such acts of kindness from and toward black soldiers became part of a broader postwar mythology about the good Germans who had suffered Hitler's tyranny and now led the Federal Republic on the path to redemption.

Yet a closer look reveals that the stories cast Bernhard and Hildegard as parental benefactors even as they purport to applaud black lives and identities.[82] Hildegard tries, in vain, to teach the North Africans to use the indoor toilet, rather than simply relieving themselves in the meadows surrounding the barn—a trope that was common throughout colonial literatures about African resistance to public sanitation measures.[83] The passage transforms the black soldiers from racial threats into naïve children awaiting European instruction in modern technology. They even write a letter to Hildegard after the war with a photograph displaying the water closet they built back home.[84] Narratives of German kindness toward African American soldiers had a similar power to insult those they sought to celebrate. This was especially evident in West German reactions to the "mixed-race" babies known as "occupation children" resulting from sexual relationships between African American soldiers and German women. These children became the objects of widespread scrutiny and socio-psychological investigation—much of it by the protégés of racial hygienists who had served under the Third Reich.[85] Most West Germans decided that these "mixed-race children" would fare much better if adopted by African Americans in the United States. In Germany, they argued, the children would face the challenges of adapting their inborn characteristics to the dictates of the "dominant" culture.[86] Discussion of cultural integration, in this sense, still hinged on immutable properties of "racial difference"—a distinction that had made Nazi anti-Semitism possible and palatable in the first place. The locus of racial anxiety in the Federal Republic shifted from Jews to blacks without confronting the Nazi regime's broader racial underpinnings.

Grzimek was deeply moved by the plight of occupation children, especially after seeing the 1952 melodrama *Toxi*, a movie about the plight of an abandoned occupation child that spurred him and Hildegard to adopt an occupation baby.[87] Bernhard and Hildegard named their adopted son Thomas, even though many speculated at the time that the boy was Grzimek's own love child from one of his many extra-marital relationships in Africa.[88] Grzimek's personal story reinforced the couple's magnanimity toward Africans and African Americans and rejected the dominant view that "half-castes" were inferior.[89] Long passages about Grzimek's sympathy toward people of color were undoubtedly designed to distract from his dalliances with the Third Reich. But they also signaled a special—and paternal—affinity for persons of African heritage when advocating for national parks in Africa. "Because of my interest in these people and their life, it was not long before I also came into contact with the black politicians of these countries, got to know their problems and fears, and could sometimes do more for the development and safeguarding of the great national parks in Africa than official European institutions," he wrote in 1978.[90]

The inevitable blurring of "races" as part of modernization reinforced Grzimek's conviction that only the non-human world retained its authenticity. For him, the bombed-out cities and destroyed agricultural fields of Poland and Germany revealed not so much the folly of Nazism's specific ideological vision but the ephemeralness of all political ideologies, cultures, and social norms. When his homeland Silesia fell into Polish hands after the war, Grzimek saw it as part of the ceaseless dispossession and uprooting that had taken place there since early modern times and would no doubt continue into the future.[91] Sentimental *Heimat* films of the 1950s extolled the virtues of rural areas and the integration of true-blooded outsiders, but for Grzimek and others displaced by the bombings of 1944–1945, emotional attachments to homeland were futile.[92] Only animals retained organic connections to territory; only they deserved a permanent refuge from human violence.

At Home in the Zoo

Quite by accident, Grzimek found a lasting sanctuary for animals at the Frankfurt Zoo, which he successfully transformed from a bombed-out ruin with few surviving animals into one of the largest zoological institutes in Europe. Wilhelm Holbach, whom the Allied administration named interim mayor of Frankfurt in 1945, had published many of Grzimek's animal stories in the city newspaper and asked him to take over the position. Grzimek quickly demonstrated his lifelong penchant for showmanship by introducing mass entertainment onto the damaged zoo grounds, including building a makeshift dance hall platform, cinema, and stage for theater and circus performances. He even relocated a rollercoaster from a defunct amusement park in the Black Forest and appropriated (without permission) nearby parcels of land and leftover rubble to expand the zoo's space and building materials.[93] These efforts alienated him from the staid directors of Germany's other zoological gardens, but Grzimek always viewed the spectacle as a necessary evil to earn money—visitor by visitor—so that the zoological garden could repair or rebuild critical structures and replenish its array of animal specimens. The strategy worked. In 1946 alone, the zoo attracted two million visitors.[94]

The role of zoo director gave Grzimek an ideal opportunity to pursue his interests in animal behavior, but the day-to-day care of zoo animals ultimately stimulated broader ecological questions about how to replace or mimic their former living spaces and social worlds in captivity. The field of ecology (*Ökologie*), as originally conceived by the German Darwinist Ernst Haeckel in 1866, studied the relationship between organisms and their environment and with each other. Ecologists investigated the means by which they adapted—or failed to adapt—to changing surroundings that enabled only the fittest to survive.[95] In Central Europe, animal geography and behavioral studies inspired by Alexander von Humboldt's holism and geared toward understanding the symbiosis between climate, wildlife, and vegetation were also important themes.[96] Key principles of what we might term today "community ecology," particularly Karl Moebius's concept of the *biocoenosis* (later referred to by ecologists as the "ecological community," or *Lebensgemeinschaft*) developed in non-university settings. In zoological gardens, natural history museums, and grade schools in provincial cities throughout Germany, naturalists sought ways to encourage a "biological perspective" that moved beyond the confines of traditional taxonomic organization and toward displays of animals' dynamic relationships.[97] Grzimek's zookeeper's ecology, driven by practical questions of how best to mimic the wild within the confines of the zoo, emerged from similar circumstances.

Figure 1.2 Dancing on the Zoo Terrace amid the ruins of the Frankfurt Zoo, 1946. Grzimek used unconventional methods to attract visitors to the zoo in order to raise money for rebuilding and purchasing new specimens, moves that alienated him from Germany's more conservative zoo directors. Institute for the History of Frankfurt, S7 Ko No. 127, Photographer Fred Kochmann.

When Grzimek first visited the Frankfurt Zoo before the war, he was dismayed to find an "outdated row of cages" holding individual or, at most, pairs of specimens organized according to taxonomic categories.[98] In his view, zoos were not museums that needed to preserve and display an exemplar of every species on earth. Indeed, by the 1930s, zoos in Germany had begun to shift away from these displays and toward open-air ensembles, replete with vegetation and rock formations intended to simulate animals' natural surroundings, which suited a new era of zoological gardens as scientific institutions for study and species conservation.[99] "We zoo-people, at least the more progressive ones," he wrote in his autobiography, "no longer want to keep animals alone, but rather in pairs, groups, herds, in natural communities."[100] In such communities, the animals needed to perceive their paddock as their own territory (*Eigenbezirk*) or, even better, their own possession (*Eigentum*), especially when they found everything within it that they depended on in the wild—food, partners for reproduction, and most importantly, space to move around.[101]

Following in the footsteps of famous Hamburg animal trader Carl Hagenbeck, Grzimek quickly used the opportunity of war destruction to seize territory on surrounding city blocks in the late 1940s and restructure the zoological paddocks as cageless, open-air communities of animals arranged according to biogeographical zones. Hagenbeck had pioneered the use of such cage-less "panoramas" at the Berlin Industrial Exposition in 1896, which he then developed into an animal park in Stellingen, outside Hamburg.[102] The park consisted of bar-free animal enclosures built up as stages one behind the other, separated from the public by concealed moats and artificial rockworks that gave the impression of a wild habitat.[103] While a number of scornful zoo directors vowed never to capitulate to the "Hagenbeckization" of their own zoos, they could not fail to note that he had over one million visitors annually, even before World War I and given limited public transportation to the site.[104] Making animals and their communities robust not only enhanced the visitor's experience but also encouraged the animals to breed, a sure sign of their sense of well-being in the ersatz living space of the zoological garden and a source of pride for zoological institutes worldwide.[105]

To create sufficient room for such large-scale paddocks, the zoo's staff began to reduce its numbers of specimens—from a high point of 965 species shortly after the war to 676 by the 1960s. Grzimek even made room for two hippopotamuses—an incredible dedication of space given the zoo's urban location—by finding a full-grown mate for the zoo's two-ton male, Toni. Like Toni, Gretel had survived Allied bombing raids by diving into the pool of water provided by her keepers, though she lost her mate and child and still had visible burn scars on her legs.[106] Even the predators had for the most part returned to the zoo after the air raids, never once hunting down humans for food as the press had erroneously reported. As proof of the animals' contentment with their zoological home were the zoo's deer populations who could easily leap over six feet into the air but never bothered to scale the hip-height fences surrounding their enclosure.[107] Like their displaced human counterparts, the refugee animals wanted nothing more than to put the war behind them and settle into a stable home territory.

Such concern about the wards of the zoological garden was a far cry from the brutality inflicted by nineteenth- and early twentieth-century specimen collectors under commission by Hagenbeck and others. Hunter-naturalists such as Schomburgk and Carl Schillings had isolated prized juvenile specimens by slaughtering adults in the surrounding herds, and scores of baby elephants, hippopotami, and lions died on the weeks-long journey back to Hamburg, the main port of call for zoo specimens in that period. The final moments of enraged elephant bulls protecting their young were then captured on film, while the poor creatures' "horns, skins, or bones" found their way to trophy walls or as specimens for natural history museums.[108] With the development of the tranquilizer or "capture" gun developed by veterinarian Toni Harthoorn in the 1950s, the procurement of animals for zoos became a mundane and commercialized affair, with buyers' agents purchasing live animals from European settlers who had trapped the creatures themselves or bought them at a low price from local Africans.[109] The cargo was then loaded onto a steamship or plane and shepherded along by an experienced handler; hunter-collectors' tales of adventure and endangerment were pure bunk, as Grzimek had reminded his readers.[110]

While developing his garden, Grzimek was keenly interested in Basel zoo director Heini Hediger's theory that animals did not roam freely in the wild but perceived, structured, and defended spatially delimited territories as their own. Drawing on the animal geographical studies of Ernst Marcus and Richard Hesse, the game management philosophies of Aldo Leopold, the animal cognition studies of Jakob von Uexküll, and the ethological research of Lorenz, Hediger argued that animal species lived in networks of overlapping spaces that included their geographic range, habitat, and living space. Individuals of each species also inhabited and defended territories, or personal living spaces, in which they fulfilled physiological requirements (e.g., acquiring food, excreting wastes, drinking water) and psychological needs (e.g., refuge from predators, courtship, and mating).[111] "The beasts of the jungle," Grzimek surmised, "are really no freer than we humans, with our frontiers, customs barriers and passports and all the other impedimenta of international usage."[112] These overlapping biotopes and territories, in turn, contained a biological hierarchy of diverse species as well as an intraspecies social hierarchy, all of which regulated animals' distribution in space and time. For Grzimek, the zoo was one of the last places where humans could connect to a biological past of which they were once part.[113]

Of critical importance for Hediger's theories of animal welfare in a zoo setting was Jakob von Uexküll's assertion that animals actively selected from and reshaped the reservoir of stimuli in their environment. For Uexküll, this process of niche construction went beyond a Darwinian drive toward species preservation; animals, he believed, subjectively shaped and reconstituted their own world through paths and path markers, uniquely constructed dens or nests, and strategically placed scent trails. Animals not born into captivity had to construct a fresh subjective world, and the job of the zookeeper was to provide the right amount of space, stimuli, tools for flight responses, forage, unexpected encounters with other animals, and choice of mates.[114] For Hediger, the animals in zoological paddocks were "owners," rather than "captives," a rhetorical move designed to defend zoological institutes against animal rights detractors who viewed zoos as nothing more than animal prisons.[115] For Grzimek, Hediger's zoological biology offered fresh insights into the relationship between animal behavior and biogeography—insights that he yearned to test in the animals' "native haunts" abroad.[116]

The gradual recovery of animal populations in Frankfurt and other zoological gardens symbolized not just municipal reconstruction but also the possibilities for redemption after the destruction of so much human life in a senseless war. Grzimek's faith in nature's unique regenerative capacity, which was forged in these troubled postwar years and then globalized as he began collecting expeditions to Africa, would soon lead the zookeeper to fashion himself as a second Noah, leading the animals to safety amid the rising tide of humanity.[117] In 1950 Grzimek was one of only three German zoological directors invited to join the International Union of Directors of Zoological Gardens (today's World Association of Zoos and Aquariums) at its international conference in London, presided over by its new president, Heini Hediger, who had become Grzimek's mentor and friend. In that year, Grzimek also helped to establish the Society for the Friends of the Frankfurt Zoological Garden, which was later re-christened the Zoologische Gesellschaft Frankfurt am Main, gegründet 1858 (Frankfurt Zoological Society, founded 1858, hereafter FZS).[118] The organization helped the zoo to raise funds and use the influence of its board members to maintain its independence from city administrators who, from Grzimek's perspective, meddled too much in the institution's scientific affairs.

The study of animal territoriality eventually led Grzimek to expand his zookeeper's ecology beyond Frankfurt—to the homelands of the zoo's "owners" in Africa. "When one keeps thousands of animals in captivity, one often wracks one's brains how best to replace their life in the wild. But how do these animals actually live in the wild? That one has to observe directly in their *Heimat*."[119] Despite scores of nineteenth-century natural history accounts documenting the discovery of new species in Africa, Grzimek ascertained, very little was known about the behavior or habitats of animals in their native environments. When he consulted the well-respected Brehm series of animal encyclopedia for basic information—for example, on gestation among lions—he found that the data came from observations from other zoos, not from observation in the outdoors.

Given the lack of field data about animals, Grzimek leapt at the chance to visit the African continent after being invited in mid-1950 by a German-Jewish acquaintance, identified only as the former Frankfurt jeweler "Mr. Abraham," who had fled Nazi persecution in the 1930s and eventually taken up residence in Bouaké in the Ivory Coast.[120] After overcoming numerous bureaucratic hurdles—some a result of lingering French suspicions about a German traveling abroad—Grzimek found himself in the homelands of the Baule, a Tano-speaking West African community.[121] He and his sixteen-year-old son Michael spent three months there. In his 1951 memoir of the journey, Grzimek presents the Baule as content with French colonial administration, having prospered through French schools, hospitals, and markets for the area's rich harvests of coffee, cocoa, and yams.[122] Local villagers helped the Grzimeks and their French-speaking guide locate a number of animals for observation and, despite protestations in the opening pages that this was not a collecting trip, offered them for sale to the Germans. Michael returned from the Ivory Coast on a steamer filled with chimpanzees, antelopes, and monkeys bound for the zoo but also picked up an unidentified tropical fever that almost killed him.[123]

During their stay, the Grzimeks investigated Toni and Gretel's "brothers and sisters," whose behaviors conform perfectly to Hediger's theories about territoriality and animal *Heimat*. Hippos "mark the confines of their territories by a species of scent-boundary, the bulls using their short tails with a propeller-like movement and spraying dung and urine plentifully over the adjacent bushes." The result, he averred, was a clear demarcation telling other animals that they were "trespassing on occupied territory" and would have to "engage in bitter battle' to remain there.[124] The Grzimeks also confirmed how Toni and Gretel survived Allied attacks; the hippopotami used the nearby river as a refuge and "stampede blindly" whenever disturbed or threatened on land. "Once in the water they fear nothing," Grzimek remarked, "one often has no difficulty in approaching quite close to them with a boat."[125] Such "flight reactions" became a cornerstone of the Grzimeks' animal behavior research in the years ahead. Grzimek was astonished how quickly the portly hippos could scramble up steep river embankments or use their gaping mouths to threaten humans and crocodiles. All of these reactions became fodder for further refinements and naturalizations of the hippopotamus paddocks back home, ensuring Toni and Gretel even greater success at producing young in the zoo.

The problem with zookeepers' narrow focus on mating in captivity, it soon became clear, was the rapid depletion of animals in the wild. Hippos had almost completely disappeared from northern Africa, and their territories south of the Sahara were dwindling every year. Agricultural expansion had doomed many of the zoo's most popular species to extinction; by the end of this century, he lamented, "our grandchildren may well come to know the elephant, the rhinoceros, the okapi, tiger, tapir and so on, only by seeing them in books and at the cinema."[126] Data gathering about the movements, behavior, and reproduction of species in the wild thus served another, more urgent purpose: to ease the transfer of populations whose habitat was destroyed permanently. Hippos might make it a bit longer than lions or giraffe, he thought, for their "damp and swampy" habitats would be the last to succumb to agricultural cultivation. [127] The sobering fact that Africa's large mammals were doomed shifted Grzimek's attention from increasing breeding in zoo paddocks to preserving habitat abroad. Such destruction of habitat made humans—including ordinary zoo-goers—"the most dangerous predator on earth" as a mirror installed on the zoo grounds attested.

Figure 1.3 Grzimek in front of the installation "The Most Dangerous Predator" at the Frankfurt Zoo from the 1960s. Institute for the History of Frankfurt, S7C No. 1998-29.840, Photographer Philipp Kerner.

This shift from zoological refuge to scientific conservation abroad became clear as Grzimek identified the one glimmer of hope for giraffes, lions, rhinos, and zebra on his Ivory Coast journey: the forty-thousand-acre Nimba Mountain Reserve (today's Mount Nimba Strict Nature Reserve), tucked into a corner of the territory bordering Liberia and what was then French Guinea. The Nimba was a result of French initiatives that began in 1944, and characteristic of the French and Belgian models of nature conservation, as the sanctuary prioritized scientific research over tourism. Grzimek admired especially that "neither black nor white is allowed so much as to set foot" on the reserve without special, temporary scientific permits issued by the University of Dakar.[128] After experiencing the cacophony of chimpanzees in the reserve who lived more freely and more authentically than Ulla ever could, Grzimek dedicated himself to research and fundraising among the "handful of enlightened men . . . [who] . . . are doing their best to organize animal reserves, in which our hirsute brothers can live and flourish unmolested."[129] Such natural zoos, he averred, would also require careful observation to be sure that the animals were not merely dropped in, but could flourish in their surroundings. Grzimek predicted that "civilized generations of Negroes will thank the French administration for its foresight" in creating the reserve, which otherwise might become a target for development should precious minerals or uranium be discovered in the area.[130] The French idea of a scientific reserve—a gigantic zoo where researchers could observe animals freely living in paradise—remained Grzimek's benchmark throughout the 1950s. Only a strict preserve, he argued, could protect the animals from the devastation unleashed by the new global hegemon: the United States.

On the Equality of Degenerates

Grzimek's fear that American materialism would destroy the *Heimat* of Toni and Gretel paralleled his conviction that the Baule were losing their authenticity due to the same forces of "coca-colonization" that were engulfing Europe in the 1950s. The introduction to *Dr. Jimek* promises to bring German readers out of their "minute patch of the globe" and tell them about the "bipeds, black and white" that he had observed alongside the quadrupeds who were the usual subject of his writings. "Man, too, is a very interesting animal," Grzimek notes, "even if he has become more degenerate and domesticated than our pigs, cattle, and dogs."[131] As in *Genghis the Wolf*, Grzimek used paternalist and exotic clichés of the "primitive" African to turn the tables on his smug European readers—though he never quite succeeded in freeing himself from these same racial stereotypes.[132] As a general rule, he wrote, "a white man cannot help but feel a certain superiority in the presence of Negroes," as is evident when his servant "boy," Joe, appears to conflate the Christian trinity with the gods of animist traditions even as he claimed to be a devout Protestant.[133] For those Europeans who found animal totems silly or mocked the superstitious ways of the Africans in the "bush," Grzimek reminded his readers of their own superstitious nonsense, particularly the many Germans who regulated their lives according to astrological calendars.[134] Underneath the skin, Europeans and Africans were all just higher primates: "Such emotions as joy, hate, astonishment are the same all over the world and as easy to read on a black face as on a white—not to mention the chimpanzee."[135]

Such depictions reflected long-standing imperialist images of the "noble savage" as a foil for European culture, but Grzimek's narrative reflected a 1950s mode of travel writing in which all the world's "blank spaces" of fantasy were gone.[136] Unlike traditional ethnographic travel writing, which was premised on a denial of the coeval status of the "primitive" in relation to the European field researcher, *Dr. Jimek* sees simultaneity across vast distances, revealing what German reviewers of the book called an "odd and even dangerous mixed condition" created by Africans' speedy transition from a primitive state to an Americanized modernity.[137] On their bumpy ride in lorries across the vast interior, the Grzimeks conjure up images of the waning days of the American frontier to describe the African countryside. "In a land which is now blossoming forth, as did America in the days of the old pioneers," he wrote, "there is a great deal of money to be earned for the asking. Any wretched starveling, provided he is prepared to work hard, can become a rich man in a few years."[138] No longer subject to the forced labor regimes of early imperialism, Baule men were emerging as home-steaders, eschewing traditional communal landholding and arranged marriages in favor of cultivating their own freehold plots and wooing a girlfriend of their choosing. Hollywood melodramas were the cause of the Baule men's abandon-ment of tradition, Grzimek claimed, which they consumed just as readily as the Wrigley's Chewing Gum hawked by young boys at the open-air cinemas across the African interior.[139] Africans facing this "dangerous mixed condition" emerge as a distorted reflection of the postwar European self: consumerist, alienated, impulsive, and environmentally destructive.[140]

For Grzimek, the triumph of American materialism was an outward sign of a deeper, somatic "degeneration" of Baule culture caused by "race mixing" in the interior—a vision uncomfortably close to Nazi portrayals of the United States as a "bastardized" society infecting the rest of the world.[141] One evening, Bernhard and Michael stayed overnight at the house of a recently deceased Alsatian, who had been an "enthusiastic follower of Hitler" but, in moves that did not conform "with the racial principles he had ostensibly endorsed," carried on a liaison with an émigré German-Jewish woman and then purchased "six 'native' wives" who had borne him a 'host of half-caste children.'" The Alsatian soon went entirely "native," sleeping on the ground and serving guests snake cutlets. After his death, Grzimek maintains, his seventy-year-old mother found that her son had left her a "rich heritage" of "colored" grandchildren. Like the Grzimeks, the grandmother "rose to the occasion" and adopted the children as her own.[142] Such interra-cial polygamy nonetheless haunted Grzimek's imagination, reminding him of an article he had read in the Nazi SS journal, Das Schwarze Korps, discussing the possibility of multiple wives as a solution to a man-impoverished postwar world. Grzimek quickly dismissed such an arrangement in a Western context, for it would be far too difficult to "cut out the paramours of twelve women, buy each of them new and better clothes, and take them out to the cinema and to restaurants."[143] Grzimek then imagined the horrors awaiting the "hen-pecked" harem leader in the West—a disturbingly lighthearted evocation of patriarchy and racial terror in a postwar travel book. Grzimek's obsession with the prolifer-ation of racial "hybrids" in the Ivory Coast signaled that Africans, like Europeans before them, had become unmoored from "natural" laws of purity and equilib-rium that once regulated the organic and social realms.[144]

Lurking behind Grzimek's obsession with sexual practices was the deeper biopolitical fear that such uncontrolled human reproduction would lead to ever-diminishing space for wild animals. As he expanded his contacts in Africa, he fixated ever more on imperial authorities' pro-natal campaigns that sought to

lower infant and adult mortality rates and boost the number of African workers.[145] Such welfarism, he averred, had breached the laws of "natural selection,"
creating a stark imbalance between rising population numbers and the existing land resources for people and animals.[146] Coupled with French "pacification"—meaning no more wars among the "natives"—Grzimek foresaw that
the mechanisms of rapid population growth were locked into place. "The globe
is suffering the same fate at the hands of the human race as a dog attacked by
scurvy," Grzimek wrote. "The scurvy mites multiply and spread more and
more . . . until at last not a speck of healthy surface remains."[147] Grzimek noted
that the export of modern medicine and hygienic standards to the colonies had
brought down rates of infant mortality and conquered the majority of deadly
tropical diseases, leading to a "shockingly rapid rate" of population growth. "In
the last hundred years more human beings have been born on earth than during
the whole 500,000 previous years of the existence of our degenerate species,"
he noted.[148] Drastic measures were necessary to be sure that the "mites" did not
infect all the remaining healthy tissue.

Grzimek was not alone in his obsession with demography and space in the
1950s, however. Bernhard read and admired eugenicists such as Fairfield Osborn
Jr., who, in the wake of war, quietly shifted from advocating for hereditary health
at home to promoting family planning in the Third World.[149] In *Our Plundered
Planet* (1948), Osborn seized on statistics about declining infant mortality in
the Third World to depict a "silent war" on nature more potentially devastating
and permanent than the obliteration of cities in Europe and Japan.[150] Osborn
warned that soil erosion caused by spiraling population growth threatened the
capacity of the land to feed, clothe, and shelter humans and provide habitat for
wildlife. "The tide of the earth's population is rising," Osborn continued, while
"the reservoir of the earth's living resources is falling."[151] Grzimek also cited
R. C. Cook, who wrote *Human Fertility: The Modern Dilemma* (1951) and Erich
Hornsmann, the author of *Sonst Untergang* (*Otherwise Collapse*, 1951), both of
whom feared the unsustainable demands these new mouths would soon place
on already exhausted soils and depleted natural resources.[152] Cook cautioned
that the explosion of new babies in the Third World would destroy the planet's habitability far more quickly than the atom bomb. Such depictions made
a humanitarian gesture into a crime against nature: by offering Africans inoculations against smallpox or treating tuberculosis, European doctors and nurses
had unwittingly repeated the mistakes of late nineteenth-century Europe, throwing population numbers and the land available for animals out of whack. Such
pronouncements came just as African nationalists were demanding autonomy
and rights as citizens on par with their metropolitan peers, rendering the quest
for self-determination epiphenomenal in comparison to the great war on nature
that threatened to engulf humanity as a species.[153] Africans were still "junior

brothers" in the postcolonial order who needed Europeans' mature perspective to navigate the excesses of modernization.[154]

Suspicions about whether Grzimek was an "avocado" environmentalist can easily miss this disquieting association of "degeneration," Malthusianism, and nature conservation across the post-1945 Western conservation community. Such commonalities, in fact, enabled Grzimek to join the cosmopolitan networks of late colonial conservation without having to confront troublesome continuities with his Nazi past.[155] Grzimek, Heck, and Riefenstahl all found their way to Africa in the 1950s, part of a cohort of German academics, artists, and writers with questionable ties to the Third Reich who breathed new life into their careers by filming, photographing, and writing about a continent "leaving the bush" for the uncharted coordinates of Western modernity.[156] Heck focused his attention on the former German Southwest Africa, a mandate of the Union of South Africa, which he lauded for apartheid policies that prevented "interbreeding" and kept intact colonial-era reserves that stopped indigenous peoples from destroying precious wildlife at Etosha and Kruger National Parks.[157] Riefenstahl found her way to the Sudan, where she photographed the Nuba and Kau, resurrecting the sensuous appeal of the athletic nude found in her fascist-era filmography.[158] Grzimek, meanwhile, initiated a series of journeys into the Belgian Congo that discovered signs of the rogue human primate decimating vegetation and animals. The humble traveler of *Dr. Jimek* soon gave way to a vision of himself as a "new Noah" who would protect endangered creatures' last refuge: the vast rainforest of Central Africa.[159]

No Room for Wild Animals

The swirling, ever-rising tide of humanity is today drowning the wild
animals just as surely as did the Flood in the Bible. But this flood kills
more surely and lasts much longer. Creation is in dire need of a second
Noah. Someone, then, must enter the lists on behalf of the animals; and
not for the animals' sake alone, but for the sake of all mankind.
—Bernhard Grzimek, *No Room for Wild Animals*, 1954

Bernhard Grzimek's bestseller *No Room for Wild Animals* (*Kein Platz für Wilde
Tiere*) opens with a startling series of statistics:

> During the few minutes which it takes you to read to the end of this
> chapter, the number of people on earth will have increased by 4,000.
> By tomorrow at the same time the earth's population will have risen by
> almost 100,000—roughly the population of Offenbach [in the English
> version, Oxford]; and, to produce the food required to feed the new
> arrivals of a single month, new arable land has to be found equal in size
> to the state of Württemberg [equivalent to Surrey, Sussex, and Kent].[1]

With a predicted global population of five billion by century's end, he warned,
such multiplication of humans would soon outpace the meager 2 percent of the
earth's surface available for cultivation. One by one, the world's great civilizations
had fallen by outstripping their lands' carrying capacity through deforestation
and overgrazing, turning the "desolate Sahara," formerly the "granary of Rome,"
and Mesopotamia, the cradle of the "Garden of Eden," into desert wastelands.[2]
Signs of the latest collapse littered the American Great Plains with abandoned
homesteads and depleted fields, the result of a dustbowl that had sent the richest
topsoil in the world aloft.[3] With Africa's population poised to double within the
next fifty years, he predicted, its fragile tropic soils would share the same fate. As
rainforests gave way to fields of cassava, sweet potato, and cattle, the habitats of
baboons, lions, and hyenas would also be destroyed. "That is the reason why the

Our Gigantic Zoo. Thomas M. Lekan, Oxford University Press (2020). © Oxford University Press.
DOI: 10.1093/oso/9780199843671.001.0001

wild animals of Africa are doomed to die, why *all* the wild animals on earth will be compelled to yield to the 'Human Locust.'"[4]

The documentary film based on the book that appeared two years later employed nightmarish scenes of bulldozed forests, cold-hearted trophy hunters, and imperiled animals to drive home Bernhard and his son Michael's message. It opens with a depiction of a red, glowing earth viewed from outer space, populated by allegorical figures of the first male and female human inhabitants. The slow spread of humans across the earth—reaching only eight hundred million by 1800—explodes at the dawn of modernity amid a staccato of images: misshapen skyscrapers, skeletal figures on the march, and an atomic bomb detonation.[5] The film then cuts to actual footage from Léopoldville (today's Kinshasha) and Nairobi, where the narrator Victor de Kowa explains that the "children of technical science" have replaced the "abode of gods, snakes, and demons" with the "signal of our age": the traffic light.[6] Alongside a scene of children begging with outstretched arms alongside the camera crew's moving truck, de Kowa laments that they had been wrenched from their primitive existence, forced to share in the West's "culture of the day after tomorrow." On this emerging continent there is increasingly no room for virgin nature, for human children, and "above all, no room for wild animals."

The only sanctuary from such rapid development lay in national parks and forest reserves. In the Albert National Park (now Virunga) and the Ituri Forest Reserve, the Grzimeks discovered a "forbidden paradise" in which the animals live unfettered by strife, while the Batwa-speaking indigenes, the "pygmy" *Mbuti* (in the *No Room* text, the "Bambuti") live much like the creatures of the forest, unaware of the catastrophe that awaits them outside their sylvan homeland. Like the Nimba Reserve in the Ivory Coast, Albert National Park was a strict scientific reserve—not a tourist attraction like Yosemite—established and managed from the start as a "world laboratory" signifying scientific universalism and international cooperation.[7] From there the Grzimeks could envision a "cultural heritage of all mankind" that every person, "black or white, capitalist or communist," might cherish and protect.

In *No Room for Wild Animals*, Bernhard put aside the lighthearted modesty of the Ivory Coast adventure and embarked on the conservation quest that eventually led him and Michael to the Serengeti. What began in the early 1950s as a collecting expedition to bring the Okapi, a rare "forest giraffe," back to Frankfurt, became in time a world-historical mission led by a self-appointed "Noah" to protect national parks throughout Africa as sanctuaries from the "rising tide of humanity."[8] In both the text and film, the Grzimeks used doomsday prognoses and the jaundiced eye of the zoologist to challenge exotic and adventurist depictions of the continent that had long dominated the European imagination.[9] Africa would appear, in their words, "completely raw," the victim of the relentless corrosion of industrial-urbanism and the seductions of American consumerism.[10] Such depictions overturned the colonialist hunting film that featured "the jungle" as the abode of marauding elephants and lions. In the Grzimeks' hands, the rainforest and its noble creatures appeared instead as victims of reckless hunters that needed immediate protection.

Bucking dominant views of their time, the Grzimeks blamed rapacious Europeans, not African subsistence hunters, for the "great dying out" of wild species that was afflicting the continent. They charged Europeans with parasitizing Africa's resources to keep their bloated numbers at home afloat and lambasted previous writers for racist stereotypes that underestimated Africans' capacity for progress. Yet the Grzimeks never liberated themselves from imperial discourses of "saving Africa." Rather than amplifying their insight about colonialist parasitism into a broader critique of unjust resource extraction and First World consumption, the Grzimeks' biological determinism led them to fixate instead on African fertility as the greatest threat to the global environment.[11] The threat of overpopulation served as a proxy for their continuing fears of Americanization and "race mixing," all of which portended Africans' loss of organic connections to the rainforest and its creatures. Glossing over the history of King Leopold II's ignominious "Red Rubber" regime, they depicted a sylvan refuge where animal sorrow took precedence over reckoning with the Congo's past.[12] African homelands became a "cultural possession of the *whole* human race" still in need of European scientific stewardship even as the imperial order began to crumble.[13]

Africa Leaves the Bush

The 1950s witnessed a resurgence of German media, diplomatic, and economic attention to the Dark Continent that shaped the visual repertoire and critical perspective of No Room for Wild Animals. A flurry of angry, post-Versailles calls for Germany to reoccupy Africa had dissipated in the 1930s as the National Socialists' pursuit of "living space" in Poland and the USSR had shifted attention away from maritime colonialism.[14] In the texts of modernizers and boosters for investment from the Federal Republic, "Africa" emerged as a hopeful space where primitive villagers were "leaving the bush" for blossoming cities, creating potential markets for West German goods and services and allowing for new diplomatic ties between the Federal Republic of Germany (FRG), its European imperial allies in the European Economic Community (EEC), and non-aligned and newly independent African nations.[15] No region embodied these hopes for the New Africa more keenly than the Belgian Congo, the main setting of No Room for Wild Animals and a battleground between the conflicting midcentury visions of conservation and development on the brink of decolonization.

No Room for Wild Animals appeared in cinemas in 1956, just after the FRG had gained back full control over its domestic and foreign policy from the Western Allies and hoped to project an international image as a democratic, can-do nation. West Germany regained its national sovereignty within the framework of a European Common Market that assumed the need for sustained European presence in Africa—even continued imperial rule where possible. The 1957 Treaty of Rome, for example, envisioned a European solidarity that bound the Continent to its "overseas colonies" and pledged the European Community to "ensure the development of their prosperity" as these territories made their way toward a distant future independence.[16] The FRG, which had lost its own African territories at Versailles in 1919, saw itself as an important scientific advisor and economic engine for this more enlightened imperial endeavor.

The Common Market development fund, established in 1958, received one-third of its budget from West Germany, a sure sign that the FRG wanted to participate in this effort with funding and technical advice. As one business owner wrote to the Foreign Office in Bonn about his trip to French West Africa and Equatorial Africa, "in comparison to the much-maligned word 'colony,' the formulation 'under-developed' peoples expresses a duty of all highly civilized and wealthy peoples to do something for those innocent and left behind . . . . This recognition of duty runs parallel to the demand for social development of under-privileged parts of the population in modern states" and a "feeling of shame about the weak, without any racial discrimination."[17] Myths of the former "good German colonizers" were never far behind such affinities. In a 1956 Foreign Office letter about the former German protectorate of Togo, now in French hands, a previous colonial governor described being regularly approached by Togolese who "gladly remembered the German period."[18] Despite the formal onset of decolonization in the 1950s, West Germans imagined a "modernized . . . idea of the White Man's Burden" to legitimize a renewed presence in Africa—a situated globalism that deflected attention from the Third Reich's still-recent visions of a European racial empire by focusing on African welfare.[19] Small wonder, then, that we find Grzimek lauding the French in *Dr. Jimek* and the Belgians in *No Room* for bringing peace, education, and prosperity to Africa, since EEC imperialism had created new bonds between West Germany and its allies after World War II.

The fascination with an emergent Africa led to the re-founding of the German-Africa Society in 1956 by future Bundestag president Eugen Gerstenmaier, an organization whose mission included educating the public about the potential economic value of Africa.[20] Gerstenmaier signaled the renewed hope among West German business, trade, and commercial interests that Africa could become a prime consumer of West German goods and services—a critical goal for an exporting country still largely shut out of domestic markets in France and

Britain and their overseas territories. Indeed, in the 1950s and early 1960s, the West German Foreign Office sponsored a number of trade exhibitions that traveled around the continent showcasing the Federal Republic's emergence as an economic powerhouse and a model of humane "social market" capitalism for the developing world.[21]

The creation of the European Economic Community during a period in which France and Belgium still controlled wide swathes of territory in West and Central Africa revived a long-standing German discussion of "Eurafrica."[22] Boosters for Eurafrica envisioned a unified trade and administrative zone that would combine European technical know-how and Africa's "untapped" natural resources to create a supranational state with the ability to challenge US and USSR hegemony on the world stage and stem the spread of Islam on the African continent.[23] America, the Eurafrican boosters maintained, was too materialist and immature to take over the mantle of Christian-humanist civilization and lead Africa into the modern age, while the USSR and its Asian-Communist allies were working to thwart the continent's development, exacerbating the conditions of penury and fomenting unrest to spread the world revolution.[24] The vision of Eurafrica provided an economic rationale and moral justification for Europeans to salvage the positive technical, scientific, and cultural achievements of the "civilizing mission" and for West German advisors, scientists, and tradesmen to restage their country's benign global presence.[25] Gerstenmaier and others noted that this would require a growing budget for technical assistance and development aid that would reorient African states toward free trade rather than colonial monopolies of exploitation, a commitment that gained momentum as the FRG tried to contain the German Democratic Republic (GDR) on the European and world stage.[26] The Grzimeks worried that such development aid would backfire, endangering the continent's ecology and destroying its fragile forests and soils.

As the many scenes in No Room of Central Africa crisscrossed by roads, railroads, concrete bridges, and hydroelectric dams attested, the Grzimeks feared the rapid modernization of the Congo taking place in the mid-1950s. The lurid images of tractors and highways eating their way through the rainforests of Central Africa in No Room for Wild Animals served as an intentionally stark counter-image to the Congo emerging in the texts of Eurafrican boosters. "What Canada stands for on one side of the world," wrote the Austro-German journalist Anton Zischka in a 1954 article, "lies the Congo on the other: an undeniable example of the indefatigable vitality, creative potential, and effectiveness (Leistungsfähigkeit) of Europe and the superiority of its economic methods."[27] A former NSDAP member who had gained prominence for promoting the Third Reich's economic development policies, Zischka saw in the Congo a colony too busy to hate, where race relations remained calm and European settlers and investors would be assured healthy returns and a standard of living unimaginable in Europe. In Zischka's eyes, the Congo had put the legacies of Leopold II's brutality behind it and forged a stable and prosperous colony that was the envy of other European powers.

Zischka's account echoed Belgium's paternalist vision of itself guiding "Notre Congo" toward maturity and emancipation.[28] Here, blacks and whites were working together to harness the colony's staggering mineral wealth of timber, copper, and diamonds. It was also well known that the colony contained large stores of uranium, lending credence to exaggerated accounts of Central Africa's leap from the "stone age to the atomic age."[29] What is more, the territory was experiencing high rates of urban growth fueled by an influx of European expatriates and Africans in search of work.[30] Such growth and migrations created a stark contrast between the "darkest region of the dark continent" and a bevy of new metropolises—Léopoldville, Elisabethville, and Stanleyville—connected by new roadways.[31] In 1954, the capital Léopoldville contained 265,000 inhabitants, the first skyscraper in Africa, and King Bauduoin Stadium, featured prominently in *No Room*, which had space for seventy-two thousand "black football enthusiasts."[32] Such movement into cities confirmed Europeans' expectations that Africa was finally entering the historical mainstream, recapitulating the early stages of British industrialization and, thus, progressing toward the endpoint assumed by modernization boosters.[33]

The Grzimeks found the Belgian Congo's increasing emphasis on public welfare and medical care especially worrisome, as they threatened to upset the delicate balance between human and animal populations. In the late 1940s and 1950s, a period that scholars often refer to as the Second Colonial Occupation, all of the remaining imperial powers in Africa—Britain, France, Belgium, and Portugal—transferred postwar ideologies of social welfare to the colonies with a renewed technocratic zeal for technical education, veterinary treatment of livestock diseases, soil conservation measures, and public health outreach.[34] Such investment reflected, in part, an effort to make good on promises in the 1948 United Nations Charter affirming self-determination for all European colonies and calling for colonial powers to prepare their possessions for independence. This trend also reflected imperial powers' desire to boost their own ailing postwar economies by exploiting colonial resources, creating stable supplies of critical resources and markets for European finished goods.[35]

But no imperial power invested as much as the Belgians, whose *Plan Decènnal* for 1948–1958 foresaw $500 million in development and medical funds.[36] The Belgian outlays reflected a sense that this country had more to atone for than the other powers given the international reporting of King Leopold II's brutal rule of the Congo Free State from 1885 to 1904.[37] In the "Red Rubber" regime of that era, Leopold's agents had forced Congolese men to tap rubber plants or

Figure 2.1 Léopoldville apartment blocks under construction, 1953. Scenes of such high modernist "dwelling machines" in *No Room for Wild Animals* symbolized the Congo's rapid shift from the "stone age to the atomic age." Getty Images.

labor in processing plants by threatening to mutilate them or taking their wives and children as hostages and sexually assaulting them.[38] Belgian colonial officials remained distressed about the unusually high rates of infertility, venereal disease, and childless families that were the results of Leopold's tyranny (in which about half of the territory's population died), as well as the decades of overwork that followed.[39] As a consequence, labor shortages prior to the war had threatened the basis of the Congolese economy, so Belgian administrators in the Second Occupation developed the continent's best rural neo-natal and primary care clinics, designed to boost the life expectancy and well-being of current and future workers.[40] Zischka depicted the Congo's gleaming new clinics and infirmaries as showcases for the colonial government's success in encouraging Africans to get vaccinated against smallpox or treated for gonorrhea, stemming the spread of waterborne diseases through better sanitation, reducing infant mortality by supplying infant formula in villages, and clearing tsetse-infested bush to prevent sleeping sickness. With malaria deaths down by more than 50 percent in just a few decades, he averred, the Congolese were better off under enlightened Belgian rule than the "poor and underdeveloped" independent African member states in the United Nations.[41] All that was missing, Zischka suggested, was the labor power necessary to crank up the Congo's economic engine.

No Room is replete with images of "primitive" Africans gazing at hydroelectric dams or succumbing to the pleasures of urban dance halls, but Grzimek saw these new health clinics and infirmaries as modernity's greatest threat to the territory's future. Echoing eugenicist arguments about the excesses of European "welfare," Grzimek stated that the medical profession around 1850 started to "meddle with real success in Death's affairs." Doctors managed to reduce infant mortality and banish "plague, cholera, typhus, smallpox" from laying waste to human populations.[42] The result was a global population about to skyrocket from 2.4 billion in 1954 to five billion before the end of the century—with widespread famine and starvation as a result. "To die of starvation is a slow and painful death. Plague and cholera were more merciful," he stated.[43] In Africa, he insisted, colonial officials interested in boosting the labor pool had also been "meddling" too deeply in natural selection through free inoculations and outreach campaigns designed to contain the spread of bilharzia and sleeping sickness. Within just fifty years, the continent's population south of the Sahara was on track to double.[44] Bernhard lamented that unchecked human fertility would soon overwhelm the resources and space available for wild animals, dooming mammals and birds to extinction. The time had come, once again, to save Africa from itself, only this time by salvaging the last natural zoos reserved for Africa's wild creatures.

National Parks as Natural Laboratories

Lucky for the Belgian Congo, the territory already contained extensive refuges from relentless urbanization and overpopulation, found in the continent's best network of national parks and game reserves. By the 1950s, the Belgian Congo contained some of Africa's largest and most biologically rich national parks, which held special significance for internationally minded conservation groups because of their transnational origins, strict policies with regard to indigenous people, and scientific research goals.[45] Carl Akeley, the famed American taxidermist, nature photographer, and collector for major American institutions such as the Field Museum of Natural History and the American Natural History Museum, had visited the Congo in 1921 to hunt down gorillas for the American Museum's collection, shortly after a German officer, Oskar von Beringe, had "discovered" the magnificent creatures.[46] When news of this discovery spread, Akeley knew that museums in Europe and America would rush to collect specimens and pleaded with King Albert, son of Leopold II, to set aside a nature reserve where the small population of gorillas could find refuge from hunters and scientific collectors. Luckily for Akeley, the king had recently visited Yellowstone and Yosemite National Parks and in 1925, moved quickly to proclaim the establishment of Albert National Park by royal decree, the first on the African continent.[47] Akeley and his wife Mary convinced the American paleontologist John C. Merriam and the Belgian ambassador in Washington to support Albert's vision, hoping that well-endowed institutions like the Rockefeller and Carnegie Foundations and the affluent members of the Boone and Crocket Club in the United States and the Society for the Protection of the Fauna of the Empire in London would provide the funding for an international field laboratory dedicated to natural history, field biology, biogeography, geobotany, and ethnography.[48] Adding to the park's biological diversity was dramatic scenery, including two of the world's most active volcanoes, idyllically sheathed in cloud forests and framing Lake Edward—a counter-world to Zischka's modernizing eye.[49]

Such cosmopolitan origins and scientific purpose set the Belgian Congo's parks apart from other sites in sub-Saharan Africa, such as Kruger National Park in South Africa, where "penitent butchers"—hunters who lamented the rapid decline of big game that had accompanied colonial expansion— made the first moves toward establishing game reserves.[50] Like the other European imperial powers in Africa, the Belgians had signed international conventions in London in 1900 and 1933 that regulated both European commercial hunting and African subsistence hunting. The 1900 Convention for the Preservation of Animals, Birds and Fish (hereafter 1900 London Convention) committed the Belgians to strengthening their game laws, creating a list of endangered species protected from all hunting (along with juveniles and breeding females of all game species), setting minimum weight for the sale of elephant tusks, and establishing game reserves protected from encroachment.[51] The 1933 convention went even further, doing away altogether with the notion that vermin—harmful and unattractive animals—could be killed at will and prohibiting the unsportsmanlike shooting of animals from cars or airplanes.[52] The 1933 signatories also targeted African hunting practices deemed especially "cruel" and "unsportsmanlike," including the use of snares, staked pits, and poison arrows—indeed many blamed the "natives" for Africa's extinction crisis.[53] Though never ratified by all parties, the two London Conventions underscored that the Europeans powers saw the protection of African nature as part of their "civilizing mission."[54]

At the 1933 conference, the Belgians stressed that their reserves were neither hunting reserves nor national parks dedicated to tourists on the American Yellowstone model. Instead, like their French counterparts, they saw their imperial parks as scientific reserves. Similar to the Nimba Reserve in the Ivory Coast, the French and Belgians considered their national parks to be extensions of natural history museums in the metropole, as "integral nature reserves" (*réserves naturelles intégrals*) whose primary purpose was research and study, not recreation.[55] Belgian scientists cordoned off the reserves from humans; they admitted a few scientists and monitored and controlled their movements.[56] The Belgians eventually did allow a handful of tourists into Albert and Garamba but confined them to small, well-demarcated areas—and only after Hediger had conducted pioneering "flight reaction" studies showing that the animals could tolerate automobiles in their presence.[57] For the Grzimeks, such continental conservation reflected the best features of Eurafrican partnership, as they established science—and not sport—as the basis for international cooperation in saving African nature.

The Belgians also centralized the administration of the parks so that provincial administrators did not have the power to make ad hoc policies or accommodate African needs on a case-by-case basis. Victor van Straelen, the director of the Brussels Museum of Natural History, created the Institute of the National Parks of the Belgian Congo in the capital city in 1933 and presided over the creation of new national parks at Kagera in 1934 and Garamba in 1938.[58] Van Straelen argued that Albert and Garamba provided areas of "original purity" whose climax associations of plants and animals allowed scientists to investigate Africa in its primeval state. In such parks, scientists would be able to investigate "the laws of animal and vegetal life," whereas outside the grand nature reserves the landscapes were "increasingly diverted from their original state."[59] The Belgian parks were, in this sense, natural laboratories that shielded relics of the earth's evolutionary past.

The language of original purity masked the steps van Straelen had taken to remove African settlements and "invasive" species to restore the parks' "primitive" character. He and his staff evicted thousands of local Wahutu and Watutsi during the 1930s out of a conviction that these communities posed a dire threat to local vegetation. Van Straelen reported that the Tutsi pastoralists kept their cows for reasons of "social standing," rarely slaughtering them for daily use, leading to an overpopulation of people and cattle close to the parks' borders.[60] The creation of the park excluded pastoralists from the uplands forests, leading to a severe shortage of dry season forage in the highland meadows and regular infractions against park regulations. Van Straelen complained that he lacked the manpower to keep the Hutu and Tutsi herds out of the gorilla's main habitat in the park.[61] He did allow a small number of "primitive" Mbuti to remain inside Albert and Garamba, but even their activities were restricted considerably over time.[62] Van Straelen contemplated sealing off the entire park with by planting agave plants to prevent contact between its large mammals and the livestock outside park borders, and his team suppressed fires that might disturb the area's delicate biological equilibria. For Belgians, scientific universalism and international cooperation meant that most tourists, invasive species, and local Africans should remain permanently outside the parks.

European conservationists were not immune to the symbolic power of the Congo forests in making their case for supporting van Straelen's restoration effort. Beyond the ecological value of the "jungle" was a rich symbolism reaching back to the early years of Europeans' "discovery" of the Dark Continent—one that unfortunately distorted Africans' own connection to and transformations of the tropical landscape. The untamed and "lost world" character of the Congo basin's equatorial forests often led Western authors to depict them as a "green hell" in need of European "taming" or as an idyllic foil for the corrupting or emasculating effects of "civilization."[63] Henry Morton Stanley, well known as the first white man to traverse Africa from east to west, traversed the "dark jungle" of the Ituri in his stories about the search for David Livingstone, while Joseph Conrad featured the Central African rainforest as the "heart of darkness" that caused Mr. Kurtz to go mad in his enigmatic 1902 story.[64] Yet the savage jungle of the European imagination hardly matched the diversity of environments, shaped in part by human labor, found in Central Africa's woodlands. Grzimek, like Stanley and Conrad, assumed that Congolese "in the bush" had simply lived off the fruits of nature, with little sense of the arduous planting and gathering necessary to maintain human life in the forests. Europeans envisioned the equatorial forest as a hostile wilderness where geographic barriers or the lethargy caused by a hot, humid climate left the Congolese isolated and "underdeveloped."[65] Yet the primeval rainforest was a cultural landscape shaped by long-standing exchanges between Batwa and Bantu communities and centuries of harvesting, felling, metalsmithing, fishing, and agricultural cultivation—especially for palm fruits and bananas—that had made the inhabitants into savvy "forest specialists" who had established myriad villages, hunting camps, pathways, and fields long before Europeans arrived on the scene.[66] Such diverse activities had also produced dynamic forms of environmental knowledge, spiritual practice, and community identity in the Congo basin that structured how local inhabitants perceived, evaluated, and gave meaning to the forest.[67] Myths of wild Africa tended to overlook African landscaping of the region, turning instead to tired stereotypes about "tribal warfare," inter-African slavery, or unchecked tropical diseases to legitimize land grabs and forced labor.[68]

Accounts of Central Africans moving rapidly from the "stone age to the atomic age" also erased over six hundred years of political development, economic specialization, and participation in global markets along the Congo Basin. This region witnessed the consolidation of centralized political units in the thirteenth century, the entry into the Atlantic economy through Portuguese traders in the fifteenth century, and the expansion of European imperialism to fuel the industrialization of the North in the nineteenth century.[69] Congolese middlemen served as critical intermediaries in the slave and ivory trades— Stanley found a river abuzz with commercial activity in his infamous 1876 journeys into the interior. Shortly thereafter, quinine, steamboats, and Maxim guns gave Europeans the upper hand as they pressed into the Congo Basin in pursuit of profits and "unwashed souls" and pushed out rival Zanzibari caravan traders from the East. European "pacification" was driven by a recognition that African middlemen were savvy negotiators who were outcompeting the Europeans for access to resources and setting prices too high to make the newcomers the profits they believed they deserved.[70] Such stories of African eagerness to participate in capitalist trade and global commerce dropped out of European portrayals of "savage" aboriginals in the expeditionary accounts of the imperial era.

Grzimek offered an alternative to such tired imperialist accounts in *No Room for Wild Animals*. In the text and film, he and Michael transformed the fearsome jungle into a fragile ecological relic deserving protection and was more sympathetic to the Congolese who lived there than most Europeans. Yet his depiction of himself as a latter-day Noah still relied on imperial discourses of "saving Africa" as a pretext for dubious self-realization and Western intervention. Glossing over King Leopold II's "Red Rubber" regime, Bernhard depicted a sylvan refuge where the Congo's tragic human history was trivialized in favor of animal sorrow.

The Search for the Okapi

The journey that became the book *No Room for Wild Animals* began with an invitation to Bernhard from the director of the zoological garden in Léopoldville to obtain an Okapi as a gift to the Frankfurt Zoo. The animal was a goodwill gesture from Belgium to West Germany after the terrible occupation of the lowland country during World War II.[71] Only sixteen specimens of this rare "forest giraffe," which the Belgians had put under complete protection in 1933, existed in captivity outside of Africa. The first "German Okapi" promised to give the Frankfurt Zoo another star attraction, one with a fabled history as a living fossil.[72] Stanley had first heard about this horselike animal inhabiting the vast rainforests of the Congo River Basin from the Mbuti during the 1860s. British colonial officer Sir Henry Johnston, future governor of British Uganda, then learned that the Mbuti called the animal "Okapi" and was able to collect skeletal and hide fragments and ship them to the Royal Zoological Society in London, which confirmed that the animal that did not belong to any known species of zebra. Numerous zoological societies then began the hunt for the fabled creature, which resided in a narrow stretch of the Ituri jungle almost six hundred miles from the nearest coast.[73]

The Okapi was notoriously difficult to keep alive in transport, let alone in captivity. Even after the first was transferred to a Belgian zoo in 1918 it survived only fifty days. Many Okapi died after capture because of exposure to parasites, particularly the trypanosomes that cause *Nagana*, or sleeping sickness. Grzimek explained, erroneously, that the "virgin forest" was free of such parasites but the animals were bitten by infected insects carried in the narrow transport cages of the ship hold. The animals were further weakened by long journeys and the absence of the Ituri's specific foliage, which upset the delicate balance between host and parasites in the animals' guts. For the Okapi, then, the "vast, leafy roof of the Congo forest" was a last refuge, as it was for other living fossils that had retreated from "Darwinian struggle" and human encroachment—the Congo peacock, the forest hog, and the Mbuti themselves.[74] Banana plantations were invading the remaining habitat every day, and just a few hundred miles from the Ituri lay vast deposits of copper, gold, and uranium. "Woe betide them," Grzimek lamented, "if uranium is ever discovered in the actual haunts of the Okapi!"[75] The symbiosis between the Okapi and the rainforest demonstrated the necessity of expanding Grzimek's zookeeper ecology to encompass scientific conservation of habitats abroad if the species were to survive in the wild.

No Room for Wild Animals played upon audiences' anticipation of an exotic Congo adventure only to subvert their expectations with its alarming conservationist message. Finding the Okapi brings the Grzimeks to the most remote region of the Dark Continent, recalling Stanley and the many other adventurers who had risked tropical diseases and extreme heat to "penetrate" the Congo Basin. Book chapters such as "Cannibal Land," "Among the Hippopotami," and "The Bambuti" beckoned armchair travelers, yet Grzimek knew full well that the account upturned adventurers' accounts of all three.[76] Leopold II briefly appears in Grzimek's short history of the Congo as the host for Stanley and geographical societies to investigate the African interior. Yet Grzimek does not even touch upon the well-known barbarism of his reign and instead lauds him for ending the slave trade in Central Africa and building a railway in the interior. "Opinions on the effects of colonialization may often differ," notes Grzimek, "but in justice it must never be forgotten what the natives, through slavery, exploitation, neverending wars, superstitions and cannibalism, suffered under their own rulers."[77]

Grzimek pushed the narrative beyond colonial adventurism, yet trivialized African initiative by inserting himself in the familiar role of European savior— only this time on behalf of the non-human innocents.[78] He likened his mission to a calling, one that drove him to shield "fellow creatures . . . . As fine and as worth preserving as ourselves," from overpopulation and habitat destruction. "We should like to see our grandchildren standing and gazing at the shy bongo antelope . . . . That is the object . . . . I will tell the story of our doings, a story quite different from that to be found in books of discovery, adventure, big-game hunting or trapping."[79] Readers might yearn to tour this "last paradise of all our yearnings," much as Grzimek himself had as a young man—but that place was now "half electrified, spanned by radio and cut up by state frontiers."[80] To underscore their distance from safari literature, Grzimek turned the adventurism of the big game hunter on its head.[81] In place of caravans of weapons and white table cloths in the bush, the narrative portrays two lanky and underdressed scientists appearing completely out of place when they are received by Léopoldville high society. Their slapstick auto scenes of the mechanically inept pair's adventures in a leased Ford truck along Central Africa's muddy roads—including a complete tumble outside a small village—parodied older depictions of European hunters "mastering" African nature.[82]

Moving beyond colonialist adventurism led Grzimek to relegate uncomfortable reminders of German colonial interests in Central Africa to the distant past.[83] No mention is made of the German geographical societies that had helped to "open up" the region to resource exploitation in the 1870s or the Berlin Conference of 1884, which spelled out the terms of occupation that unleashed the imperial "Scramble for Africa."[84] There is also no revengefulness over the loss of colonies in 1919; Grzimek mentions in passing the loss of the territories of Ruanda-Urundi to Belgium without a hint of anger.[85] Nor did Grzimek's documentary eye note the close connection between photography, moving images, and the subjugation of Africans in the early years of German expansion in Central and Eastern Africa.[86] As the shifting borders of Poland and Germany after World War II had shown him, political regimes came and went: African chieftains were no better or worse than German or Belgian colonizers, since all of their machinations and powerplays were trivial compared to the unwavering laws of nature.

Grzimek devotes the most attention to Georg August Schweinfurth, the German botanist who investigated the interior of East-Central Africa in the early years of the Second Empire.[87] Grzimek identifies closely with Schweinfurth's pure science; indeed, *No Room* re-traces and updates the botanist's routes from the 1874 book *In the Heart of Africa*.[88] Schweinfurth "discovered" the Uele River, an important tributary of the Congo, in 1869, the first European contact (twenty years before Stanley) with the cannibalistic Mangbetu (Monbuttu). After landing at Léopoldville and spending time with the zoo director there, the Grzimeks continued on to Stanleyville, about 930 miles northeast of the capital. There they rented a truck and drove further northeastward, visiting an elephant station near Garamba National Park where efforts to tame the great beasts were underway.[89] Schweinfurth, as Grzimek notes, was among the first to sound the alarm about the depletion of elephant populations in Central Africa as the "ivory frontier" had moved ever further westward.[90] Belgian game laws outlawing the trade in ivory ensured that few elephants were killed in the region anymore, the station head notes proudly, even though Africans living near Garamba increasingly had to endure crop raiding, trampled fields, and personal injury.[91] The Mbuti then help the Grzimeks find the Okapi inside the Ituri Forest Reserve, which lay more than 125 miles southwest of Garamba.

Most of the flora, fauna, and cultures that Schweinfurth documented so painstakingly are all under threat in *No Room*. "It is astonishing how a country can change in the course of a single generation," Bernhard noted in another projection of modernist anxiety onto the Congo. Grzimek's father was thirteen when the intrepid Schweinfurth first set foot on the Upper Uele in 1869. "In the intervening years, mass migrations have taken place in [my father's] homeland of Upper Silesia, and now a different people is living there. In the hall of our house, beneath the beam which bears the date 1730 and the name of my ancestors, a different language is now being spoken. But this country here, on the upper Uele, has changed, I think, even more during the same period." Though the cannibalistic peoples in this region still filed their teeth into "sharp points," as they once did to "tear the flesh of captives," he noted, the Belgian colonial government now exacted the death penalty for such practices.[92] Prospects for the Mbuti looked gloomy. Like the Okapi, these "merry little savages," as the Grzimeks called them, had found shelter in the forest from the more powerful "Negroes" from West Central Africa who had once enslaved them and were now carving roads into the region. Grzimek, like other Europeans, universalized this "frontier" model of ethnic interaction and conquest from an imperialist history and missed the more subtle linguistic, cultural, and spiritual crossovers between Batwa and Bantu peoples that had enfolded in the region over centuries.[93] Grzimek describes the Mbuti as "small, brownish, often yellowish, men, who were obviously not of negroid race . . . . With protruding foreheads, flattened nostrils and big, almond-shaped, brown eyes, they had a puckish and gnome-like look. . . . they reminded us of children."[94] Such imagery evoked the long-held association of "pygmies" with the primordial origins of humankind, but Grzimek disputed accounts of their cognitive immaturity and cultural isolation—indeed they had become the latest victims of coca-colonization.[95]

The American documentary filmmaker Martin Johnson had claimed in the 1920s that the Mbuti were so primitive they could not recognize objects or persons in photographs. In Grzimek's text, however, they giggle as they point to and describe chimpanzees, long-tailed monkeys, and, most delightfully, the Grzimeks themselves in photographs taken in the Ivory Coast.[96] Far from living in isolation deep in the forests, Grzimek asserts, the "pygmies" resided close to Bantu speakers on the logging roads where they could trade animal products for agricultural produce or take up temporary labor assignments for wages.[97] Grzimek laments that such market intrusions into the virgin forest had corrupted the Mbuti, much as they had the Baule in West Africa. When scheduled to be photographed in their "natural" state, many Mbuti showed up in a pair of European shorts they had obtained by bartering foodstuffs, and some were even caught "preening themselves" in an "old and tattered European jacket." Shocked by such displays of vanity and sartorial pleasure, Grzimek refused to let them stand in the photographs or "get a piece of chocolate," until they donned loin cloths.[98] As in *Dr. Jimek*, such creeping consumerism signaled that the Mbuti were slowly degenerating, marrying "negroes" and losing the racial essence that bound them to the organic world. "Everything had turned out to be different from what we had been led to expect," Grzimek wrote. "The virgin forest of Ituri was no tropical hell, pregnant with fever, as the books had described it; and the dwarfs were not poisoned-arrow-shooting cannibals, but happy, confiding and friendly overgrown children."[99] With the Mbuti slowly leaving the bush, Grzimek implied, there would soon be no need to "save" them—the colony's sylvan refuges were there for innocent animals, and not people, to find refuge.

The Great Dying Out

The call to save the Okapis' tropical habitat becomes especially urgent in the book's opening chapter, "Africa's Wild Animals Are Doomed." Grzimek begins this narrative in his own ecologically impoverished Germany, which contained about forty thousand of what he estimated as the earth's five to ten million species. Most of Germany's species were "insects, spiders, and worms," a product of the "rank and cancerous growth of humanity" that began in Europe around 1800 and wiped out big mammals, even in the continent's most remote forests and mountainous regions. The first to go were the wild cattle, or aurochs, in the seventeenth century, which the Hecks' breeding experiments had shown were impossible for "puny humans" to reproduce even as a "modest copy." Arrogant Europeans followed this mass killing with the tarpan, the progenitor of domesticated horses, and the European bison (*Wisent*), hunted to near extinction in Polish forests. The "human locust" then spread its murderous campaign in various directions, taking the dodo, the passenger pigeon, the Steller's sea cow, and the great auks, a large flightless bird last seen off the southern coast of Iceland.[100] Grzimek presents human settlement as the driver of a relentless zero-sum contest between people and animals where non-humans were quickly losing the capacity to survive.

In Africa, the great dying out began with the extinction of the wild ass, the North African elephant, and, later, in the highly urbanized Islamicate cultures of the region, the Berber lion.[101] At the other end of the continent was a landscape that before 1600 "brought to mind the stories of the Garden of Eden before mankind's fall from grace," endless herds of antelope, gazelle, zebra, wildebeest, and Cape Buffalo. But the Boers saw only cheap meat, driving the quagga and Burchell's zebra to extinction by 1900.[102] The text portrays Africa's creatures being trapped in a great pincer movement moving from both the north and the south, toward the green heart of the continent. Africa's animals had to die, in this grim natural history, because Africans were gradually recapitulating the stages of development set in motion by European civilization.

Yet contradictions soon emerge between the text's insistence on the Malthusian roots of extinction and the complex interplay between colonial policies, global markets, and disease ecologies that threatened animals at regional and local scales.[103] Applying examples from the Americas and Australia directly to the Congo was off the mark, since large predators never underwent the late Pleistocene extinctions that accompanied human colonization in these other regions.[104] Africans served as stewards of their landscapes well into the 1880s, and the survival of elephants, lions, and zebra was a testament to their co-evolution and co-habitation with those creatures—not the mindless slaughter of all *Homo sapiens*.[105] To attribute the extinction of the dodo to a colonial expansion driven by bloated population numbers was dubious, since European populations in 1662 were at their nadir due to epidemics, the "Little Ice Age," and the Thirty Years' War. Many believed already in the 1950s that the iconic species' extermination was the result of the accidental release of invasive feral cats among flightless birds that had known no such predators before.[106]

As the Grzimeks journeyed into the heart of the Congo in search of the Okapi, they fixated on the expansion of European-style plantation agriculture and late colonial public health campaigns as signs of a coming population bomb. Up to midcentury, so Bernhard's doomsday narrative continues, Europeans had not yet felt the full impact of population increases because imperialism had enabled them to live far beyond their own continent's carrying capacity by sucking up the forests, minerals, and harvests of overseas lands. Central Africa's fragile soils were the last to be affected but were withering under this onslaught. Coffee, banana, tea, and cocoa plantations carved out of the rainforest lay exhausted after only five or six years.[107] Following the period's now widely discredited thinking about African landscapes, Grzimek described the "typical" African savannas they encountered as remnants of a vast forest that once covered the landscape but had died due to human-induced bush burning to cut down on tsetse flies and prepare the way for croplands.[108] As a result, Grzimek lamented, the Sahara Desert was advancing "nearly a mile a year" along a "front of nearly 2,000 miles," turning valuable bush into a dried-up wasteland.[109]

Grzimek's zero-sum portrayal of humans versus animals failed to correlate with his own examples of the violent encounters between peoples caused by colonial expansion that had little to do with population growth. Grzimek notes rightly that the decimation of American bison took place in a context in which the US Army wished to demoralize and destroy Native American cultures—a horrific political decision that had no direct connection to overpopulation.[110] The German version of *No Room* is filled with mournful images of starving bodies from a famine-ravaged South Asia, but the reader is left unsure how to link them to textual passages that describe European hunting expeditions or condemn the commercial demand for ivory in Asia and Europe made from teeth and tusks.[111] Malthusian explanations for extinction concealed the site-specific cultural and political meaning of wildlife and the "slow violence" of a wildlife trade linked to distant markets.[112]

Nonetheless, Grzimek's ruminations about overpopulation and colonialism did represent a significant departure from dominant European understandings of conservation that justified colonial game reserves by blaming African hunting for the animals' demise. Grzimek forgave hunter-gatherers for their ecological missteps and was fully aware of Africans' "cruel" methods. Indeed, he describes in gruesome detail how the Mbuti felled an elephant by creeping up behind it, severing the tendons of its hind legs and cutting off its trunk, and then leaving it to bleed to death. Other Africans he encountered had devised spears with large barbs that pierced the great mammal's abdomen and intestines; as the animal attempted to rush away, the barbs ripped open its belly and pulled its innards out. Such scenes of animal agony were clearly intended to bait readers' indignation over "native" cruelty, but Grzimek shows that such methods hardly had the capacity to bring about mass extinction.[113] Far more worrisome for him was a trend touted by Belgian officials as a sign of the colonial welfare state's "progress": prenatal care and vaccination campaigns that had reduced infant and adult mortality rates.

Before the era of colonialism, he argued, African population densities had remained low due to the slave trade, warfare, and, especially, the tsetse fly that spread human sleeping sickness. This small creature appears in a *No Room* graphic as the "guardian" of the African interior against human settlement, preventing the spread of cattle and people.[114] The Grzimeks marveled at the ability to ride their horses into the bush while on the lookout for African buffalo, for in colonial times the horses would have quickly succumbed to the disease.[115] The German microbiologist Robert Koch had made this possible by helping Africa's farmers and herdsmen win the race against rinderpest, a virus that affected cattle and other ruminant animals. Koch developed an injectable prophylaxis that could protect herds from infection, allowing Europeans and Africans to open up new pastures across Central and East Africa.[116] Colonial governments would sometimes kill off wild animals that might carry rinderpest or clear bush that harbored the insect, opening up new land for settlement—only to find that the fragile soil could not support intensive European agriculture. The worst example had just recently occurred in Tanganyika, where the ill-fated Groundnut Scheme led colonial officials to slaughter almost six thousand wild animals and plough under five million acres of semi-arid savanna to grow peanuts. Drought soon turned these crops to dust, leaving the ecologically impoverished and cash-strapped territory $102 million in debt.[117] From Grzimek's perspective, wild animals and cattle or other livestock were locked in a deadly spiral due to land clearance and veterinary "improvements," a sure sign that ever-shrinking space would determine the fate of the continent.

Conflicts over arable land would only get worse as African populations grew. As one Belgian administrator tells Grzimek proudly, between 1948 and 1952, the Congo's population had increased by 620,000, largely due to falling mortality rates, and each year 1.2 million acres of land were brought under cultivation. Sleeping sickness in 1950 afflicted only five million persons—about 0.1 percent—whereas two decades before there would have been twelve times that number.[118] At first glance, this should not have caused the Grzimeks alarm; the Congo occupied a territory more than half the size of all of Europe and had only two persons per square mile in 1954 (versus seventy-seven in the Federal Republic). Given that Leopold's regime had killed at least eight million Congolese between 1890 and 1910, most Belgians in the provinces were far more worried about a plummeting birth rate and applauded such small improvements in life expectancy.[119] Yet dread over anticipated demographic explosions saturate No Room for Wild Animals, where Grzimek conjures such population forecasts to stoke his readers' fears about extinction crises and social change in the Third World. By narrowing his invective against colonialism to misguided vaccination campaigns, Grzimek offered little serious reckoning here with colonialist exploitation or affluent countries' patterns of consumption that threatened wildlife in the 1950s.

In the book's conclusion, Bernhard and Michael gather up their charges: the Okapi they christened Epulu; Dima, a juvenile female elephant they found at the station near Garamba; five chimpanzees; two forest swine; and various antelopes. They were all bound for the safety of Germany in an "aerial ark"—a specially equipped Sabena aircraft with holding pens for the menagerie.[120] Once the plane began to make its way up the Rhine, and the red cathedral of Frankfurt was in view, the Grzimeks breathed a sigh of relief. Like Noah, Grzimek believed he had "bestowed upon future generations a gift richer than all the works of art, the discoveries and the knowledge, the religions and inventions of great men."[121] Yet this zookeeper's vision of global sanctuaries bypassed the Congolese themselves, whose wildlife offered resources to build their own economies, food supplies, and cultural identities after independence.

A Forbidden Paradise: From Text to Screen

Despite its doomsday message, No Room for Wild Animals became a bestseller in Germany and beyond. It was translated into twenty-seven languages and reached a total of seven million readers by 1960. Such a favorable reception convinced Grzimek and his son to make a film version and they set off in the summer of 1955 to the Congo to begin shooting, mainly in Albert National Park, Garamba National Park, and the twenty-four-thousand-square-mile Ituri Forest

Reserve. Though only twenty-one years old at the time, Michael Grzimek took the lead on the arduous task of producing and securing financing for the work, to the tune of a hundred thousand Deutsche marks (equivalent to $24,000) and helped to found the production company, Okapia AG. Bernhard put up collateral for the film and served officially as scientific consultant, while Herbert Lander, assisted by Michael's school chum Hermann Gimbel, did the camera work. The Grzimeks' African "boy," Hubert, cooked, cleaned, portaged, and, most importantly, translated for the production team throughout their journey, although his name did not appear in the credits.[122]

The Grzimeks' goal in moving from text to film was to engage a broader audience for the conservation cause. "Books, even best sellers, are only read by a few thousand, and at best by a hundred thousand people," Grzimek noted. "We wanted to impress millions in Europe and America with the fact that lions . . . are dying out . . . . The only way to get in touch with millions of people is by films, television, or the illustrated weekly papers."[123] The production team reworked the book's central quest of rescuing specimens for the zoo to promoting wildlife reserves abroad.[124] Fears about "race-mixing" between the "primitive" Mbuti and other Africans, meanwhile, propelled a storyline which revealed that even the most "primitive" hunter gatherers were quickly becoming part of "our degenerate species." Far more than the book version of *No Room*, the film stages racial purity as a groundwork for belonging to "nature," suggesting a failure to both decolonize and de-Nazify postwar understandings of human ecologies just as the Grzimeks and other European conservationists set out on their global missions to save African wildlife.

Transforming the scattered thirty thousand meters of 35mm celluloid into a feature-length film required outside professional editing and sound, and the Grzimeks turned to some of the best in the industry. Klaus Dudenhöfer, an editor at the prestigious Real Film studios in Hamburg, helped to shape the film's plot line. With his direction, the search for the Okapi was dropped as the leitmotif; instead, he helped the Grzimeks to create a tripartite structure centered on the national parks as wondrous refuges for threatened creatures, with hippos and the "primitive" Mbuti taking center stage. For sound, the Grzimeks turned to Wolfgang Zeller, well known in West Germany for providing the music for Veit Harlan's notorious 1940 anti-Semitic film *Jud Süss*, to score the film. The narrator, de Kowa, had recently appeared in *Des Teufels General* (1954) and as the voiceover for James Stewart in the German version of *Harvey*.[125] The Grzimeks expected to make no profit from the film, but they did enter it into the 1956 Berlin Biennale prize competition. There, despite terrible storms and a nearly empty theater on the day it opened on the Kurfürstendamm, *No Room* received considerable acclaim. The film beat out Disney's *The African Lion* (1955; *Die Geheimnisse der Steppe*, 1956), part of its True Life Adventure series, for both the jury and audience prizes as best international documentary, including a cash award of twenty thousand Deutsch marks. In the same year, *No Room* received the prestigious Federal Film Prize (*Bundesfilmpreis*), eventually playing in over sixty-three countries by the early 1960s.[126]

Bernhard was as surprised as anyone to take first prize over Disney Studios, for he recognized that without Disney's reinvention of the wildlife film genre in the 1950s, he and Michael would never have found a global audience.[127] As Grzimek was well aware, most safari films or still photographs of animals came from hunting or zoological collecting, usually taken by Brits and Americans in colonized territories in Africa, such as Martin and Osa Johnson's *Congarilla* (1932) as well as by Germans such as Alfred Lindgens. The close connection between the language of hunting and camera work stemmed directly from this earlier symbiosis of hunting and film—from "loading" the camera to "shooting" a reel.[128] Still photographs became hunting trophies in themselves, as many of those who felled an elephant liked to be featured with a foot planted firmly on the carcass in a pose of domination.[129]

By the 1920s, major natural history museums such as the American Natural History Museum or scientific institutes such as the New York Zoological Society

Figure 2.2 The Grzimeks receiving the Golden Bear prize at the Berlin Biennale in 1956. The pair beat out Disney's *African Lion* for the top prize. The Grzimeks used proceeds from this film to fund their aerial surveys that became the subject of *Serengeti Shall Not Die*. Getty Images.

supported the production of such films, in the hopes of attracting a popular audience and raising cash for research, conservation, and museum projects. At the same time, profit-seeking producers and distributors welcomed the genre, whose canned exoticism and action-adventure themes appealed to mass audiences. As this film category tended toward ever-greater sensationalism, including many scenes that were obviously staged, conservation-minded institutions withdrew their support.[130] Paul L. Hoefler's nonfiction travelogue *African Speaks* (1930) was a particularly egregious example; in one scene, after Hoefler orders a Maasai boy to fetch rifles, the boy is felled and supposedly killed by a lion, with a pair of legs shown protruding out from the animal's mouth.[131] By 1930, the genre had receded almost entirely into obscurity. The Walt Disney Company reenergized the wildlife film in the late 1940s, first as introductory shorts before other feature films, then with its own full-length movies.[132]

Such dubious staging of adventure was familiar to German audiences as well. Interwar German expedition movies, especially the popular "hunting film" (*Jagdfilm*), frequently associated African animals with the dangers of the jungle or glorified the hunt for bloodthirsty "beasts."[133] These films were often produced in the studio rather than open air, where the Great White Hunter overcomes poisonous snakes, cannibalistic tribespeople, or infectious diseases to kill a marauding elephant or man-eating lion that threatens the helpless African villagers.[134] The privilege to hunt was an important part of the colonial imaginary in many British and German hunting films, because it suggested that white control over an unruly nature justified imperial rule. As the only ones capable of freeing Africans from the shackles of a hostile environment, Europeans saw hunting as a right of occupation while denying Africans similar access to animals for trade and subsistence.[135] Interwar hunt films often staged Germany's imaginary reconquest of African landscapes, usually justified by Germans' unique love for the continent's forests and steppes and with the enthusiastic approval of Africans who wanted their German father figures back.[136] As Hans Schomburgk reminded his readers in 1922, "we must never despair . . . that we once owned and then lost colonies."[137]

Disney broke the mold of the wildlife film by presenting breathtaking imagery and animal behaviors and interactions in time-lapsed sequences that would be impossible to witness through casual observation.[138] By cutting, splicing, and juxtaposing scenes filmed at different times or locations, such films made prosaic activities—feeding, mating, giving birth, or fighting off predators—into storylines of dramatic encounter.[139] Films such as *The Living Desert* (1953) and *The Vanishing Prairie* (1954) presented nature and the animals who resided in various ecosystems as fascinating and precious. Such films acknowledged that nature was at risk, yet always reassured the viewer that the threat had been contained through nature's resilience or wise state intervention.[140] Grzimek lauded

Disney for reshaping the genre but complained about the tendency toward an Americanized happy ending. The zookeeper even wrote to Disney directly to request that the studios acknowledge that their images of wild animals came exclusively from national parks and that the animals and plants were gravely endangered. "What an unbelievable triumph for nature conservation might have occurred," he wrote, "had Disney nature films included even a few sentences about the threat of humans to the animal and plant worlds."[141]

No Room for Wild Animals was thus a product of Grzimek's admiration for but also frustration with the limitations of Disneyfied nature. His success proved that there was an audience willing to sit through a conservationist film filled with lurid images of ecological destruction, not just the thrill of the chase or affectionate scenes of animal-human companionship. The tone of the Grzimeks' film is sober and didactic, full of uneasiness about gullible readers, viewers, and tourists falling for exotic representations of Africa that masked the continent's rapid modernization. By featuring a rapid-fire montage of urban growth and urban squalor in the opening sequences, for example, the Grzimeks linked the abstract demographic concept of overpopulation to the growth of the modern metropolis, with Nairobi and Léopoldville standing in for urban pathology writ large.[142] "Like rust, like a disease," notes the narrator, "our civilization is corroding this continent." Africans with chain saws fell 150-foot trees for coffee and banana plantations whose yields, we can surmise, will fill grocery aisles in North America and Europe rather than the bellies of urban Africans. The bushfires set to clear land for cattle stations sweep away trees, drying up the land and causing dust storms; within a few years, the narrator asserts, the once mighty forest resembles a "dismal landscape of the moon." How this development relates back to the overpopulation of the first sequences is never explicit.

The middle sequences of the film contrast completely with the film's opening section. Here, scenes taken in Albert National Park and the Ituri Forest reveal a "forbidden paradise" into which "no one, white or colored, may step," a reference to the stringent controls that van Straelen placed upon visitors to nature reserves in the Congo.[143] In this "animal fairyland," the creatures live "unfettered by strife," with members of different species mixing and mingling, barely noticing one another's movements. The sequences focus especially on the two-ton male hippopotamus Kiboko, an "old Swashbuckler" with a harem of wives and children who bask in the midday sun; they seek nothing more than the "peace and comfort" that people do.[144] There are no quarrels with nearby species, particularly the African buffalo. Despite hunters' reports about the innate aggressiveness of this species, when left unprovoked, de Kowa notes, Mrs. Kiboko and her children can pass right in front of them. Strife only arises in this animal paradise when Thulo, an adolescent male, reaches sexual maturity and begins to "court" his half-sister, a move Kiboko aggressively blocks. Soon Kiboko and

Thulo engage in a fierce fight for dominance, but it is one marked by sporting fairness rather than revenge or cruelty.[145] Once Thulo concedes his position in the hierarchy, all aggression ceases, and he leaves the clan to find another spot further upstream, where someday he will start his own family. When killing does occur in the natural zoo, as it does in a night scene involving a poisonous viper and a field mouse, the serpent kills and eats its prey quickly, with as little pain as possible, and without tormenting the poor victim. On display in these scenes are the timeless rules of social interaction that contrast sharply with the reckless destruction just outside the park's boundaries. Given how few visitors were permitted to enter the Congo's parks, the scenes allowed viewers a privileged glimpse of a timeless and vulnerable paradise. The Grzimeks hoped that such rare footage would spur audiences to support national parks in places they could only dream of visiting.[146]

Grzimek's portrayal of hippo territory and domestic bliss set in a stable, harmonious environment undoubtedly reflected the influence of Disney's suburbanized and anthropomorphic representation of animals. Portrayals of an intact organic world in the tropics soothed anxieties about an urban-industrial, mass consumerist world in the North and offered an intimate view of animals to a society that increasingly knew nature through leisure, not labor.[147] The Grzimeks also used the sequences to demonstrate the principles of animal psychology. In their view, the harmony between and within species was a product of innate social rules that enabled animals to avoid explosive conflicts. Unlike Disney, moreover, the Grzimeks were quick to remark on the human endangerment of hippos and most other denizens of the "animal fairyland," from the crocodiles on the Upper Nile that might become a handbag or the magnificent white rhino whose horn is valued by "superstitious Asiatics" as a love potion. Entertainment was critical but so was assimilating a conservationist message to ensure that the animals survived at all.

The Grzimeks' foray into the hippos' riverine habitat also had a critical scientific purpose: to substantiate the principles of animal territoriality laid out in Uexküll's animal ecology and adapted by Hediger to zoological gardens.[148] They were especially interested in measuring animals' flight reactions in the presence of human beings. In Albert National Park, the Grzimeks are astonished how closely they can approach the animals; in this natural laboratory, men did not yet carry "the mark of Cain on their foreheads" and, thus, the animals were not afraid of them. A wildebeest takes flight at the sight of their oncoming truck, but soon its curiosity about the "bipeds" gets the best of it, and it comes closer to investigate. Yet Kiboko and his clan clearly do have a sense of their territorial boundaries—this is no freewheeling Communist paradise—one that the alpha male marks through the dispersal of urine and feces along the maze of pathways that hug the river's edge. Kiboko stands ready to defend his home against intruders or pesky juveniles who might contest his authority, but animal territoriality assures that aggression never bubbles up into catastrophe. The Belgians' world laboratory offered the Grzimeks the opportunity to confirm theories of animal territoriality and use them to create appropriate paddocks back home.

The only humans who find a similar "home" in the rainforest are the Mbuti, who appear as endangered as the wild beasts who share their Ituri homeland.[149] The Congo national parks earned their reputation as a "world laboratory" in part because scientists could study gorillas, the "most advanced" primate on the evolutionary ladder, and "pygmies," the "most primitive" human race, in one area.[150] The Grzimeks underscored this theme by presenting the Mbuti as a relic of humanity before the fall—before the processes of degeneration had crept into European society and culture.[151] They depict the wonders of the Ituri through the eyes of two young lovers, Kasimo and Epini, who hail from different tribes and must meet in secret to exchange gifts and tokens of affection. "Young men's hearts are the same everywhere," we are told, even if the loin-clothed Mbuti seem to blur the line between human and animal by creeping along the forest floor or stealthily climbing giant trees to guide the viewer toward a close-up look. The two point out Duiker antelopes and other mammals, all of whom we are told are associated with gods and spirits. Epini scales up a tree to reveal the hidden treasures of the canopy, such as long-tailed monkeys, while Kasimo crouches in the understory, uncovering pythons, scarab beetles, chameleons, and praying mantises. The Mbuti live a "carefree, childlike" existence without any drive to acquire things or kill for pleasure. In one scene, Kasimo spears a small crocodile, hiding an injury incurred in the struggle with the sharp-toothed animal and then serving it as a meal for the entire tribe.

The two lovers are finally able to wed when Kasimo, according to custom, trades his sister for Epini so that there are enough workers in the other village. Viewers witness tribal dances and the decoration of Epini's breasts and thighs with blue ochre, "the latest in bridal fashion," just as technicolor flowers burst open in sync with the young couple's love. The scene's culmination is obviously staged, especially since the two Mbuti actors could hardly stand each other.[152] The Grzimeks invite the viewer to see the Mbuti as a primitive form of "ourselves," a vestige of a distant prehistoric time when hominids were just one among many predators in the forest, taking only what was needed from the fruits of nature. More importantly, there are rules of social behavior among the forest Mbuti that are not too different from Kiboko and his family. These rules—ranging from the sharing of food to finding brides among neighboring villages—dampen conflict and keep childbearing well within the boundaries of "tribe." Ecological intactness and racial autochthony produce and reinforce each other throughout the Mbuti film sequences, making the "true" hunter-gatherers the only human denizens who can call the rainforest home.

Figure 2.3 Michael Grzimek recording the two Mbuti actors whom the filmmakers featured as the young lovers "Kasimo and Epini" in *No Room for Wild Animals*. Photo used courtesy of Getty Images.

Unfortunately for the Mbuti, the "hour of doom is upon them," the narrator explains, due to the worrying trend toward inter-tribal sex along the logging roads. "Bantu" road builders, who considered the Mbuti "inferior" and easily exploitable, were enriching themselves purchasing ivory for a pittance from gullible pygmies. They used the money to purchase Mbuti girls, creating an ever-growing number of "mixed-race" children. Unable to secure a wife in this new commodified sphere, the pure-blooded pygmies were disappearing altogether, while the "forest Negroes" were becoming fair-skinned and shorter.[153] In the film, just after Kasimo and Epini's wedding, the camera cuts to a sequence in which an "African" in a Western safari suit and hat walks away with two pygmy girls he has purchased from a lumber village in exchange for "greasy notes" and a goat. Along the forest road leading into the village, the Grzimeks encounter the result of such trafficking in young girls: hundreds of "half-caste bastards" dressed in European clothes, a "jolly band of beggars" who have not yet learned that money must be earned.[154] The growing number of "half-castes" was a sure sign that the Congolese, like the Baule that the Grzimeks had encountered in the Ivory Coast, were degenerating under colonial patronage—leaving them vulnerable to the temptations of consumerism and hastening their social dissolution.

Soon they would face racial extinction, much like the animal species that sought shelter in the Congo's last stretches of intact rainforest.

Yet the cultural and sexual interaction between Mbuti and other African communities that fueled the Grzimeks' fears about racial decline had occurred for millennia in the Congolese forests.[155] Just as Grzimek had insisted during the Nazi era that there was no vestige of a "Germanic" race in his Silesian homeland, there was also no "pure race" of pygmies facing ruin in the 1950s. Grzimek's conflation of threatened animal species and endangered "tribes" reveals how readily interwar fears of racial degeneration still structured the postwar imagination, even as he and other travelers disavowed racism as unscientific. The Grzimeks' search for natural purity made it impossible to conceive of or value the Ituri as an ecological and linguistic patchwork where multiple cultures and animal species coexisted side by side.

The debasement of African cultures by mass consumerism reaches a crescendo in the film's unsympathetic portrayal of European tourists who appear hoodwinked by canned displays of tribalism. Just after depicting the demise of the pygmies along the forest road in No Room, the camera cuts to the "warrior dance of the Watusi." As the camera closes in on a frenzy of combatants in bright red costumes, elaborate golden headdresses, and synchronized ankle chimes, the narrator describes a "proud, unapproachable race, the undisputed lords of their land" who dance in preparation for raiding another tribe for women and slaves. The camera then moves back artfully to frame a bench that is largely occupied by white female spectators taking snapshots. "No more, no more," notes the narrator in an exasperated tone, "times and customs have changed . . . . Today the dance is just a commercialized show put on to cash in at the box office." The women clap politely, and the narrator reveals that one can buy cheap souvenirs of the dance "made in Birmingham" and take a picture with the tribal leader, who "likes American cigarettes" and "says hello politely into the camera, for he is a very much filmed man." The presence of female viewers, long associated with gullible consumer behavior in European culture, reinforces the message that Africa was now a place for sightseers, not the discerning travelers of old.[156] What stands out, though, is the close-up of the mocking face of the "tribal leader," who appears to delight in duping the European visitor—a clear sign that she will only find fearful projections of the European self "in the bush." By associating Africans with consumerist ways of life in this sequence, the Grzimeks implied that they, too, had been "seduced" by American salesmanship—leaving only "Europeans with black faces" to encounter the visitor.[157]

The Grzimeks feared that such canned exoticism had also transformed the once-proud imperial hunt into another type of "commercialized show," one that threatened vulnerable animal populations even further. For the Grzimeks, the embodiment of the crass tourist was the globetrotting American safari hunter who came to Africa "between business trips to shoot a few elephants or lions, even if he has never had a rifle in his hands before coming here." Once a rite of masculine passage for European adventurers, the hunt had become mere entertainment in the hands of déclassé Americans, such as the "button factory owner from Scarsdale," who was said to have killed three hundred animals and blown the head off a leopard in a particularly gruesome shot.[158] Hunting scouts coached such men to track and shoot their prey, sometimes even steadying the gun on their shoulder.[159] Grzimek implied that vacationing "big game hunters" were as gullible as the women viewing the Watusi dance: both had succumbed to the commercialized blandishments of the tourism industry.

Grzimek's focus on the American sportsman may seem curious given the low numbers of American travelers to East Africa in the 1950s, but his sentiment meshed well with a decades-old critique of Americans' rapacious and profligate use of nature. American president Teddy Roosevelt's well-publicized 1909–1910 expedition to East Africa involved two hundred trackers, skinners, porters, and gun bearers, and Roosevelt shot, preserved, and shipped to Washington, DC, more than three thousand specimens of African game. When the photographs of the expedition appeared, the British colonial governor regretted issuing a special license for such wanton killing—and German newspapers reprinted details of the expedition with a note of horror.[160] Echoing the longstanding anti-American sentiments of German nature conservationists and Eurafrican advocates of the 1950s, Grzimek wrote that the noble animals' "extermination" should not be "prostituted" for the amusement of "dilettante sportsmen."[161] Elephants, lions, and zebra might have to give way to development, but "a few places should be preserved for them .... Where the animals have to cede they should be treated with dignity."[162] Africa's new hegemonic power could never be trusted as a guardian of Africa's wildlife—a stance that conveniently left Germany's own colonial expansion unexamined.

By lingering on these scenes of gullible tourists and an Americanized hunting industry, the Grzimeks once again upended audience expectations of a heroic Congo journey. One needed a discerning eye to make sense of the new Africa, the Grzimeks implied. Only non-partisans like themselves, who sought neither profit nor pleasure, could reveal the "truth" of the continent's sad predicament. The Grzimeks created a counter-world to the colonial hunter's milieu and its fantasies of domination. As Bernhard noted scornfully, "People in Europe and America are deluded by films and books." Upon viewing *No Room for Wild Animals*, he explained, "the film experts [in Berlin] complained that our portrayal of wild animals was too peaceful. They were accustomed to other Africa films in which a predator killed its prey every few seconds . . . and maliciously attacking elephants being shot just in time." As zoological scientists, the Grzimeks wanted to show how these creatures lived in reality, not to suit the tastes of "the thrill-seeking public."[163] Only by presenting the Congo's forests as idyllic and vulnerable could Grzimek move his viewers to support and justify the Zoological Society's emerging role in scientific conservation abroad.[164]

In the final sequence of No Room for Wild Animals, the narrator mentions the controversy over the Serengeti borders as the next battlefield in the quest to protect the last natural zoos in Africa. The pair had visited smaller parts of Uganda, Sudan, and Tanganyika during filming, which enabled them to glimpse Mount Kilimanjaro and learn that the Serengeti was threatened with division to accommodate cattle-herding Maasai. "Now the British mandate government is forfeiting two-thirds of the nature protection region of the Serengeti Steppe, the only national park in Tanganyika," notes the narrator with alarm, "one of the most famous animal paradises on earth, an ideal possession of all of mankind, is thus being destroyed."[165] The Grzimeks offered the Tanganyikan government the twenty-thousand Deutsche marks prize money from No Room to purchase land outright in Tanganyika for wildlife habitat. But when the park's game warden, Peter Molloy, suggested using the money instead for conducting aerial surveys of the great migration, the scientific quest that became Serengeti Shall Not Die was born.

The Serengeti mission had its origins in Congo journeys that revealed a continent on the brink of decolonization and destined to recapitulate Europe's pathological shift toward modern ways of life—urbanized, brutalized, and above all, overpopulated. The Grzimeks realized it would never be possible to rescue animals one by one in zoos. Rather, their zookeeper's ecology evolved into a plea for the global community to salvage and expand national parks established by colonial authorities but now belonging to "all mankind." With its massive networks of strict reserves, the Belgian Congo appeared as the model state for the rest of Africa, a place where the combined energies of blacks and whites were creating both a robust economic engine and an enlightened conservation corps. Unlike most of their contemporaries, the Grzimeks blamed Africa's environmental ills on European rapaciousness rather than African cruelty, offering a book and film that tried to undermine imperial hunters' tales and collectors' adventurism with portrayals of a continent under siege by midcentury brutalism and consumerism.

Yet their "completely raw" aesthetic never broke free from the imperialist visions of African nature that had justified European intervention and guided conservation measures in the first place. By sidestepping both Leopold's cruelties and Germany's colonial past in Central Africa, the references to a new Noah merely dusted off old scripts about white saviors rescuing the continent from contemporary evils. Europeans were the cause of Africa's ills; as such, they were dutybound to help the continent avoid the worst missteps on its path to modernity. The Grzimeks framed this obligation as another universal: as "the only rational being in this world," the final scenes noted, enlightened humans were responsible for our "brothers" in creation. The doomsday portrayals in *No Room*, moreover, tried to vanquish any lingering romanticism about "primitive" Africans living in harmony with nature. A vision of human equality emerged in which all persons, black or white, had broken their bonds to the organic world. From this Eurocentric perspective, becoming "just like us" had made Africans economically and reproductively successful but racially degenerate, no longer deserving of special consideration when it came to traditional land use. Africans were still culpable for the wild's destruction, only in a more abstract way: creating too many babies for too little space.

Africans appear only as victims in *No Room for Wild Animals*—of the slave trade, missionaries, European traders, urbanization, and racial decline—with little capacity to realize a *Heimat* on their own terms through working the land, exchanging goods, or finding sacred refuge. With so little capacity to act on their own behalf, it was a short step to replicating the same distorted portrait of Africa "leaving the bush" as the modernist boosters that the Grzimeks despised. Now that Africans had succumbed to the temptations of the "culture of the day after tomorrow," they were doomed to follow Europeans down the predetermined path of ecological catastrophe, necessitating a sharp divide between landscapes of production and development and those of consumption and conservation. Even before decolonization had arrived, such European anxieties imaginatively disenfranchised the Congolese, removing them from decision making about how best to steward the wildlife populations that would fall under their care. *No Room*, as the next chapter shows, globalized West German environmental awareness and began the "greening" of the country's political culture. But the film offered few resources for a trans-regional exchange in the opposite direction—one that affirmed the need for African environmental self-determination in the decades to come.

Thinking Locally, Acting Globally

> Entangled in laws and regulations, ensnared, like flies between the
> threads of a spider's web, in frontiers, railways, and trunk-roads, men
> turn their eyes toward the Dark Continent, wild, virgin and unex-
> plored, where it is not taxes and politicians that they must be on their
> guard against, but lions and rhinos. . . . No matter how the Great Powers
> divided it up, Africa really belongs to all who take comfort from the
> thought that there are still wild animals and virgin lands on earth.
> —Bernhard Grzimek, *No Room for Wild Animals*

The Grzimeks' Congo journey forged an ecological contact zone between
Germany and Central Africa that connected zoos and nature reserves, scientists
and imperial administrators, and filmgoers and wild animals across vast distances. Yet this space of interaction left little room for the Congolese to imagine their own environmental future. The bleak Malthusian depictions in the
book and on screen integrated them into a global story of overpopulation and
degeneracy that made the Congo's wild animals the only creatures worth caring
about. West Germans, on the other hand, found abundant places to debate the
significance of the Grzimeks' expedition in book reviews, newspaper editorials,
and radio listener feedback. They discovered a sphere of ecological engagement
beyond the existing ideologies of right and left, a chance for post-fascist Germans
to follow their country's Second Noah by saving animal lives from destruction.[1]
The country was still decades away from the green movements of the 1980s, but
the Grzimeks' advocacy in Africa spurred deeper reflection on ecological threats
at home, ranging from the loss of heritage landscapes to the deleterious effects of
pollution.[2] Yet even as sub-Saharan Africa stood on the brink of decolonization,
there was no reckoning with the colonialist longings expressed in Bernhard's
assertion that the continent "really belonged" to those seeking comfort in "virgin lands."[3] This chapter examines the inequalities that emerged as the Grzimeks
spoke on behalf of the world's animals (and peoples) from their own culturally
and historically situated position in Germany and the misalliance that resulted
from "thinking locally and acting globally" in their quest to save African wildlife.

Our Gigantic Zoo. Thomas M. Lekan, Oxford University Press (2020). © Oxford University Press.
DOI: 10.1093/oso/9780199843671.001.0001

The Grzimeks' project won over critics and audiences because their depictions of Africa meshed with many West Germans' anxieties about modernization and American influence in postwar Europe. Bernhard and Michael were masterful at connecting ordinary people to African wildlife across a variety of media—illustrated weeklies, radio, documentary films, and television.[4] In their hands, anthropomorphized stories about peace-loving animals replaced interwar narratives of marauding beasts, renaturing animals in German media spaces even as their habitats abroad dwindled.[5] During the 1950s, the hard times of reconstruction were giving way to unprecedented economic growth as West Germany was transitioning to a postindustrial society dominated by cross-class media consumption, automobility, and outdoor recreation.[6] In this context, the dwindling wild spaces of Central Africa became what one scholar has described as a "projection screen" for conservative anxieties about the dark side of the West German economic miracle: the social dislocations of urbanization, the hollowing out of traditional ways by mindless consumerism, and the potential fanaticism of mobile mass crowds.[7] Without their help, African might also succumb to these dangerous currents. Wild Africa still lived on in films and adventure tales, Grzimek told his audiences, but "in reality it is already beginning to disappear."[8]

The Grzimeks expanded the contours of German cultural conservatism to include ecological concerns in tandem with a new generation of apocalyptic environmental writers who warned that their tiny country's economic upswing would stall in the face of water shortages, soil exhaustion, atomic radioactivity, and mass extinction.[9] The elder Grzimek's writings energized discussions about how citizens of the Federal Republic might escape the "diseases of civilization" in nature parks and leisure spaces suitable for automobilists seeking respite from the city.[10] He took this impulse one step further. He used his experiences in Africa to make room for animals back in Germany, renovating the zoo environs to mimic natural habitats abroad and featuring live animals as studio guests on his TV program *A Place for Animals*. He even called on his fellow citizens to adopt the African national park model back in the homeland, rewilding their living space with species that had vanished in Germany over the past two centuries.[11]

Not all Germans welcomed the Grzimeks' environmental message. Both father and son knew that *No Room for Wild Animals* would rile critics and make enemies—and they were right.[12] German hunters who had long seen themselves as stewards of the *Heimat* landscape were outraged at the film's scenes of reckless, "impotent" men on commercial safaris. They attacked *No Room* in editorials, articles, and books, arguing that the Grzimeks' doomsday portrait exaggerated the decline of wildlife, dishonored their community's long-standing commitment to nature conservation, and diverted attention from more pressing conservation problems at home. Bernhard used the battle with the hunting lobby to link recreational hunting to tawdry consumerism and Nazi aggression,

Figure 3.1 The First German Okapi, with the name Epulu, 1954. Grzimek acquired the rare creature from the Belgian Congo. The Frankfurt Zoo's success in breeding them helped to cement its reputation for popular attractions and scientific conservation. The notion that Grzimek was a new Noah gained traction, especially once the Belgian Congo descended into civil war after independence just six years later. Institute for the History of Frankfurt, S7C Nr. 1998-29.875, Photographer Egon Matthes.

paving the way for wildlife scientists and camera safarists to dominate visions of Africa's wild spaces. Yet both the zookeeper and his critics sidestepped the colonial violence and paternalism that had created African game reserves. In the 1950s, debates about World War II still overshadowed the colonial past, leaving European fantasies about African nature completely intact.[13]

Spectacular Animals

The Grzimeks' Congo journeys cemented Bernhard's position as one of Europe's most important zoo directors and established the Frankfurt garden as a leader in animal care and technical innovation. The success of *No Room* put Allied inquiries into Bernhard's Nazi past and lingering threats of career suspension far behind him.[14] Scientists and film reviewers lauded the filmmakers for their sobering portrayal of African wildlife. Researchers at the Max Planck Institute for Behavioral Research—including prominent students of Konrad Lorenz—confirmed the film's authenticity and praised its ability to render large-scale environmental problems emotionally engaging for lay audiences.[15] Film reviewers, meanwhile, commented on the film's "optical majesties." The skillful use of color, light, and time-elapsed sequences to capture the "tropical flora sprawling unimpaired" on the rainforest floor even made one reviewer think immediately of packing his bags to see this last untrammeled space.[16] Newspaper columnists drew parallels between Grzimek and the most famous "good German" of the time, the Nobel Prize–winning ethicist Albert Schweitzer. In his quest to save African wildlife from extinction, noted one article, Bernhard embodied better than anyone else the "doctor of Lambarene's" appeal to "reverence for all life."[17]

Energized by the Congo expedition, Bernhard popularized the conservation mission in radio broadcasts, illustrated articles, and editorials that presented the pair's observations about animal behavior and outlined the uncertain prospects for wild animals' survival.[18] Bernhard noted with pride that the Frankfurt Zoo had "Germany's first Okapi"—one of only ten outside Belgian-controlled zoos. Criticized by the zoo's board of directors for the high costs of the Congo journey—particularly the specially outfitted Sabena aircraft—Grzimek retorted that the Okapi would bring in an extra twenty-five thousand visitors in the first year. This estimate was far off the mark—"Epulu" ended up bringing in fifty-five thousand visitors in just the first three months of 1955.[19] Just three years later, the West German foreign minister Heinrich von Brentano— also a Frankfurter—helped him to procure a female mate for Epulu from the Congo. Grzimek beamed with pride when "Safari" gave birth to "Kiwu," the first of its kind born in a German zoo.[20] Monies generated by the star quality of such new attractions enabled Bernhard to clear the last ruins from the war on the zoo grounds, expanding room for his charges and creating additional cageless enclosures or specialty houses for lions, giraffes, antelopes, and gorillas. The Frankfurt Zoo also opened an "Exotarium" in 1957 that combined aquariums, terrariums, and avian enclosures into a synthetic experience of fish, reptiles, and birds. Though never one of Europe's largest zoos, Frankfurt became renowned for its technical innovation and ingenious use of its limited urban space, offering visitors "quick-changing impressions" of animals in a variety of habitats: an African savanna, rocky mountain ledges, and rainforests, with buildings for staff scientists and maintenance facilities tucked into artificially created hills and cliffs.[21] In that same year, the zoo received its highest number of visitors to date, over 1.5 million, making it "the most visited site in West Germany."[22]

The Exotarium was completed just in time for the zoo's hundredth anniversary in 1958. Grzimek and his team hosted an international zoo directors' conference that showcased Bernhard's renovations and allowed him to present his cutting-edge findings about habitats and behavior abroad as well as the care of large mammals in captivity.[23] The anniversary also witnessed the re-founding and renaming of the Society of the Friends of the Frankfurt Zoo as the Frankfurt Zoological Society (FZS). Grzimek saw its new mission as a nature conservationist NGO charged with fundraising and advocacy for wildlife abroad, especially in East Africa. With well-heeled Frankfurt bankers, industrialists, and officials of the Common Market on its board alongside a base of ordinary television viewers, the FZS was able to amass millions of Deutsche marks to support conservation projects in the decades that followed.[24]

Grzimek's reliance on armchair conservationists—the "little people" who sacrificed what they could for the poor animals of Africa—gave FZS fundraising its moral punch. Yet the initial idea for a television series about animals came from producers at the Hessian state broadcasting company, not Grzimek himself. In 1956, the journalist and TV editor martin Jenteconvinced Bernhard and Hildegard to let the company's crew follow a day in the life of the four gorilla babies who lived in the Grzimeks' apartment. Gorillas Want to Sleep, Too, which aired in 1956, was a huge hit, and Jente approached Grzimek about a weekly series. To his surprise, Grzimek equivocated.[25] After seeing a constant stream of television ads on a visit to the United States, Grzimek associated the medium with America's crass commercialism and wanted nothing to do with it.[26] But West German TV was different. Viewers paid a fee for having a television set, which limited the advertising to short periods between programs, and Grzimek never needed a commercial sponsor who might influence the content of his program: He had "only the animals to sell."[27] Eventually, Grzimek relented, agreeing to a monthly, forty-five-minute format for the program.

Much like Marlin Perkins's Zoo Parade in the United States, A Place for Animals initially focused on the habits and quirks of live animals brought into the studio from the zoo.[28] Grzimek soon added still photographs and edited footage from his African journeys, supplementing and amplifying the central themes of No Room. Through television, viewers experienced animals more intimately than in cinemas, as the device connected living room audiences to live creatures across vast distances. This allowed for glimpses into foraging behaviors and mating rituals that were difficult to witness firsthand. In German-speaking Europe, wildlife television helped to catalyze ecological consciousness as well, as Grzimek and other colleagues demonstrated the plight of endangered animals at home and abroad.[29] Grzimek enhanced this sense of being part of the action by cultivating a stern countenance and unscripted style that gained viewers' trust. Impeccably dressed in a professorial jacket and tie and his famous gold-rimmed glasses, Bernhard appeared like a nerdy uncle returning from Africa with an exotic pet or a home slideshow.[30] Viewers could sometimes detect an animal growl in the background or hear a chair tip over—all of which enhanced the spectacle of familiarity. Grzimek seemed professorial, naïve, even a bit jittery at times; his sentences sometimes trailed off or jumped to a new topic as his soft, nasally voice described an animal's quirks or set the scene for an image. All was part of the show effect.[31] Grzimek insisted on a single camera that remained fixed on him—there were no "two shots," musical interludes, or subtitles.[32] A cheetah might leap across his desk or off the stage, but the zookeeper remained unflappable: knowledgeable, dependable, and yet modest.[33]

A Place for Animals became so popular that it catalyzed the growth of television as a medium. Regular television broadcast began in West Germany in 1951; by 1955, only a hundred thousand households had a television set. By 1957—in part due to the success of Grzimek's show—the number had reached one million. By the mid-1960s, when 90 percent of West German households had a TV, Grzimek had about thirty to forty million viewers: about 70 percent of the available viewership in that time spot. By the time it ended in 1987, *A Place for Animals* had featured 170 episodes—making this the most successful documentary series in the world.[34]

Figure 3.2 On set at *A Place for Animals*, 1957. Grzimek's program became the longest-running documentary series in television history and a key way for Grzimek to raise funds for his animal protection campaigns. Getty Images.

The Globalization of German Anxiety

Amid his successes in broadening the zoo's conservationist mission and developing a successful television program, Grzimek remained deeply ambivalent about the contradictions within modernity that had made the zoological garden popular in the first place. Grzimek was quick to point out, for example, that zoo directors' pride in the successful breeding of rare species in captivity went hand in hand with the industrialized death of domestic livestock destined for the disassembly line—cows, pigs, and chickens—which gave birth to their young and died under horrific conditions in modern slaughterhouses. Far from ignoring these barnyard species in pursuit of charismatic megafauna, the contact zone between Germany and Central Africa enabled Grzimek to connect the mutually reinforcing processes of consumption and imperilment that drove animal suffering across different regions and scales. The industrialization of livestock accompanied the fetishization of pets, he argued, while the bulldozing of tropical forests in the Congo went hand in hand with the sale of animal figure sets replete with plastic palm trees.[35] Grzimek proposed that animals might even have the capacity to reflect on their ignoble fates in the zoological garden: "If one takes a moment to think about this profession, one can easily feel like a prison director . . . . even as a zoo director makes his daily rounds, he is often blinded and dulled to what is really going on there. A person can even get used to a concentration camp, I was once told," he added—once again evading specific German crimes in a general story of brutalization and incarceration.[36] Much better to be a ranger at a national park among free-roaming animals, he mused.[37] Behind Grzimek's avuncular television image lay a deep cultural pessimism that shaped the environmental messages of No Room at home and projected them across the globe.

Trying to hit the right tone for a broad audience that included "children and university professors" also left Grzimek, like many of his conservative compatriots, dubious about the prospects for mass society. The "animal uncle" longed to be free of the "hordes of sightseers" at the zoo and bemoaned the many who tried to pet or feed animals, asked inane questions, and littered the grounds with cigarette packets and gum wrappers. In 1954, the zoo banned visitors from feeding the animals, even charging a fine of twenty-five Deutsche marks and expulsion from the zoo for each infraction. City administrators staunchly opposed the fee, fearing a loss of visitors, and challenged Grzimek's authority to carry through with the ordinance until the zookeeper demonstrated how many animals became sick or even died from ingesting popcorn or candy.[38] Such confrontations led Grzimek to take a dim view of the give-and-take of modern society—including the FRG's new experiment in parliamentarism. "Few people . . . are actually aware of the basic principles of a democracy," he noted, "our politicians do not do what is best for the common good, but always that which will bring in the most votes at the next election."[39] Grzimek wished Germany still had a limited monarchy to help "open doors" with influential statesmen abroad and longed for the bourgeois respectability of the Wilhelmine era when "money was not the measure of all things."[40] In the liberalized public sphere of the 1950s, conservationists had to compete with unscrupulous politicians and big-money interests to make their voices heard. Small wonder, then, that Grzimek insisted on a stern image and fixed television camera: He could bypass the latest political brouhaha and speak directly to his viewers.

German filmgoers had not experienced *No Room*'s bleak images of over-population and ecological destruction onscreen before, but the film's fearsome depictions of urban pathology and "race mixing" were hardly new for post-Hitler audiences seeking an edifying "cultural film."[41] When the film appeared, the Federal Republic was about to experience an "economic miracle" that produced remarkable rates of growth, allowing for nearly full employment, long weekends, and a doubling of average household income between 1955 and 1965. By 1961, almost one-third of the country's 56.5 million people lived in cities with more than a hundred thousand inhabitants—many of which had just witnessed an influx of refugees from the East.[42] Most West Germans applauded their new-found prosperity and discretionary income. But as the phase of rebuilding drew to a close in the late 1950s, concerns about "quality of life" superseded growth at all costs, particularly in the shrunken and densely populated living space of the Federal Republic.[43]

Doomsday sequences of vertiginous cityscapes and the African urban masses in *No Room* reflected this dark side of the economic miracle, turning Africa into a projection screen for anxieties at home. In *No Room*, for example, ancient trees in the Congo are felled to create nylon and whiskey advertisements "for a certain newspaper in New York" and scantily dressed Congolese cook polenta in a fire-pit where, the narrator asks, "Who can say whether in fifty years on this spot there won't be a night club or dance hall?" Such boisterous images of Americanization provoked both admiration for ways of life unfettered by the past and condemna-tion of the shallow materialism of mass-produced culture, a theme that had its roots in the interwar era.[44] Indeed, when the National Socialists came to power, they labeled certain expressions of American culture as "degenerate" and spoke of establishing "German capitalism" as an alternative to both Fordism and the USSR's revolutionary socialism.[45] For Grzimek, like so many cultural critics of the 1950s, anti-Americanism remained trenchant—a reflection of a "conser-vative modernization" unfolding under the watchful eye of traditional cultural arbiters.[46]

One way that cultural conservatives registered their anxiety about modern-ization was to bemoan, like Grzimek, the "coca-colonization" of their country by the American occupiers even as Adenauer tried to ensconce the Federal Republic in a Western alliance dominated by the United States.[47] When viewers of *No Room* saw the Grzimeks' images of Nairobi's multistory apartment blocks, traffic jams, highways, and billboards, it reminded them of modernist rebuilding processes in German cities that carved access roads into downtowns, stripped ornamentation from historic façades, transplanted brutalist structures into traditional neighborhoods, and even led some cities, especially Grzimek's adopted home of Frankfurt, to copy the American skyscraper on its way to becoming West Germany's "Mainhattan."[48] Both Germany and Africa appeared to be under assault by US materialism, and it was up to Germans and other Europeans to sound the alarm about the new empire on the horizon. Fears about industrialized technology and consumerism eating their way through the African countryside enabled conservatives to assail Americanizing trends at home without running the risk of being seen as antimodern or antidemocratic in a public sphere dominated by the Allies and Cold War geopolitical alliances that favored closer ties with the American behemoth.[49]

At the same time, the Grzimeks' doomsday portrayal of the African urban masses meshed with the pronouncements of post-Hitler conservatives who feared the potential for political demagoguery to emerge out of Africa's detribalizing societies.[50] In the pages of *Atlantis*, the well-known travel writer Werner Krug questioned whether Africans had received sufficient time to absorb external changes on their own terms. On the surface, they had acquired the accoutrements of a European lifestyle, with the "petroleum canister" replacing the handcrafted earthen jug, and radio stations blasting news about European conflicts to both urban workers and "half-naked aboriginals" in "grass huts."[51] With their customs, social networks, and "pagan" beliefs destroyed, Krug maintained, Africans were ill-equipped to bear the psychological burdens of modernity. The Congolese could only imitate—never build on their own— the machinery and infrastructure that allowed cities to hum. As a result, they remained under the yoke of white bosses, spurring hopelessness and resentment. "The Negro finds himself in a vacuum," Krug wrote, "and should he want to escape, he becomes confused by new taboos, new commands, and new customs." Many African urbanites returned to the "bush" in short order, but others slid into the "negro proletariat," loitering on street corners or turning to thievery or prostitution to get by.[52] Small wonder that this "mob" was vulnerable to political "agitators" from among the educated Congolese who were "resentful" of their European betters.

Fears of this undifferentiated "mass" becoming politically radicalized were hardly new in the 1950s, as European writers had already diagnosed the dangers of the roving "savage crowds" as "barbarians" in the midst of European cities around the turn of the century.[53] Mapped onto Africa, however, this fear of political fanaticism took on a more sinister cast, as it raised fears about modernization and social dislocation spurring the growth of "totalitarianism" across the globe. Conservatives feared that the "massification" of society was creating "uprooted" individuals prone to "impatience, intolerance, [and] rash judgments" and "a willing victim of loud propaganda."[54] Such sentiments reflected a view of Nazism that blamed the uprooted and atomized "mass man" for falling prey to demagoguery, conveniently forgetting cultural conservatives' own support for the Hitler regime.[55] Anxiety about mass seduction also enlarged the specter of Communism abroad, leading to a vision of Africa in which vulnerable populations still needed European guidance. To avoid "chaos" and "catastrophe," Krug recommended a Eurafrican solution: Whites and blacks needed to work together so that the modern institutions brought by Europeans could be "adapted and transformed by the black man to suit his own condition."[56]

Grzimek broadened the contours of such cultural criticism by projecting West German environmental anxieties onto Central Africa as well.[57] The 1950s marked a turning point in the emergence of German environmental consciousness, as the media paid growing attention to the unpredictable and synergistic effects of industrial effluents, radionuclides, and other toxins unleashed in the country's air, water, and soil.[58] Conservationists produced dozens of films about the local and regional environmental threats, but none of them could convey ecological themes like Grzimek, who galvanized viewers with his sorrowful stories of imperiled animals in the green heart of Africa.[59] In the film *No Room*, the Grzimeks' references to Lake Edward on the Ugandan border as "untroubled by sewage from human factories" offered an Edenic contrast to life in Europe's urban areas where citizens existed "beneath blankets of dirty grey miasma." Grzimek described Europe's cities as places that "swell like evil boils, suck up the groundwater from the land and then pollute the rivers with the disgusting effluents which they discharge."[60] Such pollution imagery had clear associations with the lurid pictures of fish kills and paralyzing detergent scum along the Rhine in the 1950s.[61] At the same time, Grzimek's insistence that newly planned hydroelectric dams in Africa would destroy animals' watering holes echoed the fears of limnologist Erich Hornsmann, who predicted that similar projects in Germany had produced a "water emergency" that might lead to the country's desertification. Hornsmann's *If We Did Not Have Water* (*Hätten wir das Wasser nicht*, 1957) asserted that West Germany was already in the midst of a water emergency that threatened to stall postwar economic recovery. With more frequent bathing and industrial needs, he noted, water had become a commodity in short supply.[62] Grzimek did not see desertification as a problem for Africa alone but also as part of an unfolding global catastrophe that threatened Europe.

Germany, like Africa, seemed to be drying out in the 1950s, resurrecting fears of a "steppification" (*Versteppung*) that had long haunted environmental discourses about Imperial Germany's easternmost regions. Such fears had played a critical role in landscape architect Alwin Seifert's controversial and highly public 1944 critique of overzealous hydraulic engineers in Robert Ley's German Labor Front, whose efforts to drain wetlands and canalize streams during the war had dropped many regions' water tables to dangerously low levels.[63] In November 1959, after West Germany had faced its driest summer since 1890 and implemented widespread water rationing, Der Spiegel printed an eleven-page feature on the country's water scarcity and pollution problems, graphically depicting the causes of water over-consumption, the sources of water pollution, and the hydrological consequences of streambed regulation.[64] Conservationists warned that Germany's "excrements of civilization" had become "life-threatening" due to the greedy overuse and environmental mismanagement of the nation's natural resources.[65]

The Grzimeks' focus on protecting creatures' *habitat* abroad was especially critical, as it transformed concerns about animal welfare into a deeper assessment of ecological threats in Germans' own backyards. In the pages of *Das Tier*, an illustrated monthly that he published along with Lorenz and Hediger, Bernhard used his column "Battle for the Animals" to report on the Zoological Society's efforts to protect gorillas' "living space" in Ruanda-Urundi or to criticize missionaries in the French Congo who tried to sell juvenile chimpanzees to zoos, rather than nurturing them in their own biotopes.[66] Yet Grzimek and his companions put these articles side-by-side with essays about the joys and imperilment of species close to home. Lorenz satiated his "yearning for paradise" by observing wild ducks and geese in ponds behind his country house, noting he had "no rational explanation" for the "ineffable satisfaction" that came from being alone on the moors and having such waterfowl answer his call.[67] In the Upper Harz region of Lower Saxony, a farmer had made wild deer "as tame as pets" by feeding them in the winter—a delight for nearby automobilists who came to the local guest house in droves to observe the shy creatures.[68] These natural zoos were under threat throughout West Germany, however. As another article noted, magnificent storks—which spent three months in South Africa each year—were "dying out at home" due to callous farmers in Europe who destroyed their nests in barns, rooftops, and chimneys.[69] Moving back and forth across the contact zone, Grzimek showed that migrating animals were losing their last refuges in both Europe and Africa.

Such global threats made Grzimek a pivotal figure among the cadre of "apocalyptic" environmental writers in the 1950s who warned about impending ecological collapse from nuclear and chemical contamination, overpopulation, and strains on natural resources. Günther Schwab, for example, pointed to atomic fallout and radioactive wastes as some of the most insidious problems facing postwar societies, ridiculing the "peaceful" use of the atom for inexpensive and "clean" power generation.[70] Schwab's 1958 book, published in English as

Dance with the Devil, dramatized the ecological crisis in the form of an interview between the devil, his helpers, and four human characters. The demons outdo each other to convince human beings to do the devil's work by destroying the environment to the point where life is untenable, including emitting toxic pollutants, destroying traditional agricultural practices, cutting down forests, and proliferating nuclear fission.[71] In a similar vein, Grzimek, Lorenz, and Hediger used the opening issue of *Das Tier* to lament the "militaristic exploiters of atomic science who, every month, use all means available to concoct new ways to wipe out entire peoples." Such self-destructive capacity showed that humans were "no longer the measure of all things;" it was imperative to show how the "four-legged and flying" among the earth's creatures "are conditioned and . . . get along with one another."[72] Saving animals, in this sense, offered a chance to redeem humanity with organic insights on ways to structure a society without violence and retribution. Seen in the context of this postwar wave of apocalyptic writing, the contact zone forged by the Grzimeks' journeys challenged the parochialism of traditional nature conservation. As much as they projected German anxieties onto Africa, they also used Africa's endangered habitats as a benchmark to spotlight the threats to living spaces back home.

The Last Monuments of Nature

No issue galvanized conservationists' outrage about West German ecological deficits more than the country's lack of national parks in which to experience "untrammeled" nature. As one conservationist wrote,

> Nowhere is the number of idealists who want to preserve God's pristine nature higher than in Germany. We discuss, write, and read more about animals and their problems than any other people. Yet we have done the least to ameliorate the challenges to the very existence of the free-living animals we so love caused by humans.[73]

Particularly galling to the "idealist" German was the comparatively superior record of the United States, the land of unfettered materialism, which had managed to put 10 percent of its territory into conservation areas—three times the proportion that the Federal Republic devoted to *Naturschutz* regions. Germany had over 360 small and medium-sized nature reserves—a legacy of the local activism of turn-of-the-century *Heimat* movements—but not one met the IUCN standard for a national park.[74] Small wonder that the Grzimeks' "forbidden paradises" in Central and East Africa were so enticing to Germans of the postwar era.

The desire for a German national park dated back to the 1890s, a time when a newly united Reich was experiencing the first wave of its dynamic industrial expansion and urban growth. After visiting the Rhine-hugging cliffsides, forests, and medieval ruins of the Siebengebirge nature park south of Bonn in 1898, Breslau school teacher Wilhelm Wetekamp, a member of the Prussian Assembly, called for a "declaration of untouched areas as state parks similar to the national parks of the United States."[75] Wetekamp's appeal led the assembly to commission botanist Hugo Conwentz, the head of the West Prussian Provincial Museum in Danzig, to establish the State Office for Natural Monument Preservation in 1906.[76] Yet Conwentz found America's national parks inappropriate given Germany's economic conditions, size, and population density; a park the size of Yellowstone would have encompassed the entire Kingdom of Saxony. The Nature Park Society (Verein Naturschutzpark, or VNP), a private organization founded in Stuttgart in 1900, did raise money to secure the first parcels of land for national parks in the Austrian Alps and the Lunebürger Heath and considered more in Germany's African colonies, yet promoting such large-scale reserves remained the exception before 1945.[77] Unlike the National Park Service, the Prussian State Office evolved into an advisory agency for a decentralized array of regional and local efforts to secure individual natural objects or smaller conservation regions. Conservationists argued that small-scale and easily accessible nature reserves provided hikers with a respite from the industrial era's class and political strife—an important prelude to Grzimek's upscaling of African nature as a "common property" (Gemeinbesitz) of the people.[78]

The discussion of West Germany's lack of a national park centered on the Federal Republic following behind international trends and standards. National parks of any stripe remained difficult to establish in the Federal Republic due to an aversion to government land grabs in the wake of Nazism, a reluctance to designate a "national" park in a nation still divided by Cold War hostilities, and a tendency to believe the country was better served by a network of smaller parks spread across different regions.[79] Yet the Federal Republic's feeble efforts stood in sharp contrast to the record of its peer nations. During the 1950s, Great Britain opened ten national parks, bringing its total to twelve, while Japan established four more, with a total of twenty-eight. The densely populated Netherlands added another national park to the two already in existence, while Italy's Gran Paradiso National Park encompassed more land than all of the Federal Republic's 360 reserves put together.[80]

German conservationists were successful, however, in promoting recreationally oriented "nature parks" throughout West Germany in the 1950s.[81] Hamburg business mogul and VNP chair Alfred Toepfer saw these parks as "oases of calm" in the countryside that would allow urbanites to escape the noise and air pollution of the burgeoning cities and promote love of homeland among FRG citizens and newly arrived expellees from Poland and Czechoslovakia.[82] Toepfer argued that the FRG did not have the "luxury" of setting aside vast landscapes as national parks.[83] Yet, like many physicians at the time, the millionaire argued that recreation in nature was essential to combating "managerial diseases": the chronic fatigue and stress produced by long hours, bureaucratic procedures, and alienating office life.[84] Toepfer noted that West Germany's existing network of nature reserves was simply inadequate to meet the demands of a new generation of hikers and campers, who were increasingly inclined to take to the woods in their cars, rather than by train or on foot, and needed adequate spaces for introspective hiking. If they could not find adequate recreational space at home, many tourist promoters warned, they would seek it beyond Germany's borders—a loss of revenue for local operators and for homeland attachments that might otherwise bind a seemingly unmoored society.[85]

When *No Room* appeared in 1955, West Germans were not yet the "world champions of travel" (*Reiseweltmeister*) they became in the 1960s, but mass tourism was on the horizon. As a result of National Socialist initiatives to break down class barriers to leisure travel for middle-class, lower-middle-class, and some working-class Germans, the growing motorization of the country in the 1950s and 1960s, and the expanding number of package tours to domestic and international destinations, West Germans of the "Miracle Years" were beginning to devote substantial amounts of their discretionary income to holidaymaking.[86] Buoyed by generous paid vacations and expanding affluence, many Germans turned to nature, combing the Alps, the Harz Mountains, the Baltic seacoast, and, later, the Mediterranean for places to hike, camp, and enjoy the outdoors. The leader of the German Camping Club in Munich noted that the Federal Republic had added about one hundred camping sites to its existing stock of two hundred campgrounds in 1953 alone, but even more were needed: France had over three thousand sites. Contrary to a widely held view," he wrote,

> [I]t is not America that is the home of the camping movement, but England. Germany, thrown out of the development by the war and by a period in which people were not particularly enamored of individual hiking, is now connecting up again. But the individuals with the urge to separate themselves are now invariably bunching together into new masses on the campgrounds.[87]

Such "bunches" of nature-hungry campers needed more and more space to realize their yearnings. But without careful supervision and designated zones of activity, Toepfer and others feared that the masses might overrun fragile natural areas and deface them with litter and graffiti.[88]

For the most part, the nature park program found support among federal, state, and local leaders across different political affiliations.[89] Toepfer and the VNP put up some of the funding for the parks and received additional funds from private foundations and state subventions. Between 1957 and 1963 alone, twenty-six parks encompassing over fifteen thousand square miles were established across the country, particularly in the heavily industrialized northern states of North Rhine-Westphalia, Hamburg, and Hesse.[90] The nature parks were supposed to balance nature conservation and recreation; there was even talk of calling them "national parks." But these privately administered reserves were hardly a "wilderness" according to the benchmarks established by the London Convention in 1933. Conservationists complained that the balance had tipped too far in the direction of recreation. During the 1960s, 80 percent of the funding for nature parks went to trails, parking lots, restrooms, picnic grounds campgrounds, and other structures; some even included mini-golf courses and water slides.[91]

The Grzimeks' critics worried that *No Room for Wild Animals* would exacerbate West Germany's nature shortage by diverting audience's attention from the national park campaign at home. They accused Bernhard and Michael of "throwing stones in glass houses": fixating their fellow citizens on the plight of Africa to avoid reckoning with West Germany's woeful environmental record. As their detractors noted, the popularity of the Grzimeks' film showed that West Germans all too easily transferred over their "compassionate spirit to the abuses in other countries," forgetting in the process the "deficiencies" of German conservation. Indignant about the killing of elephants in Africa, the writers continued, Germans quite readily put a "live lobster into boiling water"—a symbol of the many "daily sins against nature" they committed at home.[92]

Such criticisms were off the mark. Grzimek never ignored domestic environmental concerns in favor of Africa and parlayed his experiences as a zookeeper and global conservationist to advocate for new wildlife spaces within West Germany. With the help of Georg von Opel, heir of the famous Opel automobile fortune, Grzimek sketched plans to transform the millionaire's wildlife reserve in the Taunus Mountains into an open-air "sister zoo" for the Frankfurt Zoological Garden.[93] The idea behind this safari park, or *Tierfreiheit*, was to expand the central zoo's capacity and lure automobile tourists from the Rhine into the interior of Hessen. In African and some US national parks, Grzimek maintained, animals became accustomed to motorized vehicles, offering visitors unparalleled opportunities to view them and their habitats from behind the wheel. Guests in such "safari zoos" would need to stay inside a vehicle, since the creatures would be allowed to roam free inside vast enclosures, without fear of hunters or poachers and without the potential for mass tourists to degrade their habitat.[94] Grzimek proposed that the species in the *Tierfreiheit* include cold-tolerant exotics from

Africa and Asia along with large European mammals wiped out long ago in Germany's forests and meadows.[95] Like Toepfer's nature parks, the safari zoos were an expression of conservative modernization; proponents argued that a *Tierfreiheit* offered a healthy and managed recreational alternative for laborers who might otherwise spend their precious weekend hours watching TV, listening to the radio, or reading comic strips.[96] Despite many setbacks, Grzimek never stopped believing that African parks offered models for rewilding the shrunken landscapes of home, packaged in a form that was fully compatible with a motorized, consumerist society.

Bernhard's effort to expand the African safari park model to Germany nonetheless ran afoul of local conceptions of leisure and landscape. District officials blocked the plan to acquire the Opel reserve because it violated local zoning codes but offered Grzimek the opportunity instead to purchase the state-owned "Weilburger Game Park," also in Hessen. An extended public debate then ensued over the conditions of the purchase and local residents' concerns about exotic animals "disfiguring" the *Heimat* landscape, with many arguing that this "miniature translation of the African Serengeti" did not belong in the German landscape.[97] District officials then scrapped the plan for the Weilburger Park as well.[98] Undeterred, Grzimek immersed himself further in domestic affairs by becoming the chairman of the German Nature Conservation Circle, a loose network of conservation, hiking, and beautification societies with a substantial number of conservation-minded hunters as members and activists.[99] In this role, he threw his support behind a plan to create a national park in the woodlands in the "Bavarian Siberia" along the sector border between West Germany and Czechoslovakia. Grzimek lobbied hard—and ultimately unsuccessfully—for a rewilded habitat that might have existed in medieval times, when buffalo, beaver, lynx, and wild boar roamed the woodlands and streams.[100] Foresters, wildlife biologists, and members of the VNP once again pilloried this "Bavarian Serengeti" as wholly inappropriate for the homeland landscape and argued for allowing selective human activity—timber harvesting, small-scale agriculture, hunting, and the harvesting of herbs—to continue in some zones while letting nature take its course in regenerating the forest in others.[101] Critics often conflated the *Tierfreiheit* and national park proposals, mistakenly arguing that elephants and giraffes would soon roam the German woodlands, destroying their native plants and animals.[102] As the Bavarian government moved toward acquiring the land for the mixed-use national park in 1969, Grzimek disavowed the entire project. This "national park," in his view, had failed to create a habitat for wildlife that met even the least stringent international standards for such a reserve.[103]

The failure of the *Tierfreiheit* and national park projects revealed the potential frictions between "thinking locally and acting globally" as the Grzimeks moved across the German–African contact zones in the 1950s. Dealing with political factions at home, Grzimek argued, forced him into confrontations with hypocritical fellow citizens who claimed they were "friends of nature" but did nothing to stop the destruction of German animals—from butterflies to falcons—when a new autobahn was proposed.[104] But at a deeper level, Grzimek's vision for the *Tierfreiheit* and animal habitat–centered national park clashed with a much longer tradition of conservation in Germany. This was a tradition that envisioned the landscapes as a natural-cultural hybrid that still prioritized regional identity and assured recreational opportunities over zoological concerns about species conservation. Grzimek concluded that it was far more expedient to make headway in Africa, where it was still possible to cordon off imperial nature parks from "the ubiquitous biped" without having to confront—at least not yet—African citizens with their own ideas about nature, culture, and environmental sovereignty.[105] Yet even on this "global" stage, Grzimek had to confront conservation-minded Germans who had long considered themselves the real guardians of both European and African wildlife and who still claimed Africa's wild spaces as proof of European superiority: big game hunters.

A Commercialized Mockery

The Grzimeks knew they were courting trouble by including a searing critique of trophy hunters in the final version of *No Room*. Big game hunting in East Africa remained a popular and lucrative industry in the 1950s, a favorite among the Federal Republic's newly affluent industrialists, financiers, and government officials. Even the chairman of the Society of the Friends of the Frankfurt Zoological Garden, Georg von Opel, indulged in this sport. Like other "Africa hunters" at the time, von Opel wrote about his kills upon returning home from safari in Kenya in 1955—two elephants, two rhinos, three buffaloes, and assorted other wild game.[106] Moreover, hunters had long counted themselves the principal stewards of Germany's wildlife. Without hunters' care and feeding, many of Grzimek's critics noted, there would be no game reserves and thus, no red deer, roe deer, or wild boar left in Central European woodlands.[107] Hunting was not just a sport; it was a calling to maintain *Heimat* nature for future generations.

German colonial officials had also been at the forefront of wildlife protection in their East African protectorate before 1918. Led by enlightened trophy hunters and their code of conduct emphasizing respect, responsibility, and restraint (known as *Waidgerechtigkeit*), territorial administrators had sounded the alarm about African wildlife "going the way of the buffalo" and rescued lions, elephants, rhino, and hippos for posterity.[108] Penitent hunters such as the writer Carl Georg Schillings, for example, had warned his compatriots about Africa's dwindling wildlife in best-selling books and packed slideshows on the eve of World War I, advocating for hunting concessions for sportsmen with long-term leases and the establishment of "nature protection parks" throughout German East Africa.[109] In a similar vein, beginning in 1896, the German East Africa governor Hermann von Wissmann had promulgated a series of ordinances that limited the taking of animals by skin, ivory, and trophy hunters. Modeled on the customary laws of the aristocratic German hunting estate, the ordinances outlawed the hunting of females and foals, established hunting seasons and mandatory licences for various species, and called for game reserves to allow large mammals to seek refuge and breed.[110] Von Wissmann's efforts paved the way for German and British colonial officials to join forces at the International Conference for the Preservation of Wild Animals, Birds and Fish, which was held in London in 1900 in a cooperative effort to regulate the hunt and encourage scientific exchange across imperial boundaries. Though never ratified, the convention created a foundation for game regulations throughout imperial territories in the decades that followed.[111] Such German traditions of homeland and imperial stewardship posed a significant obstacle to a zookeeper's ecology premised on scientific conservation and global administration.

Bernhard feared that the growth of mass tourism had destroyed the ethical foundations of sport hunting, transforming the ostentatious big game hunt into a tawdry American-style package tour. Before the opening credits begin in *No Room*, the Grzimeks showed hippopotamuses, zebras, and lions fleeing in terror as the narrator cuts to an advertisement crying "Safari, in Africa!" and between shots of the rifle, "$3,000, and you get an air passage with a guarantee that you'll shoot an elephant!" If unsuccessful, the naïve sportsman could even head to one of dozens of shops in modern Nairobi and purchase a "leopard skin for a beautiful lady," telling her: "yes, I shot it myself dear!" The feckless hunter in this sequence hits and wounds an adolescent female, a travesty under German conventions of *Waidgerechtigkeit*, because of her future capacity to breed.[112] The hunter could not even be bothered to give her a merciful final blow; in the film's final sequences, she slowly drowns as she enters a lake seeking relief for her bloody, excruciating wound. Once a symbol of aristocratic status, worldliness, masculinity, and imperial hegemony, trophy hunting had become "commercialized mockery" in the hands of unscrupulous safari companies catering to parvenus.[113]

After the film's release, the Grzimeks quickly distanced themselves from any hint of connection to the Great White Hunters of the past. In all press notices about their journey, he and Michael mentioned that they had brought no guns with them. There was no danger to be had; wild animals did not stand a chance against such modern weapons. Crowded onto ever-dwindling nature reserves and pressed on all sides by farms and timber plantations, wild animals were easy targets—unless someone was a "fool or drunk." When a Viennese relative showed Bernhard a picture of a female hippo he had killed in Africa, Grzimek asked why he did not simply shoot a few cows grazing in an Austrian pasture, since it was so easy to approach the giant beast on the banks of a stream in Africa.[114] Better that such bloodthirsty, "impotent" men seek employment in slaughterhouses, he observed.[115] "Nor let it be thought for a moment that one has to go sweating around in the bush in search of one's victims," Grzimek noted.

> All one has to do is go into Nairobi and hire oneself a 'safari' from one of the agencies. Everything is then laid on—a hot bath every evening in the city of tents in the middle of the bush, ice-cold drinks, and excellent cuisine—and the wild animals brought to just the right stance from the gun to ensure that they can be shot dead without any danger.[116]

Widely available emergency kits including penicillin also meant that the main threat to prewar hunters—infections in the bush from being grazed by a bullet or a fall while trekking—were a thing of the past.

Given what many hunters considered their proud legacy of conservation and animal protection in both metropole and colony, most were outraged by the antihunting scenes and emasculating commentary in *No Room*. In the wake of the film's release, articles condemning hunting as a violent and outdated "Sunday hobby" for "parvenus" appeared in major newspapers and magazines such as *Deutsche Zeitung* and *Revue*.[117] Those returning to Germany hoping to publish their stories about heroism and adventure found themselves ridiculed, creating a growing consensus that this "sport" was on the wane.[118] In 1959, when a German actress condemned Bundestag president Eugen Gerstenmaier's hunting trips to East Africa as an "international scandal" in the pages of the *Stuttgarter Zeitung*, the hunting lobby saw Grzimek's handiwork and went on the defensive.[119] Hunting enthusiast and "radiator manufacturer" Manfred Behr convinced Hans Otto Meissner, a former National Socialist diplomat and author of several books on big game hunting in East Africa, to co-author *Have No Fear about Wild Animals* (*Keine Angst um Wilde Tiere*, 1959) to save the honor of trophy hunters. The highly respected University of Munich zoologist Theodor Haltenorth wrote the forward to *Have No Fear*, supporting the pair's "counter-propaganda" against the steady stream of "falsehoods and nonsense" about the natural world.[120] In Behr and Meissner's eyes, the Grzimeks' limited experience in Africa had led Bernhardand Michael to neglect the measures that hunters had already taken to save African wildlife through regulations, reserves, and the employment of wardens. The release of *Have No Fear* unleashed a new round of controversy about the German colonial provenance of protected areas and the real status of wildlife on the brink of decolonization.

It should be noted that Grzimek was hardly sentimental about animals and never opposed to all hunting. He praised "penitent butchers" such as the Serengeti warden Myles Turner—the same type of gentleman that Behr and Meissner lauded—as some of the greatest advocates of conservation in Europe and Africa, with valuable on-the-ground knowledge of animal behavior and movements.[121] In the early 1960s, he even partnered with his former critic Gerstenmaier in proposing long-term hunting leases for parts of Tanganyika under the assumption that wealthy foreigners could serve as stewards of the natural heritage—a plan that crumbled when the revolution in Zanzibar and the leftist turn in the Republic of Tanzania in 1964 led to soured relations with West Germany.[122] Only those with a long-term stake in the land could earn such a privilege, Grzimek argued: the animals should not be prostituted for the amusement of "parvenus and rich snobs."[123]

Yet Behr and Meissner pierced the heart of the Grzimeks' claims to scientific accuracy and representational authenticity by underscoring their limited experience in Africa. For one thing, Behr and Meissner argued, there was still plenty of wilderness left off the beaten track. The high urbanization rates in the Congo had actually depopulated vast stretches of the territory, leaving thousands of acres filled with elephants, bongo, and zebras.[124] Countering the Grzimeks' portrayal of emasculate, feckless hunters, Behr and Meissner homed in on a photograph of Michael from *No Room* being carried across a stream by African porters to imply that such "prissy newcomers" who stayed on the well-worn paths of roads, rail, and airlines were not hardy enough to track down lions in the bush. Only old-style safaris—trekking on foot with African game scouts in tow—revealed tropical nature in its raw state, still replete with the danger of charging elephants or "negro tribes" practicing cannibalism and holding slaves.[125] Deep in the jungles near Lambarene, Behr and Meissner noted, Albert Schweitzer had noticed this rebound in wildlife numbers: "Elephants have become a plague in our region," wrote Schweitzer, "the growing destruction of planted fields is becoming a catastrophe."[126] The other problem was the Grzimeks' dubious staging of animals in distress. Behr and Meissner accused the Grzimeks of forging the notorious scene of the young elephant's demise in *No Room* to win sympathy for conservationism, noting that the wound on its leg did not seem to come from a bullet.[127] Turning the tables on the Grzimeks' fulminations against "commercialized mockery," Behr and Meissner accused them of exaggerating the threat to animal populations and forging scenes of animal cruelty to sell more books and movie tickets.

Behr and Meissner also countered the Grzimeks' depictions of hunters' wanton slaughter and the endangerment of animals, noting, quite correctly, that national parks had their origins in imperial conferences organized by hunter-naturalists. The days of the ruthless commercial slaughter of elephants for their tusks and other species for their meat, skins, and hides were long past, they argued. The animal murderers of the early 1900s had become repentant butchers—"old sinners" who had led the assault on African animals in the early years of colonization but had mended their ways to become conservationists' staunchest allies.[128] Behr and Meissner reminded readers that it was mostly hunters who gathered at London in 1933 at the world's first "Congress for Animals": the Convention for the Protection of African Fauna and Flora, which established the Grzimeks' cherished national park as the gold standard of nature protection.[129]

At London, the remaining colonial powers in Africa, along with international observers from the US and the Netherlands, updated and expanded Germany's beneficent legacy of wildlife conservation. The Belgian crown prince Leopold III—grandson of the notorious Leopold II—spoke at the gathering, noting that "wild game do not belong to us . . . . They are an inheritance of Nature, entrusted to us to preserve for those who come after us."[130] The conference participants banned commercial hunting altogether, agreeing to put some species—such as the Okapi itself—completely off limits. The 1933 convention laid the groundwork for modern protected areas throughout Africa, ranging from controlled zones that allowed licensed hunting of some classes of animals to strict reserves open only to scientific researchers.[131] The delegates declared that national parks and scientific reserves should have permanent boundaries that encompassed the entire range of endangered animals—including migrating ones such as wildebeest.[132] The convention made the ecological habitat, not the whims of territorial administrators, the benchmark for wildlife conservation efforts.[133]

Meissner had written to a safari company in Nairobi in 1958 about the pair's upcoming "anti-Grzimek" book, which he promised would "ruin" the zookeeper's reputation and save the hunting industry from further harm.[134] Meissner noted that a number of "rich" and prominent persons had helped to finance the book, out of fear that their favorite pastime was under assault. Unbeknownst to Meissner, the company promptly forwarded the letter to Grzimek—almost a year before the book appeared—so the zookeeper had plenty of time to prepare his response. Bernhard warned the press about a potential lawsuit for libel; he even presented details of Meissner's letter to the illustrated *Revue* and mobilized scientists and journalists to back up his own observations about the impending threat to African wildlife.[135] Once the book appeared, most scientists agreed with the Grzimeks. As one commentator in the Congo noted, this "exceedingly odd book" strained credulity by painting European hunters—who had managed to wipe out wild animals from entire districts in the space of five decades—as the key to their future survival.[136] Others, including the well-known Freiburg biologist Otto Koehler, condemned his colleague Haltenorth for taking kickbacks from a "big game hunting, millionaire first author," including an all-expense paid trip through Tanganyika.[137] Nonetheless, after the publication of *Have No Fear*, German media outlets stoked the controversy. *Der Spiegel* printed a twelve-page article casting doubt on the Grzimeks' doomsday tone and noting that Gerstenmaier was quite happy to see the zookeeper taken down a notch.[138] Such articles, editorials, and reviews were part of an expanding discussion about wildlife and habitat that stretched German ecological awareness even as it unveiled the frictions between global nature's competing spokespersons.

Never one to shy away from the public spotlight, Grzimek answered the recriminations against his work with strategic rhetoric and plenty of vitriol against his enemies. Not only did he draw attention to shameful attacks on Michael, but he also referenced Meissner's checkered Nazi past and his ties to the former "master of the Hunt," Hermann Göring, to discredit a book glorifying the good old days of colonial domination and gun-wielding violence.[139] Meissner was in fact well-known in West Germany for his expedition books, and even though Grzimek's press releases did not describe their contents in detail, the writings were filled with viciously racist depictions of Africans, justifications for white rule, and even scenes describing a "cleansing action" against a "degenerate" gorilla that had killed local villagers in French Equatorial Africa.[140] Such language went too far for postwar audiences for whom such masculinist bravado and Darwinist rhetoric struck a nerve after contemporary revelations of Nazi atrocities. In 1959, an anti-Semitic wave had resulted in the desecration of the Cologne synagogue, while just a year later, the trials against former execution squad commanders on the Eastern Front made public the racist-inspired atrocities by ordinary men, opening up uncomfortable questions of culpability beyond the Nazi elite.[141] Unnerved, West German viewers were not inclined to follow an author who called for "cleansing actions," though the racial fears that animated so many disquieting sequences in *No Room for Wild Animals* slipped viewers' and reviewers' attention.

Grzimek, for his part, eventually admitted that the juvenile elephant was not the victim of unscrupulous hunters. Instead, the film crew had come upon the elephant in question accidentally and she had likely been injured by poachers' traps—but those details hardly mattered for most filmgoers.[142] The heart-wrenching scene was a critical turning point in German wildlife history. Filmgoers who once saw elephants and lions as marauding beasts now viewed them as innocent, peaceful creatures threatened by human beings who had proven their violent, rapacious ways in the last war. Even the GDR recognized *No Room* as an antimilitarist film and allowed it to be screened throughout the "Soviet Zone of Occupation"—reinforcing the sense that nature conservation stood above Cold War squabbles.[143]

The Swirling, Ever-Rising Tide of Humanity

Despite the acrimony on both sides of the 1950s wildlife debates, the parties involved missed the opportunity for a deeper reckoning with the imperialist mentalities that had shaped national park expansion and sidelined African livelihoods. References to Meissner's Nazi sympathies, for example, evoked uncomfortable memories of the recent war but avoided any confrontation with Germany's own ecological imperialism, which was premised on the violent exclusion of Africans from game reserves and contact with wild animals. Couched in terms of a white man's burden to guide immature Africans in the ways of enlightened environmental stewardship, the 1900 and 1933 conventions prohibited African hunting practices that were deemed "cruel" or "unsportsmanlike," including the use of poison weapons, snares, gins, pits, nets, and fire. European trophy hunters viewed these methods as an affront to aristocratic codes of sportsmanship that called on hunters to ensure the well-being of their game.[144] In their view, African hunting practices were too "primitive" to warrant attention or accommodation, indicative of peoples at an earlier stage of human evolution. Even though European overhunting had wiped out elephants and other large mammals in several districts, Africans bore the brunt of game ordinances that German officials and their British successors used to control "native" access to wild animals under the pretext that locals were a growing threat to animals.[145] Not surprisingly, imperial diplomats, hunters, and naturalists were the only ones invited to wildlife conferences, establishing "conservation without representation" as a guiding principle in international environmental conservation.[146]

Europeans justified such measures as part of their moral duty to guide the wise use of African natural resources but such soaring rhetoric masked the unsettling reality of European hunting conventions: to convert wildlife from a "locally used and customarily managed" resource into one that Europeans possessed as an exclusive right.[147] By criminalizing African hunting, Europeans hoped to solve the ongoing "problem" of scarce labor for export agriculture by coaxing African laborers away from free-range hunting and toward wage-earning jobs on European plantations. Cut off from "supplemental" harvesting of animals, plants, and other resources, Africans would be lured into the cash economy— the bounty of too much "nature," in this view, kept them from "advancing" to a higher level of social development. Curtailing access to wild meat and other bush products and moving people off the land to make way for nature reserves fit well with the late colonial need for taxable labor and the integration of African producers and consumers into the cash economy.[148]

Such assumptions about Europeans' civilizing mission and African development continued unabated into late 1950s even as decolonization loomed. Between the film release of *No Room for Wild Animals* in 1956 and the appearance of *Have No Fear* in 1959, two sub-Saharan nations, Ghana and the Republic of Guinea, had achieved independence, while candidates from Julius Nyerere's Tanganyikan African National Union (TANU) had gained a significant number of seats in Tanganyika's Legislative Council despite significant opposition from European and Asian constituencies.[149] In 1960, just as the debate about *No Room* was winding down, the Congo itself achieved independence, stoking fears about what would happen to the Belgian legacy and its "world laboratory" once Africans were in charge.[150] The decolonization process was thus proceeding far more rapidly and unpredictably than conservationists had expected.

Grzimek feared that "weekend safari hunters" would leave the wrong impression about European intentions in these newly decolonized spaces. At issue for him was not the number of animals that hunters killed, but rather the *psychological* impact of conspicuous slaughter on Africans who already viewed game reserves as hated symbols of Western imperialism.[151] "Black people have hunted since time immemorial," Grzimek insisted, "and cannot understand why it should suddenly be forbidden in parts of their own country."[152] Africans who would soon be asked to set aside more land for animals in national parks needed enlightened examples of how to curtail their desires in the interests of "higher" values. But how could the "natives" be expected to understand why they would be punished for hunting, he exclaimed, when they "see the cars of the wealthy Europeans, filled with trophies, pass through their villages?"[153] The continuation of the hunt would make all European conservationists into ecological hypocrites.

Though less overtly racist than Meissner, Grzimek's worries about "setting the right example" were no less paternalist. Grzimek feared what would happen to the animals when Africans' own motive for hunting inevitably shifted from subsistence needs to status attainment, as it had in Europe and North America.[154] In the Grzimeks' view, European racism had blinded Western observers to Africans' capacity to imitate more advanced societies and cause destruction commensurate with the early phases of European industrialization.[155] Grzimek worried about poaching, of course, and the Grzimeks' films contained disturbing scenes of zebras entrapped in horrible snares or elephant feet for sale as wastepaper baskets. But Grzimek did not see poachers as a long-term threat to animals; after all, he insisted, poaching could ultimately be limited through proper enforcement. What was necessary was a campaign of public enlightenment in which Africans would learn to appreciate the motives behind conservation and to value their natural heritage on the same terms as the rest of the "civilized" world. He feared the sudden collapse of European control, which was likened to the era of the 1848 revolutions in Central Europe, a time when peasants took up arms and wreaked revenge on their aristocratic oppressors by slaughtering animals in game parks.[156] Once this revolutionary phase was over, Grzimek predicted that "black chieftains who have acquired wealth" would "dress in European clothes, drive large American cars, build pretty villas—and will go elephant shooting, just as they have seen the rich Europeans do."[157] Conspicuous slaughter, in this grim analysis, would complete Africans' transition to consumer modernity—a vision of development that straitjacketed past and future interactions with wildlife to ensure that European zoological and conservation paradigms would predominate after 1960. The Congolese became an unwitting foil of the European self, without an environmental history—or future—of their own.

Despite the gap between Behr and Meissner's benign vision of colonialism and the Grzimeks' scientific conservation, neither side owned up to Germany's own ecological imperialism, leaving the idea of "conservation without representation" unquestioned. All assumed that the "natives" were not capable of thinking much about the future, driven as they were by meat hunger and other short-term needs. As such, both pairs of observers thought that Africans still needed Europeans' guidance to cherish and manage their wildlife. In addition, both Behr and Meissner and the Grzimeks believed that overpopulation was the greatest long-term threat to the continent's animal heritage. They argued that colonial medical officials' well-meaning efforts had backfired, disrupting the "natural" checks on human demography that kept Africa's human and animal populations in dynamic harmony. Malthusianism sidestepped a deeper reckoning with the colonial past, as it took the debate about conservation to a "global" scale beyond the German–African contact zone altogether.

Despite the centrality of the "overpopulation" theme in both *No Room* and *Have No Fear*, Malthusian themes generated surprisingly little comment in the public arena, partly because fears of a population bomb did not resonate as yet with existing tropes of German cultural criticism or audience expectation.[158] The locus of anxiety in interwar Germany had been the mismatch between its burgeoning population and truncated borders after Versailles, which the Third Reich would use as a justification for Germanic expansion into the East.[159] The Grzimeks and the Behr/Meissner team envisioned instead a *Raum ohne Volk*—a place where animals could find refuge from burgeoning human populations who were using up more than their share of the earth's resources.[160] As Grzimek put it: "The swirling, ever-rising tide of humanity is today drowning the wild animals just as surely as did the Flood in the Bible . . . . Creation is in dire need of a second Noah."[161]

Even as Behr and Meissner continued their attacks on Grzimek, the energies of global conservation concern were shifting away from hunter-naturalists and imperial wildlife conventions and toward a burgeoning network of scientific conservationists worried more about habitat protection than hunting quotas. In calling Africa's remaining wildlife a "cultural possession belonging to the *whole* human race," the Grzimeks drew inspiration from a transnational green network of North Americans and Europeans that was just beginning to coalesce in the "curiously utopian moment" after World War II.[162] Their appeal to the natural heritage of all mankind echoed the words of fellow Malthusian and future collaborator Julian Huxley, who in 1947 became the head of UNESCO. Huxley helped to found the International Union for the Protection of Nature (IUPN) at Fontainebleau just a year later, an organization of concerned scientists that hoped to save wildlife and ecologically significant landscapes as cultural amenities and sites of scientific research.[163] In 1949 Huxley helped to organize the United Nations Scientific Conference on the Conservation and Utilization of Resources at Lake Success, which brought together over five hundred delegates from forty-nine countries—including Victor van Straelen and Fairfield Osborn—to discuss wildlife conservation alongside topics ranging from pesticide use to habitat protection.[164] Unlike 1930 and 1933, which focused almost exclusively on hunting regulations, Lake Success considered a range of ecological stresses on the global habitat, all of which required new regulations and land management strategies to overcome.[165] By 1956 the IUPN had changed its name to the IUCN—the International Union for the Conservation of Nature and Natural Resources—a reflection of international bodies' growing recognition that a "wise-use" perspective toward wildlife protection was needed to enhance economic development in the postcolonial age.[166] The Grzimeks yoked their mission to this green network of international conservationists, which eventually pushed them to support the IUCN's vision of protected areas as catalysts for tourism, regional development, and ecological planning in the post-independence era.[167]

By the time that filming for *No Room* began in 1955, therefore, the Grzimeks had reshaped an earlier zookeeper ecology focused on enhancing animal welfare in zoos to one that embraced scientific conservation as the key to wildlife's future. Through a series of films, illustrated weeklies, and television, they forged a contact zone in which models of conservation moved fluidly between Germany and Central Africa across vast distances. Imagining urban-style zoological gardens in Léopoldville, Nairobi, or Lagos would be a catastrophe, they argued; only the protection of natural habitats in vast national parks could save the earth's biodiversity. At the same time, African protected areas offered templates for rewilding the German homeland, allowing proposals for a *Tierfreiheit* and a national park to gain traction. West Germans responded favorably to these visions of paradise because they offered a projection screen for their own anxieties about modernization, particularly as America's consumer empire threatened to engulf both Europeans and Africans in a shared environmental tragedy. In the Grzimeks' hands, Africa's animals became a cultural possession of all humanity, an appealing alternative to the usual vitriol of German partisan politics and Cold War brinkmanship. Bernhard even triumphed over the hunters who stood in the way of this peaceful globalist vision, sidestepping this group's critical role in the

establishment of protected areas—and their role in the colonial state's exclusion
of Africans from wild nature. In Grzimek's view, these once brave men had succumbed to the temptations of the Americanized package tour—leaving intrepid
scientists to face Africa's postcolonial future.

The Grzimeks' triumph over the hunting lobby was part of an international
shift from imperialist hunter-naturalists to UN-inspired scientists and nongovernmental groups as arbiters of wildlife policy. Yet the vision of parks as global
heritage repeated the imperial error of insisting on "conservation without representation" just as the Congolese were embarking on their own search for
political and environmental sovereignty. This desire to assist Africans in wildlife protection shifted the cultural meaning and environmental significance of
national parks but never addressed the environmental inequalities left by imperial conservation. From a local perspective, it mattered little if the bounding of
nature reserves served trophy hunters or camera hunters, as both responded to
European, and not African, needs for revenue or remorse. "Thinking globally"
from the situated space of West Germany and European zoological knowledge
left the intractable problem of environmental sovereignty unaddressed: how
could those who spoke on behalf of global nature ever succeed without accom-
modating Africans' own desires for these spaces after independence?

4

Serengeti Shall Not Die

> Neither today, nor tomorrow, but in three or four generations' time
> when Bolshevism and Capitalism have long been forgotten and Eastern
> or Western blocs no longer matter, many people may be glad that dur-
> ing our era someone gave a thought to the wild animals in Africa. . . .
> In a hundred years time Khrushchev and Eisenhower, political anxiet-
> ies and hatreds will only have a printed existence in history books, but
> men will still consider it important that wildebeest should roam across
> the plains and leopards growl at night.
>   —Bernhard and Michael Grzimek, *Serengeti Shall Not Die*

Along the well-traveled road from the Ngorongoro Conservation Area Visitor
Center to Serengeti National Park in northern Tanzania, just past a popular
overlook for taking in the blue-green hues of the caldera teeming with animals
below, stands the pyramidal stone memorial that marks the Grzimeks' gravesite.
Michael and Bernhard had come to the Serengeti region in 1957 to conduct the
first aerial surveys of East Africa's last great migrations of wildlife, at a time when
they had just finished their Congo journeys and committed themselves to saving
Africa's national parks. Michael died over the nearby Malambo Mountains on
January 10, 1959, when his zebra-striped Dornier DO 27 collided with a griffon
vulture and crashed into the side of the crater, killing the twenty-four year-old
instantly.[1] The epitaph is a testament to the young man's sacrifice for the wildlife
protection cause: "He gave all he possessed, even his life, to save the wildlife of
Africa."[2]

The melancholia evoked by the Grzimek gravesite can easily lead visitors
to overlook the explosive political controversies that brought the Grzimeks to
British-controlled Tanganyika and led to Michael's death. In 1956 the British
colonial government had decided to separate the Ngorongoro Crater, the surrounding Ngorongoro Highlands, and the Eastern Serengeti Plains from the
existing frontiers of Serengeti National Park to create a mixed-use form of
nature conservation. This would be a particular form in which Maasai cattle
and wild animals would share the same territory (see Figure I.1). The colonial

Our Gigantic Zoo. Thomas M. Lekan, Oxford University Press (2020). © Oxford University Press.
DOI: 10.1093/oso/9780199843671.001.0001

Figure 4.1 The Grzimeks' gravesite at Ngorongoro. The epitaph speaks to Michael's martyrdom for the wildlife protection cause, but the marker's position also suggests that the father and son still watch over a landscape that has remained a flashpoint of controversy over African customary land rights in the region. Photograph by the author.

government's decision to divide the park came after years of wrangling over whether the Maasai were a part of "nature" and could continue their traditional pastoralism within the park boundaries or whether their growing heads of live-stock overstretched the Serengeti's carrying capacity and interfered with its tourist amenities.[3] The division fueled protests from conservationists in London as well as their American and European allies in the International Union for the Conservation of Nature and Natural Resources (IUCN) and other big NGOs.[4] The conservationists lamented that Maasai cattle and goats took up precious space, trampling fragile grasslands, crowding out wild animals' access to watering holes, and hastening the march of deserts.[5] "You cannot keep men, even black and brown ones, from multiplying and cannot force them to remain 'primitive'," the Grzimeks fumed. "A national park must remain a piece of primordial wilderness to be effective. No men, not even native ones, should live inside its borders."[6]

With great passion and moral conviction, the Grzimeks hurled themselves into a controversy over the Serengeti's boundaries that had been brewing since the British had established the national park in 1951.[7] At first the pair planned to give the Tanganyikan Game Department money from their earnings from *No Room for Wild Animals* to purchase compensatory land outright. In light of the impending decisions on the park boundaries and the uncertainties of previous ecological studies of the region, however, Peter Molloy, the Serengeti National Park's director, recommended instead that they count the animal herds and research their migrations so the park could fulfill its mandate to protect the itinerant animals throughout their life cycles.[8] Using their own funds, the Grzimeks launched a series of aerial surveys and vegetation analyses of the Serengeti Plains from 1957 to 1959 that promised the first baseline survey of this "primordial wilderness."

As the contact zone between Germany and Africa shifted from the rainforests of the Congo to the savannas of Tanganyika, however, the Grzimeks encountered a cultural landscape replete with traces of German colonial histories— "ghosts of land use past" that belied the portrayal of the region as a primordial wilderness.[9] The Grzimeks arrived in the Serengeti just five decades after the German colonial government had established East Africa's first game reserves and contemplated the creation of "nature protection parks," both designed to protect the animals and keep Africans out. Such reserves evoked revanchist memories of "good German colonizers" who had understood this land and its people on an intuitive level, leaving behind a bountiful agricultural and forested landscape.[10] Africans who had witnessed the German colonial period knew better, and their elders' memories were still raw: the lingering impact of devastating rinderpest epidemics that destroyed pastoral communities, evictions for white-owned plantations, exclusion from hunting grounds, and the destruction of farms, towns, and roads in the latter days of the Great War.[11] To become a wilderness park, the Grzimeks needed to free this storied landscape from uncomfortable reminders of wartime traumas, colonialist violence, and African pastoral and agricultural use.[12] Small wonder the pair tried to soar above the conflicts on the ground with breathtaking images taken from a new technological wonder featured prominently in their film: the Dornier DO 27, which they affectionately called "D-Ente" or the "Flying Zebra."

This chapter analyzes the frictions that emerged between lofty ambitions designed to overshadow "ephemeral" politics and the gravitational pull of terrene

Figure 4.2 The Flying Zebra over the plains of the Serengeti. The Dornier DO 27, used by the authors for the game census, was capable of extremely slow airspeeds and landing on rough ground. The usual flying altitude was higher than shown here. The lines on the ground are trails made by the animals. Wildebeests and a single zebra can be seen in the foreground. The Grzimeks argued that the plane hardly bothered animal herds or bird flocks—a technological companion rather than an alien presence in the landscape. Okapia Ltd.

perspectives enmeshed in troublesome histories and intractable land-use controversies. The Flying Zebra promised viewers an overarching perspective of the plains unavailable to Africans who toiled on the ground or demanded the right to graze or farm on lands promised to them by British colonial officers. Unlike *No Room for Wild Animals*, the Serengeti quest was not an attempt to rescue individual animals but rather to save an entire ecosystem whose borders merely existed "on paper." Through their trial-and-error efforts to count, track, and analyze the foraging habits of migrating animals—often at great risk of injury—the Grzimeks hoped to follow the 1933 London Convention mandates by demarcating the entire habitat of the dwindling populations of wandering wildebeest and zebra. Unlike previous naturalist surveys, the Grzimeks depended on the arsenal of scientific wildlife management—aircraft, tranquilizer guns, vegetation and soil samples, and cameras—to establish a firm scientific baseline for future conservation efforts. They referred to the Serengeti and Ngorongoro as "our gigantic zoo," one created by God to hold the animals in self-regulating cycles of rain, desiccation, predation, and rebirth so long as humans, including pastoralists and poachers, remained safely out of the picture. Yet politics drove the film's urgency and moral appeal, as the Grzimeks insisted that only the precise ecological demarcation of natural borders could withstand the impending shift from colonial to independent African rule.[13] The Grzimeks' airplane was not merely a prosthetic extension of everyday sight, in this sense, but the very platform by which the Serengeti could become a wilderness capable of being measured, salvaged, and even loved.

The chapter then examines film technologies, behind-the-scenes photographs, and field notes to show how the Grzimeks utilized aerial filmography to respond to the unprecedented aesthetic challenge of making audiences care about entire animal populations and their habitats.[14] The Grzimeks made full use of their specially equipped aircraft to achieve a "bird's eye" perspective of the savannas, one that resulted in breathtaking images of stampeding animal herds and de-territorialized space.[15] Back on the ground, the Grzimeks used their camera and text to "rewild" historical terrain, rendering the remaining vestiges of African, German-colonial, and British-colonial landscapes ephemeral and insignificant by showing them succumbing to more powerful natural forces of weather, sand, wind, vegetation, and time. In the final sequences of their film, the Grzimeks used their celestial panorama to claim the "last remaining herds of African game" as a "cultural heritage of all mankind" on par with the Acropolis, St. Peter's, or the Louvre. "No man—black or white—should ever be allowed to endanger" this serene wilderness: a formulation designed to temper African assertions of self-determination and environmental sovereignty.[16] *Serengeti Shall Not Die* succeeds only to the extent that the viewer succumbs to this fantasy of experiencing the Serengeti from the cockpit.

Becoming Wilderness

At the center of *Serengeti Shall Not Die* is the Grzimeks' heroic quest to document the number and mobility patterns of the earth's last migrating herds of zebras, wildebeest, and gazelle. According to W. H. Pearsall, an ecologist commissioned by the park's board of trustees in 1957 to survey these lands, the animals moved in tandem with the bimodal rainy seasons in East Africa, descending at the beginning of November from both the "corridor" east of Lake Victoria and the highlands of the Ngorongoro Crater to feed on newly sprouting grasses. During the brief dry period in December and the longer rainy season that stretched from January to May, he proposed, over one million animals met in the center of the plains to feed on the grasses, mate, and calve their young. Pearsall argued that the animals then retraced their route back to their former habitats once the rains were over and the grasses of the central Serengeti Plains shriveled and browned.[17] The assumptions about this rather orderly east–west trek led British park administrators to believe that the proposed new boundaries for the park—which sheared off the Ngorongoro Crater and Highlands as Maasai territory and created a new northern extension of the park—could protect the majority of itinerant mammals.[18] Pearsall had based his recommendations mostly on preexisting estimates, observations from the car, and short reconnaissance flights. But he had not visited large sections of the park due to the impassibility during the rainy season and was not able to reach the northern districts of the territory due to the anticolonial Mau Mau Emergency just across the border in Kenya.[19] The Grzimeks hoped to build on Pearsall's study by covering a much larger expanse of territory and identifying the underlying ecological mechanisms that guided the herds' movements. Both surveys created a baseline that excluded ecological history and human ecology—a critical step to the Serengeti "becoming wilderness" in the 1950s.

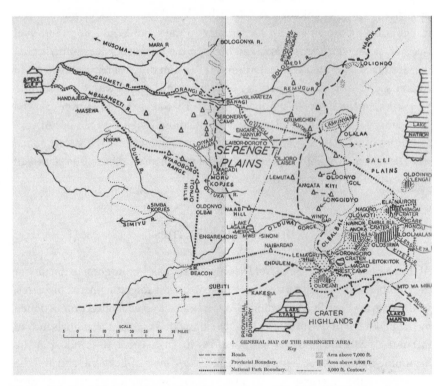

Figure 4.3 Pearsall's general map of the Serengeti area, 1956. The British plan of 1956 envisioned turning over the area around the Moru Kopjes (center) to ranchland development and making the Ngorongoro Crater into a strict nature reserve. Note also the location of the Salei Plains, named after the Maasai clan that British ethnographers considered the original "Hamites" to come to this region in the eighteenth century. Courtesy of Fauna and Flora International.

The Grzimeks had first planned to give the proceeds from *No Room* directly to Tanganyikan colonial authorities to purchase conservation land at the foot of Mount Meru—in the Momella hunting estate of the recently deceased Margarete Trappe, dubbed by many as "the greatest German huntress."[20] The pair had little previous contact with this territory, having only glimpsed Mount Kilimanjaro and a few other sites during the filming of *No Room for Wild Animals* in 1955.[21] Writing of their decision to survey the park, the Grzimeks noted:

> The plains of the Serengeti are said to harbour more than a million large animals, and these are constantly roaming in large herds . . . . There are many hypotheses about this migration, and the proposed new borders of the park are based on some of these theories. Up to now nobody has found out how to follow the wandering animals . . . . The government has no funds to spare for such research—but what government on earth ever had money to spare for lions, giraffes, zebras and wildebeest?[22]

By the late 1950s, it was quite common for cash-strapped British colonial governments to commission "strangers" to fill gaps in ecological knowledge and to put park management on a sound scientific basis. There was no dedicated national park research staff in any part of British East Africa and game department officials complained to the Colonial Office that their staff was too overtaxed to undertake systematic surveys.[23] Most wildlife biologists and ecologists came to East Africa from North America, often with the assistance of the National Science Foundation, the Fulbright Foundation, and the American Wildlife Management Institute. Critical to the Grzimeks' study was the American rangeland ecologist George Petrides, who worked for the Kenyan government in the mid-1950s and argued that the long-term aim of national park management should be protection of *habitat*, not just stopping poachers.[24] Bernhard and Michael's zookeeper's ecology made them especially qualified to tackle the question of how to study and protect animals' biotopes. The Congo journeys had given them a good understanding of the relationship between biogeography, animal physiology, and animal behavior, which the zoo staff needed to mimic animal habitats back in Frankfurt. "Natural zoos," they maintained, still needed everything for animals to thrive over the long haul: sufficient forage or prey, an adequate choice of mates, and an ability to create a dwelling place in the wild.

National parks also had to be self-regulating: large enough to encompass diverse populations of various species without overshooting the "carrying capacity" of such ecosystems, particularly during times of drought. According to this scheme, there were a host of factors that delimited the number of grazing animals on a given tract of rangeland, including climate, soil, and the type and abundance of natural vegetation.[25] When the animal population remained at or below the ideal numerical capacity, the inhabitants had room to grow, and the system could eventually reach a point of oscillating equilibrium between predators and prey, grazers and grasses, soil and vegetation. Once the animal numbers exceeded that capacity, however, overconsumption of the grasses would tip the system out of balance, leading to accelerating ecological decline and widespread animal starvation.[26] In the arid and semiarid savannas of East and Central Africa, the main worry of most scientific "strangers" was that livestock grazing on the grasslands of the Serengeti plains outcompeted wildebeest and antelopes for forage and water—leading to overgrazing, thinning grasses, soil compaction—and finally permanent desertification. To halt the degradation of habitat, Petrides recommended that the British initiate a "peaceful process" of using the US technique of declaring eminent domain over territories to push African cultivators and pastoralists—most especially the Maasai—off the most ecologically productive savannas.[27] National park proposals from outside experts, in other words, justified land alienation and resettlement as necessary for ecologically sound management.[28]

As the Grzimeks prepared for their journey, however, it became quickly apparent that they could not easily transfer their knowledge of tropical environments from the Congo's rainforests to the East African savannas. *No Room for Wild Animals* had focused on the fate of the Okapi and other creatures of the seemingly timeless jungle, whereas the Serengeti mission required a holistic investigation of animal movements, shifting mosaics of semiarid grasslands and open forests, and complex weather systems that never seemed to settle into predictable patterns. Situated on a vast plateau in the African interior, the forty-five-hundred-acre Serengeti National Park that the Grzimeks encountered was a triangular-shaped reserve, roughly the size of Connecticut, which stretched in a southeasterly direction for about 120 miles from the Speke Gulf (named for John Speke, the first European to identify the source of the Nile) on the southern end of Lake Victoria to the highlands of the great craters that run up the eastern spine of the Great Rift Valley known as the Gregory Rift.[29] Pearsall divided the park into three zones of investigation: the aforementioned western "corridor," a narrow alluvial region situated between the Grumeti and Mbalangeti rivers, which flowed only in the rainy seasons; the central Serengeti Plains, a terrain of gently undulating grasses with shallow top soils that served as a critical habitat for the wildebeest migration; and the Crater Highlands and the Rift Valley in the east (see Figure 4.3).[30]

Bordering the corridor, along the park's northeastern border near the eastern park warden's headquarters at Banagi, lay rolling acacia woodlands that Chief Game Warden Myles Turner described as the "sleeping sickness belt at Ikoma": tsetse-infested bushlands inhabited by African communities known for their skill as hunters.[31] The most geologically noticeable feature of the central plains was a number of granitic tors, also known as "inselbergs" or "kopjes," which were the residual mountains of metamorphic rocks.[32] The most famous of these inselberg landscapes were found south of Seronera in a region known as the Moru Kopjes, which was already noted in the 1920s for its abundant wildlife, especially lions, which liked to lie on the outcroppings in the hot midday sun. Beyond the kopjes, the Serengeti matched its Maasai description as *Siringet*, an "extended place;" when the German geographer Fritz Jaeger encountered the inhospitable, waterless terrain in 1906 he wrote in his journal: "Grass, grass, grass, grass, and grass. One looks around and sees only grass and sky."[33]

The eastern part of the Serengeti National Park—the site of so much controversy over indigenous land rights—contained the highlands of the great volcanic craters and the wall of the Gregory Rift. With an average height of eight thousand feet, the highlands contained moist montane forests that provided water sources for the whole region yet created a rain shadow that kept the inland plains so arid.[34] The Ngorongoro Crater itself was about ten thousand feet above sea level along the rim and fifty-seven hundred feet on the crater floor, giving it a perennially mild and malaria-free climate. To the north of the Ngorongoro caldera was Lake Natron, where the Grzimeks filmed flamingos and other colorful bird species during their surveys. West of the Ngorongoro highlands lay another key area of interest: the Olduvai Gorge, a deep canyon that snaked its way across the Olbalbal depression in the Eastern Serengeti Plains.[35] It was here that the German butterfly collector, Wilhelm Kattwinkel, spotted fossils of the three-toed horse, *Hipparion*, making the area into a treasure trove of fossils from the area's paleo-ecological past. Such natural boundaries effectively cordoned off the Serengeti Plains on all sides, leaving the impression of uninhabited badlands free from human influence. Apart from a few nomadic Maasai and wandering bands of Waikoma hunters, Turner noted, the "Serengeti had always been an uninhabited game area."[36]

In such a semiarid environment, the Grzimeks quickly discerned that rainfall and evaporation rates meant life and death, determining the availability of nutritious grasses and thus the timing and extent of wildebeest migrations, the calving of young, and the offtake from predators. The Serengeti's "short" and the "long" rains were zenithal in their occurrence, peaking shortly after the sun passed south of the equator in September and then again in March. Between those two rainy seasons was a small but not very distinct dry season. In the longer dry season that extended from around late May to November, the central Serengeti became completely dry, with a yellowish-gray appearance on which animals appeared only infrequently. During the long rainy season, the plains turned verdant and the herds returned. Such patterns were not predictable, however, as they were nested in broader extremes that could merge the rainy seasons into one long wet season (creating sheets of water across the plains) or link up the dry ones into an extended drought, as was common in the 1950s.[37]

The rain rarely fell in gentle showers but tended instead to be sudden and "torrential," sometimes producing five inches of rain in just three hours.[38] Pearsall had not found rainfall data for his scientific analysis, but in a stroke of luck, the Grzimeks discovered that the ranger's station at Banagi had kept daily rainfall records since July 1937, enabling them to make comparisons across decades. These records showed that over a twenty-three-year period, it rained in the Serengeti Plains about 30.4 inches on average—more than London's 24 inches or Berlin's 23 inches, but concentrated into cloudbursts on 82 days, rather than the 177 rainy days in London or 203 in Berlin.[39] Such patterns suggested that the main migrations would not pass the same parts of the region in the same order and at the same time each year, making the Grzimeks' tasks of mapping the "animal state" unusually complex and fraught with potential errors.

Because no reliable maps of the Serengeti existed at the time of their surveys, the Grzimeks turned to colonial-era expedition reports, memoirs, and interviews—many drawn from the German colonial period—to orient themselves in this new landscape.[40] The most important surveyor of the Serengeti was Oscar Baumann, an Austrian geographer who led the German antislavery expedition from the coast to Lake Victoria in 1891–1893 on foot using porters and armed *askaris*.[41] The entourage traversed Ngorongoro and Serengeti, noting the wildlife, vegetation, and cultures they encountered. Baumann arrived in March, normally the beginning of the wet season, but at that time bone dry; ostriches were the only large wildlife he encountered on the eastern plains. As the caravan made its way to the western bushlands near Lake Victoria, the members saw vast herds of zebra and antelope and "astoundingly many rhinos."[42] Alarmingly, however, Baumann also recorded seeing the skeletons of hundreds of wildebeest and buffalo across the plains near the lake.[43]

Nor did Baumann report seeing any elephants in the Serengeti, as the pachyderms had already been decimated by the expansion of the Zanzibari and, later, European ivory trade over the course of the mid- and late nineteenth century due to demand in Europe for piano keys, billiard balls, knife handles, and other luxury items. The market for tusks was so large that elephants had become scarce throughout East Africa by the 1890s despite German colonial efforts to introduce quotas and licenses.[44] Between 1814 and 1890, population biologists estimate that about two-thirds of the African elephant population disappeared, a massive loss of a keystone species responsible for the shape, size, and distribution of vegetation across the savannas.[45] The Maa-speaking Ndorobo, who did not cultivate or keep cattle, were among the most skilled African hunters to procure elephants for the ivory trade; European accounts place them occupying territory throughout the central Serengeti woodlands in the 1860s. It was not until the 1950s, partly as a result of decades of colonial conservation efforts and partly due to shifts in demand, that elephants made a comeback: in 1958, at the time of the Grzimek surveys, there were approximately eight hundred elephants in the Serengeti.[46]

Baumann also visited the Ngorongoro Crater during his journey, noting that he was received "in the friendliest fashion" in the Maasai *bomas* that dotted the floor of the great caldera. Indeed, pastoralists had long been part of the Serengeti environment, having appeared in Africa already some six thousand years ago and had moved southward, roughly along the Great Rift Valley, displacing hunter-gatherers in many regions until they reached East Africa around 2000 BCE. Among these migrants were Nilotic speakers such as the Maasai, who had occupied the dry grasslands and plains along the Great Rift Valley, reaching Ngorongoro and its environs in the nineteenth century.[47] The Maasai had adapted well to this semiarid landscape, with its unpredictable rainfall and frequent droughts, by working together in small, ambulatory herding units consisting of men within a certain age, who shifted the herds according to the seasonal weather patterns that determined the availability of water holes and semipermanent rivers. They spread out with their herds across the treeless eastern Serengeti plains during the wet season—avoiding wildebeest herds that might be carrying a malignant catarrhal fever deadly to their cattle—but retreated back to well-watered montane forests or spring-fed pools as the weather became hotter and drier. The bomas that Baumann saw were another ingenious adaption to this landscape. They consisted of houses and corrals (or kraals) constructed with sticks and plastered with mud and cattle dung and encircled by thorn fences to keep predators out, allowing for seasonal grazing without permanent encampments. The key to survival for pastoralists, like the animal herds, was the flexibility afforded by mobility.[48]

When Baumann arrived in Ngorongoro in 1892, however, it was clear that something was disturbingly awry. Baumann described Maasai women who had taken refuge there as "walking skeletons," accompanied by children "resembling deformed frogs and warriors who could hardly crawl on all fours."[49] Starving Maasai ate anything available, even the skins, bones, and horns of cattle. He and his porters shared what they could, but their meager rations were clearly overwhelmed by the need.[50] "You wallow in milk and meat," cried an elderly Maasai, "and shoot at us, who are dying of hunger. Curses on you!"[51] The Grzimeks commented on these terrible scenes, noting "such starvation has since occurred only during wartime, when the Germans and later the British ruled Tanganyika."[52] In their Malthusian framework, such famine was a fact of life in precolonial Africa—a means to rebalance the human population with available resources. Their account quickly moves on from the starvation scenes, describing a crater "unchanged by the passage of seventy years," and delighting in locating the acacia forest, the wild animals, and the Maasai kraals that Baumann had first witnessed.[53]

The Grzimeks' fixation on famine as a "natural" check on population growth missed the unnatural catastrophe that was unfolding in the region in the 1890s due to the ravages of a European-introduced disease that Baumann referred to as the "cattle plague": rinderpest. Indeed, Baumann knew that the crater was filled with "refugees from Serengeti where starvation had depopulated whole districts" whose cattle had died and were now reliant on their cousins in the crater for food and shelter. A highly contagious panzootic viral disease, rinderpest was likely brought from India to Ethiopia by Italian invaders as they tried to conquer these lands in 1887. It eventually killed 95 percent of the cattle and countless wildlife in Africa as it spread southward and eastward into the continent through 1897, expedited by colonialism, leaving starving families and social dislocation in its wake.[54] Rinderpest exacerbated a famine caused by drought, as well as locust infestations and bovine pleuropneumonia, which were already afflicting East Africans at the turn of the nineteenth century.[55] With their nutritional intake down and immune systems weakened, many Maasai who did not succumb to thirst or hunger eventually died of smallpox or leishmaniasis. The Austrian estimated that about two-thirds of the precontact population had perished in what local Maasai still remembered in the 1950s as the "Time of Troubles," or "wipe out" (*Emutai*): a socio-ecological disaster on par with bubonic plague in Europe in the 1350s or smallpox in the New World after 1492.[56] The vast, orchardlike appearance of the plains that Baumann described in his journals was the remnant of an African pastoral landscape experiencing unprecedented catastrophe.

Though many Europeans were aware of the devastating effects of rinderpest, they did not consider how the relative absence of people and wild bovines had shaped the baseline conditions they encountered in the 1950s. As a result of *Emutai*, pastoralists could not burn the bushlands to create grazing pastures, which allowed the regeneration of young trees and the regrowth of dense vegetation that attracted tsetse flies (*Glossina* spp) and spread trypanosomiasis, or "sleeping sickness."[57] Rinderpest epizootics occurred every ten to twenty years over the decades between 1900 and 1960, keeping cattle, wild bovines, and pastoralists at low numbers; only those ruminants unaffected by rinderpest, most especially zebra, had relatively stable numbers throughout the period. Humans and cattle could only return to the Serengeti after the British colonial government began mechanically clearing and burning the bush between 1930 and 1950.[58] Then, as a result of a cattle vaccination campaign that was just being developed and implemented by the British in the late 1950s, the rinderpest virus was slowly disappearing from the plains and populations recovered more rapidly—just as the Grzimeks were arriving in the area, fearful that overpopulation and over-hunting had brought wild animals to the brink of extinction.[59]

Lack of attention to the region's historical human ecology also led German and British colonial governments to establish protected areas atop once extensively used pastoral and hunting landscapes. The Germans had designated the Northern Highland Forest Reserve near the crater in 1914 and even debated the establishment of a "nature protection park" there before the Great War derailed these plans.[60] Despite UK officials' subsequent indictment of Germany as a politically inept "parvenu" that had relied on forced labor, brutality, and war to maintain control over its East African protectorate, British officials had long admired the German conservation model of licenses, closed seasons, and sanctuaries for protecting wildlife.[61] The two imperial powers had already cooperated in sponsoring the 1900 London Convention , which attempted to create a common framework for imperial game protection.[62] As one critic put it: "She handled Nature better than she handled man; that is the truth of it."[63] Germany had established fourteen game reserves by 1914.[64]

The British picked up where the Germans had left off shortly after taking over Tanganyika Territory. In 1921, Tanganyika promulgated a game ordinance that built on Hermann von Wissmann's 1896 German wildlife laws by requiring that European trophy hunters carry licenses and banning Africans from hunting any animal except when defending their person or property. In 1923, the Ngorongoro Crater became a "complete game reserve" that outlawed all hunting, fishing, camping, cutting of trees, or burning of grasses.[65] In 1929, the Tanganyikan government declared the Western Serengeti a "closed game reserve" that restricted hunting to license holders only and hired a game warden, Major Monty Moore, to enforce the new regulations.[66] Moore's headquarters were at Banagi Hill, which remained the headquarters for the Western Serengeti until 1959. The British expanded this closed reserve in 1930 and again in 1932 to encompass eventually the western Corridor, Ngorongoro Highlands, and the Loliondo district as far north as the Kenyan border—a vast area spreading across nearly the whole of north-central Tanganyika.[67]

Unlike the Grzimeks and their fellow zoologists, the British officials who created game reserves in Tanganyika came from a wise-use perspective: they imagined game animals as an economic asset that needed to be efficiently exploited and sustainably harvested to make the colony pay for itself, not lock up its "resources" behind fixed boundaries or leave them to Africans' "primitive" and "unproductive" uses.[68] The Serengeti Closed Reserve was established primarily to stop the wanton destruction of lions by foreign hunting expeditions in an area that many considered British Africa's "last virgin game fields."[69] Animals lovers were particularly incensed about reports in the London press about the baiting of animals behind automobiles in the Serengeti Plains, which were more easily reached as a result of a tourist road constructed by an American entrepreneur in 1920.[70] Intense lobbying from Moore led the government to establish a fully protected Serengeti Game Sanctuary for lions in the corridor area in 1935, encompassing a large nine-hundred-square-mile protected zone.[71] Sport

Table 4.1 **From Game Reserve to National Park: A History of Protected Areas
in the Serengeti Region**

1887–1897	Rinderpest introduced on the Horn of Africa kills bovines across the continent. Maasai pastoralists are among the many communities devastated
1892	Oscar Baumann explores the Serengeti region as part of antislavery commission
1896	German colonial governor Hermann von Wissmann promulgates first game ordinances to regulate the ivory trade
1900	London Convention for the Preservation of Wild Animals, Birds, and Fish
1914	German colonial administration creates a forest reserve and proposes creation of "nature protection park" at Ngorongoro
1921	Tanganyika Game Ordinance
1923	Ngorongoro Complete Game Reserve established
1929	Serengeti Closed Game Reserve created
1931	Hingston report recommends Serengeti become a national park
1933	London Convention Relative to the Preservation of Fauna and Flora in their Natural State
1940	Tanganyika Game Ordinance declares Serengeti National Park but shelved due to World War II
1948	Revised National Parks Ordinance creates Serengeti National Park
1951	Tanganyika Government gazettes Serengeti National Park

hunting ceased in this area, to be replaced by animal photography and filming—with the Serengeti emerging as a famous production site for interwar wildlife films. Despite such moves toward species protection, neither Moore nor the Game Department sought to dismantle the lucrative trophy hunting industry altogether; game reserves allowed animal populations to recover so they could be sustainably "harvested" for profit over time.

For the British, moreover, the enclosure of land for animals went hand in hand with rebooting the European "civilizing mission" in East Africa—by force if necessary. The British believed that wild animal populations had gotten out of hand due to German mismanagement and were determined to bring these wild populations back into line. Under the auspices of the League of Nations mandate and, later, UN Trusteeship that authorized their presence in Tanganyika, the British cast themselves as benevolent guardians of a Tanzanian population still suffering the effects of German exploitation and brutalization.[72] More often than not, this guardianship meant *controlling*, not protecting, wild animals. When wild animals got in the way of farm expansion or, even worse, were identified as vectors for the transmission of sleeping sickness to domestic livestock and people, the staff was quite willing to shoot them en masse.[73] Similarly, game officials were ready to use force to control Africans' "excessive" or "cruel" hunting practices, blocking them from hunting, gathering, or collecting firewood inside of game reserves.[74] Small wonder that local Africans associated wildlife and game reserves with the violent hand of the colonial state: their Swahili name for the Serengeti Closed Game Reserve was Shama la Bibi (literally, "grandmother's fields," a reference to Queen Victoria).[75]

When Bernhard and Michael set out to document the Serengeti's baseline conditions, they did not connect game reserves to colonial domination over Africans, leading them readily to dismiss calls for customary access as trivial "politics" rather than an outcry against historical injustices. Indeed, while hunting and forest reserves disrupted local human ecologies, national parks went further in promoting a fully dehumanized landscape as an ideal state. The most important group lobbying for the establishment of national parks in British East Africa was the British Society for the Protection of the Fauna of the Empire (SPFE), founded in 1903, just after the 1900 London Convention. Many of the Society's members were "penitent butchers," aristocratic and upper middle-class hunters who shared the Grzimeks' conviction that Africa's large mammals stood on the brink of extinction.[76] In 1931 the Society commissioned Major Richard Hingston to tour Tanganyika Territory and other colonies in East and Southern Africa to explore the potential for nature preserves. Hingston's original proposal for the Serengeti National Park was more than ten thousand square miles of territory stretching from Lake Victoria in the west to Lake Natron in the east—roughly the size of Belgium and containing seventy thousand Africans. Hingston argued that without immediate intervention, several species of wild animals—most notably the white rhino, the elephant, and the hippopotamus—would face extinction in less than fifty years due to overhunting and human population growth.[77] Given such dire warnings, the SPFE pressed colonial administrators in Tanganyika to transform the existing Serengeti complete game reserve into a national park with permanent boundaries.[78] The government declared its intention to create a national park in 1937 and did so in a 1940 ordinance—which sat on the shelf as it arrived just in time for the onset of World War II.[79]

Beyond a passing reference to Michael Grzimek reading a book on the Mau Mau Emergency in *Serengeti Shall Not Die*, no mention is made in the film or the book about what came next: anticolonial and independence struggles that rocked this part of Africa in the 1950s and informed the British decision to divide the park.[80] The British colonial government's 1948 charter for the national park envisioned that indigenous peoples, including 140,000 Maasai who pursued their "primitive" ways, could remain within its borders, much like the Mbuti who were likened to the "fauna" of Albert National Park. Once the colonial government gazetted the park in 1951, however, officials began to argue that only those who were born in the region before that year could remain. All others would have to move to the Loliondo region on the border with Kenya so that their livestock did not overtax the park's watering holes.[81]

When hundreds of Maasai herders refused to leave, the British contemplated a massive forced removal in 1954 but backed off from this plan under pressure from the anticolonialist Mau Mau uprisings in nearby Kenya. The British were also under fire from the United Nations Trusteeship Council, which was investigating land rights abuses stemming from the eviction of Meru people from their farmsteads in 1951 to make way for British beef and dairy farmers.[82] The Serengeti Committee of Inquiry turned to Pearsall's 1956 report to conceive of a revised strategy that banned cattle grazing, agriculture, and hunting in a truncated Serengeti National Park but dedicated the Ngorongoro Highlands to a multiple-use strategy that included both Maasai pastoralism and wild animals.[83] This compromise provoked a wave of international outcry among conservations and catalyzed the Grzimeks' decision to come to the Serengeti. "The Masai were the cause of all our hard work," Grzimek remarked ruefully. "Because of them we had to learn to fly. They were the reason why we were so far from Frankfurt and why we had been counting, marking and dyeing animals for the past weeks and months . . . . The Serengeti cannot support wild animals and domestic cattle at the same time."[84] Just how much room the animals needed to sustain themselves on the plains in large numbers remained the central puzzle of the Grzimek's mission to Africa.

They Came in a Flying Zebra

Given the uncertainty of the terrain, the conflicting numbers, and the long-standing need for a holistic, "unbiased" perspective of the Serengeti environment, the Grzimeks decided that their research demanded aerial surveys, which they conducted between December 1957 and January 1959. Using their prize winnings from No Room, they purchased a specially outfitted Dornier DO 27—the first aircraft that the Allies allowed to be produced in West Germany after a ten-year halt to the aviation sector. With a length of only about nine meters; a cantilevered, unbraced wing affixed to the fuselage; and a maximum airspeed of about 138 mph, the Dornier combined a reasonable speed for a long-distance journey with the ability to take off and land over short distances. The

Dornier's adjustable flaps also maximized airflow around the wings, enabling the Grzimeks to hover close to the ground in observing animals and coast at speeds of only 30 mph.[85]

The Grzimeks added several features to the basic design, particularly an extra gas tank for long-distance trips and wilderness conditions, special brackets for mounting their Arriflex camera under the wing, and the iconic zebra striping. Zebra-striped planes had appeared in wildlife films before, particularly in Martin and Osa Johnson's 1935 *Baboona*, and the Grzimeks were no doubt aware of this symbolism.[86] The Johnsons had playfully featured modern technologies on safari, such as record players or automobiles, to suggest a Western mastery over an otherwise precarious situation—until Martin had met his end in a similar light aircraft in 1937. The Grzimeks thought the striping would assist rescuers in detecting the plane in case of an emergency and make the aircraft less threatening to the animals they wished to study. Since the Serengeti had only two airstrips, at Banagi and Seronera, the plane was specially outfitted with a non-retracting skid undercarriage to land on rough terrain using special brakes and struts, so that Michael could sample vegetation from around the region in the hopes of finding ecological connections between the migration routes and the available forage. Otherwise, the plane revealed its spartan, military origins in the lack of passenger comforts, deafening cockpit noise, and constant leaking in rainstorms. When the plane set off from Frankfurt on a cold December morning in 1957, the Grzimeks had only a compass and a handheld map to chart their way across often brutal winter storms in Europe and rainstorms along the Mediterranean that forced them repeatedly to turn back or find new routes along the six-thousand-mile journey.[87]

As in *No Room*, Michael assumed the role of lead cameraman for the film's production. The film crew included his former classmate Hermann Gimbel, along with Richard Graf and, a bit later, Alan Root.[88] Holdiger Hagan served as the film's narrator. The film begins in the cockpit as the Grzimeks depart from Frankfurt, following the contours of the Rhine Valley as did so many on the nineteenth-century Grand Tour, noting that from this middle range "one gets to see something of the earth." Characteristically, Bernhard expresses his anti-heroic reservations about the daunting task that lies ahead, noting that he is not a "technical enthusiast" or a "sport type," and yet found himself learning to fly at forty-eight years old—and without much training for handling emergencies in a wilderness area. Using an animated trick sequence common in World War II documentary shorts, viewers follow the plane as it casts a shadow over a map of Africa, moving stepwise from Frankfurt to Cartagena, then along the Mediterranean coast from Oran to Alexandria, hugging the Nile before landing at Juba in the Sudan and then Entebbe in Uganda—and finally from Nairobi into Tanganyika.[89]

Once they land at Arusha, the trick sequence continues briefly so the Grzimeks could demonstrate their pioneering method of dividing the Serengeti into thirty-two narrow, thousand-yard flyover strips to count the herds.[90] They compared results from two independent passengers on each side of a strip in conjunction with select aerial photographs to ensure accuracy. Viewers then return to the cockpit, glancing over the shoulder of the passengers in the plane (who included Molloy along with wardens Myles Turner and Gordon Harvey) as they make hash marks for different animal groups. Because the Flying Zebra had no wing struts that reduced visibility (a trick Grzimek had learned from Leni Riefenstahl), viewers feel themselves quite literally to be part of the "discovery" of the stampeding herds below as they glance over the men's shoulders and outside the cockpit.[91] Together, they reach a sobering conclusion: the Serengeti did not contain a million animals, as previous studies had reported, but only 367,000.

Like *No Room for Wild Animals, Serengeti Shall Not Die* self-consciously evokes features of the imperial expedition report only to subvert audience expectations in the name of science and conservation. The mysteries of the steppe beckon these heroic white men to darkest Africa, but the Grzimeks had no interest in posing as colonial hunters and explorers. Among earlier German trekkers in Africa, from Carl Schillings to Margarete Trappe, it was common to stand proudly over a freshly killed animal in a photograph, declaring loudly "I was there."[92] But the airplane achieved a higher and more certain ecological truth than such terrene optics. Myles Turner, one of the "penitent butchers" who had taken up the wardenship of the Western Serengeti in 1956, recalled the day that he learned two German biologists would be arriving in the Serengeti by plane. He began clearing an airstrip near his homestead at Banagi but had completed only about half the job—the rest of the strip being downed trees and thorn bush—when he heard the drone of an engine coming in over the trees. Turner looked up to see a single-engine plane painted with zebra stripes, Michael Grzimek at the controls. 'They'll never land here," thought Turner at the time. "But land they did, using every inch of the cleared strip. Michael Grzimek was a skilled but reckless pilot," he recalled.[93] The scene captures well the shift in the late 1950s from hunter-naturalists to scientists dominating not just what was known about the Serengeti but which instruments validated such knowledge: a transformation that Turner later lamented but found impossible to halt.

The removal of the Grzimeks from scenes of the Flying Zebra and the distance they could achieve from the land below seemed to guarantee the nonpartisanship of their vision, free from "dogma" or the "teachings of philosophy and religion."[94] Such depictions of the nonaligned German naturalist working in Africa had their own long tradition. Before the German Empire began to acquire colonial territories, a number of German-speaking explorers, including

Heinrich Barth and Gerhard Rohlfs, were hired by British geographic societies, much as the Grzimeks were under contract to the British colonial government to document the great migrations.[95] Michael planned to assemble the research into a dissertation—a use of Africa as a laboratory that had been part of German academic culture before the wars.[96] "English readers will be struck by the fact that the Grzimeks could never have been anything but Germans," reads Alan Moorhead's preface to the English version of the text:

> The thousands of little packets of soil and plants sent back to Germany for analysis, the precise criss-crossing of the ground that went on until every yard was photographed from the air and every head of game was counted, the improvisations, the dangerous experiments, the careful notetaking, the endless checking of repetitive facts and figures—who but a German could throw himself into this work with such untiring gusto?[97]

Through science, the Grzimeks aimed for an internationalism beyond the imperial and the recent past, one that could disentangle their observations and experiments from European avarice and domination. "Men have other ideals for which they are willing to die: freedom, glory, politics, religion, the rulership of their class or the expansion of national borders," wrote Bernhard. "But in the long run Michael and I will be proved right."[98] The Serengeti research was more like a "calling" than a mundane scientific survey—a quest made possible by the celestial panorama.

Great Migrations

Much of *Serengeti Shall Not Die* focuses on the precarious trial-and-error methods the Grzimeks developed to select and capture animals designated for tracking from the air without harming the creatures. At the end of the 1950s, American veterinarian Toni Harthoorn had developed a prototype of an anaesthetizing dart, later called the "Cap-Chur" gun. This device allowed researchers to use a projectile syringe at close range to temporarily immobilize large animals, study them, administer an antidote, and later release them back into the wild without harm when scientists wished to weigh, measure, tag, trace, or even relocate them for veterinary or ecological surveys.[99] The Grzimeks discovered that tranquilizer guns worked well with smaller mammals such as gazelle and antelopes but were less effective for their larger cousins. For zebra, buffalo, and wildebeest, the research team had to rely on high-speed car chases to capture and immobilize the animals, resulting in harrowing sequences that only heightened the

Figure 4.4 Capturing the Animals. The Grzimeks took great risks to capture animals targeted for tracking, heightening the sense of scientific adventure and seriousness of purpose within the film narrative. Okapia, Ltd.

heroic affect.[100] In one sequence, the Grzimeks and their Tanganyikan assistants attempt to lasso a zebra running at full speed. Just before Michael can secure the end around the zebra's head, the pole hits the ground, resulting in a severe neck injury for Michael and a week-long stay in the hospital. After efforts to mark the animals using a powdered dye as well as ear tags failed, the Grzimeks settled on using brightly colored neck collars, each linked to a particular species, to follow the animals across the savannas from the air.[101]

Using these tracking methods, the Grzimeks largely confirmed Pearsall's findings about the movements of animals out of the corridor, but they also found vast herds following north–northwestern routes in the summer and fall that lay far outside the proposed boundaries of the park. They found no evidence that the herds lingered in the proposed "northern extension," whose woody habitat, they argued, did not allow for extended grazing—making it useless as compensatory habitat. Unlike subsequent researchers, they did not see the connection between the Serengeti herds and the wildebeest and zebra that fed north of the Mara River, in Kenya, during the dry season, which made the extension more valuable than they had realized. Most alarmingly, the Grzimeks could not locate wildebeest or zebra that moved in and out of the Ngorongoro Crater or highlands and into the Central Ol Balbal depression. Instead, they argued, the crater population of wildebeest, zebra, and gazelle remained nearly constant through-out the year.[102] Making the Ngorongoro into a mixed-use conservation territory, in their eyes, would thus jeopardize the future existence of these populations of animals.[103]

The most original contribution of their work lay in identifying the underly-ing biogeographical reason for the animals' preferred range and movements. Michael used the aircraft to land at seventy-nine remote locations, sampling grasses, measuring the nutritive value of the plants, determining the composi-tion of the soil, and hypothesizing about why the animals visited particular spots and not others on their seasonal wanderings.[104] Such "untiring gusto" yielded a second sobering discovery. Grasslands that the animals depended on were far outside the proposed park boundaries, leaving them vulnerable to hunters, encroaching farms, and competition with pastoralists' livestock. Nor could the park wardens erect fences or ditches to channel the animals toward other grazing grounds, as some had proposed. The animals' movements were choreographed to synchronize with the sprouting of specific grass species, so not just any patch of land would do. "It is therefore not possible for the surviving large game con-centrations to receive the protection that the National park intended to give them," the Grzimeks concluded.[105] Human populations around the park in the 1950s were still sparse, they noted, so the borders needed to be ecologically pre-cise before their sizes exploded after independence.

The uneasy balance between scientific calculation and moral appeal in the Grzimeks' work is also evident in the plane's first expansive landscape scenes, which unfold in the contested Ngorongoro Crater. The narrator describes Ngorongoro as a "natural zoo," larger in area than Berlin and all of its suburbs, which God himself had created with two-thousand-foot walls to fence in the animals from marauding humans. "It is impossible to give a fair description of the size and beauty of the crater," Bernhard wrote, "for there is nothing with which one can compare it. It is one of the Wonders of the World."[106] The Grzimeks and other conservationists feared that without immediate protection, the Ngorongoro's fauna would go the way of the American buffalo. "A hundred and fifty years ago the gigantic herds of other types of animals thundered across the prairies of North America and Canada in similar abundance," the Grzimeks wrote. "That was life on earth before man was fruitful and multiplied and 'sub-jugated nature.'" Future visitors to Serengeti could witness this "splendour that was nature, before God gave it to man to keep and cherish," the Grzimeks noted ominously, but "only *if* they are still moving then."[107] The Grzimeks' reference to the Serengeti animals going the way of the buffalo suggested that the savannas of sub-Saharan African would soon be consumed by the same forces of modern-ization that had transformed the North American wilderness and destroyed its iconic creatures.

Yet the depiction of the Ngorongoro as a "natural zoo," as an intact biotope shaped by ecological processes rather than human hands, belied the Crater's critical role in the expansion of German colonialism in East Africa. The German frontiersmen Adolph and Friedrich Wilhelm Siedentopf, who had tried to tame zebras and drive wildebeest out of the Ngorongoro to create a vast cattle-herding station, receive only a few paragraphs in *Serengeti Shall Not Die*, even though the Grzimeks used their farm as their headquarters for lodging and research analysis while inside the crater.[108] Other German farmers, meanwhile, had already touted Mount Kilimanjaro as "Germany's highest mountain" in the early 1900s so they could attract Europeans from the coast to visit inland areas for hiking excursions. Neglected by the metropole and insecure about their status within the so-called German protectorate, small farmers argued that it was their hard work—not that of big plantation owners or Africans—that was transforming East Africa into a *Heimat* abroad.[109] The Serengeti was indelibly marked by traces of German occupation that belied the Grzimek's portrayal of a pristine nature devoid of human presence.

The film's longest sequence is devoted to the biannual cycles of desiccation and rain that dominated grassland ecology and shaped the migrations of its inhabitants. Dramatic scenes of a grass fire—set accidentally by a group of African honey collectors—move across the plains, destroying sparse woodlands and drying out the already thin, vulnerable soils. Nonetheless, storm clouds appear on the horizon, bringing healing waters and newly sprouting grasses to the charred landscapes. As the ungulates return to the steppes to feed on the sweet grasses, they give birth to their young by the thousands, some of which become prey for lions, hyenas, and wild dogs—"happiness and death are constant companions in this world," the narrator reminds the viewer. And yet the killings are depicted as minor episodes in a finely tuned balance of predator–prey relations. In a particularly striking sequence, the Grzimeks follow lions as they track down and kill a helpless juvenile zebra that is shared among all members of the pride, even the frail, injured, and elderly, under the shade of the Dornier's wing. "It is true that lions kill and devour peaceful animals, just as we do," notes the narrator. "But they do not kill each other, and there are no murderous wars amongst them. That is one of the differences between lions and us. The world would be better off if humans behaved like lions."[110] The large cats are featured later in languid moments of domestic bliss, as cubs playfully attack their parents' tails. Indeed, it is difficult to tell just what the normal parental roles are when the mothers do most of the hunting and the males stay back with the pride, and all adults in the group seem to tolerate the frisky cubs. Such admiration for gentle, gender-bending lion families went too far for West German rating boards who later demanded that Bernhard cut the scene to get their highest accolades.[111] But Grzimek refused. For him, the comments were necessary to reinforce the notion of Africa as an untouched refuge in a world where humanism had met its demise on the killing fields of Europe.[112] The lions' social behavior reflected millennia of evolution, Grzimek noted, whereas humans' increasingly lethal weaponry had exceeded their capacity to exert ethical, diplomatic, or legal checks on aggression.[113]

By privileging the unending cycles of death and regeneration on the "remote" savanna, the Grzimeks presumed a baseline of ecological stability that overlooked the layers of African history and transregional exchange that had shaped this cultural landscape for millennia. The book about their journey excludes any mention of the millennia-long migrations from other parts of Africa to this region, including Bantu speakers from West and Central Africa, such as the Sukuma who came from the Congo forests to the region around Lake Victoria in the mid-sixteenth century; the Cushitic-speaking Iraqw, who came from northeastern Africa five hundred years before and were thought to have constructed the Engaruka urban-irrigation complex near Arusha; and the Maa-speaking branch of the Nilotic clans who arrived in the Serengeti region in the late eighteenth century.[114] Readers learn a bit about the Zanzibari ivory and slave traders who braved confrontation with Maasai warriors in the region, a sign that East Africa was already well integrated into transcontinental trade networks before European arrival. How this integration of the Serengeti into the Indian Ocean economy shaped the population sizes and distribution of a number of species, most especially elephants and rhino, is left unexamined in both the book and the film.

In depicting the horrors of fire on the savanna, the Grzimeks also missed the adaptive role of controlled, low-temperature burns and the subtle ways that Africans had shaped the composition of the Serengeti's woodland-grassland mosaic before European colonization. Previous to the 1890s, as we have seen, the Maasai and other pastoral groups had used fire to encourage new grasses for their livestock and create a no-contact zone between tsetse fly–infested bush and their own cattle and homesteads. Such a fire-induced zoning had also helped to contain the spread of sleeping sickness in people and *Nagana* in domesticated and some wild animals. As domestic animals died during the rinderpest epidemics (along with even-toed ungulates such as buffalo, eland, wildebeest, and larger species of antelope) and people stopped firing the grasslands, the African bush began to spread.[115] Soon thereafter, shrubs, trees, and recovering wild animal populations overtook vast stretches of formerly managed and cultivated lands. This oversight had also led the pair to underestimate the potential of the proposed northern extension as habitat. The Grzimeks' aerial photographs of this area, full of hilltop thickets, dense acacia woodlands, and "tsetse-infested bush," missed that this region had once been a more open grassland dotted with well-spaced acacia trees.[116] No matter how much the Grzimeks wished to soar above the plains in their quest for scientific truth, the subtle traces of land use past pulled them back to the earth's messy and politically contested terrains.

Bird's Eye Nature

The Flying Zebra revealed new ways of understanding the dynamics of the Serengeti ecosystem, but its most memorable scenes invited viewers to engage with the animal herds aesthetically and emotionally. As a zookeeper and television personality, Grzimek had long believed that contact with animals, even on screen, answered to a primordial need of modern humans to connect with their biological past. *Serengeti* included a vignette about Bushiri, a juvenile male zebra that the Grzimeks freed from a poacher's snare, only to find himself in a fierce battle with his half-brother over his status in the herd. Another famous sequence revolved around the African honey guide, a small bird that guides Ndorobo residents to honeycombs found deep inside trees in the *miombo* woodlands on the park's western borders. Too weak to pry open the bark and cambium that encases the bee colonies, the honey guide relies on its foraging human companions to share some of their find, an avian-human symbiosis that models the possibility of harmonious hunter-foragers living amidst the animals in rural East Africa. And yet *Serengeti Shall Not Die* is not primarily a film about individual animals. The Grzimeks knew that the Serengeti's mammals and their terrestrial island of grasslands and extinct volcanoes could not be rescued one creature at a time, as the pair had attempted by using a Sabena aircraft as a "new ark" in *No Room for Wild Animals*. Saving the Serengeti required viewers to appreciate entire herds as ecological treasures worthy of global attention.[117] Forging these affective bonds required the plane and the camera to work in tandem to stage the herds and their habitat as objects of expressive sympathy and wonder.

Aerial photography and filmography provided the Grzimeks with these new tools of ecological apprehension, for they allowed Bernhard and Michael to depict entire populations of animals in artistically composed shots "never before seen" in still photographs or movie theaters. For aerial shots, the Grzimeks relied on a highly sophisticated Fairchild camera whose winding, conveyance, and shutter release were completely automatic.[118] This camera was widely used for military photography in the latter part of World War II; indeed, it was this device that captured the notorious mushroom cloud over Hiroshima when mounted on the *Enola Gay*. The Grzimeks transformed the Fairchild into an instrument of ecological surveying. The camera made an exposure every few seconds as the pair flew over the Serengeti, which the Grzimeks calibrated to overlap with previous and succeeding exposures by about 50 percent, creating large strips of films they hoped to reconcile later with human counts to get the most accurate estimates. Originally, the Grzimeks had proposed assembling thousands of these acute-angle overhead shots into a map mosaic, a photogrammetric technique that surveyors had begun using after World War I to construct highly accurate topographical maps.[119] The vastness of the Serengeti and its lack of distinguishing topographic features quickly showed this method to be cost prohibitive, so the Grzimeks turned back to airplane passenger notes to count the wildebeest herds—increasing the chances of error due to over- or undercounting.

Nevertheless, the Grzimeks did convey other findings based on acute angle photography that revealed sharp differences from scientific surveyors who still worked on the ground. Cruising over Lake Natron, slightly northeast of Ngorongoro, the Grzimeks reported that they had identified about 164,000 flamingoes inhabiting the salt marshes—a far cry from the one million birds described by the renowned ornithologist Leslie Brown working in the same territory. Brown had relied primarily on surveys of nests on the ground and computations of the length and breadth of colonies from a "normal" aircraft— a technique the Grzimeks found passé in this new age of aerial innovation. Because the camera was mounted to the floor of the airplane, moreover, the Grzimeks could photograph at an angle that dispensed with the linear perspective of the picturesque tradition. Instead, the pair produced an image of flocks of flamingoes from twenty-four hundred feet up, merging the reddish-pink avians into a single, amoeba-like superorganism with choreographed movements and fractal complexity at every scale.[120] In these images, the Grzimeks successfully de-familiarized viewers' on-the-ground sensory apprehension of the bird flock in order to reveal their own mechanical reproductions as moments of astonishing natural beauty—perhaps even better than the real thing.

The blurring of technology and nature in the bird's eye view provided the Grzimeks with new techniques for documenting the flight reactions that were critical to Bernhard's research on animal behavior as well. The Grzimeks were amazed to report that solitary animals—including kongonis and topis—reacted only slightly to the presence of the plane overheard, even when it came to within thirty feet of their herd; resting Thomson's gazelles did not even stand up. Small herds of zebra and gazelles reacted a bit more vigorously, running about a hundred yards away as the plane came to within sixty feet. Only the wildebeest were more skittish about the plane, so the Grzimeks made sure to fly sufficiently high so as not to startle them. Small birds, they reported, were curious about the plane, moving only ten to twenty yards to the side and about 120 feet above the aircraft, while large birds of prey such as vultures and buzzard hawks merely eyed their strange new techno-companion, since "in the air, these birds may feel that there is nothing to endanger them."[121]

The animals' nonchalant reaction to the aircraft sharply contrasts to what the Grzimeks observed about some animals' reactions to the local Maasai. Casting doubt on the colonial government's belief that the Maasai had completely given up their tradition of hunting lions to prove their "manhood," the Grzimeks claimed that the big cats still showed a distinctive "flight reaction" when approached by a tall Maasai youth carrying a spear. They also observed that eland antelope and Cape buffalo fled from both Maasai and the Grzimeks' jeep, while zebra, wildebeest, and Thomson's gazelles could easily be approached by a car. In the national parks of Uganda and the Belgian Congo, where no Maasai resided, both eland and buffalo remained "tame" and approachable. The Grzimeks surmised that the Maasai hunted far more than British ethnographers or district officials had realized. Even if the herders mostly lived on their own cattle and domestic livestock for sustenance, they occasionally also hunted and ate eland and buffalo, the Grzimeks claimed, since Maasai considered these wild bovines "to be related to their cattle" and therefore "fit to eat."[122] Such findings cast further doubt on the long-term prospects for a mixed-use conservation area surrounding Ngorongoro, as it would doom species that the 1951 borders of the park now protected. Even more strikingly, the Grzimeks implied that the animals could better accommodate cars and airplanes in their midst than rural Africans trekking across the savannas. Far from distancing the viewer from nature, motorized technology was the key to a new kind of cyber-organic fusion with the animal world.

The Grzimeks underscored their belief that airplanes could achieve a more perfect union with nature than non-industrial human activities through a short ethnographic sequence that showed how the Maasai carefully bled their cattle for human consumption and moved from place to place in search of sweet grasses for their flocks. Hovering over the grasslands, the D-Ente reveals a landscape in which the Maasai "recklessly cut down trees" for their enclosures and then burn the makeshift structures as they move on, often resulting in scorched earth for miles beyond the compound. Such environmental destruction is completely unintentional on their part; after all, "what race of shepherds, black or white, has ever given even a remote thought to the fate of their country?"[123] The Grzimeks even denied male viewers the pleasures of a lingering "goona-goona" shot of naked Maasai girls splashing in a stream before being chased away by a threatening leopard. As the young women scramble up the embankment, one girl's glance at the camera gives away the careful direction of the scene Alan Root filmed using eight Nairobi prostitutes as extras. Root could not find any Maasai girls in the Serengeti region willing to do the scene since they did not customarily appear in public with their upper bodies uncovered and disapproved of such flagrant sexuality.[124] Yet Bernhard insisted on including the footage, feeling it was necessary for promotional materials and to entice viewers accustomed to "primitive" African female nudity—even though the film subverted that same message by arguing that the Maasai girls did not belong to the natural order of the Serengeti.

The tendency of the Grzimeks' airplane to camouflage their political intention to disenfranchise the Maasai in the guise of a beatific vision of the Serengeti plains has led many film scholars to locate *Serengeti Shall Not Die* within the imperialist tradition of travel writing and expeditionary filmography that "aims to take possession of a landscape even as it purports merely to describe it."[125] The Grzimeks' documentary reveals traces of the militarist gaze in the repeated description of large animal herds as "armies" or "marching columns," though the Grzimeks used these metaphors to draw parallels between wandering animals and the millions of displaced persons after World War II. The film's subtitle, *367000 Tiere Suchen einen Staat* [367,000 animals in search of a state]— suggested that animals, like people, needed a state, a homeland, to be safe and secure.[126] Michael's heroic place in the Serengeti story transformed the image of the fighter pilot into a warrior for nature. The media of the interwar era had portrayed airmen such as Charles Lindbergh in America and Italo Balbo in Italy as modern Apollos, "youthful gods whose missions took them above and beyond

Figure 4.5 Michael Grzimek as Gentle Warrior, 1959. Advertisements and marquee posters for *Serengeti Shall Not Die* foregrounded the Flying Zebra but reworked interwar myths of the godlike fighter pilot to feature young Michael Grzimek as a gentle warrior for the innocent animals of the Serengeti. Okapia, Ltd.

the mundane life of earthbound mortals."[127] Posters and marquees for *Serengeti* drew upon this tradition by featuring young Michael with the iconic D-Ente hovering in the background. But such images could also be menacing. Shots of the Dornier's shadow gliding above a map of Africa or the steppe lands echoed a detail that the Grzimeks almost certainly borrowed from scenes of Hitler's plane casting a shadow across the Romanesque and gothic spires of Nuremburg in *Triumph of the Will* (1935).[128] The Grzimeks intended these visual affinities to draw connections between the majesty of cultural and natural monuments, but the scenes pointed to the power and contested legacy of the airman's gaze—at once romantic and mastering, sublime and surveilling, holistic and violent.

By describing animals as marching columns, Grzimek implied a direct relationship between wandering African animals and the many displaced persons who lacked a home in the wake of wartime deportations and Nazi "ethnic cleansing." Such rhetoric drew parallels between migrating ungulates victimized by arbitrarily drawn park borders and the Jews, Poles, and ethnic Germans who found themselves stateless as a result of hurriedly crafted national frontiers. One glaring omission in this attempt to link animal and human suffering in the wake of war was the lack of any sympathetic attention to Africans' independence struggles in the landscapes that surrounded the Serengeti itself.[129] Indeed, Grzimek questioned whether the "overly hasty conversion of coloured colonies into independent democratic States was good for the inhabitants."[130] Democracy in Europe, after all, had "taken thousands of years to come to full flower," with many transitional stages, including the Prussian three-class voting system. This was an odd choice, as the system had skewed votes on the basis of landholding to keep conservatives in power—though such continued aristocratic control fit nicely with Grzimek's assertion that a "colonial nation must be half-literate before it can govern itself in a modern way."[131]

One sign that Africans were not quite ready to assume the mantle of statehood was the poaching rampant in the Serengeti, which only European aircraft could help colonial territories to solve. In one of the film's most engrossing sequences, the Grzimeks use the D-Ente to assist Myles Turner and a squad of British park rangers on an antipoaching raid. The Grzimeks dive toward the poachers—who fire poisoned arrows at the plane, clearly startled by being detected from the air—before dropping a smoke bomb to alert the antipoaching brigades to the location of the poachers' lair. The Grzimeks mounted the Fairfield in the tail-gunner position to capture the release of the smoke bomb, much like the wartime photography of bombing raids.[132] The pair refer to the poachers as "human hyenas"—a dehumanizing portrayal magnified by Michael's comment that "I'd like to have a machine-gun that fired through the propeller" to kill the poachers in their tracks. On the ground, Tanganyikan assistant wardens spring from their vehicle and capture the poachers, twenty in all, who will soon face charges in

Figure 4.6 The poacher's lair: a grisly scene of the wire snares and poisoned arrows used by poachers featured in *Serengeti Shall Not Die*. The airplane became a critical instrument for surveilling large tracts of land with only a few rangers. Okapia, Ltd.

court. The poachers' hideout is a hellhole of animal suffering filled with grisly snares, tortuous traps, and drying bushmeat. Injured and lame animals, including a lion missing a limb and an antelope with a grievous hind quarter wound, hobble across the screen, no doubt reminding European viewers of the wounded and disabled in Allied newsreels.

The wardens then burn the whole encampment to the ground, leading the Grzimeks to comment in the book on the horrifying futility of it all. "Year after year thousands of animals are killed by these gruesome methods," they note. "Only a tiny portion of the meat is utilized; most of the victims of the poachers only provide tails, ivory, a few hides and rhino 'horn.' What is the use of the Serengeti National Park when the protected animals have to leave it every dry season, only to be killed in huge numbers?"[133] Properly managed wildlife control areas on the frontiers of the park, Bernhard argued, could provide villagers with bushmeat containing far more nourishing protein per acre than any domesticates.[134] Instead, the animals' bodies were wasted on status symbols—horrific, luxury décor such as elephant feet fashioned into wastepaper baskets or leopard skins used as floor rugs. Such statements missed poachers' myriad motives, which sometimes included trade in body parts but also often reflected local demand for meat, especially during times of famine or drought that put additional pressure on hunting grounds.[135] The Grzimeks never considered these older moral ecologies of meat procurement and framed animals instead as objects of fantasy, rarity, and wonder for outside audiences—commodities for sale in world markets. In this sense, the airplane and the camera worked in tandem as modernizing agents, accelerating the trend toward African alienation from the wild that the Grzimeks found so worrisome.

Rewilding the Serengeti

Aerial filmography that dislodged the Serengeti from battles over borders or the rights of indigenous peoples reinforced the Grzimeks' claim that nature stood above political whims and power fantasies. Yet the Grzimeks encountered numerous traces of the German colonial past and World War I on their journeys—ghosts of a violent human past that challenged their depiction of the Serengeti as a primordial wilderness. To subdue these troublesome colonialist and wartime memories, the Grzimeks staged historical ruins to reveal nature's capacity to erode or green over even the most troublesome elements of land exhaustion and battlefield violence.[136] Such dramatization of organic processes only raised more questions about the human values guiding the process of rewilding former cultural landscapes—political questions that became hard to dismiss or ignore.[137]

The process of cinematic rewilding began early in the journey as the airplane glides over the former battlefields of North Africa. The Grzimeks argue that nature was reclaiming these killing fields from the "last war," shifting Europe's bloody conflict just fourteen years prior to the distant past. While gliding above Cyrenaica in Libya, for example, the Grzimeks discovered a verdant countryside crowding out war wreckage in the desert, including abandoned minefields, burned-out houses, a six-hundred-mile stretch of railway, an airport from the National Socialist occupation, and the ruins of Mussolini's Marble Arch. The green carpet was a result of the accidental introduction of grasses from the Australian semi-desert in horse fodder:

> While abandoned tanks rusted away, the desert around El Alamein started to grow green . . . . The new green life adapted itself to the Mediterranean conditions and prospered, particularly among the deadly mines which Italian, British and German soldiers laid in a hundred mile strip along the coast . . . . It is the only good thing left by the war.[138]

In this rendering, the Grzimeks showed that the uncomfortable reminders of a New Rome or a thousand-year Reich would quickly capitulate to more powerful nonhuman forces.

Through the film and book, traces of German imperial rule succumb to the dust and bush of the savannas. At one point in the narrative, the Dornier is grounded after the plane's wheel hits a warthog hole, and the Grzimeks discover the ruins of Fort Ikoma, a picturesque "European castle" like "one along the River Rhine." The fortress was once a slave-trading post along one of the Zanzibari routes, but the Germans had seized it as a government fort during their colonial occupation of East Africa. In 1901, Maasai raiders attacked the outpost, leading the Germans to build a massive fortress on the hill, replete with watchtowers on all sides.[139] Yet the fort's shell-scarred walls and watchtowers bore witness to another history: ferocious battles between German and their African *askaris* and Belgian-British troops in 1916 and 1917 due to its strategic location on the road to Mwanza that left a pile of bodies on nearby hillsides, according to the Grzimeks' Ikoma driver, Mgabo.[140] "As we drove across the old, weed-infested road," the Grzimeks wrote, "we saw a gap in the thick high walls . . . . [through which] . . . three startled zebras galloped . . . . Michael dug into the N.C.O.'s living quarters and unearthed a few coins. After cleaning them he could see the inscription: 'D.O.A. [Deutsche Ostafrika] 1916. Fünf Heller.' "[141]

Figure 4.7 The ruins of Fort Ikoma. The discovery of Ft. Ikoma, evoking the memory of colonial wars, challenged the notion that the Serengeti was a pristine wilderness untouched by human violence. Here nature overtakes the troublesome ruins of the past. Okapia, Ltd.

Michael and Bernhard ponder in these passages how lonely the German troops must have felt so far from their *Heimat* and recount how the fort's misty-eyed former commander, retired Lt. Paul Diesener, reported that he was charged during colonial times to defend the "natives" against Maasai raids and "hold court over the Africans," never imagining that he would see Ft. Ikoma in full color on screen after departing in 1913. In the film, Ft. Ikoma's appearance is brief, as the Grzimeks reenacted the airplane injury to show how it was possible to survive overnight in the wilderness by digging into an old stream bed for water, much as elephants do, and setting up a lean-to that faced no real menace from lions or other predators, since "we are not their normal prey." The fact that the Grzimeks could call up multiple retired colonial officers for stories about the region, however, indicates just how close to the surface the colonial past remained in the Federal Republic even as the film staged the fort as if it were an ancient ruin. Ft. Ikoma later became a tourist lodge, further distancing it from an uncomfortable history of colonial domination and war on the northwest fringes of the park.[142]

The discovery of Ft. Ikoma offered the Grzimeks the opportunity to present in the book a short history of Tanganyika that appears to affirm the revanchist "colonial guilt lie" even as the narrative distances itself from imperial mentalities. Their history includes a host of peoples who criss-crossed the region: Chinese seafarers and Omani slave raiders and ivory hunters who had plied the coast a thousand years before, followed by Portuguese slave traders, nineteenth-century European missionaries and explorers (including David Livingstone and Henry Morton Stanley), and American, French, and British merchants who desired to trade with the sultanate in Zanzibar.[143] The Grzimeks note Bismarck's reluctance to acquire colonies and the machinations of the German Colonial Society to send the unscrupulous Carl Peters to create a trade protectorate. They acknowledge Peters's notorious brutality and intimidation of "natives" but in a footnote cast doubt on stories of his wanton killing.[144] And they comment that another German from Silesia, Emin Pasha (born Eduard Schnitzler), a Muslim convert who had served as governor of the British province of Equatoria in Sudan, did much to disrupt the slave trade. After the Maji Maji rebellion, many German military administrators were replaced by civilian ones, whom, Grzimek indicates, post-1919 British administrators lauded for a school administration "far ahead of all neighbouring colonies" despite being latecomers to the colonial scramble. "It is only fair to add," they state, "that many German officials were interested in the people they governed; they were sympathetic to them and took a conciliatory attitude" despite numerous rebellions.[145] It is clear from these passages that the reclamation of land and history go hand in hand, obscuring any deeper reckoning with Germany's colonial past in Tanganyika.

The Grzimeks refer to the Waikoma themselves as a "frontier tribe, as unruly then as they are today," overlooking the role that this skilled group of farmers and hunters had played in shaping the Western Serengeti before Maasai and European hegemony. Agro-pastoralists such as the Ikoma, Ikizu, and Nata had occupied the Western Serengeti's short-grass savanna and *miombo* woodlands for centuries before famine, drought, Maasai raids, and smallpox made them vulnerable to European colonization. Oscar Baumann described their homeland as a vast open prairie in the 1890s, only dimly aware that the orchardlike appearance of the open savanna with small groves of trees was a remnant of these groups' burning of the grasslands. Such burning attracted and sustained wildlife for the hunt, controlled tsetse- and tick-infested bush, and facilitated an extensive economy of gift giving, shared labor, and cross-zonal trade. The nearby woodlands and water holes served as repositories of memory for ancestral and spirit worship for those seeking fertility, healing, and protection.[146]

When Turner took over as Serengeti warden in 1956, he described conversations with Waikoma elders who described the precolonial chiefdom lying thirty miles north of Seronera. The community had used the area around Seronera and Banagi for centuries as a dry season hunting area and the landscape remained full of old dug-out pits into which they drove large mammals. Such dry-season hunts were timed to take advantage of the animals' seasonal migrations as they moved from the central plains to watering holes in the north. The father of one of Turner's game scouts use to "regale" the company with stories of the Ikoma success in using poisoned arrows, which felled so many beasts that the pits were full of animal bodies that the rest of the herd could run over while fleeing in terror.[147] The effects of the caravan trade, European colonialism, and disease had nonetheless cut the Ikoma off from the animals and prohibited them from using fires to keep a balance between the domesticated homestead and the bush. The result was tsetse infestation, heightened pressure on game, and an increase in sleeping sickness that imperial authorities blamed on African mismanagement of the landscape. Far from being a Garden of Eden inhabited by "unruly, frontier tribes," the Western Serengeti was a *Heimat* of the Ikoma and other African communities.

Alongside the staging of ruins, the Grzimeks edited out cultural landscapes that might distort. One of these landscapes was found at the Siedentopf homestead in the middle of the Ngorongoro Crater, whose layers of Maasai memory and European "development" were a stumbling block for those seeking untrammelled nature. Adolf Siedentopf had come to German East Africa in the early 1900s as part of a small wave of European settlers to establish a cattle station that eventually consisted of a farmhouse, shed, and stable along with thousands of cattle and sheep and dozens of Maasai and Iraqw employees. His brother, Friedrich Wilhelm, established a smaller farmstead in the southeast corner of the Crater, near the spring-fed Lerai Forest. The Siedentopfs bred ostriches, tried to tame zebras, planted Australian eucalyptus trees and alfalfa, dug irrigation canals, created tracks for ox wagons, and erected kraals for livestock. The pair were both commercial hunters, killing numerous elephants for ivory and wilde-beest for their tails and earned extra money leading small safari hunting parties in and around the crater.[148]

Maasai were living in the crater when the Siedentopfs established their ranch and looked on with horror as the pair decimated wildlife to protect their cattle from malignant catarrh—and asked the brothers to stop the slaughter.[149] The Maasai had inhabited the area around the farm for generations, and it was an important sacred grove for fertility, rainmaking, and the burial of elders intimately tied to indigenous memories of place.[150] The Siedentopfs nevertheless convinced district officials to expel Maasai from the crater in 1907, declaring it "crown land" that the "nomads" could not claim as property because they had not developed it properly.[151] After the Siedentopfs failed in their cattle ranching and afforestation efforts and stood accused of worker mistreatment and unpaid wages, a strong con-servation lobby group led by Carl Schillings tried to have Ngorongoro declared a "nature protection park" (*Naturschutzpark*) in 1913 for well-heeled hunters will-ing to pay high fees—all made possible by the previous expulsion of the Maasai from the crater floor. But the government ran into difficulties raising money and support for the scheme, leading the colonial governor to open the crater once again to private entrepreneurs who lined up for the rights to lease farmland.[152] The farm itself was declared enemy property and sold to an American millionaire, who retained it as a hunting lodge until it became part of the Serengeti complete reserve in 1929.[153] By severing the national parks from this history of failed colo-nial experiments and land expulsions, the Grzimeks could fashion themselves as globetrotting zoologists unencumbered by the imperial past.

A Global Heritage of Mankind

The more traces of human habitation that the Grzimeks encountered in the Serengeti, the higher the Flying Zebra soared. The greening of colonial history shaded into the post-1945 era, blurring any assignation of guilt for the "recent war" by presenting it as a calamity of human frailty. In one particularly striking passage, Grzimek noted that:

> Millions feared Hitler and millions were enthralled by him. Millions laid down their lives for him and other millions died fighting against him. Today when German school children are asked questions about Hitler most of them know very little about him and cannot even name his henchmen . . . . Only Nature is eternal, unless we senselessly destroy it.[154]

The Grzimeks saw nature as a source of aesthetic wonder and awe beyond any national, ethnic, or economic community. Such privileging of nature's eternality bypassed uncomfortable questions about specific Nazi crimes and German wartime responsibility in favor of an abstract appeal above ideology and race.[155] Palaces could be rebuilt after wartime destruction, as the experience of London and Berlin in the 1950s had shown, but "once the wild animals of the Serengeti are exterminated, no power on earth can bring them back."[156] In their final staging of the Serengeti, the Grzimeks wanted viewers to experience it as a monument of evolutionary history whose aura outshone the greatest works of human ingenuity.

In one shot, when introducing the Ngorongoro, the Grzimeks flew directly toward the outside rim of the crater and then glide almost motionlessly as the camera mounted under the wing reveals a vast and featureless crater floor interspersed with the black silhouettes of clouds. In the distance the viewer can gaze at the curvature of the earth's surface, framed at such an oblique angle it is difficult to tell up from down.[157] The camera cuts to a scene on the crater floor itself, panning sideways from a camera mounted high atop their zebra-striped jeep to reveal a natural zoo consisting of animals from different species and sizes. Both

Figure 4.8 Celestial panoramas: the Ngorongoro Crater. The Grzimeks used a camera mounted on top of their companion zebra-striped jeep to achieve panoramic shots of animal herds that attempted a seamless connection between celestial images aloft and the "natural zoo" on the ground. Okapia, Ltd.

scenes had few direct precedents in imperialist filmography, as the Grzimeks' goal was not the visual possession of tropical nature but the awe inspired by the inability of the viewer to impose normal categories of experience onto the planetary vistas achieved by the ingeniously mounted cameras.[158] Framed as a celestial panorama, the Serengeti would be free from imperialist scrambles and "petty" ethnic conflicts. The Dornier invited viewers to experience the park from a distance that merged ground-level waterways, grasses, acacias, even mountainsides, into a kaleidoscope of intricate patterns from which it was impossible to discern territories shaped by human hands.

The Grzimeks had long been intrigued by what a glimpse of the planet might do to environmental consciousness. In the expository shot of *No Room for Wild Animals*, the pair had imagined the earth from outer space as a glowing red ball—a paradise for hominid ancestors and wild animals alike until modern humans began their rapid and destructive expansion. Such Malthusian themes about the threat of globalization remained critical to *Serengeti Shall Not Die*, but they receded in favor of illustrating the vastness and vulnerability of the park as a global monument to the earth's biological past.[159] The immediate reference for the Grzimeks' call to salvage world heritage had taken place in Egypt in 1954, when the newly independent government of Gamal Abdul Nasser announced plans to construct a dam across the Upper Nile near the city of Aswan. Heritage preservationists from around the world were immediately in an uproar, because the resulting reservoir would drown several historical sites, including the Great Temple of Ramses II at Abu Simbel and the Sanctuary of Isis at Philae. UNESCO stepped in at Abu Simbel with an ambitious salvage operation that promised to relocate temple structures—stone by stone—to higher ground.[160] In 1960, after a successful appeal by the Director General of UNESCO to member states for financial assistance to "save the monuments of Nubia," thousands of archaeologists and conservationists began the tough work of excavating, coding, and relocating temples, stoneworks, and artifacts. The Abu Simbel campaign helped to launch the designation of "world heritage sites," monuments whose significance transcended national, ethnic, or Cold War interests—but signaled a distrust that emerging nations were up to the task of protecting precious sites.

The Grzimeks knew about the Abu Simbel effort. They had taken an "honorific lap" around the Aswan Dam during their flight to Tanganyika and during the height of the Serengeti controversies suggested that the United Nations should step in to stop the division of the park.[161] Aswan served as a prime example of ecological folly, as few predicted its catastrophic effects: lowering the water table, cutting off prime farm land from floodplain nutrients, and salinizing irrigated fields.[162] In this sense, the Grzimeks' references to saving the Serengeti from the "rising tide of humanity" was more than just metaphorical. For them, the rising Nile waters were a symbol of what might occur in Tanganyika if an autonomous government repeated the mistakes of other newly independent African nations bent on ambitious irrigation and rural electrification schemes.

By framing the Serengeti as a cultural monument on par with the Egyptian artifacts, the Grzimeks accentuated its value as a global resource just as Europeans' direct control over colonial territory was slipping away. Bernhard argued that a "clever man" such as TANU leader Julius Nyerere might be persuaded to recognize the value of wildlife for a future independent state. But the Grzimeks remained deeply skeptical that "immature" Africans would follow such a moderate politician. They lacked the capacity to realize animals' higher value—after all they had only recently been wrenched from a "well-adjusted primitive existence" and remained "ninety-eight percent illiterate."[163] For people at such a primitive stage of civilization, they averred, animals meant nothing more than "so much meat, hides and grazing land."[164] However stridently Nyerere might call for the end of colonial oppression, the Grzimeks insisted, an "overly hasty conversion of coloured colonies into independent democratic States" because of costs or political squabbles shirked Europeans' responsibility toward the "governed peoples." "*We Europeans must teach our black brothers to value their own possessions, not because we are older or cleverer, but because we do not want them to repeat our mistakes and our sins*," the Grzimeks wrote.[165]

The god's eye perspective gave the international community of enlightened conservationists a new tool for justifying their role as advisors and technical experts during the transition in national park management from imperial rule to independence. Decolonizing peoples still needed Europe's guidance to realize the Grzimeks' vision of an alternative environmental modernity. They could not yet be trusted to serve as stewards of their wildlife heritage, for colonialism had left them just too vulnerable to the seductions of Western modernity. Even so, many Africans that the Grzimeks encountered remained skeptical about whether a call to protect global heritage answered their growing desire for political *and* environmental sovereignty. As one medical student remarked upon hearing the Grzimeks' call to teach their "black brothers": "there still remains a bit BUT. . . . What happens in our countries is *our* concern—even if we ruin them. We'll manage all right, because we *want* to manage, but first of all we must be free!"[166]

The realization that Africans would one day take over the national parks led the Grzimeks to slowly abandon their hope of recreating the Belgian strict reserve in the Serengeti. In their book they hint at a new way to convince Africans to protect their heritage: tourism. The relative ease with which their small Dornier conveyed them to Africa was a sure sign that airplanes would soon transform global travel, with bigger and faster jets replacing the luxury steam liners that had kept Africa an exotic and expensive destination, affordable mostly by aristocratic hunter-naturalists. For the Grzimeks, the masses who streamed into the Frankfurt Zoo and watched *A Place for Animals* had made the animals into a "commodity in search of a market," and they wanted to be sure to alert up and coming African leaders about their potential.[167] As urbanization deepened and Europeans became ever more alienated from contact with animals and wild nature in their everyday lives, the Grzimeks argued, the herds of the steppes would become even more precious. "Large cities continue to proliferate," the Grzimeks wrote. "In the coming decades and centuries men will not travel to view the marvels of engineering, but they will leave the dusty towns in order to behold the last places on earth where God's creatures are peacefully living." Countries that preserved such places, they averred, would be the "envy" of other nations and would be visited by "streams of tourists" making a "pilgrimage" to the wild.[168]

The Grzimeks argued that hunters—the same persons who had just recently slammed his and Michael's story of animal imperilment in *No Room for Wild Animals*—were mostly to blame for Africa's failure to become a tourist destination. Their exaggerated accounts of adventure in the bush scared off potential First World visitors by claiming that one "needed to wear long boots to protect against poisonous snakes, or that at night they would be threatened by lions and scorpions."[169] The Grzimeks used their film to convince conservation-minded viewers that Africa was safe for those who wanted to experience wildlife through the lens of the camera rather than the barrel of a gun.[170] As the Grzimeks rumble across the plains in a safari jeep or fly low over the Ngorongoro caldera, the audience can see that wildebeest, gazelles, and zebras abound. This assured the viewer that even an amateur photographer will have a successful hunt with the camera. And for those who did not travel, sublime images of the elephants in grasslands silhouetted by Kilimanjaro presented a powerful image for raising funds or arousing political protest in the name of conservation. "Comparatively few tourists come to Africa nowadays to *shoot* animals," the Grzimeks noted. "There are already tens of thousands who would rather *see* them in their wild state than in zoos."[171] By comparing the Serengeti to the Acropolis, the Grzimeks suggested that Africa's national parks were ready for inclusion on the emerging "pleasure periphery" of northern industrialized states.[172] The Flying Zebra served as the technological vanguard for a new kind of environmental regime in which globally minded tourists and scientists, not the "native tribes" or hunters of the imperial past, would come to dominate how the savannas "ought to be seen."[173]

———

The Dornier DO 27 appears in over twenty scenes in *Serengeti Shall Not Die*, far more than the Grzimeks themselves or iconic lions, wildebeest, or elephants.

By experiencing the Serengeti from the Grzimeks' cockpit, viewers felt themselves part of the heroic mission to unlock the great mysteries of the plains. How many animals still inhabited the region? Where had they moved in their great migrations? And most importantly, what ecological reasons underlay their choice of particular grasses and not others? The answers to these questions offered insights that might rescue the Serengeti from narrow-minded border disputes. In this search for the true borders of a 367,000-animal "state," the Grzimeks recognized their fellow creatures' plight as no different from ongoing efforts to resettle displaced persons safely in their ethnic homelands. The appeal to unending cycles of nature offered war-weary West Germans and other Europeans a refuge in East Africa that consigned "Hitler and his henchmen" to the distant past and eased the tensions of a Cold War that had begun along the sector boundary in Germany and spread to postcolonial Africa. From their lofty perspective, the Grzimeks could stage the animal herds as complex superorganisms greater than the sum of their parts, an evolutionary achievement that no person, "black or white," had the right to endanger—or claim as their own. Even though some of the Grzimeks' conclusions later proved inaccurate—the animal counts were far too low and the migration maps missed the importance of both the northern extension and dry season grazing across the Mara River in Kenya—their aerial techniques, sampling methods, and insights about ecological connections served as a model of baseline ecological surveys for decades to come.[174] But the Grzimeks' most remarkable achievement was to make wandering wildebeest the real stars of the show. These herds drove the Serengeti's ecosystem dynamics, its status as a national park, and its future as a global heritage of humanity.[175]

The staging of the Serengeti's herds as global heritage could only be realized by an equally powerful strategy of historical erasure, as the vestiges of African and European cultural landscapes succumbed to the vines of the woodlands or the black sands of the volcanic plains. From further aloft, the patchwork of landscape created by human, ungulate, and domesticate interactions melded into the shadows of cloud formations or vanished into the horizon. The zebra striping that aided Michael after several emergency landings also camouflaged the plane from animals on the ground and avians charting their own migrations, convincing the Grzimeks that vultures, lions, and buffalo would welcome this new mechanical beast as one of their own, allowing observation without intrusion. Their flight reactions in the presence of Maasai, meanwhile, showed that indigenous people were not part of the "fauna;" they were intruders into an otherwise harmonious and self-perpetuating system. What happened in the villages bordering the park or the cities further afield did not make into the frame at all, as the Grzimeks saw the animals as the only inhabitants worth salvaging in East Africa.

One of the deep ironies of such tourist promotion was that it alienated Africans even further from their wildlife, accelerating the very modernizing trends the Grzimeks abhorred. The global icon that emerged in *Serengeti Shall Not Die* built on layers of imperial conservation and control that could not easily be erased by two citizens of a former colonial hegemon in East Africa—no matter how breathtaking their scientific ambition and filmic imagination. The Serengeti was established as a game reserve not only to limit European sport hunters but also to stamp out African hunting so that British colonial administrators could cut off common resources and redirect African labor to farms and plantations. National parks served a similar purpose. The Colonial Office and the territorial government embraced the national park model—despite the evidence that wildlife was increasing in number after the rinderpest epidemics—because it meshed with the goal of sedentarizing Tanganyikans and developing their lands for export. *Serengeti Shall Not Die* was not simply romantic escapism from the ills of Cold War modernity but an agent of modernization itself, heralding the division of the landscapes into zones of production and consumption without offering a sustainable middle ground that wild animals, livestock, rural peoples, and urban visitors might occupy together.

Michael's death, in a collision with a vulture no less, served as a warning about escaping the surly bonds of terrestrial life in search of ecological truths beyond the humanist imagination. Bernhard and the crew's proposition that Michael had martyred himself so that the Serengeti might live heightened the moral certainty that animal herds were as precious as Egyptian or Greco-Roman heritage yet did little to recast the conservation mission in anticipation of Tanganyika's impending decolonization. Indeed, *Serengeti Shall Not Die* did the opposite. By declaring the Serengeti a global natural monument unmoored from its deeper human-animal past, the Grzimeks reenacted some of the most dubious colonialist assumptions about African land stewardship and their capacity for self-government. In such a scenario, Tanganyikans could only emerge as immature Europeans, forced to recapitulate a Western path of modernization that would doom the continent's fragile ecology and necessitate a permanent separation of cherished wild animals from local inhabitants.

A Weakness for the Maasai

A Masai spits on civilization, quite literally. He will never wear a
European hat or buy a car.... If you must have natives inside the Park,
the Masai are the least of all evils.
　　　—Bernhard and Michael Grzimek, *Serengeti Shall Not Die*

Bernhard and Michael Grzimek had a deep affection for the Maasai. Like so
many previous European visitors to these remote steppes, the Grzimeks found
themselves enthralled by stories of these unrepentant cattle raiders who deemed
themselves "God's chosen people." The Maasai belief that non-Maasai had
no right to own cattle, the Grzimeks claimed, had made the herders into the
"scourge" of their neighbors, as they took whatever they needed during times
of drought or famine.[1] Bernhard especially respected their disdain for European
technology.[2] Other Africans seemed quite impressed by the Grzimeks' Flying
Zebra, and both father and son expected that the Maasai "would also come
running to admire our wondrous striped bird." But when the pair landed near a
Maasai encampment, the men were away herding, and the women merely said
"hello" (*Jambo*) and carried on with their work. "We found this lack of interest
almost insulting," Bernhard wrote bemusedly, until he learned that the Maasai
considered the smiths who manufactured objects made of metal to be unclean.[3]
Other "odd" customs, according to the Grzimeks, made the Maasai especially
good neighbors for wild animals. The Maasai only ate the meat of their own
cattle, sheep, and goats, Bernhard remarked: "If you must have natives inside the
Park, the Maasai are the least of all evils."[4] As Harold T. P. Hayes remarked in his
1976 memoir of journeys with Grzimek, "No people could have been less suited
for the role of antagonist" in the Grzimeks' quest to save the Serengeti.[5]

For globally minded conservationists, their "problem" with the Maasai had
nothing to do with personal animosity. Instead, it stemmed from a deep well of
nostalgia and regret: the misfortune of an ancient "nomadic" culture out of sync
with the winds of change. Pearsall had noted that the trampling hooves and grazing habits of increasing numbers of cattle were likely to compact thin tropical

Our Gigantic Zoo. Thomas M. Lekan, Oxford University Press (2020). © Oxford University Press.
DOI: 10.1093/oso/9780199843671.001.0001

soils and denude the seasonal vegetation of the Serengeti. "The pastoral mode of life of the Masai is inevitably, if locally, harder on the grasslands," he wrote, "than the presence of a similar number of game."[6] In *Serengeti Shall Not Die*, however, the Grzimeks ramped up this threat of deserts on the march. The Maasai could "never own enough cattle," they noted, and during their wanderings across the plain the herders would cut down lone shade trees to build new kraals and cordon off wild animals from watering holes to make way for their bovine intruders.[7] Such patterns exemplified the tragedy of the pastoral commons. As Bernhard wrote, "Pastoral people, whether black or white, never consider the soil and its vegetation, they never think of the future. The barren hills of Italy, Spain and Greece, and the new deserts of India, are evidence of this."[8] Few noticed that such "status symbols" were a logical buffer for subsistence herders against the vagaries of the savanna environment and a medium of exchange when needed in the short-term for foodstuffs or manufactured products.[9] In the Malthusian logic of the 1950s, wildebeest migrations and pastoral mobilities were on a collision course due to the limited space and resources of the semiarid savannas.

This chapter looks at how midcentury scientific and administrative misunderstandings of pastoralist ecologies and savanna resilience created the land-use

Figure 5.1 Ethnographic photograph of a Maasai family from German ethnographer Moritz Merker, 1910. Merker's carefully posed photographs reflected the available technologies at the time as well as an ethnographic impulse to document "native" inhabitants for museums dedicated to *Naturvölker*—the "primitive" peoples who did not command a written language of their own. Getty Images.

Figure 5.2 Michael Grzimek with Maasai friends, 1958. The Grzimeks claimed to have a "weakness" for the Maasai and such intimate still photographs are abundant in the visual archives of their journey. Such photos belie reports of personal hostility toward the Maasai, whom the Grzimeks called upon frequently for help orienting themselves in the landscape or seeking shelter after various mishaps during the research process. But the photos also suggest no need for Merker's ethnographic distance—for the Grzimeks, the Maasai, like other Africans, were quickly losing their traditional culture. Okapia, Ltd.

conflicts that lay outside the aerial frame of *Serengeti Shall Not Die*. It emphasizes the politics of landscape from the ground up, gleaned from the perspectives of herders, hunters, and colonial officials who gazed up at the Flying Zebra without always fully grasping how this new instrument of surveillance was transforming local skirmishes over indigenous access to national parks into an international scandal right on the brink of decolonization.[10] These battles had begun in the 1930s, when London conservation lobbyists described the Serengeti as the crown jewel of British Africa and demanded that the territory demarcate it as a national park that banned all but the most primitive inhabitants.[11] By 1958, British imperial debates about the status of the Serengeti reserve had mushroomed into an international controversy as the IUCN, US-based NGOs, and the Grzimeks called for the UN to step in and administer this piece of global heritage. Any attempt to "appease" the Maasai, international conservationists argued, would jeopardize the integrity of national parks across the world.[12]

Between 1948 and 1958, however, the park's trustees put forward a series of three contradictory border proposals that attempted to find a middle ground in which "authentic" pastoralists could remain in the Serengeti. In the first phase (1948–1953), British officials and park managers sought to limit the Maasai's "rights of occupancy" to those who had inhabited the park before 1951. Such accommodation of a small population of cattle herders inside the park reflected, in part, the legacies of indirect rule, which had first evolved in West Africa in the 1920s as a remedy for the failure to establish viable white settler colonies and export-driven plantations. This administrative system was based on the idea of devolving certain administrative functions to "tribal" authorities, which British colonial officials assumed to be fixed ethnic units with primordial origins that lived under cohesive and ancient systems of customary law.[13] Such tribes, British ethnographers and officials argued, had been destroyed by slave traders and German officials' ruthless suppression of "native" interests, even though Europeans' invented traditions had little resemblance to the "kaleidoscope" of interests, stories, and overlapping identities that predominated in East Africa.[14] For those tribes deemed to be especially "primitive" and living in a state of nature, such as the pygmies of Central Africa or the Maasai of the savannas, there seemed to be little threat to wildlife—and no need to alienate them from their customary lands.[15] Indeed, some conservationists argued that they were part of the "fauna" of the national parks that deserved protection from the encroachment of modernity.

Yet the British soon discovered that it was impossible to determine exactly which Maasai among the many clans and family networks they encountered enjoyed "traditional" rights of access, partly because they relied on a "pastoral myth" that was ill-suited to the mobilities and interdependencies necessary to survive in an oscillating, semiarid environment. In the second phase (1954–1956), British officials decided to remove all cultivators from the park in the hopes of recalibrating the human and animal populations to the land's carrying capacity. "True" Maasai pastoralists, they averred, did not cultivate, reinforcing an ethnic stereotype that relied on surprisingly crude notions of indigeneity and a deep misunderstanding of the extensive land-use and flexible ecological knowledge that pastoralists needed to thrive in the drylands. The perceived tension between Maasai seeking a place to pasture against the pressure of wild animals seeking room to migrate became so fraught that it brought the Serengeti to the brink of dismantlement by 1957.[16]

The Grzimeks descended upon the Serengeti just as this middle phase was coming to an end and as the effects of poaching and recent drought were becoming severe. Lacking a deep knowledge of East Africa and the provisional adaptations that pastoralists made during drought conditions, the Grzimeks' book, film, and photographs exacerbated British imperialists' misreading of the landscape with sweeping Malthusian pronouncements and dubious depictions of racial "corruption" that accelerated the drive to expel that Maasai from the park. By eliding evidence of previous Maasai inhabitation, the father-son pair presented an image of the Serengeti as an endangered slice of wild Africa ready for film audiences and tourists to enjoy. The Grzimeks believed that removing the Maasai from the Serengeti would restore the region's climax communities to a primordial state. This vision of permanence was difficult to reconcile with a restless plains environment that never equilibrated as expected and whose human ecology depended on synergies between cattle raising and wildlife migrations and between herding and farming that confounded European expectations of race and space. In the final phase (1958–1960), control over this "wicked" situation slipped away from British colonial officials as independence drew near. International organizations and NGOs such as the FZS quickly stepped into the breach—but without better tools for mastering the human conflicts over customary tenure or subduing the non-human agents that made the Serengeti so dynamic, breathtaking, and intractable.[17]

Bounding the Serengeti: Debates on Residency, 1948–1953

As recent anthropological work has demonstrated, the Maasai have developed their own narrative about the origins of Serengeti National Park (SNP) that stands in sharp contrast to the Grzimeks' depiction of an untrammeled wilderness. In this account, a German man who wanted to keep lions asks Maasai elders if they would give him some land to keep them on. The elders agree, giving him a small parcel of territory, but when they return, they discover that the German had taken even more terrain for the lions. "Each time the elders went to visit him," notes the anthropologist Ben Gardner in relaying this narrative, they discover that the German "had expanded the area for his lions. Eventually the government used this as an excuse to create Serengeti national park, where foreigners pay the government to see the man's lions." As Gardner notes, the story highlights the deep irony of the Maasai predicament. They had given up land for something they do not inherently value: the protection of lions. Yet the German continues to take up more and more territory for his animals without permission, aided by a state willing to pass laws and use force to keep them out of the lionkeeper's domain. In examining the Maasai narrative, one is struck by pastoralists' deep sense of belonging and the powerful figure of the "German" who links colonial hunting reserves to postcolonial national parks. For the Serengeti Maasai, it mattered little whether the Serengeti was designated a game reserve, a national park, or an international biosphere reserve, since in all three cases, outside interests justify, broker, and finance land grabs. Such "core spatial images" of loss, constriction, and enclosure serve as powerful reminders of the tensions between human rights and conservation efforts that crystallized in the Serengeti during the controversies of the 1950s.[18]

The disjuncture between outside conservation interests and local subsistence needs in the Maasai narrative reflects a history of environmental injustices across sub-Saharan Africa. These injustices emerged as Europeans tended to blame Africans for environmental problems caused by colonial expansion and to carve protected areas out of landscapes with long histories of extensive human use for agriculture or pastoralism. Yet for a brief period in the 1950s, Tanganyika's territorial administrators and district officers—informed by (but without the critical participation of) local African constituencies—did explore the possibilities of a "middle ground" between fortress conservation and sustainable traditional use. While no less condescending toward the Maasai than international conservationists, a circle of park administrators and advisors, many with decades-long experience in the Serengeti districts, tried to find a compromise between the needs of wildlife and those of "natives." After the war put Tanganyika's 1940 Game Ordinance on hold, Tanganyika's legislative council passed a National Parks Ordinance in 1948 that designated the Serengeti as the territory's first full-fledged national park and established an independent board of trustees. It was not until 1951, however, that the board turned to the difficult task of specifying the new reserve's boundaries.[19] This fluidity on the ground, in turn, opened up differences of opinion *within* the colonial state about the priorities of wildlife conservation in a mandate territory under the watchful eye of a UN Trusteeship Council eager to promote the human development of Tanganyika and prepare it for independence.[20] The tensions between international conservationists, colonial government officials, and rural Africans unfolded against a backdrop of drought, demographic changes, and political unrest that turned the Serengeti into a hotbed of environmental conflicts in the 1950s.

The Grzimeks' experiences in the Belgian Congo had left them ill-prepared for the myriad human conflicts that erupted in the Serengeti between game officials and national park advocates over customary land rights in a protected area. As Bernhard noted in their field notes, the Belgians had been willing to transplant "whole villages . . . at the outset in order that the land might be totally free of human inhabitants," an action fully in line with their vision of an integral nature reserve.[21] Such measures were not undertaken in Tanganyika, however, where officials believed that "primitive man was part of nature" and enjoyed rights of customary tenure. The 1948 National Parks Ordinance that established the Serengeti did not call for restricting the Maasai's grazing and water rights and allowed free access to those "whose place of birth or ordinary residence was within the Park."[22] The Grzimeks agreed with the spirit of this British assessment, noting that this "point of view seemed eminently justified particularly as they decline to adopt European clothes and civilization and are not habitual hunters."[23]

The Tanganyikan government did consider the complete removal of the Maasai from the Serengeti region in order to conform more closely to the 1933 London Convention.[24] The Serengeti, as one board member lamented, was the only national park to start its existence under the "severe handicap of a resident population of Maasai with their cattle."[25] Yet the board maintained that the Maasai deserved rights of occupancy because their traditional ways did not conflict with the goals of wildlife protection. As one proponent of native rule noted, "The rights of the Masai are protected by law and cannot be abrogated. Government relies on the elders to co-operate with the Park Warden, to follow his directions and keep the Park Laws."[26] The government reported that in 1951 there were roughly 21,000 Maasai in the park along with 120,000 head of cattle and 230,000 small stock—sheep, goats, and donkeys.[27] The government hoped that it could persuade a large number of Maasai to de-stock their "surplus" herds or evacuate the region altogether through an ill-defined and never-executed plan to improve watering and grazing opportunities for cattle outside the park.[28]

Though the Maasai were the only ethnic group recognized as having traditional rights of occupancy, the ordinance's wording left open the possibility that farmers and hunters on the western edges of the proposed park might be able to remain as well.[29] In his 1931 report, Major Hingston stated that the western zones contained "few native inhabitants" and that no serious objections would arise if they were transferred outside the boundaries—a phrasing that gave little thought to the Sukuma, Nata, Ikoma, and Ikizu who would be cut off from the bushmeat, plants, honey, wood, and sacred sites they depended on.[30] In the Serengeti, the establishment of a station at Banagi with a permanent European ranger in 1929 had already resulted in an increase in convictions for illegal hunting.[31] But as Myles Turner's game officers began to crack down on illegal hunting in the western zones, confrontations between them and western Serengeti villagers escalated.[32] Field officers found themselves threatened with pistols or being chased away by angry villagers who refused to recognize the legitimacy of the new national park.[33]

A sizeable contingent of district officers had always feared the escalation of such conflicts and argued that the national park ordinances went too far in policing customary access to game animals. When the Serengeti was still a game reserve, district officers and even game wardens found it difficult to prosecute African men bringing home meat for their families to supplement meager fruits and vegetables or "squatting" on land their families had occupied for generations.[34] Indeed, in a 1929 circular sent to district commissioners, the Governor insisted that officials not go too far in prosecuting African cultivators. "The native should be regarded as having a *moral right* to killing or procuring game for food even if he has not license," noted one official. "We do not obstruct the native cultivator in his measures in protection of his plantations from depredations by game."[35] Several administrators had also criticized Hingston's national park proposals as an abrogation of "native" land rights protected under the League of Nations Trusteeship.[36] On the eve of the Serengeti's designation as a national park in the late 1940s, in fact, many district officers even ridiculed London conservationists' doomsday reports about the state of wildlife in East Africa. In their estimation, the destruction in World War I and the failure of tsetse control measures had allowed the bushland that harbored both the insect and large mammals to reclaim vast stretches of former farms and ranchlands.[37] They felt besieged by the return of nature—not its demise.

Given field officers' tendency to look the other way when Africans procured animals for food and the contrarian animal counts they reported to the Colonial Office, members of the Fauna Preservation Society (FPS), the successor to the interwar SPFE after World War II, argued that the Colonial Office should centralize authority over imperial parks and hire trained wildlife ecologists to determine the proper use of land.[38] They feared that the 1948 ordinances establishing the Serengeti did not restrict human activities enough, as they contained no provisions to limit future immigration into the park or stem population increases of "natives" and their herds.[39] Of particular concern was the perceived large number of people who had entered the park between the Game Ordinance of 1940 and the revision of borders in 1951, which FPS members argued had doubled the number of Maasai residing within the park and increased those engaged in cultivation. By 1954, according to Myles Turner, over two hundred families—eighty-two of which were Maasai—were growing maize and tobacco on the crater floor near Seronera "diverting streams for irrigation and destroying vegetation" (see Figure 4.3). Apart from the original Serengeti Maasai, Turner noted, none of the "new arrivals" could claim "traditional rights of occupancy in the Park."[40]

Based on their experiences in the Congo, the Grzimeks warned that it would be impossible to force locals to remain "primitive" inside the new park. If given the right to stay in the Serengeti, they predicted, the Maasai would quickly abandon their role as "children of nature," by refusing to "hunt with bows and arrows" and incorporating "imported motor-cars into the National Parks . . . [and covering] . . . their roofs with tin cut from petrol canisters."[41] Like the Mbuti they had met in the Congo, the Maasai would eventually be corrupted by modernity—and turn off visitors expecting *shuka*-clad cattle herders and thatched *bomas*.[42] Both Pearsall and the Grzimeks reinforced these arguments by noting that bovine vaccination campaigns—particularly against rinderpest—would leave "no natural brakes" on the number of cattle, leading to an inevitable clash with wild animals over resources and space.[43] For the Grzimeks, national parks should remain an open-air zoo dedicated to the welfare and observation of animals, not people.[44]

One way to resolve the conflicts between metropolitan and local officials was to concentrate administration in the hands of an impartial body of superintendents. The 1948 national parks ordinance created an autonomous governing body, the Serengeti National Park Board of Trustees, to oversee its administration.[45] The board comprised seventeen seats, including three ex-officio members—the local territorial administrator, the park's game warden, and the chief conservator of forests—who proved particularly vocal in the debates of the 1950s due to a growing conviction that Tanganyika's forest reserves were under siege by fire-wielding peasants and pastoralists.[46] The trustees then appointed a board of management to oversee the park's day-to-day operations. Tanganyika's Arusha-based chief game warden served as that board's chairman, alongside a park warden whose residence was located near the visitors' camp at Ngorongoro and who oversaw a small staff of assistant game wardens and park scouts.[47] The board of management drew upon the competencies of the game, forest, and geological departments and was designed to stand above partisan squabbles—a noble dream that quickly dissolved amid the competing goals of international conservation lobbies, centralized administrators, district officials, and rural Africans.

The board found itself ill-equipped to establish standardized operating procedures in an unruly landscape of highly variable topography, diverse biotopes, and most importantly a climate that refused to cooperate in conservation schemes premised on maintaining a harmonious balance between wild animals and livestock.[48] To be sure, colonial officers were well aware of climatic oscillations that made the Serengeti appear degraded and denuded during drought times and lush and verdant in just a few years once rains returned.[49] But during the early 1950s, an extended dry spell followed the foundation of the Serengeti National Park, spurring Maasai from surrounding districts to bring their herds into the park in search of forage and water.[50] In 1953, for example, rainfall amounts plummeted from a normal average of 30.4 inches to only 18.4 inches.[51] Government attempts to divert the Maasai away from the park by boring water holes outside the Serengeti boundaries failed because the water became too salty.[52] As water holes salinized and wild pastures withered, Maasai herders from around the region followed a long-established transhumant pattern of moving their herds from low-lying plains to find dry season pasture in the well-watered Ngorongoro Crater Highlands that lay inside the park's official boundaries.[53] This movement put them on a collision course with forestry officials trying to protect these upland forests from human incursion, as well as European farmers who had recently gained access to these prized lands after a series of land alienations designed to "free" these parcels for agricultural development.

As the Maasai moved deeper into the highlands and other sectors, conservationists feared that their temporary adjustments to the parched conditions were causing irreparable damage to wildlife habitat, spurring fears that another high plains dustbowl was imminent.[54] In some places, the Grzimeks feared, the Maasai were preventing thirsty herds of wild animals from reaching watering places by fencing them off for use by their own cattle.[55] They also built new boma compounds with high fences of thorn scrub to protect herds at night against predators, a practice that many worried would exacerbate the scarcity of trees. On leaving their bomas in search of new grazing areas, the Maasai would then burn the huts and the thorn fences, killing off acacia woodlands in the Serengeti hills. The Grzimeks believed such practices had destroyed a once-mighty forest that covered the region before the arrival of pastoralists, not recognizing that the area was a shifting woodland-savanna and not a remnant of the rainforests they had encountered in Central Africa.[56]

Quarrels over water holes, burning practices, and woodlots led to countless skirmishes between herders and park wardens, all of which eventually filtered up to the board and, in some cases, the central colonial government in Dar es Salaam.[57] Maasai leaders were dismayed by their lack of representation in the capital and rejected proposals to limit their activities and cattle stocks given that the decline in wildlife had been caused by European hunters in the first place.[58] "We let the wild animals live in peace," noted dismayed Maasai representatives that the Grzimeks encountered. "Only last week we saw a safari with a car load of antlers and lion skins, yet they forbid us to hunt lions."[59] As a result, the board found itself quite unexpectedly preoccupied with "constant and vexatious clashes of interest" regarding the status of human inhabitants, rather than its original remit of managing "natural" resources.[60] Indeed, by early 1954, the board of managers admitted that the 1951 ordinance was completely out of sync with local conditions and that its members were overwhelmed by the tasks at hand.[61]

A good portion of the board's exasperation stemmed from the park's competing mandates and confusion over which historical baseline—pre-Maasai, precolonial, post-1919, or 1951—represented the most desirable state of the Serengeti to which national park managers should calibrate their preservation efforts. The FPS recommendations and the Grzimeks' scientific investigations started from the 1933 Convention's premise that the park's primary goal was to demarcate the borders necessary to protect animal migration routes. In the ground reports from this era, however, Tanganyikan administrators focused primarily on the provision of tourist amenities.[62] The protectorate's officials recognized that the Serengeti encompassed breathtaking scenery, geological landmarks, archaeological treasures, and historic rangelands—a hybrid form that did not conform easily to international standards of a strict reserve.

As Chairman of the Serengeti Board of Trustees Barclay Leechman explained in a 1954 article, the Serengeti merged the features of former game reserves such as Kruger with the sublime scenery usually associated with North American parks such as Grand Canyon—a unique mix that made administration challenging. The Ngorongoro Crater, with its two-thousand-foot sheer cliffs, was an "astonishing feature" that was "worthy of protection" even if it did not contain any animal life. Another geological wonder was the Olduvai Gorge, a thirty-mile, 295-foot crevasse which snaked across the eastern plains; nearby were two enormous volcanic sandhills whose black, crescent shapes appeared like shadows moving across the earth's surface. At Olduvai, Louis Leakey had discovered a treasure trove of fossils dating back 250 million years, adding to the park's archaeological significance.[63] Once his wife Mary discovered the two-billion-year-old fossils of the hominid *Zinjanthropus boisei* (popularly called "Nutcracker Man") in 1959, interest in the human evolutionary history of the Serengeti soared as scientists recognized that East Africa might be the birthplace of the human race.[64] Park administrators had already commissioned projects to attract visitors to these features. The National Park Camp at Ngorongoro contained comfortable beds with ample drinking water supplies and park employees had built earthen dams designed to attract animals near the roads where tourists could view them more easily.[65] Park administrators called for the extension of paved roads all the way to the western corridor and had also made plans for a new campground at Naabi Hill.[66] Bernhard Grzimek often took credit for inaugurating tourism to East Africa, but his efforts built upon these late colonial efforts to transform nature into a package of "sights" for middle-class visitors.

Leechman's emphasis on a multifaceted visitor experience reflected territorial administrators' hope that tourism would generate substantial foreign currency and reinvigorate imperial networks. Kenya, Uganda, and Tanganyika banded together to establish the East Africa Tourist Travel Association (EATTA) in 1947, a consortium of travel, shipping, airline, and hotel companies charged with promoting visitation to the area and freeing up visa requirements. The EATTA estimated that tourists generated about £5.5 million in revenues for East Africa (about $15.3 million), with the largest share, £3 million, going to Kenya. Only cotton, coffee, and sisal brought more revenue to East Africa, and tourist receipts outpaced revenues from tea, cashew nuts, pyrethrum extract, gold, and meat combined—enough to pay for all of the three colonies' imports of food. Most strikingly, the EATTA statistics showed that less than 10 percent of the approximately twenty thousand Europeans and Americans who visited Kenya in 1952 bought hunting licenses, despite the "glamor" of the safari industry. If the territories could generate £3 million with so few hunters, they stood to gain enormous sums just by protecting their wildlife stocks for passive viewing. Outside consultants recommended that all three territories should rapidly

expand their number of national parks and put them under centralized administration that resembled the US National Park Service.[67]

Many district officers doubted the Serengeti's tourist potential. Unlike Kruger
and Hluhluwe in South Africa, the Serengeti lacked a European population with
easy rail or automobile access.[68] There were no hotels outside Dar es Salaam,
Arusha, and Tanga, no reliable roads to the parks, and the railroads in the region
had been built for cargo, not tourist passengers. Nonetheless, after the war, the
British placed renewed emphasis on tourism as a potential way to build trade
networks and affective communities across the remaining parts of the empire.[69]
As a 1948 guidebook to Tanganyika explained, jet air services from Air France
and other carriers, along with cheaper steamship travel and the wider availability of autos for hire, were enabling middle-class visitors only "vaguely aware" of
different parts of the empire to visit and appreciate the colonies.[70] The spread of
commercial air service and lingering British war debt—which the Americans
insisted be paid in dollars—also pushed the Colonial Office to make East Africa
an especially friendly place for those willing to spend the world's currency liber-
ally.[71] Though the EATTA's main function was to promote the region's attractions
abroad, the organization soon began to lobby governments to defend wildlife
as a tourist asset, reporting instances of "native slaughter" to game departments
and creating another layer of pressure on the districts.[72] The Serengeti emerged
as a national park amid this conservation boom fueled in part by tourism development and postwar debt.

Though the Grzimeks tended to dismiss African "tribespeople" as corrupted,
the iconic Maasai were initially considered valuable to this tourism mission.
British park administrators seemed ready to integrate the story of the Maasai
into their exhibits and public outreach. In 1950, the territorial governor emphasized that the Maasai were akin to "a museum exhibit, living in a kind of human
national park," while the commissioner of the Northern Province noted Maasai
herding in the Ngorongoro were "the most interesting feature of the crater for
tourists to photograph."[73] In his 1954 article, Leechman noted sympathetically
that the Maasai were not truly "nomads" but developed a strong sense of place
in their chosen area, moving deliberately and with acuity according to changing
seasons, rainfall patterns, grazing opportunities, and especially water supplies—
traits we now recognize as essential to "transhumant" versus "nomadic"
pastoralism.[74]

When the Europeans first entered the region, Leechman asserted, they
encountered one section of the wave of pastoralists that had moved down the
Great Rift Valley from Ethiopia in the previous century, a group that he called
the "Saleh" Maasai—a name that still exists for the broad plains beyond the Gol
Mountains north of the Ngorongoro Highlands.[75] Unlike Grzimek and Turner,
who insisted that the Maasai rarely entered the "thirst lands" of the Central Plains

before European contact, Leechman claimed the Saleh had occupied a broad swath of the Serengeti Plains, the Ngorongoro Crater, and the Crater Highlands in the 1860s and 1870s (see Figure 4.3). The time of troubles between 1890 and 1900, however, brought "ruin and starvation" and dispersed the original Saleh "tribe" over a broader section of what was to become German East Africa. Though Leechman missed the complex political alliances that made up the "Maasai" polity—Purko, Kisongo, Loitai, and Kaputiei—his account allowed for a more expansive conception of Maasai identities and ancestral domains than those of many contemporaries.[76]

Such depictions of the Saleh living amid the game before European contact suggested different potential baselines for understanding pastoralists' role in the Serengeti ecosystem. For Leechman, 1919—the year of the formal British takeover—offered a flexible benchmark for discussions of human-wildlife numbers and customary rights in the Serengeti.[77] After World War I, he noted, Maasai from across the region began to reoccupy former traditional areas, including many "newcomers" from Kenya who no longer found much policing of the border between two British protectorates.[78] Yet throughout the interwar era, Leechman argued, Maasai numbers remained low by historical standards due to rinderpest followed by decades of German mismanagement. The British maintained that German compulsory labor schemes, the seizure of too much land for the Kaiser, and the deployment of *akida* military officers from the Swahili coast as district administrators had destroyed "native tribal society" and discouraged the organic evolution of "native authority" based on African political conceptions and traditions.[79] The Serengeti border questions offered an opportunity to correct some of these mistakes of the past by reuniting the Maasai "tribes" with their traditional lands. Leechman and others noted that both the Ngorongoro and Embagai Craters showed signs of long-term human occupation and had served as places of sanctuary during times of drought and disease, with Maasai living "more or less permanently" in both craters and roaming less widely from them than pastoralists in other parts of the savannas.[80]

In a similar vein, the rural sociologist Henry Fosbrooke noted that many of the letters lamenting the overstocking of Maasai herds or their burning practices stemmed from personal recollections from the 1920s and 1930s. But in the interwar decades, he noted, Maasai and cattle numbers were at their nadir due to rinderpest epidemics. Previously, Fosbrooke claimed, the Maasai had occupied both the Serengeti and the Ngorongoro regions, covering the whole of the Serengeti plains "up to the fly bush on the West and the area to the north up to the Mara River." When the game reserve boundaries were first delineated in the 1930s, he noted, there were likely no Maasai in the area because the populations had yet to recover—what was taken as wilderness was a product of the expansion of tsetse-infested bushlands on fire-managed historic rangelands.[81] It was thus no accident, in Fosbrooke's view, that the twentieth century's largest populations of large mammals were concentrated in pastoralist rangelands that included people, for human incursions were among the many perturbations that kept the overall system diverse and resilient.[82] Fosbrooke's assessment raised a more important question: were the Maasai "incursions" actually a re-population of former herding territories and thus entirely natural? Unlike the Grzimeks, most colonial officials accepted, even if begrudgingly, that the Ngorongoro region—the "natural zoo" featured in Serengeti Shall Not Die—was also the Maasai's Serengeti homeland.

Inventing Traditions: The Pastoral Myth

Despite these gestures toward recognizing customary tenure, the efforts to reestablish "ancestral" tribal lands in the Serengeti built on decades of distrust stemming from native rule advocates' earlier efforts to demarcate a Maasailand pastoral reserve on the basis of specious "ethnic" characteristics and to authorize land alienations that favored peasants and cash crop production.[83] In the Grzimeks' field reports, the two scientists mentioned briefly these historical injustices, noting that the Tanganyikan government's "concessions" to the Maasai reflected a sense of obligation toward the "formerly warlike tribe," which had been violently "pacified" after the Germans took over. The Grzimeks recounted one incident of cattle raider arrest in which German colonial administrators had "shot a few hundred robbing and murdering young warriors in all their ostrich-feathered glory, in order to teach the others not to regard the negro tribes as ol nantinda, or savages."[84] Indeed, they correctly surmised the reason why there were so many new arrivals in the 1950s: a cumulative loss of grazing land resulting from decades of being pressed further south due to dubious treaties and land grabs.[85] Yet neither the Grzimeks nor sympathetic British officials realized how much they still indulged in the same baseless and romanticized portraits of the Maasai as "wild sons of the steppe" even as they tried to understand past land-use disputes and injustices.[86]

Pastoralist mobilities had long been a vexing problem for colonial officials who were determined to lay the foundations of an African smallholding peasant society. Alienating Maasai grazing territory had served as another tool for "pacifying" and "modernizing" the Maasai by turning their land over to more "productive" African and European agriculturalists.[87] In 1904, the Maasai of British East Africa had concluded a treaty with the British in the hopes of protecting ancestral lands, only to have the treaty broken seven years later as thousands were evicted from well-watered pastures to a "Maasai Reserve" in the southern part of Kenya—a loss of over 50 percent of their former territory.[88] Once British administrators moved to Tanganyika in 1919, their view of the Maasai as "beautiful Spartans" who pillaged their neighbors was one of the many questionable stereotypes used to sift out the elements of a "tribe" from the confusing patchwork of peoples they encountered in north-central Tanganyika and contain it within a newly demarcated "Masai Reserve" for that territory.[89] Conflicts with the Maasai about their status within the national park built upon the mistrust associated with this long history of colonial land alienations.

According to ethnographers who assisted with the creation of Tanganyika's Reserve, the Maasai lived an isolated pastoral existence and only rarely traded their cattle for the "fruit and grain of their agricultural neighbors"—never taking up farming themselves or resorting to hunting beyond an occasional eland or buffalo for food or a single lion or rhino as a symbol of bravery.[90] This formulation unfortunately overlooked the many Maa speakers in the region who did cultivate crops and the complex economic and cultural interdependencies between Maa-speaking pastoralists on the plains, Bantu-speaking farmers in the eastern highlands (particularly Arusha and Meru peoples), and Okiek-speaking hunters and gatherers in the forests of the region.[91] Such attempts to "ethnicize" occupational roles, alienate land, and restrict Maasai movements cut the herders off from ceremonial woodland sites, potential marriage partners, and cultural collaborators. Restrictions on movement, moreover, threatened Maasai access to cultivable lands and dry season preserves vital to making do in times of drought, disease, or other ecological stress.[92] This vision of ethnicity also justified European settlers in taking over seemingly underutilized highland forests and mountaintop watering holes and then renting these parcels back to local Maasai at high prices.[93] Not surprisingly, many Maasai herders refused to recognize the boundaries of the Masai Reserve and the attempt to criminalize their movements as "trespass," resulting in constant clashes with district officials throughout the 1920s and 1930s.[94] Colonial officials insisted it was the historical anomalies caused by war and German negligence that led pastoralists to leave the reserve in search of pasturage, water, or exchanges with neighboring peoples, rather than the "natural" order of things.[95] No one considered that traditional pastoralists—and not just the wild animals favored by the 1933 convention—needed sufficient space to find resources, build social networks, and secure shelter in a semiarid environment.[96]

Those Maasai who did not migrate out of Maasailand and tried to eke out a living inside the reserve often found themselves labeled a hindrance to rural development: obstinate, lazy, and untrustworthy "misers" who refused to sell their cattle to the African peasants that the British considered the backbone of an agricultural society.[97] Following the misguided theories of American anthropologist Melville Herskovits, many colonial administrators believed that the Maasai suffered from a "cattle complex" that led to an "irrational" accumulation of cattle as status symbols.[98] They were convinced that such overstocking created bloated stocks of "gaunt," unmarketable cows and discouraged private investment in land; the herders could never move into a "higher" stage of development without selling off "superfluous" cattle.[99] The environmental impact was even more alarming. "Scrub cattle," they argued, turned communal grasslands into dust as the emaciated bovines trampled fragile soils and overgrazed vulnerable pastures.[100] Officials knew that the Maasai vigorously bartered cattle for other goods, but without a cash transaction, colonial officials could not tax the income generated or keep records of agricultural products. The Grzimeks added that Maasai customs made it difficult to negotiate terms of occupancy that would limit such damage. The Maasai could not be fully trusted, they claimed, since the herders "hold that honour, decency and love only apply between Masai," which made it permissible to "lie to strangers, simulate friendliness and break treaties."[101] The Maasai also seemed to eschew chiefs in favor of lengthy democratic councils, making it impossible to get firm agreements about access to water holes or abandoning stretches of grasslands for wildlife.[102]

With the onset of the technocratic Second Colonial Occupation after 1945, making the drylands "productive" became a top priority for administrators and wildlife scientists. Like the Belgians, the British found themselves under fire by American and Soviet critics of imperialism in the wake of World War II, particularly after India and Pakistan achieved their independence in 1947–1948. The British were also deeply in debt to the American government, resulting in a contradictory program that extended welfare statism to African colonies yet exploited their resources more aggressively.[103] The United Kingdom also underscored its obligations under the UN Mandate to shepherd the Tanganyika Territory toward independence in three to four decades. Under the aegis of the Colonial Development and Welfare Act of 1940, many officials embraced a more scientific approach to land management that included land terracing to prevent erosion and cattle dipping to prevent infectious diseases.[104] In Maasailand, British experts promoted the Maasai Development Plan, which they hoped would dismantle the "cattle complex" and convince the Maasai to adopt sedentary lifestyles as ranchers.[105] Colonial officials cleared tsetse bush, constructed dams, drilled boreholes for steady supplies of water, and set up district livestock auction sites in the hopes of enticing the Maasai to sell off excess cattle, bolster the stock of fattened and disease-free cows, and enter the cash economy.[106] The colonial government's aggressive use of bovine inoculations, along with traps and insecticides against tsetse, did allow the Maasai to slowly reoccupy ancestral territories by setting fire to the infested brush and opening up additional lands to grazing.[107] When such increases in livestock and people put stress on individual rangelands, many conservationists failed to connect the resulting environmental problems to the previous reduction of the Maasai's grazing territory and instead blamed Maasai mismanagement for environmental deterioration caused by colonial land alienations in the first place.[108]

The Grzimeks' references to the historical injustices of British colonialism stopped short of analyzing the explosive political situation that led the Tanganyikan officials to delay Maasai evictions: the rising tide of African nationalism fueled by the politics of land rights. In 1951, for example, the same year that the Serengeti's boundaries were finally set, the Mau Mau Emergency was declared in Kenya, just a three-hour drive from Seronera. The fighting there between the African Land and Freedom Armies and the colonial government continued throughout the first phase of unrest in the Serengeti, making it particularly precarious to advocate for unpopular land alienations. Colonial officials worried about the potential spread of Mau Mau sentiments to northern Tanganyika—and not without reason. Kikuyu farmers brought from Kenya as laborers to the region established contacts with evictees from the Serengeti through the Kilimanjaro Citizens' Union, a group advocating for black citizenship rights in Tanganyika. Government officials feared that "Kikuyu-Maasai half breeds" were smuggling guns and ammunition to Maasai warriors, which might lead to outright rebellion if land was confiscated for conservation purposes.[109]

The threat of Mau Mau "infection" was heightened as a result of land disputes arising from forced evictions that also began in 1951 east of the Serengeti region, in the foothills of Mount Meru. In that year, the Tanganyika government expelled and destroyed the property of hundreds of Meru peasant farmers to make way for yet another dubious European plantation scheme.[110] Because Tanganyika was a UN Mandate territory, Meru Citizen Union leader Kirilo Japhet, with the help of jurist Earle Seaton from Moshi, petitioned the UN Visiting Mission to Tanganyika to assert that the evictions violated the British mandate's charge to develop the health and welfare of the territory's African inhabitants.[111] Later, the pair appeared in New York to lobby the United Nations to declare the evictions a human rights violation.[112] The Meru Land Case brought teams of international observers to conduct hundreds of interviews with local inhabitants. The interviews revealed ongoing British mismanagement of and local grievances toward a government that was supposed to be paving the way for independence. Residents of the territory resented the myriad conservation interventions—from land alienation to cattle dipping—that contravened local practices.[113] Though the Meru were not successful in getting back their land, the investigations exposed the failures of the supposedly benign Second Colonial Occupation and served as a lightning rod for Nyerere's fledgling independence movement to fire up support in the provinces.[114] An official concerned with the Serengeti border controversies declared that a forced eviction of the Maasai would be impossible "with the Meru problem hanging over our heads."[115]

Given the challenges to British rule around the Serengeti, the board of management seemed even more determined to freeze conditions inside it to conform to the Edenic harmony of a national park.[116] In the new conservationist regime, mundane and customary land-use practices that once barely raised an eyebrow, such as controlled burning, small-plot agriculture, woodlot collecting, and the use of scrub trees for boma construction, became "crimes against nature."[117] The chief conservator of forests accused the Maasai of flouting the 1940 Game Ordinance by illegally setting fires "with malicious intent," by brazenly de-barking cedar trees, and truculently injuring forest guards with spears.[118] Such montane woodlands were critical catchment areas for water supplies throughout the plains, the conservator noted, but the Maasai "despoiled" them during droughts by bringing their thirsty cattle and goats into the forests and carelessly setting fires that raged out of control, destroying many "first schedule" trees ready for harvest.[119] Turner found a similar worrying scene when he took over as warden in 1956. Turner depicted human inhabitants "encroaching to within eight miles of Seronera" in the heart of the park and accused Maasai herdsmen of cutting down the iconic yellow-barked *Acacia xanthophlea* trees along the river and allowing their domesticated dogs to chase after Thomson's gazelle.[120] More ominously, he accused young Maasai warriors of spearing lions around the Moru Kopjes, a region beloved by tourists for the spectacular granite formations that thrust up from the sea of grass, often providing a midday resting spot for the felines (see Figure 4.3). Visitors to the park in the 1950s complained that they were horrified to see so many cattle and so few wild animals in the park and along the Ngorongoro Crater rim. This was an unfortunate consequence of a cattle market being located close to their lodgings, not a massive displacement of wildlife by cattle.[121] Vilified for insufficiently "modernizing" outside the park and chastised for not being harmonious "noble savages" within it, the Maasai found themselves in an administrative morass created by conflicting visions of land and indigeneity that mirrored and exacerbated the precariousness of British control.

It is unclear if local Maasai had set such fires with "malicious intent," since igniting grasslands and woodlands was critical to pastoralists' manipulation of vegetation growth and helped to rid settlement areas of disease-bearing ticks. Fire burned away rough forage unpalatable to both livestock and wild species and opened up parklike forest glades in the highlands to sweet new grasses.[122] Without these measures, woodlands and thorny bush conducive to the reproduction of tsetse flies grew rapidly. Africans knew these focal points of infection and avoided them; in other cases, Maasai cattle ate the young sprouts of these scrub trees, thereby keeping the habitat for the tsetse in check.[123] Abandoned Maasai boma sites also left behind a ring of nutrient-rich patches created by human and animal dung—a factor that sometimes led Europeans to assume that soils all around were suitable for agriculture.[124] On such legacy landscapes, new grasses and patches of woodland often grew atop an otherwise featureless landscape, expanding shade trees and enriching the soil.[125] Drought conditions also tended to set an upper limit on the number of cattle roaming the plains. Severe dry conditions stressed or even killed livestock, forcing the Maasai to sell off their cattle at markets; indeed, by 1953 the number of cattle in the national park area had dropped from around 140,000 in 1950 to only 113,000, despite the availability of rinderpest inoculations.[126] Doomsday scenarios predicting millions of cattle lost and grasslands turning into deserts were overblown, since rainfall, rather than grazing levels, determined the productivity of grasslands.[127]

Misguided understandings of African tribalism and the agrarian biases of the colonial administration reinforced misaligned environmental expectations guided by fixed notions of "carrying capacity." The depiction of the Maasai as nomadic destroyers, for example, disregarded the myriad adaptations of pastoral peoples to grazing cattle in a shifting, semiarid mosaic of woodlands and grasslands that never settled down into a state of equilibrium. Far from being short-sighted opportunists constantly on the hunt for "greener pastures," Maasai herders monitored environmental conditions in one grassland to detect early signs of deterioration and then moved their livestock to a different location.[128] As Pearsall himself attested, "while the Maasai are accused by some of causing serious overgrazing and soil erosion, others commend them for employing proper methods of land-use, moving their cattle towards a water-hole on one day and away from it on the subsequent one."[129] They used a host of indicators to make the decision to move on: the quality of forage grasses, the daily milk yield and coat texture of livestock, the consistency of cattle dung, and the movement of the herbivorous wild animals. The Maasai also bred livestock selectively to develop strains suited to the plains and systematically and gradually exposed their stock to tsetse-infested bush to develop more disease-resistant strains.[130] A variety of devices proscribed overgrazing on communal lands as well— including storytelling, religious beliefs, and social rebuke—and Maasai oral histories embraced a "live and let live" policy toward wildlife that congregated near cattle and goats.[131] This did not mean that the Maasai's activities were always beneficent. Small field fires set by peasants or beeswax collectors got out of hand, herders killed animals that threatened their families of livestock, and overgrazing in local areas did sometimes result in a carpet of woody, unpalatable plants on formerly nutrient-rich grasslands.[132] Yet such subsistence activities paled in comparison to the damage of raising cattle alone in a limited area—as European colonial officials hoped many Maasai would do—which did reduce the savannas to dust. In this sense, the very mobilities that vexed colonial officials offered the best chance for the resilient denizens of the savannas to recover and flourish.[133]

Despite such evidence of sustainable traditional use, many forestry officials rejected the notion that either drought or previous land alienations were the cause of Maasai "incursions" into the highland forests and continued to blame overstocking instead. One assistant conservator noted with alarm that Maasai cattle numbers were "stocked far above the capacity of the land." Citing a stock inspector's report, the official claimed that the Maasai had roughly 175,000 cattle and 175,000 "small stock" (such as goats) in the region, which were growing at a per annum rate of 10 percent, while only 3.5 percent of the animals died or were auctioned or sold off at markets.[134] Only an immediate, forced culling of the stock to around ten to twenty-thousand head, he warned, could avert permanent destruction of the region's main water supply.[135] Those district officers who defended the Maasai's right to use the forests during drought were accused of suffering from "Masaiitis," which blinded them to the fact that overgrazing, not drought, was the true culprit in land-use clashes in the parklands.[136] "Humans and a National Park cannot exist together" was the conclusion of one board member. "Why Tanganyika should be considered an exception to this rule I cannot understand . . . unless the policy of the government and the Trustees reverts to the original idea of gradually removing all human occupants except those on duty in the park, there will be no Park or no reserve worth troubling about."[137] Either Serengeti needed to be managed as a National Park on the Yellowstone or Belgian models, or it should be downgraded to a "National Reserve" that included permanent human habitation—and face the negative publicity from the FPS and others that such a move would entail.[138]

The controversies over forest access, injuries to patrolmen, visitor complaints, and overgrazing coupled with the rancorous exchanges between the board of management and the board of trustees about aboriginal rights left the status of the Serengeti as a national park in serious doubt by 1953. In a series of circulars to district officials, Leechman warned the park's managers that in light of the prevailing political situation in East Africa, "all incidents must be avoided at all costs. If more occurred, the Park would have to cease to exist."[139] E. F. Twinning, the Governor of Tanganyika in Dar es Salaam, also underscored the urgent need for a solution to the problem of aboriginal land rights in a national park. He stated that the lack of mutual understanding between park officials and local Africans called into doubt the entire UN Mandate to preserve the park "for the benefit of all inhabitants of the territory" while also "protecting the rights of minorities" and "promoting good government and advancement of all people in the territory." If the board of management could not balance these competing interests, Twinning warned, then "I should not hesitate to rescind the Proclamation whereby the Serengeti National Park was declared."[140] Far from having preserved a small corner of paradise, the administrative landscape created by the new national park became a battleground over competing visions of conservation, pastoral land rights, and regional ecology: one in which both "nature" and "primitive" peoples appeared unruly, capricious, and unmanageable.

"Full-Blooded Maasai": Racializing Customary Land Rights, 1954-1956

Desperate to find a middle ground that could save the Serengeti from losing its prized national park status, the board of trustees weighed proposals ranging from draconian new restrictions on remaining inhabitants to de-gazetting large portions of the park to make room for pastoralists as the crisis reached its crescendo in the mid-1950s. Board members noted that no other country had found a "final solution" to the difficulties of human inhabitation inside a national park, but they remained determined to find a compromise.[141] In 1954, the board moved to remove all cultivators from the park and drastically cull cattle and goat herds in order to match the land's carrying capacity. There was no indication in the original ordinance that cultivation was incompatible with the goals of the park; indeed, the 1948 document stated that "nothing shall interfere . . . . with the rights of any person in or over any land acquired before the commencement of ordinance."[142] To justify the alienation of Maasai cultivators and other African farmers, British ethnographers, aided in part by the Grzimeks, fixated on racial criteria for belonging that implied that cultivators were latecomers to the savannas, thus limiting customary grazing access to only a handful of "full-blooded" Maasai pastoralists. The assumption behind this new strategy was that there were precious few indigenous Maasai left in the park due to inter-tribal "mixing" after the rinderpest "plague" at the turn of the century. "It was beneath the dignity of the true Masai to cultivate," asserted one official, since he was a "nomad who lived entirely on his flocks and herds."[143] Leechman insisted that a reconstitution of the original ordinance was possible if those living within the park would confine their activities to their "normal and traditional avocation as pastoralists" and "if those having acknowledged rights in the Park come to have complete confidence that those rights will be left inviolate."[144] Under this supposedly more enlightened policy, racial reconstruction was a beneficent act that authentic Maasai would recognize as impartial—a prelude to securing their permission to impose limits on cattle numbers and activities inside the park.

The British had long been concerned that rural-urban migrations and the mixing of ethnicities inside of Tanganyika Territory had not facilitated the appropriate "evolution of different types" necessary for tribal authorities to flourish. The Maasai, one observer noted in 1920, were of a "Hamitic stock" who had unfortunately "communicated something of their blood and culture" to the Bantu "tribes."[145] Leechman recognized that it had long been customary for the Maasai to adopt children, especially boys, or to take wives from neighboring tribes. But the scattering of the Maasai following the rinderpest epidemics had resulted in ever more "admixture" from farming communities, particularly the nearby Meru

Table 5.1 **Bounding Nature: Serengeti Controversies, 1940–1961**

1940	Colonial Development and Welfare Act
1948	Revised National Parks Ordinance creates Serengeti National Park with independent board of trustees
1951	Tanganyika Game Department gazettes Serengeti National Park
1951	Meru Land Evictions at Ngare Nanyuki begin
1954	Board of Trustees votes to remove cultivators from the Serengeti
1956	Tanganyikan Government proposes revised borders for Serengeti that would divide the park into three small conservation zones
1956	Pearsall submits report to Serengeti Committee of Enquiry
1957	Grzimeks' aerial surveys begin
1958	Maasai evacuate the central plains
1959	January: Michael Grzimek killed in a plane crash
	December: Ngorongoro Crater and Highlands shorn from the park; *Serengeti Shall Not Die* appears as a film and a book
1960	Ngorongoro Conservation Area (NCA) created; Turnbull promises human priorities will prevail
1961	September: Arusha Conference on Nature and Natural Resources in Modern African States
	December: Tanganyikan independence declared

and Arusha. "There is a considerable number of persons who have lived all of their lives as 'Masai,'" Leechman averred, "but who have no true Masai blood in them"—leaving only a handful of aged individuals who could trace their ancestry to the once mighty Saleh.[146] Echoing the interwar rhetoric used to define the Masai Reserve, this ethnic mythology maintained that "true" Maasai and Wa-Arusha had lived segregated lives prior to European occupation, with the Maasai keeping to the plains and the Arusha to Mount Meru.[147]

Yet there had always been a "strong tendency" among the Arusha and others to assimilate Maasai customs and social structure even if they had little to no Maasai "blood" in them. This portrait of precolonial isolationism made little sense given the long history of economic, cultural, and familial exchange between these groups and others in the plains.[148] Pastoralists had long sought to maintain a wide circle of exchange and marriage partners by inviting agricultural or hunter-gatherer neighbors within their age-sets. In addition, it was common for farmers to marry pastoral women and adopt pastoral men into their lineages.[149] The 1950s offered both pastoralists and cultivators in the Serengeti region an

opportunity to recover historic ties lost due to earlier epidemics, land alienations, and economic depression. Such a flexible definition of Maasai identity,
however, violated the invented traditions of indigeneity. Government ethnographers and sociologists lamented that "Maasai" had degenerated into a mere "cultural category" used to describe any group living a customary Maasai lifestyle.[150]
Colonial officials also worried that the Maasai harbored "undesirable traders"
and about a hundred families of Maa-speaking Wadorobo hunter-gatherers, who
kept an additional ten thousand head of cattle in the Moru Kopjes and western
Serengeti.[151]

According to Leechman, another factor leading to Maasai racial mixing had
been the land hunger in the highland regions north of the park, which led many
"cultivating tribesmen" to stream into the park after World War II. Such southward movement, Leechman claimed, had exacerbated the drought of 1952 and
1953 and the outbreak of tick-borne diseases in the Endulen grasslands east of
the crater, both of which had led the Maasai to keep their herds of cattle concentrated in the Crater Highlands (see Figure 4.3). While the government could
do little to control the unruly weather and diseases that were endemic to the
savannas, it could deal with the "interlopers" who had infiltrated the park and
set up agricultural plots. "These persons certainly have no traditional right to be
in the Park," Leechman asserted, "and their cultivation is much more detrimen-
tal to the preservation of the natural features of the Park than is the controlled
presence of livestock."[152] Other members of the board echoed this sentiment,
noting how few "true Masai" were left in the region even as the number of cultivators was skyrocketing due to fewer intertribal conflicts and improved medical
and veterinary services.[153] By 1954, then, questions about racial purity added
another layer of complexity and rancor to an already fraught search for an ecological fix to the land rights question.

Leechman blamed the movement of Arusha and Meru into Maasailand as a
result of "overpopulation" in their districts, an explanation that ignored decades
of land evictions from the rich volcanic soils and well-watered fields of the Meru
Highlands. To make way for European settlers in the years between 1896 and
1900, for example, the German colonial administration had confiscated lands and
cattle, burned down banana groves, broken up families, and introduced forced
labor and taxation schemes that drove the Arusha and Meru to seek work on
European plantations.[154] Such dispossession constrained the Meru to the upper
slopes of the mountain, south of a forest reserve that confined them behind an
"iron ring of alienated lands."[155] While the British had expelled the German owners in 1920—in some cases even selling the estates back to Meru farmers—they
had repopulated the majority of these prized lands with Greek and British settlers, all the while depicting the severe land famine among the Meru as a consequence of "human congestion" and "wasteful" cattle husbandry.[156] In 1946,

a committee of inquiry looking into land rights near Meru concluded that the "germ of the solution" to the "surplus population" was to *come down from the mountain with their stock and seek their future on the plains*" while the government secretly prepared to transfer remaining Meru lands to European settlers.[157]

In a cruel paradox, just eight years later, coming down from the mountain marked the Arusha and Meru as ethnic trespassers on Serengeti territory designated for pastoralists only. Leechman promised to commission an administrative officer right away who "had previous experience among the Masai" to use "careful enquiry" to distinguish between the "interlopers" and those who "are rightfully in the Park." The government would then need to find a suitable place for resettling the cultivators outside the boundaries of the park, although Leechman offered few specifics about where that place would be.[158] In 1953, the District Officer from Monduli, Henry S. Grant, estimated the number of such "lawful" residents at 7,357 persons—only about 5 percent of the estimated 140,000 believed to inhabit the Serengeti region in 1948.[159] In just a generation or two, Leechman noted wistfully, rural Africans would evolve in such a way that they would understand the higher "motives behind the creation of a national park" and the desirability of "preserving [certain natural features] for posterity." But for such lofty sentiments were quite beyond "comparatively primitive peoples" hungry for arable lands.[160]

The Grzimeks' published field notes indicated that "agriculturalists were removed from the crater without great difficulty at the end of 1954," but in actuality the ordinances exacerbated the shortage of the productive lands around the region. The ban fell hard on the Arusha and Meru who had begun cultivating bananas, coffee, maize, and beans in the Meru foothills near the park's boundaries. It also affected agro-pastoralists in the western districts of the park, such as the Sukuma, who found themselves cut off from lands for farming, hunting, and herding.[161] In a divide-and-rule strategy, the government attempted to avoid fueling anticolonial flames of such a radical decision by getting the Maasai Native Authority to give the notice of eviction to Ndorobo hunters, who were deported from the park in 1955.[162] Grant and other sympathetic district officials objected to further evictions, admonishing the government at the very least to provide a suitable "reception area" for evictees that did not remove them from access to the Maasai, since "many of the [WaArusha and WaMeru] have relatives by marriage among the local Maasai" and wanted to remain close to their "pastoralist relatives."[163] The government's proposed relocation site near Endulen, was "hot and malarious" and unsuitable for persons "used to living at a high altitude in healthy, malaria-free country."[164] For those Maasai permitted to stay in the park, the government devised a "bill of rights" that banned fire and cultivation because these were deemed to be "foreign" to pastoralist peoples.[165] Not surprisingly, the bill used crude stereotypes about African tribalism to impose a vision of pastoralism in which the Maasai could not use any modern weapons or firearms; they were restricted to carrying spears, swords, clubs, bows, and arrows as befit primitive peoples.[166] The park wardens were able to claim they were protecting customary rights, as outlined in the 1940 Game Ordinance, but violated the ordinance's spirit by deciding how the law should be interpreted, what counted as custom, and which groups were deemed autochthonous.

The Grzimeks, for their part, framed the story of the Maasai cultivators in the same way as the Mbuti in the Congo. In their doomsday vision, Maasai crop growing was an outward sign of degeneration: the ever-dwindling number of "racially pure" Maasai. Natural Maasai, according to the Grzimeks, looked like "young Greek gods . . . tall and slender" with a concept of beauty close to that of Europeans: "narrow hips, no corpulent or obese outlines and no exaggerated lumps of muscle."[167] But due to their "promiscuous habits before marriage," the Maasai had experienced skyrocketing rates of venereal disease, leaving many women barren. With birth rates rapidly declining, the Grzimeks explained, the Masaai were apt to adopt the children of "agricultural tribes," leading to the expansion of cultivation inside the crater in previous years.[168] The adopted children "grow up as Masai and remain members of the tribe," yet "the light-brown, thin-lipped faces of the real Masai, which resemble those of Europeans, are becoming rarer."[169] The Grzimeks' aerial surveys revealed only a fraction of the number of Maasai bomas and cattle herds assumed by the British; as in the Congo, there was little evidence of an impending population bomb. In such small numbers, the Grzimeks indicated, they might make "good neighbors," but not inhabitants, of the park.[170] Fears of "race mixing," in other words, propelled calls for land evictions, as conservationists came to believe that only a racially purified Maasai population could occupy the park lands in harmony with its natural surroundings.

In the face of the growing unrest, social dislocation, and international scrutiny caused by the eviction of cultivators, the Tanganyika legislative council issued a controversial white paper in 1956 that envisioned a "final solution" that would more closely adhere to international standards for national parks by permanently segregating pastoralists and wild animals.[171] But in a move that shocked international conservationists and district officers alike, the government proposed to accomplish this division by excising the large districts used by the Maasai from the park altogether. Based on a report from district officer Grant, who sympathized with Maasai claims, the government plan would have turned over large swathes of the central plains to Maasai development under the assumption that the herders only used the plains during the dry season when the wildebeest were not present. Grant's report reiterated that the Maasai had been given "positive assurances" that their rights would not be violated and attributed the increasing number of herders and cattle in the crater and Moru Kopjes to

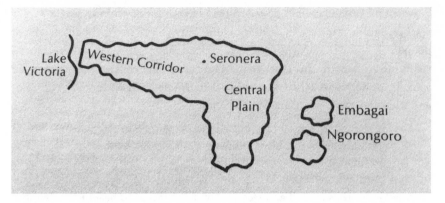

Figure 5.3 Proposed Boundaries of the Serengeti, 1956. The proposed division would have apportioned the existing park into three parts: a ranching area targeted for development, a "Maasai Sanctuary" for cattle grazing, and a small park area comprising only about 1,860 square miles (6,730 square km) of the original 4,600 (11,550 square km). The plan drew howls of protest from international conservationists and transformed a colonial debate about customary use into an international conservationist scandal on the brink of decolonization. Rudy Hoglund for Harold T.P. Hayes, *Last Place on Earth*, 27.

"cycles of poor rains" in the park's initial three years. Park officials who had tried to stop the Maasai from carrying on with their traditional ways were the real cause of "suspicion and misunderstanding" that gave rise to "antagonism and resentment" over the park's status—not the herders.[172] The proposed division would have apportioned the existing park into three parts: a ranching area targeted for development, a "Maasai Sanctuary" for cattle grazing, and a small park area comprising only about 1,860 square miles (6,730 square kilometers) of the original 4,600 (11,550 square km).[173] Grant proposed that the Maasai should receive proceeds from tourist income in return for obeying park rules and giving up on farming for good.[174]

Under the 1956 proposal, the Serengeti National Park would consist of three small parks: the Ngorongoro Crater and certain forest zones adjacent to it (about 450 square miles); the Embagai Crater (covering about ten square miles); and the Western Serengeti (fourteen hundred square miles), an area many considered a "waste land" due to tsetse infestation.[175] Ranchland development would occur in and around the grasslands of the Moru Kopjes in the Central Serengeti. The Maasai in the remaining twenty-six hundred square miles would be allowed to graze and move their herds as they saw fit, though hunting would still be banned.[176] To appease conservationists, the report created three game-control areas on the frontiers of the park—which added ninety-five hundred square miles of protected area even though most of the region would no longer qualify as a national park. "Never was the park in more danger," noted Myles Turner, "We were appalled; but luckily, so was the world."[177]

Condemnation of this "dismemberment" of the park came swiftly from the FPS, regional newspapers, and local wildlife societies.[178] The Tanganyika and Kenya Wildlife Societies argued that the proposal severely underestimated the impact of the land proposal on the migrating herds. Arguing that the ongoing drought was a severe, though impermanent cause of large numbers of Maasai in the Ngorongoro Highlands and Moru Kopjes, the societies believed that there was ample space for pastoralists, livestock, and wild animals in the central plains so long as temporary water holes did not dry up completely. But the new plan removed the headwaters of dry season creeks and springs from the national park, leaving them vulnerable to development pressures and endangering wild animals and livestock alike.[179] The societies requested that the government furnish evidence that it had bored the watering holes proposed in 1951 to entice herders outside the park and confirm whether such a plan had, or might still, decongest the park lands. Echoing Leechman, the society members argued that it was likely the post-1951 interlopers from the north who had put up the truculent opposition to park rules, not the indigenous pastoralists. If the government went forward with the plan to excise the central plains, they predicted, it would "only result in the progressive destruction of the wildlife in the proposed reduced park areas."[180] Several park wardens agreed, reciting again the charge that the Maasai search for building materials and the erosion from overgrazing meant that pastoralism was incompatible with the national park.[181]

Conservation groups outside of the empire condemned the plan in much harsher tones that registered little sympathy for weakened pastoralists. They used the Serengeti controversies to call into question the United Kingdom's fulfillment of its commitment to protecting and preserving the territory's national resources and "preparing these people by education and training" to use them properly. [182] The American IUCN representative Harold Coolidge encouraged the former Pepsi-Cola company chairman and wildlife supporter Russell Arundel to submit a strongly worded petition to the secretary of state for the colonies, Alan Tindal Lennox-Boyd, on behalf of US-affiliated conservation groups, including the Nature Conservancy, the New York Zoological Society, the National Parks Association, and the Wilderness Society. The petition suggested that the government delay its decision pending further ecological and ethnological studies and pay greater attention to the growing problem of poaching and black market trade in animal parts. Such studies would determine the extent of damage that would be caused by grazing cattle and whether some of the land already in Maasai hands could be "economically improved to permit practical grazing . . . without destroying the world's greatest national park."[183] Echoing district officials' and regional wildlife societies' fears, the Americans lamented that the removal of the central districts would leave those grasslands vulnerable to further development that would replace seasonal grazing with year-round land use, transforming the fragile grasslands into a "dustbowl" even as the Maasai moved on to damage additional acres of grassland in Kenya and Tanganyika.[184]

Questioning the assertion that the Maasai had "certain inherent rights" to land under the terms of the government's trusteeship, the petition echoed the racialized arguments to call for eviction. The petitioners noted that "it is immediately apparent even to the casual visitor" that the "Masai as a race have, by interbreeding with other tribes, by infiltration, and by absorption of the customs of others, changed materially both as a race and as a unit of social practice." Such "sentimental complications" over inherent rights, the petition went on, were "neither defined in law, described in treaty, nor etched in history"—a clear shot at the "native rule" mentality that undergirded Maasai advocates' support for customary tenure. Demonstrating their paternalist role in shepherding the mandate toward independence, the conservation groups stated: "We argue that that basic inherent right of the African is to have his natural heritage protected and defended even from his own errors."[185] The studies could be made by trained personnel from within the United Kingdom, but the petitioners assured Lennox-Boyd that the costs could be borne by wildlife associations throughout the world. Once the "global community" became involved, the language of "rights" began to shift rapidly away from the locally sanctioned, customary prerogatives guaranteed by the colonial state to ones based on universal standards of human development—imposed, if necessary, onto "backward" peoples for their own good.

The Serengeti and the Emergence of Global Environmental Governance, 1957–1960

International conservationists' sudden entry into the Serengeti controversies transformed local disputes about indigenous prerogatives within the British Empire into a referendum on the United Kingdom's capacity to rule. The 1956 proposal, wrote Arundel, "is contrary to the spirit and intent of the United Nations Mandate" which stipulated that British occupancy of Tanganyika rested on its ability to protect the "natural resources and heritage of indigenous peoples" and prepare them to "properly use and administer" them through training and education.[186] As one of Tanganyika's "prime assets," the petitioners averred, the disappearance of the Serengeti's flora and fauna would be an "irreparable world tragedy as well as a local one, and the abandonment of a natural trust which would not be forgotten while the history of man's progress is being written." The Serengeti, in this rendering, was a "natural heritage of all the people of the world" that required new forms of international environmental governance beyond the imperial order.[187] Older imperial conventions were suitable for dealing with poachers, but the colonial state was too mired in "tribal" mentalities to administer global heritage. "Can you not, therefore, find a way that the world may participate in the orderly development and protection of this area?," the petitioners asked.[188] Local debates on the park's borders had become, in Turner's words, "the hottest conservation issue in the world."[189]

Which of the many groups who spoke on behalf of nature and could be part of such world governance remained ill-defined in 1957. But it was clear to the petitioners that part of "man's progress" had been the development of a higher sensibility regarding natural heritage, one that put aside immediate material gratification in pursuit of the ideal aim of environmental protection. Such a sensibility toward nature signaled that a nation—yet to be declared in the Tanganyikan case—could enter the privileged circle of advanced civilizations, much as the youthful United States had done when it set aside Yellowstone in 1872. Yet conservationists also feared that concessions to the Maasai in the Serengeti would have a domino effect across the globe, just as decolonization had begun to accelerate and "vulnerable" wildlife resources were being transferred to black and brown majority governments throughout the Third World. In this context, splitting the Serengeti "in the face of local native pressure would have grave international results in all countries where National Parks exist." To prevent such a tragedy, Arundel recommended a permanent international committee to replace British authorities in administering the Serengeti. The committee would consist of representatives from all the remaining imperial powers in Africa—England, Belgium, and France—as well as the Netherlands, the government of Tanganyika, and the "Masai tribe."[190] These representatives would work together to formulate rules for protecting animals and plants. The petitioners encouraged the Maasai to "make use of the hereditary culture and legendary respect of flora and fauna existing deep in the Masai and contiguous tribes" to enlighten their fellow tribesmen and other rural Africans about the value of wildlife. But this "tribal" status denied the Maasai any real voice. The gesture toward "hereditary culture" did not allow any integration of traditional environmental knowledge of wildlife and grasslands, let alone enable herders to make their own decisions about how best to inhabit the grasslands. Preparation and education meant training in Western conservation science and "wildlife utilization."[191]

Faced with such a direct assault on its conservation authority in the Serengeti, the colonial government agreed with an FPS recommendation to delay the implementation of the 1956 plan pending further study. The delay paved the way for the society to commission Pearsall's report, which recommended a bipartite division that, in essence, flipped the 1956 plan. Pearsall recommended trading the Moru Kopjes, which he deemed "nodal" for wildebeest migrations and too fragile to withstand continued occupation, for the Ngorongoro Crater and highlands, in which the Maasai had long-standing ties and whose montane water sources needed to be protected in a separate forest conservation zone.[192] Pearsall knew much more information was necessary to resolve the border question adequately. The Grzimeks' 1957–1959 aerial surveys corrected some of Pearsall's findings and added a deeper ecological argument to world heritage in line with the 1933 London Convention. They explained the connection between the animals' movements and the seasonal availability of certain grasses; most importantly, they showed that the Ngorongoro mammals did not migrate onto the eastern plains but remained in many cases in the highlands or the crater itself throughout the year. In retrospect, however, their conclusions, which envisioned expanding the existing borders and evicting the Maasai from the crater, were untenable given the fraught political atmosphere that accompanied Tanganyika's impending decolonization. British administrators who had once admonished former German colonial occupiers for their grave "mismanagement" of the protectorate now found themselves under fire from a conservation community that turned environmental mismanagement into a referendum on colonial authority writ large.

The final decision to set the boundaries of SNP awaited the Serengeti Committee of Enquiry's assessment of the Pearsall survey, which resulted in a third and final white paper.[193] That report set the boundaries of a park that resembled the one tourists encounter today, including a large area of what was assumed to be the wildebeest migration route and excluding human settlement (See Figure I.2).[194] As Pearsall recommended, the park included the contested zones of the western and central plains, including all of the Moru Kopjes. As compensation for the loss of the Ngorongoro region, territorial administrators added the northern extension to Kenya, which the Grzimeks deemed a wasteland but was later shown by Lee Talbot to offer critical dry season access to the Mara headwaters across the border in Kenya: a stroke of luck for the animals.[195] The Ngorongoro Crater Highlands and Eastern Serengeti plains were removed from the park to become a managed conservation unit where the Maasi could continue grazing their animals as a concession for the loss of the Western Serengeti plains, while the floors of the Ngorongoro and Embagai craters had special status as nature reserves.[196]

After the decision to divide the Serengeti, the park system began to withdraw staff and equipment from the area designated as the Ngorongoro conservation unit and systematically evicted, against considerable opposition, Maasai, Sukuma, Ikoma, and Ngoreme people who still lived in the central and western zones of the park.[197] On April 21, 1958, twelve Maasai elders signed an agreement to vacate what was to become the Serengeti National Park, renouncing their customary claims to the Moru Kopjes and Seronera in the central districts of the park. "We understand that as a result of this renunciation we shall not be entitled henceforth in the years to come to cross this line which will become the boundary of the new SNP and which will be demarcated," the document stated. "We also understand that we shall not be entitled to reside in or use in the future the land lying to the west of this line, which we have habitually used in the past."[198] The Maasai agreed to move themselves, their possessions, and their cattle by December 31.

But in a 1993 interview with investigative journalist Raymond Bonner, Tendemo ole Kisaka, one of the original signatories, claimed that six large trucks came only a few days later and loaded the Maasai and their few belongings onto the flatbeds and carried them outside the new park with little time to prepare and mourn. The Maasai elder never returned. "I cry when you ask me about them," he said, when Bonner began to talk about Seronera, adding: "We were told to sign. It was never explained to us. None of the elders even knew how to read and write. You white people are very tough."[199] The Grzimeks' Maasai interlocutors were similarly dismayed by plans to remove them from the central plains. "If we move out the neighbouring people will come with their poisoned arrows and snares," they exclaimed, presciently. "They dare not enter our land now, for they know that we would chase them off like dogs. We let the wild animals live in peace."[200]

The British government nonetheless appeared ready to develop the Ngorongoro region as a pastoralist homeland. Tanganyika's governor Richard Turnbull, in a speech to the Maasai Federal Council in August 1959, reiterated that the Ngorongoro unit was designed to protect Maasai land rights: "I should like to make it clear to you all that it is the intention of the Government to develop the Crater in the interests of the people who use it."[201] Nonetheless, the debate over Maasai rights in Ngorongoro continued as the FPS, the FZS, the IUCN, the Nature Conservancy, and other conservation groups demanded that the crater be kept within the park and the Maasai excluded from access. Their cries for revisiting the park's division, however, came just as the colonial government realized it would have to turn over the colony to Nyerere's TANU party much earlier than expected. Additionally, the government did not know how it would pay for the park's needs when it faced the need to cut other social services for lack of funds. The compromise about the fate of the Serengeti National Park remained fragile as Tanganyika veered toward independence in 1960.

Given that these critical decisions about the park's status occurred at roughly the same time the Grzimeks were completing their research, it is not surprising that their pleas to save the Serengeti flipped from skepticism about "too hasty" independence to condemnation of the British mandate. Realizing that the park's trustees were moving ahead with the division before their surveys were even complete, Grzimek warned that the division of the park would result in an almost "total absence" of large herds, whose forays outside the new boundaries would leave zebra and wildebeest vulnerable to poachers and other illegal activities. Molloy expressed the trustees' "sincere appreciation" for the Grzimeks' "valuable scientific data," even as the committee of enquiry rejected their conclusions about the border question.[202] In this context, the Grzimeks' claim to the Serengeti as a "cultural heritage of all mankind," though far from novel, tried to imagine a new scale of governance and authority that superseded imperial factions and "native" authorities.

While they lost their battle to keep their last refuge intact, the release of *Serengeti Shall Not Die* on the heels of this controversy allowed the Grzimeks to present audiences with a spectacle of untouched nature. The image of global heritage enfolded the wicked, multi-faceted Serengeti controversy into an easy-to-analyze Malthusian story already familiar to readers and viewers from the pair's 1951 and 1954 missions to West Africa and the Belgian Congo. "You cannot keep men, even black and brown ones, from multiplying and cannot force them to remain 'primitive,'" the Grzimeks lamented in the pages of *Serengeti Shall Not Die*. They predicted that herds of cattle, sheep, and goats would outcompete the zebras, wildebeest, and gazelles for shelter and watering holes and trample the grasses on which the native animals depended. Thereafter, desertification would be unstoppable:

> Africa is dying and will continue to die. Old maps and remnants of settlements and animals show that the Sahara has advanced 250 miles northward on a 1250 mile front during the last three centuries .... So much of Africa is dead already, must the rest follow? Must *everything* be turned into deserts, farmland, big cities, native settlements and dry bush? One small part of the continent at least should retain its original splendour so that the black and white men who follow us will be able to see it in its awe-filled past glory. Serengeti, at least, shall not die.[203]

The reference to black and white men is key here, since the Grzimeks' stage-theory of African development envisioned a postcolonial world in which industrious Africans, long held back by British policies, would move to cities, develop their lands—and lose all ties to wildlife. Without immediate intervention, children in both Berlin and Dar es Salaam would see wildlife only in zoos, not on the open range. Such operatic pleas ensured the Grzimeks a place at the table of the "world" conservation community that took on the task of administering the Serengeti as British imperial hegemony crumbled.

The vision of the Maasai "problem" as a product of overpopulation and a zero-sum battle between cattle and wildlife used the global threat of desertification to defuse intractable local and regional questions about appropriate land use and environmental sovereignty. Such overarching explanations blamed the Maasai for a series of historical missteps and ongoing environmental changes that had little to do with pastoralism, including a warming climate, previous European land alienations, dubious settlement schemes, and failed ranchland and cash-crop experiments.[204] Numerous British observers noted that Maasai pastoralists saw beyond "meats, skins, and competition for their hungered cows" but the Grzimeks' doomsday vision of overpopulation and modernization subsumed complex interactions between pastoralists and wild animals into a global degradation narrative, reinforcing the belief that "native" peoples had no place in a landscape designated by God to protect the animals.[205]

Despite their advanced gadgetry, Bernhard found his and Michael's work scrutinized continually for animal counts that were far too low and maps of the great migration routes that were far too prescriptive. The Grzimeks' faith in aerial technology overlooked well-known sources of error, many scientists claimed, leaving census data and theories about migrations and grass species open to contestation and refinement for decades to come. Yet their work was not a purposeful misrepresentation, as some have argued, but part of an array of European wildlife management that had continually tried, and failed, to render the plains legible and manageable.[206] Determining the exact numbers and migration routes of East African animals had long bedeviled colonial officials, and the Grzimeks made these counts more precise and connected the dots between animal movements, rainfall, and vegetation. Yet they shared a late colonial European assumption that saw tropical savannas as especially vulnerable to overgrazing and soil erosion, which led all involved—from Hingston through the Grzimeks—to target pastoralists, not poachers, as the greatest long-term threat to the Serengeti as an ecosystem. European observers consistently underestimated the ability of the plains to bounce back from drought and overestimated the capacity of rural pastoralists to inflict permanent damage.[207]

The unruly, "disturbance-mediated" qualities of the Serengeti's ecosystems that made causal explanations so daunting were quite evident to those closer to the ground: the district officers, game scouts, and rural Africans who wrestled with shifting conditions that never settled down into the equilibrium state predicted by the scientific wildlife managers. Nature surfaces in colonial reports as capricious and unwieldy, stymying efforts to protect wandering animal herds, police the borders of the park, and manage its amenities for tourists.[208] The park's administrators confronted wide oscillations in rainfall, a patchwork of different biotopes, and animals, cattle, and people constantly on the move in search of water holes—and never mastered them. The dearth of reliable data on the plains and its peoples presented intractable and insurmountable challenges to territorial environmental governance. Government officials and park wardens seemed unsure which animal counts to trust, which herders had a "right" to remain in the park, and which historical baseline best served the preservation interests of the park and balanced the priorities of wildlife conservation, traditional pastoralism, and tourism. Only a handful of observers, such as Leechman and Fosbrooke, recognized that subsequent efforts toward a final resolution to human rights claims in the Serengeti missed the deep entanglement of people and animals as they had co-evolved on the plains before the establishment of colonial rule.

More troubling was the effort to use the national park designation not only to "rescue" wild animals, but also the mythical Saleh Maasai, from extinction. Much like ecological notions of climax community or carrying capacity, the park's administrators tried—and failed—to isolate a racially pure segment of the Maasai who would benefit from the gift of preservation. Such efforts left as little room for Maasai cultural and political autonomy as the detribalizing effects of migrant labor and urbanization that so many colonial observers feared. The British and post-independence government's efforts to distinguish "full-blooded" Maasai pastoralists from their "mixed-race" cousins who cultivated missed the long-standing connections between pastoralists, cultivators, and hunter-gatherers in the tapestry of human life on the savannas. Such racial tinkering became part of the intractable forms of exclusion that local Africans associated with national parks, which constrained their movement and access to family networks far more than the spottily enforced restriction that British colonial reserves had placed on hunting, farming, and gathering. Instead, as the next chapter demonstrates, the Maasai learned that they were now part of a national community for which tribalism—and the customary land tenure guaranteed by indirect rule—were a shameful legacy of imperialism.

An Honest Broker for the Animals

> Will the black politicians, who come and go, consider that the wild animals belong to their future? And do the white politicians, who want to help them, realize that Africa's animals will be admired by people around the world?
>
> —Bernhard Grzimek, *Rhinos Belong to Everybody*

In January 1960 Bernhard Grzimek met Dr. Julius Nyerere, the head of the Tanganyika African National Union (TANU), which was leading the territory's drive toward independence from Britain. The three-hour meeting took place at the party's headquarters on the same day that *Serengeti Shall Not Die* premiered in Dar es Salaam, a film that the zookeeper hoped would convince Africans to protect the precious wild heritage they were about to inherit. Grzimek already admired Nyerere as "Africa's most intelligent politician," poised to be the next prime minister of "our former colony German East Africa."[1] Disarmed by Nyerere's casual appearance and eagerness to hear his views on conservation, Grzimek implored the young prime minister to expand Tanganyika's tiny network of national parks and game reserves. "No African, nor even any Briton who has lived a long time in Africa, can realize how the attitude of the masses toward animals has changed in the big cities of Europe and America," he recounted saying in his 1962 book *Rhinos Belong to Everybody*. "This is the first time since there were men in the world that so many of them have lived completely cut off from nature and from wildlife."[2] Such alienation from the wild had created pent-up demand for contact with an intact organic world. "Today a flight from Frankfurt to East Africa takes eleven hours but in a few years it may take no more than three," he noted. "Holiday travellers, who are always looking for new places to go, will then come out here, unless of course Tanganyika's wild animals have all been wiped out by then."[3]

Like most other Western conservationists entering the hopeful "development decade" of the 1960s, Grzimek was counting on these nature pilgrims' dollars and Deutsche marks to substitute for Tanganyika's potential earnings from agricultural and mining exports.[4] Gone were the days when Grzimek feared

Our Gigantic Zoo. Thomas M. Lekan, Oxford University Press (2020). © Oxford University Press.
DOI: 10.1093/oso/9780199843671.001.0001

tourism's "commercialized mockery" of a once-authentic Africa. Postwar economic prosperity, the rise of inexpensive air travel, and a growing desire to escape
humdrum mass culture would make East Africa a prime tourist destination,
many conservationists hoped.[5] All that was needed was a "broker" who could
bring the Western "buyers" of wild animals together with their "sellers": newly
emancipated Africans in the free marketplace left open by the end of imperialist trade monopolies.[6] Grzimek remained unsure if Nyerere had really understood his proposition to transform Tanganyika into a "wilderness exporter"
until he learned about a *Daily Telegraph* interview Nyerere gave just a few weeks
later in London.[7] "I personally am not very interested in animals," the African
leader told the correspondent, "but I know that Europeans and Americans love
to be able to see elephants and giraffes. Tanganyika has the most wild animals
in the whole of Africa. I will make sure the tourists will be able to see them."[8]
Grzimek was pleased by this response. Rather than exuberantly pledging what
he *thought* the Europeans wanted to hear—that he was a great animal lover—
Nyerere presented his case based on a "sober," transactional assessment of the
value of wildlife, noting that after sisal and diamonds, wild animals would likely
become Tanganyika's third most important source of income.[9] Thus began a
twenty-seven-year friendship that Grzimek's former colleague has characterized
as being based on "great mutual respect."[10]

A year and a half after his initial meeting with Grzimek, during a landmark
symposium in Arusha organized by the Switzerland-based IUCN and sponsored by UNESCO and the United Nations Food and Agriculture Organization
(FAO), Nyerere co-signed a manifesto that made Tanganyika the first country in
the world to dedicate itself to the protection of its wildlife resources.[11] The Pan
African Symposium on the Conservation of Nature and Natural Resources in
Modern African States, which convened in September 1961, brought together
140 participants from 21 African and 6 non-African countries.[12] Held only a
year after independence in the neighboring Belgian Congo had turned violent,
the conference reflected the anxieties of many European delegates that newly
independent governments might evict Western advisers. They also feared these
new governments would look the other way as ordinary people slaughtered the
animals in nature reserves long viewed as despised symbols of Western imperialism. But their fears melted into "tumultuous applause" when Nyerere's minister
for water, Nyamwezi Chief Abdallah Said Fundikira, read the prime minister's
opening statement aloud:

> Wild creatures amid the wild places they inhabit are not only important
> as a source of wonder and inspiration but are an integral part of our
> natural resources and of our future livelihood and well-being. In accept-
> ing the trusteeship of our wildlife we solemnly declare that we will do

Figure 6.1 Partners in conservation: Grzimek and Nyerere, ca. 1963. Grzimek was delighted that a prime minister once skeptical of the idea of vacationing to see animals would spend his own holidays in the Serengeti and other national parks. Okapia, Ltd.

everything in our power to make sure that our children's grand-children will be able to enjoy this rich and precious inheritance.[13]

The language of trusteeship in the manifesto was striking, for it implied that Tanganyika—itself just emerging from UN Mandate status—did not previously "own" the wildlife.[14] Wildebeest and giraffes were, in this formulation, a "gift" of the world community, bestowed upon a new polity that stood ready to take its place among the family of "civilized" nations.[15] Recognizing the enormous outlays that such a task would require, Nyerere and his compatriots noted that wildlife trusteeship would require "specialist knowledge, trained manpower, and money" and looked "to other nations to cooperate with us" in executing this world-historical task.[16]

Environmental historians have long considered the Arusha Conference a watershed in international and East African conservation affairs. Proponents have lauded it as the first coordinated international effort to protect wildlife as a global resource unshackled from imperialist domination.[17] In this view,

wildlife offered a wellspring of foreign currency for newly independent countries; the animals could prove their right to exist by "paying their own way," as
one observer put it.[18] Critics of Arusha, on the other hand, argue that Western
participants imposed a neocolonial Western conservation logic onto decolo-
nial territories that betrayed the promised land reforms of the independence
movement, marginalizing local and indigenous needs in favor of globetrotting
tourists.[19] Nyerere's words also suggested that he was requesting the assistance of former colonial masters in serving as a trustee over wildlife. Nyerere's
Manifesto, in this view, re-inscribed the imperial era's paternalistic emphasis
on Africans' unpreparedness to manage their own lands and made the young
nation dependent upon foreign financial assistance and scientific paradigms
for decades to come.[20]

Both critics and detractors have largely focused on the "Anglo-Saxon" agendas
that dominated the IUCN and FAO meeting and enabled British and American
foundations and NGOs—particularly the African Wildlife Leadership Fund
(AWLF) and the Nature Conservancy—to call the shots in conservation affairs
long past independence in 1961. Yet beyond the London–Washington axis were
a number of "second-tier" players, including Grzimek's Frankfurt Zoological
Society (FZS), who took advantage of the fluidity around independence to
carve out their own agendas at Arusha. Nyerere's bold remarks about tourism
and calls for Western assistance convinced Grzimek to put aside his anxieties about "over hasty" decolonization and embrace the postcolony as a fertile
space to realize his self-appointed mission to save the globe's last charismatic
animals. Working behind the scenes with John Owen, Tanganyika's ex-pat director of the Department of National Parks, Grzimek built the critical institutional
networks that ensured West Germany a place at the table far beyond independence.[21] Grzimek's fundraising in postcolonial Tanganyika showed how wide
the gap remained between the IUCN's lofty aspirations and the measly colonial
inheritance, since Grzimek's modest grants-in-aid ensured FZS members and
even ordinary television viewers an outsized importance in East African wildlife
affairs. Grzimek presented himself as a globalist without imperialist ties or Cold
War ambitions, an "honest broker" mediating between the competing claims of
international conservationists and African national leaders. Working together,
Grzimek and Owen tried to remake Tanganyika, long considered the "poor sister" among Britain's three East African territories, into a "beacon of hope" for the
conservation struggle.[22]

The German-African contact zone of the early 1960s quickly brought together
conservationists, diplomats, state officials, herders, tourists, and animals in
novel relationships that linked wildlife conservation to postcolonial nation-
state building.[23] The slow pace of Africanization in the wildlife sector allowed
Grzimek (named Honorary Curator of Tanganyika's National Parks in 1961),

Owen, and Bruce Kinloch, the chief game warden for Tanganyika, to maneuver themselves into new roles as environmental intermediaries between the fledgling state and external funding agencies for projects that expanded parklands, introduced wildlife management training, and established an ecological field station in the Serengeti.[24] In a replay of the trusteeship period, all three argued that their expertise, fundraising, and global contacts were essential to preparing Africans to take over stewardship of the national park system. But Grzimek distinguished himself from the Anglo-Americans working in Tanganyika by his willingness to help the young nation with the unspectacular, everyday tasks of conservation work and to promote national pride in wild animals—especially among children. Grzimek parlayed his media fame and the rhetoric of Michael's "sacrifice" to help build national pride in wild animals and expand the country's number of national parks. Indeed, with Grzimek's help, Tanzania expanded its number of national parks from just one in 1960 to nine in 1971.[25]

Grzimek relied on Owen to relaunch his conservation mission after independence, but the striking continuities with the German and British colonial periods were counterbalanced by "rupture and dynamism" among Nyerere and his ministers, who "mined" the country's wildlife resources to create new export opportunities, pursue their own vision of national development, and appropriate the mode of state power long associated with wildlife conservation.[26] Nyerere never shared the conservationist view that wildlife endangerment was an "emergency" on par with rural poverty, health care, and education, but he did give his tacit blessing for Owen, the FZS, and other NGOs to help the country develop its protected areas and tourist infrastructure as generators of foreign currency.[27] The ministers who supported this vision included Fundikira, Rashidi Kawawa (minister of lands and surveys), Alhaj Tewa Said Tewa (minister for wildlife), and Hamed Seleman Mahinda, a chief ranger in the Game Division who had been among the first to enjoy FAO sponsorship to study wildlife management at the University of Colorado.[28] Echoing late colonial modernizers, many African statesmen accused the Maasai of "wasting" valuable land on hungry cattle that did not contribute to the export economy.[29] In the eyes of Nyerere and his cohort, wandering pastoralists were embarrassing obstacles to national development, mired in a tribal consciousness that hindered nationalist awakening and an itinerant lifestyle that stymied the provision of health care, water, and education.[30] Grzimek thus found new hope in Nyerere's African-nationalist government, which proved far less willing than the British colonial state to accommodate the Maasai and other rural Africans whom the state viewed as misusing "national heritage."[31] Grzimek's quest buttressed an African nation-building project that sought its own development priorities—and disciplinary strategies—in the transition from late empire to early independence.[32]

Censoring Animals

Grzimek's initial meetings with Nyerere came at a time when the prospects for transforming Africa's national parks into a "global heritage of mankind" appeared dim. The British government had rejected his and Michael's research findings and conservationists around the West lamented the partition of the Serengeti. But they were even more anxious about a new crisis: the reported attacks on wild animals in the Belgian Congo's nature reserves following the European evacuations of 1960.[33] Outside of a few reserves like these, Grzimek wrote alarmingly, the stand of animals worldwide had been reduced to only 20 percent of its original size due to losses of habitat. He warned of an impending planetary catastrophe that contrasted sadly with the triumphal strides that humankind was making in the space race.[34] Indeed, in *Rhinos Belong to Everybody*, a sequel to the Serengeti book, he elaborated on the theme of wildlife as global heritage. Grzimek feared that the Sputnik generation had forgotten the planet's precious evolutionary inheritance, dooming its grandchildren to viewing giraffe, rhinos, and elephants only in films. "What will they think of us when their fathers tell them what happened?" Grzimek lamented. "That we in the nineteen sixties were too busy conquering the universe to notice that Africa's beautiful animals were dying out for good? . . . These noble animals are entrusted to our protection, nor shall we find them again on any new star or planet that may be discovered."[35] Europeans could not "unload" responsibility for this mass extinction onto Africans. "We Europeans and white men bear that responsibility," Grzimek proclaimed, "our descendants will not acquit us."[36] In the early 1960s, the planetary horizons of the space age gave new meaning to the "white man's burden" right on the brink of independence.

The most worrying local example of neglect remained Ngorongoro, for which Michael had given "everything he possessed," as newspapers throughout East Africa reported in 1959.[37] The partition of the Serengeti and the influx of Maasai herds into the Ngorongoro region in 1958 made Bernhard feel that Michael's death had been for naught.[38] There, the British government had sacrificed "the most fertile grazing grounds in the Serengeti," intended as the animals' "safe refuge for all time," to a dying way of life.[39] The tone of *Rhinos* was much more bitter and personal than *Serengeti*, as Grzimek held the Maasai as a "tribe" responsible for "having succeeded in getting this region excluded in their favour."[40]

As if these twin tragedies were not enough, West Germany's cultural elites and hunters gave Grzimek little time to grieve his fallen son. In late 1959, just as *Serengeti* was about to appear in cinemas, Grzimek faced biting reviews and vitriolic op-ed pages in leading newspapers. The controversies started when Gerhard Prager, the chairman of the Filmbewertungstelle Wiesbaden (Film

Figure 6.2 "Scrub cattle" in the Serengeti, 1961. This photograph depicts the dustbowl conditions of 1961 that conservationists believed were the resulted of drought compounded by the Maasai and their "emaciated cattle" overgrazing vulnerable grasslands. Getty Images.

Evaluation Office Wiesbaden, hereafter FBW), demanded that Bernhard excise two scenes from the final cut in order to receive the board's recommendation of "worthwhile," rather than merely "good."[41] The first scene featured a pride of lions feasting on a zebra carcass while the narrator tells the audience that "the world would be better off if humans behaved like lions." The second and more significant cut was what the FBW deemed the "impermissible equation" (*unerlaubte Gleichsetzung*) between African wildlife herds and the Acropolis—the very comparison that stood at the heart of the Grzimeks' plea to see the non-human world as irreplaceable world heritage.[42] Grzimek argued that removing the two scenes would cut the aesthetic and moral heart out of his and Michael's film—and thus amounted to a form of "censorship" of the film's content.

The FBW did not have the power to censor a film in any conventional sense. Composed of an elite circle of film critics and producers, academics, and "ministerial staff with film experience," the FBW's review process was completely voluntary, aimed only at determining whether a film had technical, artistic, or educational merit. The FBW, however, did appraise whether the artistic form reflected the "moral principles of the culture" and its certificates conveyed significant tax benefits for theaters under West German law, enabling cinemas to release culturally significant films widely that otherwise could not compete with commercial films.[43] Many of the board's members viewed their role as protecting "Western" values, which were synonymous at this time with Greco-Roman humanism and Catholic universalism—traditions that had supposedly redeemed Europe from Nazi tyranny and distinguished it from Soviet Communism and American materialism.[44] By championing lions' social behavior and gender-bending family roles, the Grzimeks upended the nuclear family that was supposed to be the bedrock of social reconstruction in the 1950s. Even more threatening was the placement of animal herds on equal footing with classical, religious, and artistic treasures that symbolized Christian democracy's unwavering values.[45]

Given the tax benefits that came with the highest rating, Grzimek hired an attorney to support his claim that the FBW's refusal to give *Serengeti Shall Not Die* its highest recommendation would prevent the film from attracting the largest possible audience—and hence amounted to a clampdown on free expression. At the Swiss opening of the film in Zürich, Grzimek fumed that he would never make another documentary film in West Germany due to the "strong and anonymous" censorship being exercised there by an "uncontrollable anonymous committee."[46] The well-regarded writer Georg Ramseger accused Grzimek of getting "uppity" with such remarks.[47] After all, noted Ramseger, the FBW's recommendation did not mean that *Serengeti Shall Not Die* could not be shown in West Germany; Grzimek would just have to forgo the tax subsidies that came with a higher rating.[48] Yet Grzimek's incendiary claim about "censorship" transformed aesthetic questions into political ones, reminding readers of the horrors of dictatorship and leaving the FBW scrambling to justify the necessity of its rating system in a democratic society. Grzimek's protest received so much popular attention that the FBW not only reversed its initial decision but also abandoned the practice of recommending changes altogether.[49] Yet the whole episode left Grzimek feeling bitter and misunderstood.[50] Such narrow-minded critiques, Grzimek averred, reflected the myopia that kept his countrymen from recognizing the scale of the planet's ecological crisis. How could Western organizations possibly convince decolonized Africans to forego land for grazing and agriculture, he asked, when educated Germans themselves did not see the Serengeti herds as world heritage?[51]

Green Networks

As he re-armed himself to save the Serengeti against such parochialism, Grzimek found allies among the global networks of world citizens who had joined him in condemning the Serengeti's 1958 division, including the scientists associated with the IUCN and UNESCO and nongovernmental groups such as the African Wildlife Leadership Foundation (AWLF), Fauna Preservation Society (FPS), and the New York Zoological Society (NYZS).[52] In 1960, Grzimek attended the IUCN's General Assembly and Technical Meetings in Warsaw and Krakow—an unusual move for a West German during the Berlin crisis—where scientists declared that an "impartial assessment of worldwide conservation problems" had led the organization to declare Africa's diminishing flora, fauna, and habitat as the top priority for global nature protection. As a consequence, the IUCN launched what it called the "Africa Special Project," a three-stage program for addressing the crisis that began in 1960 with a series of information surveys across sub-Saharan Africa conducted by Julian Huxley and FAO forestry officer Gerald G. Watterson.[53] With the onset of the Special Project, Africa's nature reserves became the proving ground for an environmental globalism that viewed itself unencumbered by imperialism and Cold War bipolarism—yet remained saddled with paternalist assumptions about Africans' abilities to serve as caretakers of their own lands.[54]

The IUCN surveys proceeded on the assumption that the wildlife crisis was largely a product of African ignorance and poverty. After all, those facing "hunger for meat" had no time to realize the higher values of nature. IUCN representatives noted that "these great and unique faunal and floral resources could be exhausted merely because the indigenous people had not had adequately demonstrated to them methods to gain maximum economic and cultural benefits from them."[55] Watterson and Huxley's investigation proposed that nature appreciation arose in tandem with industrialized development and that Africa could skip the most destructive phase. The four stages included "fear of or obedience to nature" (Stage 1); the "rational adaptation of the environment to different needs" which the IUCN associated with Asian rice terraces and other regionally adapted agriculture (Stage 2); and the "aggressive, unilateral exploitation" associated with industrialization, slums, and dustbowls (Stage 3). Only societies that had experienced these three stages were ready for Stage 4: "responsible (and often costly) readjustment to and unification with environmental conditions." The problem for Africa, the organizers argued, was the "sudden appearance" of Stage 3 during the period of European colonization, which had led to "heedless and prolonged" destruction of the environment without any time—or tools—for a recalibration of African economies and desires to the imposed conditions.[56]

Such stages explained why Africans had lost the capacity to manage their own wildlife. "Tribal" Africans might once have had sacred areas that proscribed the overhunting of wild animals—what Grzimek called "taboo regions"—but Christian missionaries had wiped out the foundations of animist practice. There was in Grzimek's mind no possibility of a vernacular environmentalism to emerge out of the colonial experience, no syncretic ecologies of belief and science that might serve as a foundation for an African conservation ethic.[57] In a similar vein, IUCN representatives assumed that the sudden onset of Stage 3 detached Africans from "natural" checks on demographic growth, leading to the exploding populations that threatened nature reserves even further.[58] The IUCN and its Western supporters envisioned themselves as members of an international rescue mission, armed with the ecological insights necessary to bring Africa into line with the fourth stage—"the stage of recovery"—without its people or biota having to suffer the full onslaught of modernity on their own.

IUCN leaders also hoped to appeal to the national pride and status conscious-ness of the emerging African leadership by offering a definition of "civilization" that touted the symbolic value of national parks over schools, hospitals, electric-ity lines, modern cities, and national airlines.[59] Just as Americans had learned to cherish their mountains, waterfalls, and giant trees as natural monuments on par with Europe's cathedrals and museums, Tanganyikans would also begin to see their wildlife as a global resource whose stewardship paved the way for their entry into the family of nations.[60] As Huxley reminded his compatriots in a 1961 speech:

> In the modern world, as Africa is beginning to realize, a country without national parks can hardly be regarded as civilized. And for an African territory to abolish National Parks already set up or to destroy its exist-ing wild life resources would shock the world and incur the reproach of barbarism and ignorance.[61]

Such a program created a moral distance from the colonial project of direct con-trol but left intact its unfinished goals: protecting wildlife, civilizing Africans, and offering Westerners access through science and tourism.

Such international attention gave Grzimek the legitimacy he needed to advo-cate more effectively for wildlife back in German-speaking Europe. The Special Project surveys revealed that the colonial inheritance of wildlife management and control was inadequate and that most parks were "operating on a shoe string."[62] Huxley admonished the World Bank, the International Development Association, and "the great foundations" to step in at this critical moment to resolve the extinction crisis with funding at a level commensurate with the UNESCO effort to save the monuments of Nubia at Abu Simbel in Egypt from the Aswan dam building project. Huxley insisted that animal herds and ancient temples were both part of "the world's enduring resources"—a pronouncement that echoed Grzimek's debates with the FBW.[63] Recognizing the gap between IUCN expertise in wildlife affairs and the funding capacities for global conserva-tion, Huxley was among those who issued the "Morges Manifesto" in Switzerland in April 1961 calling for a "World Wildlife Fund" to coordinate international fundraising. Working in conjunction with IUCN vice president Sir Peter Scott and director-general of the British Nature Conservancy, E. M. Nicholson, Huxley helped to launch the new organization in the same month as the Arusha Conference—September 1961—with Prince Bernhard of the Netherlands as the organization's first president.[64] Eugen Gerstenmaier, the leader of the German-Africa Society and former Bundestag president, played a critical role in the German WWF's founding, assembling a "who's who" of Bonn Republic luminaries to support the organization's mission.[65] Having emerged from the Serengeti crisis as leading voices against British imperialism, this "green network" of NGOs, UN agencies, and international foundations positioned themselves to fill the role of vanguards of environmentally aware development—so long as the promised wave of funding flowed into their coffers and outward into Africa through "technical assistance."

This funding stream did not materialize as expected during the development decade. In 1960–1961, the IUCN was still dependent on bilateral aid and private organizations to provide the bulk of its monies, a pattern that continued throughout the 1960s due to the WWF's initially limited fundraising capacity. Nicholson believed it would require $1.5 million each year for global conservation efforts, for example, but it took several years before the WWF's total funds even reached $1 million.[66] Grzimek, for his part, participated in creating the German affiliate of the WWF but refrained from taking over chairmanship of the organization. He preferred to remain independent, concentrating on building the FZS's small donor capacities in friendly coordination with the bigger NGOs but without their corporate sponsorship, expensive fundraising dinners, and bureaucratic inflexibility. The WWF's delay in fundraising capacity, meanwhile, enabled Grzimek's FZS to advance conservation and expand West German influence in Tanganyika with comparatively modest grants-in-aid.

The first example of Grzimek's scrappy brokering ability came just a few months after Michael's death. In early 1959, Tanganyikan authorities agreed to a simple pyramidal stone memorial on the rim of the Ngorongoro Crater, helped along by a gift from the German consulate in Nairobi. Just a few months later, the park's board of trustees established a modest "Michael Grzimek Memorial Fund" that quickly exceeded the initiators' expectations.[67] By August, the fund amounted to around $2,100 donated by 152 persons—including modest donations from the entire African staff of the Tanganyika Game Department. Rather than fold such heartfelt gifts into a larger fund or send them off to a third party, the board, in consultation with Bernhard, decided that a laboratory designed to carry on Michael's ecological work was the most fitting tribute to the fallen conservationist.[68] Soon enough, both the City of Frankfurt and the West German Consul General office came through with small gifts, while receipts from screenings of *Serengeti Shall Not Die* doubled the memorial fund by February 1960.[69]

Figure 6.3 The crash of the Flying Zebra, 1959. The coroner's office in Nairobi determined that Michael Grzimek's death was caused by a collision with a Griffon vulture upon ascent near the Ngorongoro Crater. The death was reported in all major East African newspapers. Getty Images.

At Grzimek's urging, the board decided to donate the five-room former residence of the Western Serengeti game warden at Banagi as laboratory space, right next to the spot where Michael and he had erected a makeshift aluminum shed to serve as their home during the filming of *Serengeti Shall Not Die*. The initial plan called for Lee Talbot to revisit the Grzimeks' animal survey work with funding from the American National Academy of Sciences. Talbot's goal was to understand in greater depth the "migratory urge" with an intensive animal marking campaign combined with in-depth study of vegetation and soils. As such, the laboratory would honor Michael's original vision of "building a new Serengeti on sound ecological lines," ensuring that the mistakes of 1958 would never happen again.[70] "Pitifully little is known about the ecology of wild life in East Africa—what the animals require in food and land for them to prosper and what causes some of them to migrate over large distances," noted John Owen in an appeal to Western donors. "It was lack of knowledge that resulted in the present boundaries of the Serengeti being drawn in such a way that many of the animals have to move outside the Park for several months each year."[71] Unlike the game reserves of the past, with their shifting and arbitrary borders, Tanganyika's new protected areas would be designated and managed on scientific principles modeled on those of the Belgian Congo.[72] Just two years later, in 1962, assistance from West German donors helped the park to open the Michael Grzimek Memorial Laboratory. Eugen Gerstenmeier came to the grand opening and deposited equipment donated by the German Research Foundation (Deutsche Forschungsgemeinschaft, or DFG) and announced an additional gift of fifty-five hundred Deutsche marks that he and Foreign Minister Heinrich von Brentano had helped to procure.[73]

Both Owen and Grzimek saw the laboratory as an international space of collaboration, a symbol that the Serengeti was a "world heritage" and not the pet project of colonial expats. Grzimek himself did not conduct research there; indeed, some of the scientific papers stemming from the lab did not confirm his and Michael's findings about total numbers.[74] Lee Talbot and his team angered Grzimek by disputing his and Michael's dire population numbers and showing that the northern extension provided valuable connections to dry season grazing grounds in the Mara headwaters in Kenya.[75] Yet the Grzimeks had provided the critical techniques and holistic perspective on animals' relationships to their habitat and to each other that would dominate ecological monitoring of the Serengeti. With the Congo's future uncertain, Grzimek and his collaborators hoped the Serengeti station would become Africa's new world laboratory, guiding the protection of wildlife and the implementation of ecologically wise land-use policies for decades to come.[76]

Martyrs for Wildlife

Grzimek's scramble to institutionalize national parks and create an ecological research station in Tanganyika stemmed from the worries associated with the Congo Crisis, which global conservationists viewed as a warning for what might happen to wild animals under black majority rule. In 1960, the region had descended into a US- and Belgian-funded proxy war following Belgian withdrawal and the refusal of UN troops to assist the legitimately elected prime minister, Patrice Lumumba, who turned to the USSR for help in reestablishing a centralized state.[77] During the civil war that ensued, rumors abounded that the Congolese were "senselessly butchering" protected animals in nature reserves. Such rumors fueled conservationists' anxieties about whether "the new black masters [would] be willing and able to go on protecting their last native animals" or whether the reserves would instead "perish in the turmoil of political revolutions."[78] Grzimek grabbed headlines in 1960-1961 when he arranged for the Congolese park wardens and game scouts in Albert and Garamba National Parks—the same areas featured in *No Room for Wild Animals*—to continue

receiving their salaries despite the civil war raging between Lumumba's government in Léopoldville and the breakaway provinces of Katanga and South Kasai.
The Congo Crisis also became a proving ground for Grzimek's brand of para-
diplomatic intervention, launching him into the top ranks of global conservationists working in sub-Saharan Africa in the 1960s.

Grzimek discovered that most of the rumors of mass slaughter were false
and argued that it was possible to keep the colonial inheritance of parks intact
under independent African rule so long as Europeans acted quickly to provide
nonpartisan funding, training, and research.[79] While his IUCN peers fretted
about the fate of animals in the Congo, Bernhard heard positive news from
the American gorilla researcher George Schaller as well as the Belgian biologist Jacques Verschuren, who had braved incarceration to stay on as head of the
National Parks and witnessed Congolese resolve to protect the parks. Schaller
and Verschuren reported that the African game scouts in the two parks had
remained at their post throughout the civil war—even engaging in pitched battles against poachers from across the border in Uganda.[80] Kivu provincial judges
had even begun meting out heavy fines to the Watutsi whose herds of cattle had
"overrun" Albert (renamed Virunga) National Park during the chaos of the civil
war, with far less sympathy for the pastoralists than the Belgian administrators
had displayed.

When Kivu provincial leaders turned to Grzimek for financial assistance
and help in recruiting tourists back to Rwindi and other tourist lodges near
the Ugandan border, Bernhard and his former cameraman Alan Root decided
to slip across the frontier at Ishasha in early 1961 to investigate the contradictory reports for themselves. Sensationalist headlines in Germany proclaimed
Grzimek and Root "missing" in the Congo.[81] In actuality, the pair met up with
Verschuren and staged a small memorial ceremony near Rwindi honoring the
bravery of the Congo rangers wounded or killed in their battle with the Ugandan
poachers. Grzimek asked one ranger to take off his coat and show his bandaged
arm, a scene that later appeared on *A Place for Animals* as an example of the "gal-
lantry" that had "given new hope to many people all over the world" who worried
about the fate of African wild life. "All of this may sound a little out of proportion
in a world which busies itself with hydrogen bombs and inter-continental mis-
siles," Grzimek wrote. "But when small men in Africa offer their lives to defend
a paradise which we hope will one day give joy to men and women of all races,
colours and creeds, they deserve a little kudos and recognition. They should be
assured that there are people on all continents who will be heartened by their
behavior."[82] Grzimek and Root barely missed being captured by Lumumba loy-
alists who ransacked the lodge, but the zookeeper felt ashamed about worries
over "his own skin" compared to the bravery of the Africans. Indeed, Grzimek's
ceremony made it clear that the international conservationist cause depended

on African sacrifice—not just that of whites like Michael—a powerful symbol of the new forms of partnership that shaped the postcolonial German-African contact zone.[83]

The bravery of the Congolese game scouts convinced Grzimek that emancipation from colonial rule might be a time of opportunity rather than lamentation. As he put it, "well educated and energetic" leaders in the Congo seemed eager to build on the Belgians' world-class conservation legacy, enforcing regulations in the name of emerging national pride as well as a craving for international respect. Grzimek and Verschuren were unsure how the Congo government in Stanleyville could possibly keep funding the 250 ex-servicemen who served as rangers in Albert and Garamba—a force larger than the entire staff of the national park system in Kenya—along with the dozens of personnel in now-empty lodges and tourist facilities.[84] Unless the international community acted right away, Verschuren noted, newly independent countries would perceive an "ominous sign" about the ability of European and North American countries to act decisively on behalf of wildlife. The parks only needed $40,000 to $60,000 to fund salaries until the end of the year, when the UN hoped the government in Léopoldville might reestablish its power base. Verschuren hoped Grzimek could mobilize the conservation community to help the Congo parks in their time of need.[85]

Unlike the IUCN's Africa Special Project, Grzimek was not dependent on the UN or hamstrung by diplomatic protocols to press forward with requests for grants or to court the emerging cohort of African statesmen. Indeed, shortly after Lumumba's assassination in Stanleyville in January 1961, Grzimek received Marcel Bisukiro, a minister who represented Antoine Gizenga's Communist-backed government that had taken over leadership of the regime in Stanleyville, at the Frankfurt Zoo offices. Grzimek's account of their dialogue in *Rhinos* portrayed the meeting as an African appeal for a partnership that the zookeeper so desperately hoped to create throughout postcolonial East Africa. "The animals in our national parks are a common possession of the Congo people," Bisukiro is quoted as saying, "indeed of all mankind. We want to carry on what the Belgians have built, we want to preserve the parks for humanity as a treasure of wild life. Rhinos belong to everybody, to all mankind . . . . But our coffers are empty."[86] Amazed and delighted that "these Gizenga people here" had come down on the "right side" despite an indifferent Cold War world, Grzimek concluded "a solemn agreement, a sort of state treaty between the director of a zoo and an African government" that promised to secure the funding in exchange for "continuing a task on which the Belgians had worked so admirably for decades."[87] Grzimek took this compact seriously and cabled and phoned all over the world in search of funding, but no government or organization was willing to help in a region governed by a Communist-friendly regime that would not cooperate with the

UN and the central government in Léopoldville. Using donations from his tele-vision series and behind-the-scenes funds from Foreign Minister von Brentano, Grzimek raised the necessary monies and transferred them to Verschuren to make sure they made it directly to the game scouts.[88] "No one knows what will happen next in the Kivu and the other national parks in the Congo; for no one can predict what political developments will occur there. But the Africans have certainly shown that they can protect their country's wild animals in nature reserves and want to do so—at least where the Europeans in their country have given them a good example."[89]

The hyped-up Congo sojourn made Grzimek's FZS the most important European player in African conservation, as no other organization was so closely associated with a leader ready to enter the field himself to get things done.[90] By raising funds and ensuring accountability for the Albert and Garamba game scouts, Grzimek successfully cultivated an image as an honest broker above Cold War ideologies, ready to act swiftly and decisively as events unfolded on the ground, unencumbered by the large boards of directors, expensive overhead, or black-tie fundraising that enriched but also encumbered the larger NGOs.[91] Organizations such as the Friends of Africa in the United States turned to him for advice and support; the New York Zoological Society awarded Grzimek its gold medal for his conservation work in 1962.[92] Decolonization quite unexpect-edly became an opportunity to reinvigorate Grzimek's quest to save the conti-nent's wildlife by setting a "good example" of a European outsider who cared. His new mission was to convince African statesmen that national parks were not legacies of the hated colonial past but resources for the future state: a global com-mons that belonged to "everybody" but held in solemn trusteeship by African states. Environmental protection became a marker of political maturity—of the self-abnegation necessary to govern other facets of the state. As Grzimek put it, every rising "barbarian" people is "anxiously striving not to appear uncul-tured"—much as the German peoples themselves once felt in relationship to Greek and Roman civilizations.[93] With the political situation in the Congo still rocky, Grzimek and his allies set their sights on Tanganyika to become the new model conservation state.

Our National Parks Are the Envy of the World

As much as Grzimek had vilified the British colonial administration during the Serengeti controversies, the creation of the Michael Grzimek Memorial Laboratory and his experiences in the Congo led him to re-activate his ties to East Africa's British expatriates to press forward with conservation efforts in Tanganyika. These individuals had managed to hang on to leadership over wildlife affairs despite angry calls from the trade unions and radical voices within TANU ranks for more expansive Africanization of the civil service.[94] The Nyerere and Kawawa governments resisted such calls in the early years because many British civil servants had administrative and budgetary skills, international contacts, and fundraising capacities that African statesmen were perceived to lack in the short run.[95] Numerous memoirs have described Grzimek's close friendship with Myles Turner, the legendary Chief Game Warden who secured the new park's borders by creating an armed and disciplined brigade to fight the Serengeti's "poaching wars" between the late 1950s and 1970s.[96]

Less well known, but far more consequential, was Grzimek's close working relationship with John Owen, who took over leadership of the recently created National Parks Department from Molloy in 1960. Owen oversaw the rapid expansion of park lands during the following decade, largely by supplementing Tanganyika's "impecunious" resources with outside aid from big foundations and NGOs across Europe and North America.[97] The son of a missionary to Kenya and himself a former colonial officer in Sudan, Owen had spent his whole life in Africa. He quickly developed a reputation for his aggressive fundraising on behalf of Serengeti and other parks: "He could bite anyone's ear for money," recalled former park warden Gordon Harvey, "one reason he lasted so long."[98] Grzimek had special sympathy for such European Africans who knew their time was short due to impending Africanization: "Who wouldn't have sympathy for the Englishmen who now had to go? . . . the land was also their *Heimat*."[99] While the two did not always see eye to eye on conservation measures, Grzimek was Owen's most stalwart supporter, "pulling strings on the outside." Grzimek did everything in his power to keep Owen in place and delay Africanization—a move that reinvigorated the Anglo-German wildlife alliances forged in the imperial era to save animals in the postcolonial regime.

In Grzimek and Owen's view, Tanganyika's relative "underdevelopment" in comparison to its British territorial neighbors made it an especially suitable place for fostering wildlife conservation and nature tourism. Unlike its neighbors, Tanganyika could avoid monstrous dams, blighted cities, and smoke-stack industry—leapfrogging over the worst stages of development on its way to modernity.[100] Owen shared Grzimek's belief that European conservationists only had a short window of opportunity before wildlife affairs passed into African hands; nothing less than "an immediate and all-out effort" would do.[101] As a consequence, Owen and his staff sought to gazette national parks as quickly as possible in those areas of the country still rich in game but "unencumbered by human rights" and the threat of poachers. In 1960, the parks administration had four areas under consideration—the Ngurdoto Crater (the core of a future Arusha National Park), Manyara, Tarangire, and Mikumi. Owen envisioned a future with numerous other parks but recognized that in its "present stage of political evolution" and scarcity of funds, the Tanganyika government necessarily prioritized health and other social services.[102] The only way to make up the shortfall in the near term was international assistance. After reading *Serengeti Shall Not Die*, Owen boarded a plane to Frankfurt and asked if Grzimek could help prepare the country for Africanization by assisting with the establishment of new parks.[103]

Grzimek convinced Owen that the immediate aim should be to acquire a light aircraft to survey and police the Serengeti's fifty-five hundred square miles with a small staff.[104] In Grzimek's estimation, the airplane would give Tanganyika a comparative edge, avoiding the dilemma of paying for the Congo's bloated cadres of African staff by allowing wardens to shuttle quickly between monitoring sites or aid visitors in emergencies. The planes also became indispensable for bringing foreign dignitaries and donors into the parks. And so, the Zoological Society helped the National Parks administration secure its first airplane, and Owen and Turner learned to fly. "It is probably not an exaggeration," Owen later wrote, "to say that the future maintenance of the game herds is dependent on our having the means of controlling poaching from the air."[105] Airplanes gave the park staff the leg up over poachers with "modern weapons"—rifles, cars, and wire cable snares—with which they carried out their "cruel destruction of the wildlife."[106] Like Grzimek, Owen erroneously believed that it would be quite easy to reduce poaching to "negligible proportions" over the longer term through public enlightenment—and made education and training the priority for the postcolonial parks department.

Working in tandem in the months ahead of the Arusha Conference, Grzimek assisted Owen in outlining a "crash progamme" with six critical objectives for conservation that sought to rebrand colonial nature reserves as sources of African national pride. The program included a number of critical elements: "awakening African public opinion" to the economic and cultural value of their unique heritage of wildlife; training African staff to serve as game scouts and wardens; expanding park habitats to preserve existing species of animals; building up the tourist potential of parks; increasing the stock of animals by putting in water supplies and fire breaks; and controlling poaching more aggressively by creating a heavily armed "ranger force."[107] The call for training resulted in the establishment of the College of African Wildlife Management in Mweka, which received a portion of its initial funding from the FZS and the German ministry for economic cooperation and development.[108] "Naturally we aim to put our own citizens in charge when we have men of sufficient caliber and training," noted one park service report. "The Beefeaters guarding the Crown Jewels are British."[109] One day soon, Mweka's leaders assured Tanganyikans, Africans would be ready to take on the solemn responsibility of administering their wildlife heritage.[110]

Grzimek and Owen's public outreach focused on countering the notion that national parks were privileged playgrounds for white colonials. Grzimek began a wide-ranging "propaganda march" in the offices of diplomats, on the pages of *Das Tier*, and through direct aid to the parks administration to support this view. Zoological Society funds helped the national parks administrators to dub *Serengeti Shall Not Die* into Swahili and make another film featuring the beauty and significance of the national parks.[111] Under the motto "an ounce of personal experience is worth a pound of propaganda," the FZS also assisted in a public education campaign about the value of national parks for African society.[112] Since many African villages lacked a cinema and few Africans could read or attend school, Grzimek and Owen requested help from the Federal Foreign Office (Auswärtiges Amt, hereafter AA) to purchase a "filmrover"—a mobile projector and screen used in schools, agricultural shows, community centers, and public gatherings to spread the word about the "plant and animal world of their homeland."[113] By 1964, the filmrover had presented 250 shows, with an estimated 150,000 Africans in attendance.[114] Soon thereafter, Owen unveiled a poster campaign, also financed in part by the FZS and the AA and approved by Nyerere, featuring slogans in Swahili such as "Our national parks are the envy of the world—be proud of them," and "Our National Parks bring good money into Tanganyika—preserve them."[115] The FZS also worked with Owen to sponsor an essay competition whereby rural schoolchildren were offered prizes for essays that conveyed the majesty and value of African wildlife. With Ford Foundation funding, the parks administration eventually set up an education office in Arusha to coordinate outreach, particularly by bringing "tribal chiefs," "influential Africans," and even schoolchildren on group excursions to the parks.[116]

While the IUCN relied on vague promises of UN assistance to realize its Africa Special Project goals, Grzimek solicited aid directly from West German sources and television viewers during the fluid transition toward independence in 1960–1961. Grzimek put special emphasis on building a youth hostel in the Serengeti for Tanganyikan schoolchildren to visit the wonders of the park at a negligible cost. The zookeeper emphasized the links between children's love of nature and Germans' traditional regional pride, drawing equivalencies with German *Naturschutz* traditions. As Grzimek wrote to von Brentano in a plea for twenty-six thousand Deutsche marks in financial assistance for the project, "over ninety percent of the population of Tanganyika, the former German East Africa, do not know their indigenous large animals, such as lions, elephants, etc., because these animals were exterminated in the thickly settled parts of the territory long ago." Whereas children in Europe and North America had access to zoological gardens, Tanganyikan youth lacked easy access to nature study; the national parks could thus serve an important role in education and in "learning to love" the animal world of their *Heimat*. Such love of homeland nature, Grzimek averred, offered a more enduring foundation for African nature conservation than monetary rewards. "In this way," he noted, "the significance of the national parks will rise in the eyes of the African population and politicians, and they will have a stronger will to preserve them."[117] With additional help from American donors such as the Coca Cola Foundation, the parks succeeded in bringing in over four thousand Africans visitors to the parks by the early 1960s.[118]

Grzimek shrewdly emphasized the diplomatic value of the youth hostel announcement for West Germany at the forthcoming Arusha Conference. He worked furiously in the weeks ahead of the congress, promising to "multiply the material (*sachlich*) and political effect by making representatives of other African countries aware of the [West German] gift."[119] As he told the FRG consulate in Nairobi, West Germany did not want to be outdone in this region by the British, American, and Scandinavian representatives who had already announced gifts or sponsored some of the African attendees. "Through this gift," he noted, "there will be a certain equivalency (*Ausgleich*) to the advantage of Germany."[120] For West Germany, then, conservation and tourism development became a small but growing form of "technical assistance" on the brink of independence.[121]

Owen never relied exclusively on the Frankfurt Zoological Society or West German government, however, and sent his public appeals to organizations in the United Kingdom and the United States to help "extravert" Tanganyika's costs.[122] The annual subventions from the Tanganyika government were barely enough to care for and administer existing parks, and with budget deficits looming, the "world" needed to step in if expansion and public enlightenment campaigns were to succeed. "Wildlife is not a factor in the cold war and it has little propaganda value. Like any other worthy cause in the world, we need money and we need money quickly." Owen emphasized that the parks did not need much—"the price of one obsolescent modern weapon would enable us to save the game of Tanganyika for many generations to come"—but the need to prove the worth of wildlife before the Africans took over was critical.[123] Indeed, by providing the exact costs of the equipment in both pounds and Deutsche marks and offering a range of ways to help, the Parks Administration hoped to appeal to a range of donors—from £3 (a little over $10) to sponsor an essay competition to £3,000 ($10,500) for a new dam to provide dry season water for animals—each of which would bear the name of the donor.[124] Through such direct appeals and FZS help, Owen gradually built up a small state-within-a-state that tried to make up for shortfalls in annual budgets through direct assistance from abroad.[125]

The international success of *Serengeti Shall Not Die* in print and on screen provided Grzimek with additional resources to assist the Tanganyika National Parks.[126] A *Times* review lauded the Grzimeks' effort as "the best film ever made about wild animals... full of love and anger." Much of the praise stemmed from the film's technical mastery. "Don't miss this remarkable sequel to *No Room for Wild Animals*," noted the *Daily Examiner*. "For here the wild animals of the wild plains of Tanganyika display in their natural habitat a gracefulness that can hardly be matched by any human posing before the cameras."[127] But the politics also mattered. In its critique of the late imperial administration, *Serengeti* seemed to capture like no other wildlife film at the time the urgency of the decolonizing moment. As another British reviewer noted, "Recent political events in Africa give a special interest to this work."[128] Grzimek's public modesty at film openings also drew praise, as British observers commended this "simple and very sincere naturalist from Frankfurt" at his short introductions at the London showings, noting that the film was "completely free of theatrical tricks but as exciting as any Hollywood thriller." Once the film received the Oscar nomination in early 1960, even the British House of Commons screened it to a packed house of MPs.[129]

The success of *Serengeti Shall Not Die* in London and North America also drew the attention of the West German diplomatic corps, who recognized the cultural value of a German film celebrity just as the FRG was seeking to expand its influence in East Africa. Indeed, it was consul general for British East Africa, Herbert von Stackelberg, who first requested private screenings, with opening remarks by the filmmaker, in Nairobi and Dar es Salaam. An avid hunter, von Stackelberg shared many of his peers' misgivings about the sensationalist scenes in *No Room for Wild Animals* but argued that the zookeeper and his son had struck the right tone in *Serengeti*, one that might serve West German "public relations" and "good will" gestures in the region.[130] Von Stackelberg arranged for Noel Simon, the chairman of the Kenyan Wildlife Society, to introduce the film at its Nairobi opening. But von Stackelberg added his own remarks about this uniquely German quest for scientific truth.[131] In his words, the film reflected "a profound love for our animal world" and "an element of human tragic (sic)," as it was a visual monument for the "early deceased." Quoting King George IV, who had opened the 1933 London Convention with stirring words about the need to protect animals for subsequent generations, von Stackelberg wrote: "In this idea scientists, nature friends and tourists from all parts of the globe form one community."[132] Soon thereafter, von Stackelberg arranged for the Foreign Office to donate $250 toward Michael Grzimek's grave memorial.[133] Such support became another conduit for Grzimek to funnel modest grants-in-aid to the fledgling Tanganyika Department of National Parks outside of formal state-to-state protocols.

Help for the Threatened Animal World

Direct donations from television viewers also provided Grzimek with more immediate financial resources than many rival nongovernmental and international agencies in these critical years.[134] Despite the accolades for *Serengeti*, Grzimek knew television would displace documentary films as the best platform for disseminating information about the plight of African animals and raising donations for the Zoological Society's conservation efforts. "I do not intend to make any other film in Africa. That was the business of my son," he told a friend in Kenya. "Besides of that the cinemas are loosing [*sic*] so much visitors through television so that the chances for new documentary films are very bad."[135] When Grzimek's *A Place for Animals* first aired in 1956, it focused mostly on the habits and quirks of live animals brought into the studio from the zoo.[136] But in the early 1960s, Grzimek modified this formula to feature vignettes and reportage about the zookeeper's journeys to Africa and the Zoological Society's efforts to protect animals in their habitats abroad. Through television, viewers experienced animals more directly than in *Serengeti Shall Not Die*, as viewers were able to see, hear, and sympathize with the creatures that the FZS sought to protect without ever leaving home.[137] The program became more professional, too, with the station providing an editor to help Bernhard assemble the program from the massive amount of footage taken by him or other filmmakers on assignment in Tanganyika and elsewhere.[138]

Such comfort and dependability set viewers up nicely for the "pitch" that ended each show—a request not to forget the animals by offering small donations to support the Frankfurt Zoological Society's newly created "Help for the Threatened Animal World" (*Hilfe für die bedrohte Tierwelt*). Despite the television station's deep discomfort with solicitations on camera, the pitch came to have a "dramaturgical role" in the program. It offered Grzimek the opportunity to speak to the viewers directly and bring them into the virtual community of heroes fighting on the right side of history.[139] Then, in subsequent shows, Grzimek could point out directly what viewers' donations had accomplished—from funding the youth hostel in the Serengeti for African children to a new airplane for the staff of the Ngorongoro Conservation Area Authority (NCAA). Rather than berating Africans for not doing more, Grzimek always made sure to laud their governments, underscoring the sacrifices that these young countries were making to shame European donors to step up and do their part in the worldwide struggle to stop extinction. In 1962, the FZS shifted its mission from primarily supporting the zoological garden to "preserving the plants and animals at home and abroad," particularly by sponsoring the expansion of national parks.[140] Grzimek was proud that his small aid organization relied heavily on

Figure 6.4 Grzimek collecting donations for the "Help for the Threatened Animal World," 1970. The Zoological Society's separate fund enabled Grzimek to amass millions of small donations from television viewers, which legitimated the mass appeal of his conservation campaigns and enabled him to serve as an honest broker between North and South at critical moments in the Congo and Tanganyika. Institute for the History of Frankfurt, S7P, Nr.5.650, Photographer Philipp Kerner.

modest donations from "the little people," though inheritances in the millions from deceased fans also played a critical role in building the fund's endowment.[141] By the 2000s, the fund had accrued over thirty million euros (over $48 million), making it one of Europe's most important nature conservation foundations.[142] More than any other medium, television allowed Grzimek to amass the followers and money that explain West Germany's unexpectedly robust presence in wildlife affairs on the brink of independence.

Television also gave Grzimek his best leverage yet for proving that wildlife could pay for themselves—through the promotion of package photo safaris to East Africa on *A Place for Animals*. To show Nyerere and his ministers that "the tourists were already coming," Grzimek bluffed his viewers into thinking that moderately priced vacations were available to see the magnificent animals that appeared on his show.[143] The zookeeper mentioned that travelers could fly round-trip from Frankfurt to Africa and visit the Serengeti and other game sanctuaries for around $477 (two thousand Deutsche marks). Grzimek knew that no German travel agencies offered such packages—indeed, a roundtrip flight alone cost about $719.[144] But once hundreds of people inquired about the tours, travel agents went to Tanganyika, discussed terms with hoteliers, and put together the tours under the auspices of the Frankfurt Zoological Society. To overcome the lack of airfields suitable for commercial jets near the park, the tour operators chartered four-engine propeller planes, piloted by Yugoslavians, which used a smaller landing field at Arusha to bring the parties close to the parks. The first party of about eighty-five travelers arrived in December 1960; most were married couples around the age of sixty, for the equivalent of $477 was still too steep for younger West German families. Expecting primitive and dangerous conditions, two doctors on the tour brought suitcases full of drugs, not realizing that there were pharmacies all over the region.[145] The group members then found themselves in comfortable log cabins with baths and electric lighting, a magnificent view of the Ngorongoro Crater, and a comfortable car that rambled down a freshly paved road into the crater and pulled up to about five yards from a lion. Bemused by their responses, Grzimek wrote: "Reading about the disturbances in the Congo and Algeria, they imagined you couldn't go to Africa at all these days. Rather as if an American dared not visit Spain because Khrushchev was in power in Russia."[146]

Grzimek was hardly the first to tout the region's touristic potential or promote its natural wonders on the world stage.[147] The East Africa Tourist Travel Association (EATTA) was already hard at work in the 1950s promoting the Serengeti and Ngorongoro among the "magic words" recognized by safari tourists to Africa. Between its founding and dissolution in 1965—largely due to the emergence of self-standing national tourist boards and ministries in Kenya (1958), Uganda (1962), and Tanganyika (1962)—the EATTA collected statistics on visitorship, eased passport controls, customs procedures, and currency exchange restrictions for visitors, and promoted the region's natural wonders and historic sites at trade fairs in Europe, the Rhodesias, and South Africa.[148] In addition, East African Airways had worked to establish direct connections between Nairobi, Kampala, and Dar es Salaam and European capitals, opening up bureaus in Frankfurt and other big cities. The airline also published tourist brochures about the wonders of East African wildlife that appeared in several languages, including German.[149]

Paradies für wilde Tiere

Herausgegeben von der Ostafrikanischen Fremdenverkehrs-Organisation

PREIS Shs. 1/–

Figure 6.5 A Paradise for Wild Animals. Grzimek was not the first to promote East Africa's wildlife as tourist magnets as the East African Tourist Travel Association (EATTA) was hard at work in the early 1960s publishing brochures and ads touting the national parks—including this one appealing to West German visitors. Historisches Archiv zum Tourismus at the Technical University of Berlin.

In 1959, East Africa received 60,343 visitors who spent $22 million in the region—a total exceeded only by coffee exports in Kenya and the fourth most important export in the region after cotton, sisal, and coffee.[150] Yet, as Grzimek noted in his 1960 Arusha lecture, this was only a trickle of the global share. The region had not yet benefited from the overall growth in global tourism, he noted, nor diverted the tourists from the "classical" holiday resorts of the Mediterranean to its blossoming national parks. East Africa did receive visitors from a variety of nations in 1959, but of the 705,000 Americans who traveled abroad in 1959, only 6,482—less than 1 percent of the total—came to East Africa despite its natural wonders.[151] In light of these realities, the Zoological Society offered its own tours to boost the number of visitors. Despite newspaper articles accusing Grzimek of using state-run television for his own profiteering, the Frankfurt Zoo began to offer group tours led by staff, including Richard Faust, the managing director of the zoo, and Rosl Kirchshofer, the head of school groups and biological instruction.[152] The tours booked up quickly in 1960, and 1962 saw a threefold increase compared to 1961, with Swiss operators expressing interest in sponsoring their own package tours as well.[153] By 1971, the FZS had chartered almost a hundred package tours.[154] As Grzimek told Fairfield Osborn, the tours served as further evidence of his capacity to use TV to "make propaganda" on behalf of the animal world.[155]

Saving the Rhino

Media celebrity and donations from Europe gave Grzimek unprecedented ability to shape conservation debates on the ground in Tanganyika, but his tendency to focus solely on well-connected international conservationists and African political leaders confronted local land users with more powerful and well-funded opponents than the former colonial state. In 1961, Owen told Grzimek that the Maasai had requested a screening of the newly released Swahili version of *Serengeti Shall Not Die*, to be held on *Uhuru* day in December. Elders had complained that "they were always being filmed but never got to see the results," a sure sign that they recognized the challenges of representing their interests in the postcolonial period that lay ahead.[156] Their request came on the heels of months of conflict in 1960 over environmental autonomy within the Ngorongoro Conservation Area (NCA): the land promised to them as compensation for evacuating the Serengeti Plains in 1958.[157] In that year, one thousand Maasai and twenty-five thousand cattle had entered the NCA with a government promise that they would receive veterinary services, schools, and watering holes for cattle and goats as compensation for the loss of prized grazing lands. Sir Richard Turnbull assured the Maasai Federal Council that "should there be any conflicts between the interests of game and human inhabitants [in the NCA] those of the latter must take precedence."[158]

Yet government reluctance to make good on these promises manifested itself soon after the NCA's creation. The NCA committee's governance model attempted to combine Maasai participation with a more conventional colonial approach to district administration, leading to familiar disputes over Maasai access to dry season pastures.[159] The central administration committee for the NCA had nine members, including the district officer who was the chairman, four other colonial officials, three Maasai residents of the NCA, and one non-resident Maasai—a structure that was supposed to offer opportunities for significant local participation but favored top-down, bureaucratic-led authority.[160] For example, the Maasai residents pushed strongly for the water supplies they felt had been promised them in return for departing the Serengeti, but the chairman of the committee did not want to bore holes and lay pipelines for fear of hurting tourists' views. As a result, the two chairmen who served separate terms during this short period stopped calling meetings altogether after May 1960.[161]

The first real management plan for Ngorongoro, drafted in 1960, recommended that the Maasai should be moved out of the crater altogether, prompting the NCAA's first full-time conservator, Henry Fosbrooke, to protest the "daddy knows best" mentality of the British colonial administration.[162] Though the Maasai made up 98 percent of the population of the NCA, the 1960 plan ensured that they never had more than two individuals on the Authority's board of directors—a situation that ensured that local voices had few opportunities to stand up to the combined weight of global conservationism, tourism, and state development experts. Repeating tired stereotypes about the "cattle complex," the plan described Maasai attitudes as "conservative in the extreme" and the elders of the community "bigoted and conceited . . . [regarding] . . . any conservation measures adopted which prevent them from doing as they themselves wish a nefarious scheme to deprive them of their country." The 1960 plan called for the same tired formula of destocking rangelands and excluding "uncontrolled persons" from the Crater and Northern Highland Forests.[163] Even though Fosbrooke was known to sympathize with Maasai desires for autonomy and recognized the sustainability of Maasai range and livestock management practices, he created the position of conservator of the NCA to bypass the governing council in favor of an advisory board stacked with international conservationists rather than local representatives.[164]

Grzimek and his conservationist allies wanted to stop any use of this precious habitat as a pilot area for sustainable traditional use. Efforts to improve animal husbandry in the NCA held little appeal for Grzimek and Owen, who disliked Fosbrooke—whom they assumed "could hardly fail to hang himself" if given enough "rope"—and argued that the Maasai were doomed to perish as a result of desertification.[165] Among the pair's priorities for the Tanganyikan National Parks in 1960 was to convince the postcolonial administration to revisit the British colonial government's Ngorongoro compromise. "We must manage to convince the Government and people of this country," Owen wrote, "that it must be preserved as the finest game area in the most splendid setting in the world."[166] Grzimek underscored its tourist potential, describing it as "the only place in East Africa where visitors can see wild animals amid a wonderful landscape because all the other national parks are situated in semi-deserts."[167] As Tanganyika moved toward independence in 1961, the pair did everything they could to torpedo the Ngorongoro experiment and absorb the NCA back into the national park system lest "the rhino . . . join the dodo and the Great Auk in the limbo of animals."[168] The immediate postwar years thus witnessed a replay of the late 1950s debates about Maasai "overgrazing" and "overstocking," only this time in partnership with an African nationalist party far less sympathetic to customary use and "tribal" prerogatives.

To foster a sense of crisis in the Ngorongoro region, Grzimek widely publicized the reports he had received about the spearing of over two dozen black rhino by Maasai adolescents in 1960.[169] Grzimek and Alan Root learned of the killings on their way back from the Congo from Tony Mence, the chairman of the NCA administrative board, who invited Grzimek's help to identify the culprits and think about strategies to stem the losses. British colonial authorities had long claimed that the Maasai posed no threat to wildlife, since pastoral wanderings did not impede wildlife migrations, and the Maasai only consumed the meat of their own cattle. But soon after the creation of the NCA, authorities discovered skulls, carcasses, and even gravely wounded and barely alive rhino across the crater floor and rim, many with a Maasai spear still piercing the hides. After sharp denials of involvement from local herdsmen, the authorities identified several adolescents as culprits, each of whom claimed self-defense against the ferocious-looking, but quite harmless beasts, exclaiming they could only save their own lives by killing the *kifaru*.[170]

Grzimek found such explanations preposterous given the diagonal angle of the wounds delivered to supposedly charging animals. He pinned the killings instead on an old colonialist stereotype: the young men's "idleness" and boredom, "presumably to win kudos from the girls."[171] But as the killings escalated and authorities found more carcasses with their horns missing, Grzimek and Root discovered that the youths were involved in poaching for the black market for East Asian consumers, who prized pulverized rhino horn as an aphrodisiac. Grzimek recommended collective punishment for the Ngorongoro Maasai—fifty cows forfeited for every dead rhino found—to prevent such killings in the future, since it better fit "African custom." But British magistrates insisted on individual trials that resulted in what he viewed as a measly two-hundred-shilling fine for the trader and no sentences at all for the teenagers.[172]

Grzimek hoped that independence would sweep away such leniency. Colonial authorities routinely gave the Maasai a slap on the wrist, Grzimek argued, or naïvely accepted pleas from those convicted of trespassing that they were too poor to pay up. Grzimek advocated charging the herders as "citizens who had sinned against an important common property of the people" (*Gemeinbesitz des ganzen Volkes*).[173] Grzimek contrasted the British treatment of the idle Maasai youth—who according to "custom" did not "work" and relied on raiding other tribes—with the protectionist resolve of the Congolese authorities. The Congolese understood the value of their patrimony, according to Grzimek, and meted out harsh sentences to Watutsi herders who trespassed with their herds on park property. Grzimek argued that Maasai elders could have easily helped to identify the youth involved by the unique size and shape of the spears found. Their refusal to help was a sign that they still deemed their "tribal" loyalties more important than national citizenship, even repeating the old stereotype the Maasai were wont to break their promises to the government since "it is an old Masai tradition that oaths are only valid within the tribe, not when made to other Africans, let alone Europeans."[174] Such pronouncements justified closing the Maasai out of discussions about the future of the NCA by implying they were not yet ready to assume the rights of citizens.

In a pattern that would become familiar over the next decade, Grzimek publicized local disputes with the Maasai and other rural Africans to mobilize international outrage and force African governments to step up enforcement and fines toward poachers. A number of observers at the time disputed Grzimek's doomsday portrayal of the killings, with some arguing that the selling of horn was a regrettable, though temporary, result of a famine in the region in 1960–1961. Fosbrooke contended that the rewards for information on the sale of the horns alone would have the desired effect of stemming the killings, noting that it was far better to have the Maasai in place in the NCA to prevent more vicious commercial poachers.[175] Yet the rhino was then (and now) an important symbol of the global extinction crisis and its endangerment stirred strong emotions; in 1961, the IUCN estimated that there were only thirteen thousand left in the whole of sub-Saharan Africa. Even more alarmingly, the animals thrived best in a delimited habitat—they did not migrate and were difficult to relocate or restock. The Ngorongoro Crater had long been one of the best places in the world to see them, and tourists found it quite easy to drive up within a few yards of the fifteen-hundred-pound creatures.[176] Soon enough, every famous Western visitor to East Africa, from Juliette Huxley to Peter Matthiessen to Dennis Armand, commented on the rhino killings—a sure sign for many observers that Ngorongoro's goal of delicate balance between humans, livestock, and wild animals was beginning to collapse.[177] Huxley reported thirty-six killed or missing—and only six to eight pairs left. "Next year there may be fewer," she noted ominously. For many, the killings justified ending the multiple-use experiment and banishing pastoralists from the conservation area for good.

What these scenes of Maasai backwardness and treachery overlooked was the political and symbolic meaning behind the rhino killings: retaliation for having their herds shut out of the Serengeti Plains and their voices squelched on the Ngorongoro Conservation Area Authority's board. The fact that rhinos in the first wave of attacks still had their horns and were left with readily identifiable spears in them was a clear sign that these were the attacks of aggrieved herdsmen and not poachers.[178] The loss of the herdsmen's seats on the board exacerbated the sense of betrayal over land alienations and the failed promises of the conservation unit, whose administrators put ever-increasing emphasis on wildlife protection and tourist priorities over livestock needs. As one district chair on the board noted, "the rhino killing may be a deliberate defying and annoying of authority and an attempt to rid the Area of the chief tourist attraction," so that the pastoralists might be left in peace.[179] The Maasai retaliated, too, against the plan's major goal of controlling livestock numbers and herdsmen's movements in accordance with "scientifically planned range management"—a move that they rightly associated with further alienations of land to cultivators and forced destocking measures.[180]

Rather than take the Ngorongoro killings as a desperate plea for dialogue over the future of their historic grazing lands, Grzimek ramped up pressure on the

government to dismantle any cooperative governing structure of the NCA altogether. He proposed that a game warden be given full control over the NCAA,
repeating his arguments that law enforcement, stricter policing, and "collective
punishment" were the only solutions to prevent further attacks against the rhinos.[181] To prove that the rhinos were more important than cattle herds, Grzimek
fostered the agitation for stronger government action by encouraging tourists
on the Frankfurt Zoo's tours to send postcards to Nyerere and editorials to East
African newspapers expressing outrage over the senseless killings—in some
cases even forging tourists' names on letterhead from lodges and hotels when
they seemed too preoccupied to participate in the mail campaign.[182] Grzimek
trusted that when these tourists returned to Europe, they would be his best
ambassadors for the conservation cause. They would form a new and affluent
wing of the green network that was willing to strongarm African statesmen when
necessary.

In Grzimek's recounting of the events that followed, Nyerere summoned
him to a meeting in December 1962 after receiving an avalanche of such
letters—this time in a "new skyscraper" representing Tanzania's rapid modernization. The prime minister put up his hands in a gesture of mock defense. "In
the last few months I have been constantly criticized in the press because the
rhinoceros are being slaughtered in Ngorongoro. You are undoubtedly at the
back of it."[183] Grzimek warned him that he would go on working for the preservation of Tanganyika's wild animals by mobilizing public opinion through press,
radio, and television. "As I went out of the air-conditioned room," he wrote in
Rhinos, "I met a delegation of simple peasants in the sultry heat of the ante-room.
I wondered what cares they would be unloading on him in a minute or two—
and hoped he wouldn't forget mine, which were Tanganyika's too."[184] The most
"secure path ahead," in Grzimek's estimation, was to transform the area into a
national park and force out the Maasai altogether.[185]

Tanganyika did not dismantle the NCA and make it a national park as
Grzimek hoped, but the growing international pressure on Nyerere did cause
the prime minister to assess the future of pastoral development. Indeed, even
before the *Uhuru* celebrations in December 1961, Nyerere called on Paul
Bomani, Tanganyika's minister of finance and the premier's self-professed "right-
hand man during the independence struggle," on a mission to visit Ngorongoro
in January 1961 to bring the Maasai into line. "I am determined that the objective of preserving and developing one of Tanganyika's greatest assets should be
promoted and strengthened in every possible way," Bomani noted. "I fully share
the public concern at the folly of a few Maasai youths in continuing attacks on
rhino . . . one of the main tourist attractions of the area and one that does no
harm whatever to the Masai or their stock." Echoing old colonialist stereotypes
about lack of ambition, Bomani hoped that tourism would lure the Maasai into

a cash economy, giving "the young men some aim and object in life apart from trying to show off or waste their talents."[186] Tanganyika's cohort of African leaders at independence had few qualms about replacing customary land privileges rooted in the hated British system of tribal chiefdoms with a form of multiracial citizenship anchored by "productive" labor.[187]

Bomani made it clear that the new government would only provide the veterinary services and new water supplies promised by the 1958 compromise if the Maasai became true stock farmers, contributing to the national economy by "making proper use of the market for meat and meat products." Such services, he continued, cost the government considerable money, which could only be raised in the short term by tourism—a circular logic that proposed that the very industry that restricted Maasai access to pasture and forests for cattle was critical to their preservation as a people. Put another way, the Nyerere government adopted the former colonial role of "trustee" over "backward" peoples within the national community, with wildlife conservation and tourism serving as justifications for the state to mobilize "recalcitrant" rural populations. The Maasai needed this guidance to be "freed" from poverty and ignorance, and African nationals were much better equipped to emancipate them from such suffering than the colonial governments before them. As one African politician told the zookeeper in 1961, "It's a shame about these fellows. If you could persuade them to buy cars or refrigerators or at least trousers and shoes, they might sell five percent of their cattle every year. But as it is, oh dear!"[188] Bomani supported Grzimek's proposals to reorganize the Conservation Authority in a way that would "safeguard" the interests of "not only of the Masai themselves, but of the whole country" by prioritizing tourism and conservation over customary land use.[189]

Grzimek saw tourism as the Maasai's only hope for survival—if the "tribe" did not accommodate the "winds of change" in East Africa, they would perish in favor of their politically powerful, "land hungry" farming neighbors.[190] German and British colonialists might have had a "weakness" for the Maasai, Grzimek averred, but the "civilized Africans" (who were not about to cede precious land to herders) ridiculed the pastoralists for going around "naked except for a long garment like a Roman toga."[191] Grzimek suggested that the once-intrepid warriors offer themselves as tourist curiosities, since their "red pigtails, swords and shields" placed them among the "last noble savages in Africa."[192] Yet neither Grzimek nor Bomani gave much thought to *how* the Maasai would benefit from the tourist industry. The government had no concrete plans for Maasai training in hospitality management or to ensure that they would receive part of the revenues from hotel stays and photo safaris on pastoral lands.[193] Conservation and tourism completed the enclosure of lands that had begun under the British, leaving no room for pastoralists to regain lost territory as part of their political emancipation.[194]

This emphasis on a transactional ecology that promised to "utilize" dryland environments for the productive needs of the fledgling nation soon dominated conservationist rhetoric at the Arusha Conference. In line with the multiethnic and developmentalist rhetoric of the early 1960s, citizenship depended on the ability to contribute to the community of African producers. As West German diplomats remarked approvingly in 1960, there was no other country in Africa in which independence leaders made it clear that "Freedom did not mean Idleness" and "that the day of independence will not suddenly bring about a land of milk and honey (*Schlaraffenland*)." As they put it, Nyerere paired the call for *Uhuru* with the demand for *Kazi* (hard work), slogans that served as a rallying cry for TANU youth to bring those "loafers lying in the sun" who "sleepily and automatically thanked the new leaders for their 'freedom,'" out into the fields to work.[195] Land, in Nyerere's view, was "God's gift to man—it is always there" but was never to be owned unconditionally. "A member of society will be entitled to a piece of land *on condition that he uses it*"—a formulation that made it nearly impossible to argue for pastoralists' transhumant culture.[196] Under the banner of socialist "familyhood" (*ujamaa*), the Tanganyikan government dismantled freehold land tenure and private ownership of land altogether in 1963.[197] It then reinstated the colonial state's 1928 monopoly on wild animals by casting them as national property—and moved aggressively to criminalize "unlawful" uses of animals.[198] In an era that favored a "big push" toward managed development and global conservation, the Maasai and other pastoralists found themselves squeezed between a modernizing state and international conservation lobbies, with less room for maneuver than they had under the old colonial order.

The ongoing Ngorongoro crisis thus forged a strange and precarious alliance between European conservationists wary of the spread of Western urban modernity and African nationalists hoping to "catch up" to Western levels of material well-being.[199] At independence, development became the "legitimating project of the postcolonial nation-state," and the Maasai represented all that Africans had tried to leave behind; they were an "embarrassment" due to their perceived "savage" ways.[200] In an interview just a few years later, Nyerere noted "It's 1964 for everybody in the world, *including* the Masai . . . and the pressure for all to live in 1964, including the Masai, is fantastic." As Nyerere explained, there was no room to live a traditional life, even an ecologically sustainable one. It did not matter if the Maasai were content, either. "I'm not trying to make them *happy!*" he exclaimed, exasperated, "there is a difference between clean water and dirty water. My problem is to get that woman clean water . . . . Happy! I'm not involving myself in that." For him the question was more basic: "What kind of water are the Masai drinking in 1964?"[201]

Though Grzimek's campaign to retain the Serengeti's original borders failed, the transition to the postcolonial era did not prove to be the disaster for wildlife that he and other conservationists had feared in the late 1950s. In fact, decolonization offered an opportunity to renew and reinvigorate the global quest to save charismatic wildlife from extinction by forging a novel and, at times, awkward partnership between European conservationists wary of modernization and a corps of African statesmen who embraced a high modernist vision of development. Grzimek's fears about the "overly hasty" granting of independence dissipated as Nyerere and other cabinet members gave the green light for nature tourism and national park expansion as means to earn foreign currency and enhance Tanganyika's international stature. Fears that independence would lead to widespread poaching turned out to be unfounded as Tanganyika's "developmentalist vanguard" recognized wildlife as a critical asset that the young nation could exploit economically, culturally, and diplomatically. Grzimek was convinced that had Nyerere and his cohort of TANU ministers been in charge already in 1958, they would never have allowed the Ngorongoro region to be excised from Serengeti National Park—and he was probably right.[202]

This does not mean that Nyerere and others were passionate conservationists or even prioritized wildlife in the same way that the international agencies and global NGOs at Arusha were—far from it. In cases where the colonial inheritance did not align with the state's productivist goals—as in the Forestry Division—the state did not hesitate de-commissioning reserves it felt were necessary to boost agricultural output.[203] But Nyerere did accept the territory's potential role as a "wilderness exporter" if Grzimek could deliver the hordes of tourists ready to land and see the animals. Along with Tewa, Mahinda, and others, Nyerere also began to see the possibilities for wildlife to serve as a medium of diplomatic exchange, a "wellspring" of value that might enable Tanganyikans to "leverage" a better future for themselves at home and on the world stage.[204]

In the fluid state of affairs after independence, Grzimek's key partner remained John Owen, the Brit who remained leader of the National Parks Department from 1960 to 1971. Buttressed by the growing revenues from the international success of *Serengeti Shall Not Die* and donations to the Frankfurt Zoological Society, Grzimek helped Owen devise a "crash program" of park administration, ecological research, African warden training and especially public enlightenment designed to convince Africans to view their national parks as both a precious global heritage and a source of national pride. In this race against impending Africanization, the pair pinned their hopes on Tanganyika—the "poor sister" among British East African territories—to replace the Belgian Congo as the most conservation-minded state in sub-Saharan Africa. By the time of the Arusha Conference, Grzimek's FZS, working in tandem with John Owen, had already put the institutional structure in place to expand parks, train

African game wardens, build national pride in wildlife, and jumpstart the tourist sector. Such a commodified vision of nature foreclosed any deep reckoning with colonial legacies and emboldened the developmentalist vanguard in Tanzania's elite to tighten its grip on rural commons, including the savanna drylands. For pastoralists and others, national independence dismantled colonialism's already precarious recognition of customary land tenure without offering any rights-based language by which to contest global conservation norms and the state's narrow vision of a productive citizenry.

The real victims of the reboot of the German quest to save the Serengeti in the 1960s were rural Africans, who found their desires for deeper land reform thwarted by new forms of national citizenship and international expectation that constricted their ability to participate in pastoral development and nation-building on their own terms. Proposals to shift the emphasis in the NCA from pastoralist development to tourism stemmed from a shared sentiment among European conservationists and African agricultural ministers that dryland environments and their inhabitants were difficult to render productive. The Maasai, like all other Tanzanians, were expected to pair their newfound "freedom" with *Kazi*, or else the land would be given over to more productive uses. Rather than a bulwark against capitalist encroachment, wildlife conservation accelerated the commodification of land, people, and animals and undermined the existing working landscapes that fit neither the Edenic nostalgia of European conservationists nor the utopian development schemes of Tanzanian modernizers.

Who Cares for Africa's Game?

> If the mass of my countrymen are to be enlisted in the ranks of conser-
> vationists, they will expect to see that what they are told is 'their heri-
> tage,' however valuable it may be as a cultural asset, can still be made to
> earn its keep. I believe it can—through tourism.
> —T.S. Tewa, Tanganyika's Minister of Land and Surveys, 1961

In the spring of 1968, Bernhard Grzimek read alarming news about the state
of conservation in Tanzania. Derek Bryceson, the country's brash new minister
of agriculture, forests, and wildlife, had granted permission for an architect to
erect a new hotel at the bottom of the Ngorongoro Crater—right in the "heart
of the wilderness" that he and Michael had fought so hard to save.[1] The architect, Willi Woldrich, envisioned the edifice as a four-star lodge that would rival
Kenya's famed Treetops Hotel, which had long delighted visitors inside Aberdare
National Park with a design that encouraged animals to come right up to guest-
room windows.[2] Having spent almost a decade promoting Tanzania's tourism
industry, Grzimek now found himself regretting this potential blight on the crater landscape.[3] Using the tried-and-true formula of previous campaigns, Grzimek
turned to the green network of international conservationists to write letters of
protest to Nyerere and his ministers—Sir Julian Huxley, Prince Bernhard of the
World Wildlife Fund (WWF), Peter Scott of the Fauna Preservation Society
(FPS), Fairfield Osborn of the New York Zoological Society (NYZS), as well
as scientists such as Fraser Darling and Aldo Leopold's son, A. Starker Leopold.
The younger Leopold pleaded with the minister for tourism not to follow the
example of the United States, where lodges were "depreciating" the unspoiled
natural wonders of places such as Yosemite; protecting the "crystalline beauty
of a park" was the only way to ensure the "lasting attractiveness" of the Crater.[4]
By June, Grzimek received a short note from Nyerere's assistant noting that the
president had called off the Austrian's plan.[5] Grzimek breathed a sigh of relief but
had made yet another enemy. "Grzimek appears to consider the Ngorongoro his
personal zoo," noted the architect bitterly, "he says 'No!' to the plan and other
scientific eggheads in the world go 'quack, quack' and follow after him."[6]

Our Gigantic Zoo. Thomas M. Lekan, Oxford University Press (2020). © Oxford University Press.
DOI: 10.1093/oso/9780199843671.001.0001

Grzimek's victory in the NCA was short-lived. Just over a year later, another controversy erupted, this time over an administrative order from Bryceson ceding more than thirty-two-hundred square miles of the conservation unit to the Maasai Range Management Commission for ranching and farming cooperatives. With regional and European newspaper headlines declaring "Serengeti May Have to Die," Grzimek accused Bryceson, as the "only white member of the Tanzanian cabinet," of stealing one of the "Black nations'" most precious gifts to world heritage.[7] Tanzania's president issued a stay on the plans, but the West German ambassador warned Grzimek that unfounded accusations against Bryceson and other Tanzanian ministers were alienating East Africans who resented the zookeeper's heavy-handed tactics.[8] With the Maasai and other communities growing rapidly on the edges of the Serengeti, no one—not even Grzimek—seemed sure anymore just how long the "fragile illusion" that had driven his Serengeti quest would last into the *ujamaa* era.[9]

The NCA controversies and growing East African resentment over Grzimek's meddling were a far cry from what the zookeeper and his allies had been expecting in 1961.[10] Throughout the 1960s, Tanganyika (which became known after its union with Zanzibar in 1964 as the United Republic of Tanzania) remained the conservation community's "beacon of hope" in sub-Saharan Africa, having created six new national parks right after independence and laying plans to gazette a half dozen more by 1980.[11] For Grzimek, Owen, and their allies, all signs were pointing in the right direction after the Arusha Conference. Poaching was at its lowest point in decades, and animal populations were rebounding.[12] International and bilateral pledges of support seemed assured, and many Tanzanian statespersons shared conservationists' belief that wildlife could benefit the economy through planned development.[13] As Julian Huxley remarked in 1964, the situation was "not nearly so desperate as it seemed to many people a few short years ago . . . . difficult, yes, and in some ways dangerous, but not desperate."[14] Huxley warned about "rapidly expanding populations" that might cancel out conservation's gains, but "for the moment . . . . African wild-life is not irrevocably doomed; it is merely alarmist to talk of its speedy extinction."[15]

The shift in wildlife policy from colonialist preservation to a postcolonial emphasis on exploiting animals' "biological capital" made it possible for Grzimek to attract West German agricultural development funds for wildlife conservation— indeed the FRG emerged as Tanzania's third largest foreign donor by 1964. Technical assistance from the Max Planck Institute, the Thyssen Foundation, and the German Research Foundation (Deutsche Forschungsgemeinschaft, or DFG) enabled the zookeeper to expand the Michael Grzimek Laboratory into a more expansive "Serengeti Research Project" that sponsored studies of animal population dynamics as well as dryland ecological planning. With the help of the West German Foreign Office and the German Agency for the Advancement of Developing Nations (Garantieabwicklungsgesellschaft, renamed Deutsche Förderungsgesellschaft für Entwicklungsländer, or GAWI), moreover, Serengeti researchers began investigating the possibility of sustainably harvesting animals on the borderlands of Serengeti National Park. Such "wildlife utilization" aimed to provide rural Africans with cured or canned bushmeat culled from wildebeest and zebras—a "rationally planned" alternative to "wasteful" poaching and pastoralism in these working lands.[16] The FRG saw the utilization project as a gesture of solidarity against the "Soviet Zone of occupation"—the German Democratic Republic (GDR)—which had begun its own campaign to attract supporters among nonaligned countries in Africa.[17] Despite Grzimek's insistence that wildlife protection stood above "ephemeral" rivalries, African nationalism and Cold War competition reshaped the German-Tanzanian contact zone after independence.

Despite the technocratic optimism of this era, Grzimek and his European allies never conjured the technical assistance, emergency aid, or tourism receipts necessary to sustain a park system over the long haul, leaving the Serengeti and other national parks on a shoestring budget by the time disillusioned Africans took over the wildlife sector in the early 1970s.[18] In all three areas, Grzimek found that misguided ecological assumptions and material "underdevelopment" thwarted his ability to "make wildlife pay for themselves." Development disenchantment emerged first in the wildlife utilization project, where logistical difficulties, parasites, and erratic weather stymied game croppers' forecasts of sustainable bushmeat yields. A second wave of disenchantment arrived in 1963–1964, when Grzimek and Owen realized that foreign donors would never make good on their Arusha promises—leaving Tanzania to foot the bill for park expansion and maintenance out of its own meager budget.[19] By the late 1960s, only tourism was left to make wildlife conservation profitable—but optimistic forecasts faded as most visitors chose Kenya over Tanzania.[20] Frustrated by Kenya's monopoly over the tourism industry, Nyerere closed the northern border entirely in 1977, marginalizing Grzimek and forcing out the last British expats from positions of authority. By that point, the president had learned that the zookeeper and his compatriots might never deliver on their promises of wildlife-based development.[21]

The deficits in international aid and visitation were apparent to many British expats, African bureaucrats, and even Grzimek himself well before Tanzania launched its ill-fated experiment in rural socialism known as ujamaa. Yet international development scholars have usually blamed Nyerere's ideological reorientation toward China and the Eastern Bloc for destroying the country's burgeoning tourism industry. According to this interpretation, the Arusha Declaration of 1967, in which Nyerere called for vigorous self-reliance and state planning, stifled innovation and hastened the withdrawal of foreign aid—a

time when one former British warden lamented that "everything was beginning to fall apart."[22] The Arusha Declaration was followed a few years later by
the ill-conceived scheme to villagize the country's rural population (the notorious *Operation Vijiji*), which forcibly relocated the majority of the country's
rural denizens in government-designated population centers between 1973
and 1976.[23] Vigorous displays of top-down collectivization, coupled with a war
against Uganda, scared off Western donors and tourists, leaving little money
in the coffers to stop the poachers that decimated rhino and elephant populations in the late 1970s and 1980s.[24] But the promoters of "structural adjustment programs" in the 1990s largely forgot the broken promises of the Arusha
Conference that equally explain Nyerere's disenchantment with Western conservation.[25] Indeed, by taking Grzimek at his word—that is, by overestimating
the success of nature tourism after 1961—scholars have missed the extent to
which the green network and development experts saddled the young country
with an under-utilized tourist infrastructure atop an already inadequate colonial
one. The German-Tanzanian contact zone that the Grzimeks had forged in the
1950s had dissolved by the early 1970s, leaving Nyerere and his cabinet—and
not the "world community"—responsible for the fate of rhinos, wildebeest, and
elephants.

Courting Nyerere in the Cold War

Grzimek's conviction that Tanganyika was the world's best hope for wildlife
remained unshakable in the wake of the Arusha Conference. During broadcasts
of *A Place for Animals,* and in the pages of *Das Tier,* Grzimek cultivated an image
of Nyerere as a gentle teacher-statesman and defender of wildlife.[26] The prime
minister understood the emotional value of animals for the country's future, as
he had grown up in a small village on Lake Victoria, just outside of the Serengeti's
borders. Grzimek served as Tanganyika's Honorary Curator for National Parks
and on the park system's Board of Trustees—unique positions from which to
offer technical assistance to an emergent wildlife conservation and tourism
sector. Nyerere had no plans to "replace white intolerance with black nationalism," noted a 1962 article in *Das Tier.*[27] Indeed, the role of European advisors
and British expats in wildlife affairs showed that the prime minister still valued
expertise over "hasty" calls within TANU's ranks for immediate Africanization
to redress decades of colonial oppression.[28] Nyerere's Arusha Manifesto would
one day be recognized as a watershed event in African history, Grzimek averred.

Grzimek's depictions of Tanganyika as a racially tolerant and environmentally conscious nation helped to fortify goodwill between the Nyerere and
Adenauer regimes during the height of the Cold War. Diplomatic cables and

reports from the West German consulate in Nairobi and the Foreign Office in Bonn confirmed Grzimek's favorable impressions of the new prime minister. As one foreign officer put it in a 1960 circular, "in spite of the tremendous power (*Machtfülle*) that Nyerere holds in his hands, this slender man comes across quite modest in conversation. The openness, casualness, and humor that he displays to his conversation partners can easily lead one to forget the enormous burden of responsibility for the fate of 8.5 million people that will soon fall on him."[29] Positive impressions of Nyerere soon filtered into West German newspapers and magazines as well, which portrayed Tanganyika as a shining example of how the UN mandate system had transformed Germany's former colony into the first "real black democracy."[30] As one German embassy official wrote in 1961, Tanganyika remained an "island of trust" despite the frightful events on its western border with the Congo.[31] Even though Great Britain remained the major source of foreign aid, such comments signaled that Tanganyika was developing a "sort of foster child's relationship with the West Germans."[32]

To bolster its ties to "the former German East Africa," the Foreign Office invited Nyerere for an official visit in January 1961—eight months ahead of the Arusha Conference and almost a year ahead of formal independence. As Nyerere's delegation entered the Bundestag building, the delegates stopped parliamentary proceedings and greeted them with "prolonged applause."[33] In the discussions that followed, both sides tiptoed around painful discussions of the colonial era's forced labor, land alienations, and violent repression, underscoring instead vague and positive references to "historical ties" to curry favor and cement goodwill.[34] "(West) Germany is a country that feels near and dear in the eyes of many Africans, because it doesn't possess any colonies," one foreign officer maintained. It was a model for development as well, since "twice the country lay flat on the ground as 'underdog' and yet worked its way up from nothing." As such, the colonial past could undergird the diplomatic present, since "The dark side of the former German colonial administration has been forgotten."[35]

Nyerere and his ministers, for their part, did not shy away from rose-colored reflections of the pre-1914 period. In a lecture to the German-Africa Society during his 1961 visit, Nyerere spoke positively about Kaiser officials who had helped the country develop its railway systems and propagate sisal, its leading cash crop.[36] Nyerere then headed off to meetings with Economic Minister Ludwig Erhard—architect of the West German economic miracle—to speak of development assistance. He wanted help for Tanganyika to achieve its development goals laid out in a World Bank–inspired Three-Year Plan (1961–1963), which envisioned overcoming the lack of homegrown African capital, entrepreneurs, and know-how through European donations, foreign aid, and investment.[37] Erhard recalled fondly the development plans of fifty years prior, when the Germans drew up blueprints for using the waters of Lake Victoria to irrigate the lands bordering its eastern shores.[38] The Federal Republic pledged funds to pick up where it had left off by establishing an agricultural engineering institute that would make drought-prone areas bloom again.[39]

Bonn's eagerness to court Nyerere and sidestep the colonial past reflected the global "German-German" rivalry between the capitalist FRG and Communist GDR that shaped diplomacy and development aid in 1961—the same year that the Berlin Wall was built.[40] Though this rivalry reflected in part the "bipolar disorder" that was fueling proxy wars between Washington and Moscow throughout Asia, Latin America, and Africa, the East–West German enmity had its own dynamic, particularly in nonaligned countries such as Tanganyika.[41] After the creation of the FRG and GDR as separate states in 1949, as one historian has put it succinctly: "East Germany sought the world over to gain acceptance as a legitimate state, and West Germany sought to prevent this."[42] With diplomatic recognition by only eleven countries—all of them Communist—the GDR's leaders turned to the newly independent countries of the Third World, hoping that formal recognition by even one non-Communist country would "generate an avalanche of further recognition" and lead to the "acceptance of the GDR as an independent state."[43] The FRG, however, viewed the GDR as illegitimate—a "Soviet Zone of Occupation" whose people would gladly reunite with the West if it were not for the foreign oppressors in East Berlin. In 1955, the West German State Secretary to the Foreign Minister, Walter Hallstein, articulated Bonn's guiding position, which became known as the Hallstein Doctrine. The FRG would refuse or cut off diplomatic ties with any state that recognized the GDR except the powerful USSR.

With the Berlin Crisis in full swing in 1959, the Adenauer regime encouraged Third World leaders such as Nyerere to tie the German Question to their own countries' struggle for freedom and independence under the banner of "self-determination"—in this case, a plea for the right of citizens in the East to hold free elections.[44] Yet as a "peasant and workers' state," the GDR could proclaim solidarity with former colonies abroad even as it sealed off its own citizens behind an "anti-fascist rampart." It did so by portraying the FRG as the land of the true villains, since Marxist-Leninist ideology dictated that both late nineteenth-century imperialism and Nazism were products of capitalist militarism and violent worker suppression. These fascist "remnants" of the Third Reich, the GDR asserted, remained latent dangers in the state and industrial apparatus of the West, a threat to socialist internationalism, peaceful coexistence, and anti-imperialism everywhere.[45] As the West Germans were well aware, the GDR was working to undermine their efforts in Tanzania by linking Bonn to the apartheid regime in South Africa and the bloody imperialist suppression of its NATO allies France in Algeria and Portugal in Mozambique. Such anti-imperialism resonated with Nyerere's unwavering support for pan-African liberation and public warnings about a "Second Scramble for Africa" lurking behind promises of development aid.[46] Tanganyika felt the pressures from this rivalry firsthand. Soon after Nyerere had stepped down from his premiership in 1962 in favor of Rashidi Kawawa, the GDR premier Otto Grotewohl sent the new prime minister a congratulatory note that Kawawa merely acknowledged—creating a flurry of indignation in Bonn. The Foreign Office immediately instructed its embassy in Dar es Salaam to remind Kawawa that there was only one Germany—indeed the one that had recently pledged millions of Deutsche marks for development aid.[47]

In this Cold War context, Grzimek presented wild animals and wildlife conservation as "apolitical" gestures of solidarity that hovered above "transient" political ambitions. As Grzimek had told readers in *Serengeti Shall Not Die*:

> In a hundred years time Kruschev and Eisenhower, political anxieties and hatreds will only have a printed existence in history books, but men will still consider it important that wildebeest should roam across the plains and leopards growl at night.... Nature is of abiding importance to us all.[48]

The national parks on the drawing board were, in his words, a "great cultural achievement of the young states there," noting that "poor African countries sacrifice several times more for the conservation of nature and the national parks than the USA or we in Europe."[49] In Grzimek's formulation, Tanganyika's commitment to animals appeared rational, dignified, humane, exemplary—in sad contrast to West Germany's failure to create even a single national park. Tanzania was leading the way in a "new branch of human culture" despite the squeeze from East and West.[50]

Wildlife Diplomacy in Postcolonial Tanzania

Notwithstanding such accolades, Nyerere was no pawn of Grzimek or his West German allies. The prime minister made surprisingly few public affirmations of wildlife conservation within Tanganyika itself, and those close to him knew he was no heartfelt conservationist. Nyerere balked when Grzimek and Owen asked to use his picture on the design of national park promotional materials, for example.[51] Commenting on a 1962 speech by WWF leader Prince Philip, in which the British royal admonished the former colony to put even more of its scarce resources into antipoaching, Owen wrote to Grzimek, "As I listened to it, I wondered whether it might produce a reaction in the opposite direction.... I feel that it would be wise for everyone to lay off Nyerere for the moment."[52] Yet Tanganyika's leader knew that his country's abundant elephants, wildebeest, and buffalo gave the young nation outsized heft on the global stage as a provider and protector of the precious "wildness" that fascinated industrialized nations. Indeed, as a united Tanzania evolved from a parliamentary democracy into a one-party state with a strong president, Nyerere parlayed foreigners' interest in wildlife into additional aid, a dignified international standing, and goodwill ties with the country's allies. Wildlife conservation, in this sense, served Tanzania's own search for diplomatic recognition and helped to build the state apparatus by reordering, developing, and surveilling the rural population and its animal life. On his journeys abroad in 1960–1961, Nyerere assured audiences that "we have the richest range of wild life in the world and our wild life is well protected."[53]

Such "wildlife diplomacy," as one historian has aptly called it, entailed shaping international relations between the Third World and the more powerful countries of the First and Second Worlds by broadcasting Tanzania's commitment to conservation or offering international visitors direct experience of the country's fauna.[54] When foreign dignitaries came to Tanzania, a trip to Ngorongoro, Serengeti, or Lake Manyara was a common and pleasurable experience, creating lasting bonds of friendship, particularly with world leaders who supported Nyerere's commitment to nonalignment and liberation movements in southern Africa. For those dignitaries who lacked time for trips into the interior of the country, Nyerere even kept a small zoo on the statehouse grounds consisting of Tommy gazelles and a few other animals, which he expanded in the mid-1960s into a full two-acre private zoo in the heart of Dar es Salaam.[55]

Given that TANU had ridden a wave of rural discontent over conservation to challenge British authority, grassroots party officials and their rural constituents resented these plans for currying favor with former imperialists and expanding colonial-era national parks.[56] Yet in 1961 Nyerere saw few other options in the short term given global trade imbalances, Tanganyika's "poor" land, and a dearth of homegrown capital. East African participants at the Arusha Conference bristled at the racism and paternalism on display among the European speakers, yet they also voiced support for international conservation so long as it meshed with their own nations' plans for rural development and national belonging. At the heart of the German-Tanganyikan contact zone of the early 1960s was thus an implicit bargain. Tanganyika promised Grzimek and Owen a degree of autonomy in expanding parks for wildlife protection in exchange for technical assistance funds, development grants, training, and tourism.[57]

The most vocal supporter of wildlife conservation for a newly independent Tanganyika was Hamed Seleman Mahinda, a former game scout who had worked with Myles Turner in the Game Department since the 1950s. Having completed a degree in wildlife management at the University of Colorado with FAO sponsorship, Mahinda spoke at Arusha about the themes and results of his "propaganda work" for the game division, which included educational programs and pamphlets in villages designed to instill pride in wildlife, encourage better treatment of domestic livestock, and stop poaching in parks and reserves.[58] "If the mass of my countrymen are to be enlisted in the ranks of conservationists," Mahinda noted, "they will expect to see that what they are told is 'their heritage,' however valuable it may be as a cultural asset, can still be made to earn its keep."[59] Wildlife had to prove their capacity to pay for themselves to maintain African support for conservation.

Tewa Said Tewa, the new minister for lands, forests, and wild life, also envisioned the national parks as sources of foreign capital. Tewa told conference participants that Tanganyika, like its neighboring countries, needed an infusion of money to raise its people's living standards. One of the country's most urgent needs in this context was "an industry which can bring in large sums of money from outside while making the minimum demands on our slender resources for capital expenditure and foreign exchange." Tourism seemed to fit the bill, since it had enabled a number of poorer and primarily agricultural areas such as Greece, Spain, and the West Indies to attain a more comfortable standard of living. Agricultural Tanganyika could similarly benefit. It had abundant wildlife to be sure but also a good climate, beautiful scenery, snow-capped mountains, and "many picturesque scenes of African life." Such features could be "set against the cathedrals and art galleries" in wooing European tourists to a faraway land.[60]

Despite the commonalities with Grzimek and the IUCN's promotion of tourism at the conference, the East African participants resented European comments that portrayed Africans as precocious children who lacked an appreciation of animals or the environment. To be sure, Tewa noted, the "mystical and romantic" depiction of wild animals in Europe puzzled many Africans, many of whom considered elephants especially as a "dangerous agricultural pest" and wildebeest an "unwelcome competitor" for prized grazing lands. Yet Tewa was sure that he could convince his peers that animals were "more use to them alive than dead" if tourist revenues could build schools and attract doctors to their villages.[61] Frustrated by Europeans who assumed that independent Africans were not capable of wildlife stewardship, Tewa used a feature story in Grzimek's *Das Tier* to remind readers that the country's second premier, Rashidi Kawawa, was the son of a game scout and had inherited his father's enthusiasm for protecting wildlife. But Tewa also warned that the young country still needed Europeans' direct donations, urgently: tourist monies were not enough in the short term for a country facing daunting challenges of poverty, inadequate primary education, and epidemic diseases.[62]

In a similar vein, Mahinda took umbrage at European grumblings about Africans "disliking game" because the animals interfered with agricultural fields or posed a threat to villages. Mahinda cautioned against sweeping generalizations about all 120 tribes in Tanganyika, noting that outside of pastoralist groups such as the Maasai, nearly all hunted or made use of trophies for commercial purposes—and thus had depended on the animals for centuries. Based on his experience working with the Game Department, he noted, "It is not difficult to convert Africans to recognize the value of a thing, provided it is introduced to them in the right way." Almost all appreciated good stories about how the game had maintained African lifeways in the past. Gone were the colonial days when rural African subjects would accept an order to vacate land or avoid hunting. Newly emancipated citizens needed to be presented with sound reasons for the government's preservation policies. If Europeans rushed to blame the African for wildlife decline, he warned, "He will not accept what you say."[63]

Despite certain commonalities with the IUCN agenda, therefore, the African participants at Arusha were quick to underscore that Africans themselves were rescuing wildlife from colonial neglect and mismanagement. Working along-side Owen and Kinloch, Mahinda helped the wildlife departments to portray wild animals as an essential part of Tanganyika's national heritage. As one new article reported, "Animals were a fundamental part of the individual lives of Tanganyikans and of the country as a whole."[64] Other ministers began to speak of wildlife as *Urithi*, an intergenerational inheritance that linked wildlife conservation to the building of a national family. As a 1962 article in the TANU newspaper *Uhuru* (freedom) noted, Tanganyikans had stewarded the wildlife "before the grandparents of the British and Germans had arrived in Africa and ruled our country. Our grandfathers protected these animals."[65] Such sentiments echoed those of a growing number of nationalists who contrasted African pride in animals with the former European colonizers' sad destruction of their own wildlife.[66]

Given these long-standing ecological ties to animals, Africans did not need Europeans' help to reach "Stage Four" nature appreciation. Standing for the first time on the edge of Ngorongoro in 1961, noted the Ugandan ecologist David Wasawo, brought forth an unparalleled "feeling of the greatness and sublimity of nature." Wildlife had already made its mark upon cultures across Africa, finding expression in "folklore and its dances, its masks and ceremonies, its music and in the wonderful stories illustrating human characteristics as related to particular birds and mammals."[67] The extermination of animals, in Wasawo's view, would be a loss to African cultures—not just European filmgoers. The rest of the "world," he warned, needed to remember how jealously new nations guarded their independence, taking care in "how their advice or help is given."[68] Wasawo reminded his listeners that Africans would not tolerate European paternalism for long; postcolonial conservation had to meet African needs to stay relevant.

The Arusha Bargain articulated in these speeches appeared to pay off for Tanganyika, at least in the short run. Grzimek reported the good news that he had brokered support for a series of West German initiatives designed to exploit the country's biological capital: an expansion of the Michael Grzimek Laboratory, support for the game management school at Mweka, and, most important, a "nutritional utilization" pilot project in the Serengeti that sought to "crop" wild animals as bushmeat for villages and export.[69] Nyerere and his ministers stood ready to reap the rewards of technical assistance for planned development—yet soon discovered that donor-funded projects did not always deliver on their promises of abundance.

Conjuring Development, Act I: Bushmeat Utilization as "Technical Assistance"

In terms of total funding, Grzimek had his greatest success transforming the Michael Grzimek Laboratory into sub-Saharan Africa's leading center for ecological research.[70] Working closely with John Owen, Grzimek convinced the Thyssen Foundation, the Max Planck Institute, and the DFG to join a host of other donors—FAO, the Dutch Foundation for Pure Research, and the American Ford Foundation—to convert the makeshift facilities at Banagi into a state-of-the-art field station replete with research instruments, a small library, and a permanent staff.[71] The British ecologist Phillip Glover headed up the team working on the "Serengeti Research Project," which included Hans Klingel from West Germany studying the social behavior and population dynamics of the zebra; Murray Watson from the UK investigating the population ecology of the wildebeest; and Hans Kruuk from the Netherlands, who contributed work on the hyena and predator–prey relationships.[72] In 1966, Grzimek, working with Konrad Lorenz and Niko Tinbergen, helped Owen to convince the Thyssen Foundation to boost its contributions even further, thereby laying the foundations of the Serengeti Research Institute (SRI) at Seronera. The foundation donated over 950,000 Deutsche marks (about $238,000) for plant and equipment, making Thyssen and Ford the main sponsors of the Institute over the following decade.[73] The scientists who came to the Serengeti often imagined themselves working in an ecological paradise regained—only dimly aware of the many land controversies that had preceded their time in Seronera.[74]

To sell Nyerere on the project's relevance for Tanzania's developmental goals, Grzimek and Owen promised that the Serengeti Research Project would encompass broader questions of how to manage protected areas, delineate ecologically appropriate land uses, and develop wildlife as sustainable food resources.[75] Grzimek advocated an interdisciplinary program of research that he termed "biophylaxis," by which he meant a multifaceted investigation into "conserving the future of all forms of living things." Such an ambitious program required going far beyond the usual remit of zoology, as biophylaxis connected patterns of vegetation, animal migrations, and weather—much as his and Michael's preliminary investigations had done. In Grzimek's view, the "biophylatical" approach was critical to modernizing the management of parks, which had been run since colonial times by military officials with no scientific training—resulting in park lands that were unsuitable as habitat.[76] With "Anglo-Saxons" having dominated such ecological research agendas since the interwar era, Grzimek warned, the "colony-less" Federal Republic would quickly lose its standing in the developing world without immediate attention to tropical land management.[77]

In the Serengeti, as Grzimek knew, researchers were just beginning in the 1960s to understand how savanna ecosystems supported a large and diverse array of mammal species without overshooting the land's carrying capacity. Indeed, an unforeseen experiment in the natural regulation of species populations was well underway: the "eruption of ruminants," such as wildebeest and buffalo, after the end of drought conditions.[78] In 1962, just after Mwalimu Julius Nyerere became president, the rains returned with a vengeance in the Serengeti, turning Naabi Hill in the center of the park into an island in a sea of inundated grasslands.[79] Researchers also began to notice that the dreaded rinderpest virus was disappearing from wildebeest populations as a result of late colonial cattle inoculation campaigns. The combination of improved forage and lower disease incidence doubled the yearling survival rate, increasing population sizes fivefold from 1961 to 1971.[80] Despite these exciting findings, it was unclear how Tanganyika would benefit directly from scientific research. As Tewa noted in 1963, the project brought prestige to his country but did little to convince poachers to give up the hunt or the Maasai to forgo prime grazing lands. Starving children needed an "immediate, practical demonstration" of why it is critical to preserve large wildlife herds.[81] Tewa was intrigued by Arusha Conference presentations that showcased wildlife as an antidote to rural protein deficiency: game cropping.

Grzimek had spoken to Nyerere about the lab's research on "culling" (i.e., shooting) a sustainable number of wild animals and butchering them for bushmeat. He had even published an essay about how such wildlife "exploitation" had allowed park managers to utilize hippo carcasses culled in Queen Elizabeth National Park. There, UK advisors had determined that trampled riversides and lakesides showed that population numbers had become too large for the park's habitat size.[82] Yet the zookeeper moved cautiously in linking the laboratory's agenda to such a boldly utilitarian scheme.[83] In 1963, he assisted the Foreign Office in funding and equipping a small West German research team in the Serengeti dedicated to "wildlife utilization and bushmeat exploitation" (Wildnutzung und Wildbretverwertung) for the benefit of the indigenous population. At Grzimek's urging, GAWI and DFG provided the money to send Rüdiger Sachs, a veterinary scientist with extensive experience in the former German Southwest Africa, and Ulrich Trappe—son of the famous huntress—into the

Serengeti research station at Banagi on a three-year contract.[84] Sachs and Trappe were charged with cropping a small number of wildebeest, zebra, gazelle, and topi, measuring their muscle mass, and preparing their flesh as cured or smoked meat for nearby villages. They also hoped to identify infectious diseases in wild animals that might transfer over to domestic livestock or endanger bushmeat products.[85]

The Arusha Conference had included a sizeable contingent of speakers who advocated game ranching as an alternative to ecologically destructive ranchland and crop development schemes in savanna ecosystems. The American rangeland ecologists Raymond Dasmann and Archie S. Mossman, who carried out game ranching experiments on the Henderson Ranch in the lowveld of Southern Rhodesia (today's Zimbabwe) from 1959 to 1964, showed that wild animals were more efficient converters of plant biomass into energy than cattle and other domestic livestock.[86] Using ecosystem models of energy flow and food chains in vogue at that time, Dasmann and his colleagues argued that the grassland-wild animal assemblage formed a "delicate niche structure" in which different species browsed across a variety of vegetation levels and types—many of them unpalatable to cattle—but without competition between the browsers.[87]

In Grzimek's estimation, game cropping had a number of affinities with applied biophylaxis. For one, Dasmann and Mossman's work gave a robust ecological explanation for why the Maasai and other pastoralists "overgrazed" the savannas—their cattle were alien to the ecosystems of East Africa. As Grzimek put it, the partitioning of forage niches in a natural savanna allowed mammals ranging from the tiny duiker to the mighty elephant to fit seamlessly into the natural environment "like a giant puzzle," whereas cattle created gargantuan "steamroller formations" that denuded the vegetation.[88] Secondly, Dasmann saw game ranching as a tool of land-use planning, a way to conserve the vast pastoral lands between national parks and urban areas. Aware that the tourist industry would take many years to be profitable, Dasmann argued that "rationally exploited" bushmeat provided a quick return on investment, undercutting poachers and alleviating rural nutritional deficits in protein.[89] Finally, game cropping offered an alternative to "misguided" Maasailand development schemes, since bushmeat utilization did not require costly fencing, waterhole boring, veterinary services, staff, or maintenance—the game were simply there for the taking.

With the help of veterinarian colleagues at research stations in Kenya, Sachs was able to confirm Dasmann's hypothesis that game animals transformed plant material more easily into muscle than cattle based on analyses of topi and impala carcasses. Sachs and Trappe were also able to produce an edible and passably nutritious version of the cured meat jerky known in South Africa as "biltong" during the dry season in early fall 1964 using recently killed wildebeest and zebra.[90] As such, they hoped, wildlife utilization on a larger scale might help

Tanganyika achieve greater self-sufficiency in food, enabling the country to spend precious foreign currency on agricultural equipment and manufactured goods—key West German exports. As the German ambassador in Nairobi told his colleagues in the Foreign Office, the efforts at Banagi promised an "apolitical but nevertheless favorable influence that is of great interest to East Africans and a proof of German goodwill in the region."[91] Bushmeat utilization buttressed the West German–Tanzanian contact zone of the 1960s with the promise of sustainable resource management.

Grzimek's optimism for the scheme faded quickly, however, as the Sachs team confronted unexpected logistical bottlenecks, cost overruns, and unruly environmental conditions. Many observers at the Arusha Conference had already voiced concerns about the problems of transferring game cropping experiments on private ranches close to butcheries in South Africa to the remote buffer zones of national parks in East Africa, where wild animals were not about to submit "quietly and placidly" to their own destruction. "Your protein yield per acre from game may be as high as the sky," warned Richard Turnbull at Arusha, "but it will be of little use to you unless you can secure it how you want it, and in the quantities you want."[92] Other critics pointed out the disjuncture between the "expatriate staff and administration" required for wildlife utilization and African aspirations for environmental sovereignty. As one editorial writer in the *East African Standard* complained, Africans might be employed as hunters or truck drivers, but "they will neither own the land nor the animals. This is contrary to much of the meaning of political independence and represents a sharp break with the understood practices of pastoral tribesmen."[93] The writer gestured toward the markets in which the Maasai sold or exchanged cattle for vegetables, tools, or manufactured goods—a regional economy that European images of cattle hoarders had long misunderstood and undervalued.[94]

As Turnbull had foreseen, no one—not even the charismatic Grzimek—could broker their way past the microbes, erratic weather, and remote conditions that stymied Sachs and Trappe's efforts in 1964 and 1965. Sachs found dozens of varieties of parasites inside the guts of the impala, antelope, gazelle, wildebeest and buffalo he studied, including helminths, or tapeworms. Tapeworm cysts were known to cause cysticercosis in domesticated livestock—and in some cases, people—and obviously needed further investigation before the bushmeat could be sent to market.[95] Sachs wanted to expand his investigation of the animals' rich parasitical microbiome, but John Owen had quickly grown tired of the bloodbath at Banagi. His discomfort with shooting animals for research forced the West German pair in 1964 to move the entire project to Kirawira, a borderland camp on the Grumeti River outside the park's boundaries, which lay about sixty miles northeast of Banagi (see Figure I.2). The long distance from markets and passable roads at Kirawira meant building a rudimentary research station from scratch—largely through Trappe's hard labor.[96] Sachs's letters to Grzimek and GAWI detail the herculean tasks involved in conducting research in these conditions—from a lack of potable water and electricity to periodic floods that washed out encampments and left the group stranded for weeks at a time. Sachs could not convince the DFG to ship various veterinary medications overseas, nor could GAWI find a cost-effective way to supply an amphibious Unimog vehicle to get a refrigerated container to the site. As the costs mounted and the results less promising, the West German funding agencies seemed less and less willing to speed such requests along.[97]

While Grzimek was accustomed to mobilizing television viewers with direct appeals, he could not wield these mediagenic powers to compel the weather to collaborate with the West German team. The humidity of the Kirawira region as compared to Southern Rhodesia, coupled with the unexpectedly long rainy seasons of 1964 and 1965, revealed that there was no easy way to produce edible biltong for market. At the Henderson ranch, Sachs had witnessed hunters easily cutting the bushmeat into 30 to 40 cm strips, salting it, and letting it dry in the sun where it quickly formed a crusty exterior impervious to fly infestation.[98] But in the Serengeti, the return of the heavy rains in the early 1960s meant that the moist air lingered throughout the year, causing animal carcasses to show signs of a "bacteria-infested sheen" within two days, despite all efforts to salt and even smoke the animal flesh quickly.[99] Future researchers, he told Grzimek, should heed the warning of the team's African assistant: "Africa wins again."[100]

The troubled project left Grzimek scrambling to find an alternative location in East Africa where Sachs might salvage and continue his parasitological work. But by the end of 1965, West German donors were not willing to extend Sachs's expiring contract, and the lab equipment at Kirawira was slated to transfer over to the National Parks administration.[101] By then, the Tanzanians who had supported the project felt betrayed. The agricultural ministry lobbied in vain to force the FRG donors to fund Sachs for another year, refocusing the project entirely on the marketability and distribution of bushmeat: a goal fully in line with Nyerere's desire for planned agricultural development.[102] By 1966, however, West Germany seemed eager to put the embarrassing bushmeat project behind it, shifting the agenda at the SRI back to "pure" research. The FRG's signature wildlife conservation project lay in ruins.

Grzimek's efforts to broker wildlife conservation and development projects soon faced an unexpected geopolitical hurdle as well: the breakdown of Tanganyikan–West German relations following an attempted coup in Dar es Salaam and a socialist-inspired revolution on the nearby island of Zanzibar. In early 1964, Nyerere moved decisively to abolish Africanization altogether, calling the use of racial criteria in the recruitment, training, and promotion a form of discrimination that could not be tolerated. Many army units resented this proclamation, chafing under British commanders in a post-independence military where there were few prospects for advancement into the officer corps. An army uprising came on January 20, 1964, with mutineers arresting their British officers and seizing the State House. Nyerere's government reluctantly asked the British government to crush the insurgency and on January 25, British soldiers took control of the barracks and disarmed the rebels, killing five African soldiers in the confrontation.[103]

As if the attempted coup were not enough to rattle West German donors, developments on the nearby island of Zanzibar strained Tanganyika's relationship with the FRG. After a socialist-inspired revolution toppled the island's British-backed sultanate in 1964, the GDR moved aggressively to recognize the independent government of Abeid Karume's Afro-Shirazi Party and set up its first embassy in Africa.[104] Nyerere tried to stop the creation of an "African Cuba" off his shores by absorbing the island and naming Karume vice president of a United Republic of Tanzania. Yet the GDR continued to funnel technical assistance to Zanzibar, including a team of architects to design and co-construct a "New Zanzibar" project, which promised to transform an island left "under-developed" by Arab "despotism" into a showplace for socialist modernism.[105] Amid fears of a Western-led invasion on par with the Congo to bring "order" to the barely three-year-old political experiment, Nyerere's goal of remaining non-aligned was imperiled.[106]

The presence of the East German advisors on Zanzibar strained relations between Tanzania and the Federal Republic. Nyerere hoped the West Germans would agree to a compromise whereby Tanzania would withdraw all formal recognition of the GDR and close the embassy on Zanzibar but allow the East Germans to operate a consulate in Dar es Salaam. Chancellor Erhard balked at this arrangement as a violation of Hallstein and cancelled all military aid to Tanzania. Nyerere resented this bullying. Increasingly convinced that "Western philanthropy" came with too many strings, Nyerere retaliated by ordering the cancellation of all remaining West German aid to the country in 1965.[107] As he told one interviewer, "One country most interested in helping us, because of its history, was [West] Germany. Then we clashed—over German interpretations of Tanzanian unity . . . . I was not elected to sell the blessed country to the highest bidder."[108]

Amid the increasing tensions of 1964–1966, Grzimek scurried to use his unique position as honorary curator to smooth over relations between the FRG and Tanzania. The zookeeper reminded his fellow citizens how much the Nyerere regime had done to save wildlife. He also printed bold headlines about how his Tanzanian friend had intervened diplomatically when Grzimek was taken into custody after his airplane had to make an emergency landing in Sudan due to bad weather.[109] The zookeeper tried to cast off the failed bushmeat utilization project—which had riled both West German donors and the Tanzanian government—by arguing that it fostered a potentially dangerous utilitarian mentality.[110] In his own estimation, tourism would bring "50 to 100 times more income" than meat products.[111] Given the rising tensions between his country and Tanzania, as well as the disappointment over the failures of sustainable wildlife management, Grzimek knew that the pressure was on to prove that national parks and nature tourism could attract foreign donations—and quickly. As Owen reminded him, Europeans were outsiders after independence, and their time was running out: "If we succeed and . . . . save the game for the next 10 to 15 years . . . . Africans themselves will be convinced of the economic value to their country of its wild live [*sic*]."[112]

Conjuring Development, Act II: The "Shop Windows" of Conservation

From 1961 to 1964, Tanganyika initiated the largest expansion of wildlife sanctuaries in the developing world, creating four new national parks. Together with the Serengeti, these parks encompassed more than 10,500 square miles—an area larger than Belgium. These included (1) Lake Manyara (123 square miles), a narrow north–south oriented park that bordered one of the "loveliest soda lakes in the Great Rift Valley"; (2) Ngurdoto-Momella National Park (25 square miles), a "gem among National Parks" whose caldera resembled a miniature Ngorongoro; (3) Mikumi (700 square miles), a game-rich sanctuary within a few hours' drive of Dar es Salaam; and (4) Ruaha, the most remote of the four, which sprawled over 5,000 square miles of a former game reserve near the center of the country.[113] In 1963, the country also had over 27,000 square miles in game reserves as well as 48,200 in controlled areas, including the NCA.[114] Small wonder that Grzimek, Owen, and Tanganyikan leaders believed that the system had a bright future: "Our national parks are now the envy of the world," noted chairman Adam Sapi Mkwawa in 1964.[115]

As the Arusha Conference participants had made clear, national parks were the "shop windows for all conservation efforts," and Tanganyika's protected areas were among the best in sub-Saharan Africa. As Grzimek and Owen noted in their appeals to outside donors, Tanganyika enjoyed the "most settled prospects in the difficult time which lies ahead in the period of transition from colonial rule to independence": a government led by an enlightened prime minister eager for foreign investment; a welcoming, multiracial national community; spectacular scenery ranging from the snow-capped mountains of Kilimanjaro to pristine beaches along the Indian Ocean; and of course the largest concentrations of migrating large mammals in the world.[116] Tanganyika's politicians stood ready

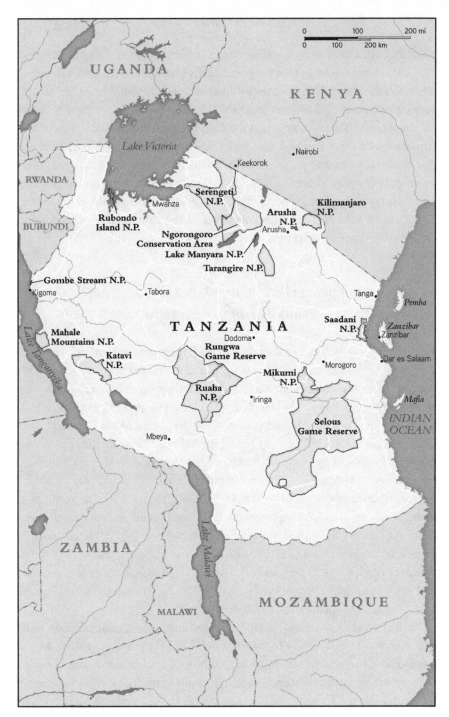

Figure 7.1 Tanzania's major protected areas as of 1980. Tanzania had proposed or gazetted a dozen national parks by this date, along with the Ngorongoro Conservation Area and major game reserves such as Rungwa and Selous featured here. Notice especially the parks and roadways that emerged in part through John Owen's collaborations with Grzimek, including Arusha National Park (formerly Ngurdoto-Momella), Manyara, Ruaha, Katavi, and Rubondo Island. Created for the author by Mapping Specialists, Inc.

to contribute a "moderate" amount on hotels, roads, and other facilities to prepare their parks for visitation "with no preconceived prejudices against National
Parks as privileged preserves set aside for the white man."[117] For a time, it seemed
like the pair had succeeded—until the scheme ran into the same troubles as the
bushmeat project: bloated promises, underperformance, and unexpected shifts
in "natural" and geopolitical conditions that derailed the fundraising efforts.

One reason that Tanganyikan politicians had fewer "prejudices" against the
national parks was the result of a unique arrangement at independence that
shielded the Tanganyika National Parks Authority (later known as TANAPA)
from the pressures of Africanization found in other state sectors. Under unique
terms established by the departing UK government, Owen and his British staff
received their European-level salaries directly from British technical assistance funds.[118] This "sweetener," as Owen called it, allowed the parks staff to
function more like "advisors" hired by the new government rather than costly
bureaucrats within it.[119] In the wake of the Serengeti controversies, moreover,
Tanganyika had established an independent board of trustees for the national
parks with the goal of shielding its "world assets" from "short-term political
vicissitudes."[120] Mkwawa, one of Nyerere's strongest supporters from among
the colonial chiefs in the former British Native Authority, became the chairman, presiding over an all-African board. Previous colonial administrators or
scientists with ties to the outgoing British served only as ex-officio officers,
while the honorary trustees were drawn from the scientists and NGO funders
that helped shape the Serengeti: the British ecologist W. H. Pearsall, for example, as well as Grzimek, Fairfield Osborn of the NYZS, and Russell Train of the
AWLF.[121] This ancillary role cast the green network as advisors, not powerbro-
kers. Unlike the Game Department, whose chief Bruce Kinloch had resigned by
1964, the National Parks Department's senior staff remained only 50 percent
Africanized in 1968.[122]

Though Grzimek's package tours brought a few dozen people to Tanganyika
in the early 1960s, he did not have a long-range plan for tourism development.
As EATTA (East Africa Tourist Travel Association) and other tourism industry
representatives at Arusha had noted, however, a country seeking nature tourists needed new roads; accommodation for various classes of visitors; a first-rate
staff of wardens, game scouts, guides, and hotel and restaurant managers; and
a vigorous anti-poaching organization.[123] Yet even this long list of items was
insufficient, for tourism was a "highly competitive international business" that
required an "all-out government effort" to construct "basic essential services"
expected by First World visitors—airports, widened harbors, functional cable
and telephone lines, and good sanitation.[124] The IUCN attendees lauded tourism for smashing "economic provincialism" and making Africans proud of their
own countries' heritage. To many African attendees, though, such costs already

seemed out of line with their countries' need for basic services such as health care, education, veterinary services, and agricultural education.[125]

At Arusha, Grzimek, Huxley, and others brushed aside concerns about how poor countries would finance wildlife tourism development. "The cost should not be too serious an obstacle," Huxley noted. "Today, it is generally recognised that the gap between the haves and the have-nots must be narrowed, and that the emergent and under-developed countries must be aided by the more prosperous nations."[126] Huxley predicted that national parks would quickly become recipients of technical assistance and World Bank loans—after all, Africa's animals were an "irreplaceable God-made cultural asset" on par with UNESCO's Abu Simbel monuments in Egypt.[127] In reality, however, Tanganyika found itself spending its own meager funds on the parks throughout the 1960s. In fiscal year 1963–1964, this subsidy amounted to about sixty thousand pounds ($204,244)—a 30 percent increase over the previous fiscal year and more, proportionate to national income, than either the United Kingdom or the United States.[128] Owen and Grzimek trusted that rich American and European foundations and international development agencies would fill in any gaps until the parks could fund themselves.[129]

Outside grants and financing looked promising for the first few years of park expansion, with grants from the FZS, the Rockefeller Brothers Fund, and Ford Foundation funding much of the heavier infrastructure. Roadbuilding proved to be the most daunting and costly task for the parks department. Tanganyika lacked Kenya's basic lorry and cargo network, meaning that TANAPA could not easily link park roads designed for tourists to existing highways. At Lake Manyara, for example, Owen's team had to build both an all-weather road that connected the park to the Ngorongoro Crater highway and one within the park for "good dry season loops"—with Tanganyika footing the extra $65,000.[130] New roads had to be laid out precisely with tough yet pliable materials, as streets and bridges had to withstand the "flailing" of the "boiling brown waters" of the wet season and the hollowing out of the ground during the dry one. To accomplish these tasks in the Serengeti, Owens's team acquired a grader, excavator, bulldozer, and a fleet of tipper trucks through a grant from the Rockefeller Brothers Fund. But even with this donated equipment and supplemental FZS and USAID grants, the yearly sum available for road *maintenance* from the Tanganyikan government in the post-independence years never exceeded $68,000—a "derisory sum" given the magnitude of the work necessary.[131] The national parks also paid out nearly $48,000 "compensation" for the Africans who "had to move from the new Mikumi National Park"—bringing its totals for 1963–1964 closer to $306,400.[132] The gap between Tanganyikan outlays and donor-funded projects was already evident during the supposed flush years of the 1960s.

Tewa invited participants at Arusha to attend the grand opening of Ngurdoto Crater (now Arusha National Park), the first national park created after independence. Tewa was proud to sever the silk tape outside the entrance with a Maasai spear at the grand opening—an odd symbolism given the government's growing skepticism toward the herders' way of life but one that showed their value as "tourist icons" for the largely European conference-goers. Working closely with Owen, the FZS provided $54,000 in direct financial support for roads, animal watering holes, and viewpoints throughout the park.[133] These funds helped Owen's team to build an all-weather roadway that linked up the crater area to a newly acquired five-thousand-acre tract of scenic lakes and woodlands from the nearby Momella Estate—the same Trappe family farm that the Grzimeks had originally planned to purchase outright in 1957.[134]

Grzimek had helped Owen to persuade German creditors to renounce their mortgage claims on part of the estate desired by the park system, which an American donor later helped to purchase outright. The Paramount set for *Hatari!* that was filmed at the former Trappe homestead, Grzimek and Owen hoped, could serve as an excellent lodge for the park.[135] For all the talk of national parks as "primordial wilderness," the FZS design team stipulated exact guidelines for maintaining "natural-looking" scenery, including keeping the vegetation along the park's curvilinear roads at a "changing and irregular distance."[136] The Ngurdoto Park and Momella Lakes were later merged with Mount Meru Crater National Park into a single "three in one" park famous for its colobus monkeys and waterfalls, with additional support from the FZS for acquiring the necessary lands and paying compensation to the "resettled" Africans.[137] Far from being vacant, "tsetse-infested" bushlands ready for visitation, national parks required considerable investment in infrastructure, maintenance, and "compensation" to become viable tourist attractions.

Owen also took the first steps toward making the Serengeti into the hub for a northern circuit that joined Tanganyika's tourist roads with points across the border in Kenya. His team urged the Public Works Department to complete an all-weather road from Ngorongoro to the eastern (Naabi Hill) entrance of Serengeti National Park, which it later connected via Seronera to Keekorok on the Kenyan side of the border.[138] Here again the work was grueling and precarious. In graveling one section of the eleven miles of the Serengeti roads, Owen estimated the trucks ran a distance of 13,000 miles—"one and a quarter times round the world."[139] Tourist vans that departed Nairobi could now take in Kenya's Tsavo and Ambeloli National Parks, head south across the border to Arusha to visit nearby Ngurdoto-Momella, and then move on to Lake Manyara, Ngorongoro, and the Serengeti itself. They could then make their way back to Kenya without retracing one step.[140] Later, this "northern circuit" would include

Mount Kilimanjaro and Tarangire. As one visitor described it, a game safari often involved spending less than a half day driving from one park lodge to the next, "leaving after breakfast, lunching at another lodge along the way, and arriving before dinner at the next well in time for a hot shower and a change before meeting for cocktails in the lounge."[141]

Back in the Serengeti, meanwhile, the onset of the heavy rains inspired new hope for wildlife survival and visitor experiences.[142] Poaching was at its lowest point in decades. In the robust rainy seasons of the early 1960s, wildebeest, zebra, and gazelle could disperse across the park instead of concentrating at watering holes that had once made them a target for "mass butchery."[143] To many observers, the Serengeti seemed like an enclave of international activity impervious to the deeper processes of decolonization and Africanization sweeping East Africa at the time.[144] Both Myles and Kay Turner's memoirs complain about the "constant routine" of administering a 250-person African staff, dealing with a growing number of ordinary visitors, and having to entertain the "high-powered VIPs" that John Owen's fundraising efforts brought to the new Serengeti Lodge, including novelist James Michener, famed aviator Charles Lindbergh, and the heads of state invited by Nyerere himself, such as Yugoslav premier Josip Broz Tito.[145] The Serengeti also enjoyed a well-heeled group of American and British donors, the Friends of the Serengeti, which cushioned it against budget deficits that affected other parks in the system. Complaints about such routines masked a deeper militarization of the park, however, as Turner had transformed the existing system of foot patrols into a motorized field force replete with radios, land rovers, and weapons, which tracked and protected the wildebeest migrations across the plains.[146]

Grzimek's Help for the Threatened Animal World Fund and other private accounts also buffered the park system. The zookeeper's annual arrival in East Africa seemed "like a visit from a rich uncle." One park warden who flew a plane partially funded by Grzimek, commanded an antipoaching team salaried by the FZS, and had children boarded in England through funds provided by Grzimek, told Harold T. P. Hayes in 1976: "I have to be careful what I ask him for, because I know he will give it to me."[147] Grzimek saw his gifts as the largesse of an "apolitical man."[148] Yet to the many critics of national parks in East Africa, the country's dependency on such Western donors kept the Serengeti a white-dominated "state within a state" long past independence.[149]

Such images of plenty before the austerity of ujamaa can be deceptive, however, when one looks at routine maintenance and administration for the park system as a whole. Owen was already quite nervous about the growing gap between Tanzania's contributions to the national parks and the paucity of Western contributions.[150] In 1964, to cite one example, the National Parks Board decided to raise entrance fees across the system to lessen the need for government subsidies

to the parks. Owen estimated that Serengeti would receive about twelve thousand pounds as a result—less than five times the costs, exclusive of overheads.
"The balance will be provided largely from the pockets of the Africans such as
those seen by visitors outside the Serengeti," he noted, "few of whom can afford
to enjoy their own parks."[151] This put Owen in a bind. If the government continued to subsidize the parks too heavily, the parks would have no hope of survival.
But without the subsidy, the park system might turn off visitors due to lower fees
across the border.[152] The parks were operating on a shoestring budget even in
the best of years.

In 1963, Owen learned that the government's promised $204,244 subsidy
would have to be cut back to $158,290 due to other budgetary priorities. He had
"little fat to spare," however, because he had needed to tap the parks' reserve fund
to repair sections of roadway washed out during the rainy season. Yet Owen had
little luck filling the gap through outside donations because—unlike Grzimek—
few of the well-endowed American funders were willing to write checks for vital
but mundane operations. Owen complained that the NYZS and the AWLF only
wanted to "pick the plums" from among existing projects or support "glamor-
ous" new ones that they could showcase in donor prospectuses.[153] Yet new projects made little sense given the uncertainties surrounding Africanization. As he
wrote Fairfield Osborn: "We do not want to run the danger of over-extending
ourselves with too many new projects . . . . most new projects need servicing
and administering and therefore bear down on our main budget which is already
over-extended." For Owen, the most critical needs were mundane: fuel and
maintenance for airplanes; tuition, salary, and housing for African wardens sent
to Mweka; or the acquisition of new land rovers. Owen pleaded with "Fair" to
check in with his attorneys to see if the NYZS could find a way to adopt these
ongoing needs as "their own." Without immediate assistance, he noted alarmingly, "We lose the present opportunities for holding the position stable, opportunities which will probably never recur."[154] Going cap in hand for routine needs
was a precarious strategy indeed.

Given all that Tanganyikans had contributed from their own pockets for
the parks, Owen soon felt the backlash from Africans who felt betrayed by the
trickle of donations. In a 1963 editorial to the *Daily Telegraph*, "Who Cares for
Africa's Game," the Tanganyikan parks director slammed his fellow citizens for
their misguided view of the parks and their lack of support.[155] Many of his fellow
Brits, he thundered, were under the misguided assumption that Africa's animals
had rested in "safe hands" under colonialism and that the transfer of power had
endangered the wildlife. "It was Europeans who wiped out most of the animals
from vast areas of South, Central, and Eastern Africa," he reminded readers,
while colonial game departments had always had few resources and tiny staffs.[156]
Now pressed to save this "world asset," Africans pointed to the remarkably poor

environmental record of Europeans at home and abroad. "If the wild life is in fact a world asset," African editorialists asked, "why does the rest of the world not help them preserve it by material aid?" Grzimek quickly translated and reprinted Owen's editorial in *Das Tier*, noting that West Germans had similar misconceptions. Africans, not Europeans, had made and were making the real sacrifices for the wild animals cherished by the industrial world.[157]

Such charges of European indifference came to a head in 1966, when Owen learned that a break in British–Tanzanian diplomatic relations over Rhodesia's Unilateral Declaration of Independence in 1965 meant that the United Kingdom planned to withdraw all technical assistance—including the "sweetener" that had subsidized the national parks staff and their pensions. Whitehall deemed the parks a "wholly Tanzanian institution," disqualifying them for short-term emergency assistance available in other settings. Owen deemed this a "mean and shabby thing to do" to those Europeans and Africans who worked "on the frontlines" to protect the country's wild heritage.[158] He warned of the "political danger" that would quickly emerge if the "Tanzanian taxpayer" were forced to bear the full costs of European game warden salaries higher than President Nyerere's.[159] As Owen expected, this move showed Nyerere that the British also had "strings" attached to their aid—making it all the more likely that Tanzania's global heritage would fall victim to "ephemeral political differences."[160] Such diplomatic skirmishes and accusations of hypocrisy left the parks in a perilous state even before the Arusha Declaration. As it became clear there would be no UNESCO emergency mission for the wildlife of East Africa, Grzimek and Owen had only one gambit left: transmuting the current "trickle of tourists" in 1960 into a "steady flood" of visitors.[161]

Conjuring Development, Act III: Animal-Hungry Tourists ... From Nairobi

Bernhard Grzimek reminded Nyerere repeatedly that his international influence and television program were responsible for making tourism Tanzania's fourth-largest source of revenue by 1970. In his letters to the president, Grzimek often reminisced about their "long talks" at the beginning of his premiership about the possibilities of tourism as a lever for development. He reminded Nyerere how he had bravely used a state-subsidized TV program to "propagate tourist tours to East Africa" and "force tourist agencies to organize the first cheap package tours" at a time when the European public still saw Tanzania as a "dangerous and savage country."[162] Tourism would become such a powerful engine of development that even ordinary Africans were "anxious to cherish the chief of their country's tourist attractions—its wildlife."[163] The Arthur D. Little consultancy, hired on a Ford Foundation grant to help with the Three-Year Plan, estimated that only fifty thousand overseas visitors a year (Kenya in 1963 had eighty-five thousand) were necessary to keep the parks afloat without government help.[164]

Grzimek liked to tout Tanganyika's superior game reserves when conjuring this vision of speedy development, but natural wonders—even the magnificent Serengeti—could not on their own overcome infrastructural disparities between Kenya and Tanganyika inherited from the colonial era. During the interwar era, Kenya was the destination of choice for globetrotting hunters, allowing Nairobi to develop into a hub for safari outfitters, African porters, and supplies.[165] Tanganyika's status as a League of Nations mandate territory and then a UN Trusteeship meant there was always some uncertainty about its future among British investors—leaving far less homegrown capital in place in 1961. Tanganyika did not tend to benefit from the East African currency and customs union either. Cargo ships loaded with East African coffee or sisal or carrying machinery from Europe usually came through the Kenyan port of Mombasa, bypassing Tanga or Dar es Salaam and the lucrative import fees and customs duties that accrued from being a favored harbor. This left many Tanganyikans feeling that they were already in a dependency relationship with Kenya at independence.[166]

Kenya's favored status in international trade also gave it the edge in attracting middle-class tourists in the early 1960s.[167] Nairobi airport was served by thirteen international carriers, and most of Kenya's major parks and reserves—Nairobi, Amboseli, Tsavo, Mount Kenya—were within a few hours' drive from the city.[168] As the first stop on travelers' journeys, Nairobi captured the market in first-night stays, the purchase of gear and souvenirs, and the arrangement of safari leaders or cars for hire.[169] The development of beach resorts along the coast near Mombasa gave tourists additional ways to enjoy their visit, combining "sun and surf" with wildlife viewing in one two-week holiday. Groups such as the Mombasa and Coast Tourist Association—established in the early 1960s to focus on both territories—put almost all of its effort into Kenyan resorts, encouraging hoteliers and travel companies to "pep up their work" to attract visitors from Europe, North America, and South Africa.[170] Splashy brochures in German that touted East Africa's beach resorts and camera safaris almost always focused on Kenya's wonders, a sure sign that Mombasa, not Dar es Salaam, would become West Germany's "African Majorca" in the 1970s.[171]

As a result of the airport hub and better rail and road connections, Kenya achieved an outsized share of the overall tourist market in East Africa during the entirety of this period. Already in 1959, for example, the EATTA (East Africa Tourist Travel Association) estimated Kenya received about $18.5 million from tourist revenues—compared to Uganda's $2.7 million and Tanganyika's $1.42 million. Almost 45,000 visitors to Kenya arrived by air in 1959, compared to only 7,539 to Tanganyika. Even though Tanganyika and Uganda outpaced Kenya in the number of visitors who arrived by road or rail—2,922 and 3,305 compared to Kenya's 1,680, respectively—this merely indicated just how many travelers flew into Nairobi (28,494), hired cars, and drove to the other territories for shorter, less lucrative stays.[172] Even Grzimek used Kenyan examples when he intended to speak of East Africa's success as a whole. "The new Hilton skyscrapers in Nairobi and other modern hotels are built by elephants, zebras, and lions," he told one conservation critic.[173] Small wonder Tanganyika created its own tourist board in 1962, putting the first nail in the coffin of a unified East African market that led to the dissolution of the EATTA in 1965.[174]

Tanganyika's legacy as the "poor sister" of Britain's East African territories meant that its natural wonders—the Serengeti, Kilimanjaro, Selous—remained largely inaccessible to the average visitor. When the UN Trusteeship Council visited the territory in 1960, the members noted that tourism offered "interesting possibilities for the future" but lamented the woeful status of the territory's roads, hotels, and communication lines.[175] In 1960, the territory had just begun building the lodge at Lake Manyara, while guest houses at Pangani and other seaside reports were still in the works.[176] Dar es Salaam still lacked a first-rate modern hotel to accommodate large numbers of visitors—making it a weak jumping-off point for travel along the coast or into the interior. As EATTA representatives wrote in 1960, Tanganyika was losing out to Kenya simply because it did not have enough hotel beds. "No progress has been made in the last year in developing Dar es Salaam as a holiday resort," the chairman lamented, "it is being bypassed in favour of the Kenyan coast by holidaymakers."[177]

The inaccessibility of Tanzania's national parks from Dar es Salaam and other major cities posed another problem. The capital city was a considerable distance from the Serengeti region, yet there was no major airfield and no highway linking it to the "northern circuit" favored by tourists.[178] Owen's determination to link the Arusha area to Kenya's Maasai Mara area encouraged tour companies to start their game safaris in Nairobi, dip into Tanzania for a short stay, and then return to Nairobi along the parabolic route known popularly as the "Milk Run."[179] Even though Tanzania had far more spectacular wildlife viewing, the country received only a small proportion of the income in entrance fees and hotel bills generated by this route—a mere 15% portion of the pie by the late 1960s.[180]

Grzimek was well aware of Tanzania's predicament. "It is in the interests of nature conservationists that the country which has preserved its fauna . . . . also profits from tourism," he noted in a 1961 speech.[181] He recommended a new airfield near Arusha—but the cost was steep, and private investors did not readily step up to help. "I have insisted several times personally to . . . [Nyerere] . . . and his government that this is the most important matter to develop tourism in Tanganyika," Grzimek told a confidant.[182] Not all agreed. The EATTA and others felt a new airline hub was impractical and would require the cash-strapped territory to invest millions without any certainty that international carriers would favor it over Nairobi. As the head of the association told Grzimek, the building of another international airport only a hundred miles from Nairobi made no sense given the capital outlays necessary along with immigration and customs facilities, meteorological services, and the precarious landing conditions in the mountain ranges of northern Tanganyika.[183] Even with substantial international aid and the fascination of tourists, Tanzania found that Kenya's infrastructural head start was hard to overcome.

Despite criticism from TANU's left wing and the lackluster performance of tourism from 1961 to 1966, Tanzania did not turn its back on the tourist sector after the Arusha Declaration, as so many have assumed. In a 1968 speech on socialism and rural development, for example, Nyerere reaffirmed the advantages of tourism for accruing much-needed foreign currency, arguing that the national parks should be "controlled and run by the public"—much like the state's collective farms.[184] In both the First (1964–1969) and Second (1969–1974) Five-Year Plans, the parastatal Tanzania Tourist Corporation (TTC) earmarked substantial public-sector investment in parks and wildlife lodges—totaling around 132 million shillings in the period between 1961 and 1974.[185] Nyerere's government also announced its plan in 1969 to hire an Italian engineering company to finally build the long-awaited Kilimanjaro International Airport near Moshi—which opened its doors in 1973.[186] By boosting public-sector investment, Tanzania hoped it might finally break Kenya's monopoly by encouraging visitors to begin and end their visits inside the territory.[187]

Still convinced that a flood of tourists was on the horizon, the First Five-Year Plan apportioned about thirty million shillings to expand parks and add new ones.[188] The Ngurdoto-Momella complex became Arusha in 1967, followed by Gombe Stream (1968), Tarangire (1970), Kilimanjaro (1973), and Katavi (1974), the last of which received extensive financial support from the FZS.[189] Grzimek was especially proud to see an area he referred to as "my personal island," Rubondo, which he helped to transform from a game reserve into a national park in 1977. Working closely with the last British game warden in the Mwanza region, Grzimek remade the narrow, 24-mile-long island—which the Game Department "cleared" of its fishing villages—into an open-air sanctuary for orphaned zoo specimens, ranging from large Guereza apes, elephants, and rhinos to smaller chimpanzees and antelope species.[190] Grzimek predicted a day when steamships would bring tourists to visit "forest game" in a spectacular open zoo—the *Tierfreiheit* he never achieved in Germany.[191] To protect these new sanctuaries, socialist Tanzania stepped up its own anti-poaching campaigns.

Nyerere chastised rural Africans who tried to "kill off wild beasts" and encouraged virtuous socialist citizens to "protect them for other people to look at."[192] Government ministers followed suit, calling on TANU in 1970 to support an all-out "shock and crack" campaign against poachers and encouraged citizen brigades to support the "noble tasks of the men of the Serengeti."[193]

Though wildlife remained an important tourist magnet, many experts thought that Tanzania should build beach resorts, since Europeans were constantly seeking out "sunny and warm" countries with unspoiled nature and "unsophisticated" ways of life.[194] A new road connected Dar es Salaam with picturesque cities along the coast, such as the old German-colonial towns of Bagamayo and Tanga, while the TTC helped to build three new hotels on the coast north of the capital as well as a new resort complex on Mafia Island in 1971—all replete with "fast-growing palm trees" to lure Europeans.[195] Grzimek used his influence to convince West Germany's Federal Ministry for Economic Cooperation and Development to support these projects from technical assistance funds.[196] By the late 1960s, it is worth noting, the Federal Republic realized it could no longer enforce the Hallstein Doctrine. As Willy Brandt, who became Foreign Minister in 1966, noted: "Every country is free to choose its friends."[197] West Germany offered Tanzania help in translating travel brochures, paying tuition for Africans to train in German hotel management programs, and most important, subsidizing road expansion and repair.[198] Grzimek recommended that FRG ministries help build an all-weather loop connecting the soon-to-open airport in Arusha with the new park at Kilimanjaro, as well another connecting Arusha to Mwanza so that tourists could enjoy the Serengeti's western corridor and Rubondo.[199]

Tanzania did see some return on its investment in parks, hotels, roads, and anti-poaching. The number of foreign visitors went from 53,707 in 1968 to 66,036 in 1969, with an average stay of six days. This was a 23 percent increase—making tourism the fourth largest sector of the economy.[200] Given Grzimek's long-standing promotion of the Serengeti and Tanzania, West Germans were well represented among the new arrivals. Travel writers reporting on their experiences in Tanzania noted that the socialist country had entered the tourist market hesitatingly (*zögernd*) and that many of its animal reserves and beaches were, as a result, relatively unknown and unoccupied—a perfect enticement for more intrepid travelers seeking natural beauties off the beaten path. As a 1972 article noted, "Tanzania offers much more than Grzimek's Serengeti—it encompasses a diversity of superbly outfitted and gazetted animal reserves with lodges and small landing strips," which made it easy to traverse the country on well-equipped small airlines.[201] Package deals from the Hannover-based consolidator Touropa-Scharnow (today's TUI) encouraged Condor and other German carriers to develop direct flights with package tours out of Dar es Salaam. These tours booked out in winter 1970–1971, generating hopes for a strong summer season as well.[202]

West German travel writers were increasingly enthusiastic about Tanzania in the late 1960s. After making their way through the national parks of the interior, noted one article, West Germans could enjoy "600 miles of coastline and 800 beds"—spectacularly empty beaches and snorkeling in the shallow reefs and azure waters of the Indian Ocean.[203] Germans along the coast had already made themselves at home in Tanzania (*schon heimisch gemacht haben*)—enjoying air-conditioned rooms, cold drinks, and fine music.[204] The Touropa-Scharnow packages envisioned these coastal paradises as an alternative to the already-crowded beaches and hotels in Kenya. "Tanzania is not so touristically developed as neighboring Kenya," noted one article, as "Nyerere's planned economy had stunted the spirit (*Élan*) of British and Israeli managers who ran the hotels, often amid real problems of supplying food and water or overcoming bureaucratic hurdles." Still, Tanzania needed the foreign currency and the German tourists, who numbered four thousand in 1972, would gladly pay to see Grzimek's wild animals while "basking under palm trees."[205]

The notion that Tanzania was still "off the beaten path" of most tourists may have appealed to intrepid West Germans, but it did little to comfort TTC parastatals that had just invested millions of precious development funds in sparkling new hotels. Putting it bluntly, as one 1974 report noted: "The economic benefits of parastatal development in tourism were simply not very great."[206] By the end of 1970, according to one estimate, total parastatal assets in the hotel sector, including wildlife lodges and beach hotels, amounted to 119 million shillings but generated employment for only 1,731 people—and an overall monetary loss of eight million shillings. Things did not look much better in 1971, when the tourism sector lost another seven million. The national parks did a bit better in terms of employment; as labor-intensive enterprises, these "fixed assets" employed 540 people in 1970. But the parks still could not pay their own way and lost 411 million shillings in that year. Even with substantial government investment, the "shop windows" of conservation simply did not generate enough income to make continued outlays worth the effort.[207]

Part of the problem lay in government parastatals' inability to compete with the private sector, which still controlled more than 50 percent of the market and was more nimble in responding to changing consumer demands. The TTC put most of its efforts into constructing expensive "international class" luxury hotels, for example, but consumers increasingly preferred modest, bungalow-style accommodations.[208] But the main problem remained Tanzania's competition with Kenya, which was able to capture an outsized share of the overall growth in the industry occurring between 1964 and 1973. In 1972, the same year that Touropa touted Tanzania's empty beaches, the operator noted that Kenya had already registered ten thousand beach guests in the hotels of Mombasa and Malindi—the majority of them from the Federal Republic. The key to attracting these golden hordes was what one article termed a huge "shake up" in costs for package tours into Nairobi that no carrier could match for Dar es Salaam. It was possible in 1969 to book a nine-day stay in Nairobi, including airfare from Frankfurt, for $256—a package whose airfare alone normally cost around $847. Such packages usually combined a wildlife safari with beach time—indeed the Touropa-Scharnow advertisements emphasized the short distances from the beach to Tsavo and Amboseli—with Tanzania's Mount Kilimanjaro easily visible across the border.[209] Such hard-to-beat prices for flights into Nairobi meant that in 1969, Kenya received 105,800 visitors, or 45.4 percent of the arrivals in East Africa, compared to Tanzania's 39,600, or 17 percent.[210]

The Foreign Office fretted about such disparities. As the West German embassy officials in Dar es Salaam noted, Bonn's support for tourism development was key to rebuffing "propaganda from the East" in this critical region.[211] They noted that the Nyerere regime had expanded the country's capacity to accommodate a hundred thousand tourists a year—and was far short of that goal. As Ambassador Norbert Hebich wrote in 1969, Tanzania was doing its best to overcome its "underdeveloped" facilities and steer tourists southward. The country even demanded licenses for travel agents who sometimes sent visitors from Nairobi or Mombasa into the northern circuit—yet failed to make clear that they were entering a separate country![212] TTC representatives reprimanded West German tourism industry representatives for extending Kenya's "monopoly" over East African tourism by sponsoring packages that dedicated only one out of five days for sites in their country.[213] Desperate to shore up the FRG's standing, embassy officials supported TTC plans to open a tourist bureau in Frankfurt and encouraged Scharnow, Touropa, and Lufthansa's efforts to expand package tours in Tanzania.[214] But this was all in vain. Tourists would continue to favor the destination with the most direct flights, up-to-date facilities, and easiest combination of beach time and game viewing—and that country was Kenya.

The Final Conjuring: Serengeti May Have to Die

Given tourism's lackluster performance, Grzimek found himself increasingly unable to use his position as honorary curator to steer conservation politics in the early 1970s—right as the country stood ready to let the last British expats go. Over the course of the late 1960s and early 1970s, a series of three showdowns with Derek Bryceson shook the foundations of the Arusha Bargain as the Nyerere regime struggled to balance its trusteeship over "world heritage" with national and regional needs. A pattern was established where Bryceson—a former farmer and fierce defender of Nyerere's authority—would authorize a development project or a modification of the Serengeti borders. Bryceson's decision would be followed by thousands of letters from Grzimek's allies arriving on Nyerere's desk. Grzimek would follow up with his own statesmanlike letter to Nyerere admonishing the president to meet the Arusha Manifesto obligations.[215] "Now that the money was running out and land hunger was growing," as Harold T.P. Hayes wrote, "the last reed ... [that Grzimek and the rest] ... clung to was the empathy of Julius Nyerere."[216]

Not surprisingly, the first two controversies focused on the NCA, where the balance between conservation and development had never been resolved since the partition of the park in 1959. On the surface, the confrontations with Bryceson over the lodge inside the Ngorongoro Crater was a classic preservationist battle, one designed to stop an unscrupulous European developer—"a former paratrooper with Field Marshal Rommel"—from destroying one of the world's great natural monuments. Grzimek worried about the ecological effects of the lodge, particularly the depletion of the Lerai Forest's spring waters. But he fixated mostly on the aesthetic impact on his "natural zoo." The last thing that tourists from Germany wanted to experience in the African wilderness, he told Nyerere, was the constant "chug-chug-chug" of diesel engines pumping water and generating electricity or the glare of lights in the evening as they gazed down from the crater's rim.[217] It would also bring additional unwanted humans into the wilderness; for every hundred beds, he predicted, the hotel would need at least a thousand service staff, who in turn would bring their "wives and children" into ugly settlements scattered around the main lodge.[218] "It was always agreed that the Crater itself should be kept totally free from human constructions," Grzimek averred, and he promised that a pristine landscape would become an "even greater source of income for the country of Tanzania and the whole of East Africa."[219]

For Bryceson and others, however, Grzimek's position seemed "perverse." After all, had not the zookeeper promised that wildlife should pay for themselves—and trumpeted the crater as Tanzania's main tourist attraction?[220] Even more problematically, Tanzania saw the Austrian plan as a chance to finally outdo its Kenyan rival—and help keep coveted tourists inside the country for as long as possible.[221] Grzimek knew that competition with its northern neighbor had driven the Treetops program but brushed aside Tanzania's complaints about Kenya's "monopoly." "It is not my fault that Tanzania does not get its fair part of this tourism," he wrote, blaming the dearth of overnight stays on the long delays building the Arusha airport and the lack of a road from the Serengeti into the Lake Region near Mwanza. Instead, he argued, Tanzania forced its visitors to leave the country "after two days" and return back to Kenya out of Seronera— the very same trek that Owen had put so much effort into completing a few years earlier.[222] The message was clear. Any blame for tourism's lackluster performance fell on Tanzania's shoulders, not those of Grzimek or his allies.

While Nyerere backed off the hotel plan, Grzimek's comments heightened a growing sense in Tanzania that the twin evils of colonialism and misguided Western advice had left their country in a permanent state of "underdevelopment" vis-à-vis Kenya. Nyerere retorted that his country was still considering other sites for the Treetops-style lodge. However much conservationists cherished the country's world heritage, his regime had to "attract tourists and give them what they want."[223] Given West Germany's fragile relationship with Tanzania and the push for self-reliance, moreover, Ambassador Hebich told Grzimek bluntly that it would have been better to approach Nyerere discretely, rather than unleash so much brouhaha (*so viel Wirbel darum zu machen*) over the hotel project.[224] The Treetops in Kenya did not appear to disturb the wildlife there, he noted, and many "prominent personalities" within Tanzania were incensed by Grzimek's audacity. "It is, at the end of the day, their business to decide what happens in their country," Hebich warned.[225] The old tactics of international pressure were starting to crumble under ujamaa as Tanzanians began to resent European oversight over their national heritage.

A second and more serious challenge to the status quo in the NCA came just a year after the hotel controversies, when Bryceson's ministry announced plans to develop the crater highlands and Eastern Serengeti Plains as rangelands.[226] In many respects, the plan resembled the 1956 blueprint for the region, as updated by a team of Canadian experts who had served as advisors to Salomon ole Saibull after Henry Fosbrooke's departure in 1965.[227] Bryceson proposed allowing the Maasai to graze and cultivate in specific zones of the NCA, excluding forested water catchment districts and areas designated as nature conservation regions. These zones encompassed the 160 square miles that comprised the Ngorongoro and Embagai craters—a move that kept the "wilderness" that Grzimek had fought for just a few months earlier intact. As in so many earlier plans, the Bryceson proposal envisioned that Maasai would give up "nomadism" and become "productive" members of cooperative ranching associations that would finance water projects and increase beef production.[228]

Grzimek was adamant that the plan would be disastrous for both the Maasai and the animals and would "impair the image of Tanzania" abroad. The move to develop the NCA would doom the unit's rhino population, he warned, reminding officials and readers of the spearings that had occurred just after independence.[229] Soon thereafter, articles appeared describing the Maasai burning the landscape, seemingly "anxious to test their new status" after years of being banned from doing so by the NCA authorities.[230] Bryceson struck back at his critics, dismissing their fears as "absolute nonsense" and noting that the area had been earmarked for development for many years.[231] The Maasai were "fed up" with not getting their promised shared of national development, he remarked, and noted that the Serengeti-Ngorongoro wildlife had flourished since independence— there did not appear to be "any cause for all this alarm from the conservation-ists." Turning the tables on Grzimek's charges of disloyalty, Bryceson exclaimed, "It is obviously in the interests of Kenya to do what they can to spoil Tanzania's tourist image and this is why this decision has been played up . . . . The decision will make no difference to Tanzanian wildlife or to the tourists who want to come here."[232] Hebich, for his part, also doubted that there would be severe ecological consequences and warned Grzimek that further "unpleasant newspaper polemics" might backfire, undoing over a decade of hard work on behalf of wild game.[233]

Hebich was right. In the third and final showdown of 1967–1969, Grzimek rallied the green network against a plan to allow Kuria and Sukuma peoples to graze their cattle and gather firewood within a recently added portion of the Serengeti, the 120-square mile "Lamai Wedge." So named for its triangular shape, this small game reserve in the very northwest corner of the Serengeti had fueled resentment when it became part of the SNP in 1967 because locals found themselves hemmed in between the northern extension, the Mara River, the Isuria Escarpment, and the border with Kenya.[234] Myles Turner described it as an unruly zone where the "fierce" Wakuria had depleted once-abundant populations of rhino, buffalo, and elephants and then launched poaching "onslaughts" into the Serengeti itself. In 1966 Owen petitioned for the Lamai to become formally part of the Serengeti National Park, and Turner's field rangers—equipped with new Land Rovers from several NGOs—began to evict and compensate Africans living in the area and destroyed their remaining huts. Yet several families refused to go and in February 1967, fifty Wakuria disregarded the new boundaries and returned, digging fields for farms. "We don't want national Parks, Game Department, or anything," they shouted at Turner and his rangers at a tense meeting. "This is our country."[235]

Just a few months later, both Turner and Grzimek thought that the issue had been resolved in favor of the park. Indeed, Grzimek applauded Nyerere's decision to "evacuate people to make room for animals," giving them a new school and a place to settle.[236] Yet in February 1972—shortly after Bryceson had become the head of national parks—Turner joined Chief Warden John Stephenson at another boisterous meeting of local Wakuria. This time the group declared the Serengeti's boundaries illegitimate, as they "were not made by the local people, but by former colonialists or Area Commissioners, who acted like colonials and not like persons sympathetic to the people whom they represented." Locals complained they were living precariously along the escarpment, where they were vulnerable to raids by Kenyan Maasai. Turner was stunned when both the Regional Commissioner for Tarime and the regional TANU leader emerged from a private palaver and declared that a five-mile strip of the wedge would be excised so that local people could graze cattle, cut down trees, and collect firewood. The meeting "broke up in turmoil, confusion, and hand-clapping," Turner recalled.[237]

Once again, Grzimek tried to mobilize world opinion to save the Serengeti, fearing that this "amputation" from the park would result in a domino effect of indigenous land claims across East Africa.[238] As wildlife advocate Michaela Denis wrote Grzimek, "it looks as though the Tanzanians are incapable of keeping law and order and will not act . . . . Or is the Arusha declaration on wildlife of which President Nyerere signed some years ago not worth the paper it is written on?"[239] Grzimek saw Bryceson's handiwork behind the decision; Owen had stepped down in 1971, and despite Grzimek's hopes for an ally of the green network to take his place, Nyerere appointed Salomon ole Saibull to replace him before installing Bryceson in 1972. "This development, which may be followed even in other African countries, is happening in a situation when Tanzania National Parks have no guidance and have become very weak," Grzimek wrote his allies.[240]

Prince Bernhard of the WWF was particularly incensed by the decision, as his organization had provided the funds for incorporating the Lamai into the SNP in the first place. After firing off a letter to Nyerere asking what the president planned to do to "ensure the integrity of the Serengeti," the prince learned that Nyerere had brokered a compromise plan with the regional commissioner.[241] Nyerere insisted that the land problems at Lamai were truly acute, as some residents had been killed by Kenyan authorities when they accidentally crossed the border while searching for pasturage. As the area did not yet appear on many maps of the Serengeti, the president thought there was a middle ground between the competing interests. Nyerere restricted the land concession to cattle grazing—no settlement, cultivation, or deforestation—on a sixty-five-mile square portion of territory, with a management scheme much like that of the NCA.[242] Bernhard replied curtly that he would have to inquire with the IUCN whether this "infringement" would downgrade the Serengeti's national park status.[243]

Though Nyerere had remained largely aloof during Grzimek's battles with Bryceson, the WWF letter got under his skin. This time the president snapped back, catching Prince Bernhard by surprise and setting the tone for a reassertion of Tanzania's environmental prerogatives. As Nyerere rightly noted, his country had set up the parks, extended them, and spent what was, for Tanzanians, a lot of money on them. "We regard these Parks with great pride, and also very much as 'National' Parks," he wrote, "if and when our policy has the support of the international community, we are very happy . . . . But such assistance does not determine our policies; we work out our policy for Tanzania in accordance with our own assessment of the needs of this and future generations."[244] Having watched Western conservationists falter in all three arenas stemming from the Arusha Bargain—bushmeat utilization, park financing, and tourist revenue— Nyerere saw in Prince Bernhard's reply a broader reflection of the environmental inequalities that had shaped the postcolonial world. His reply reads as a revision of the Arusha Manifesto in Tanzania's favor:

> [We] think it ill becomes the peoples of the developed world to tell the people of Africa, Asia or Latin America that they must sacrifice even their existing standard of living for purposes of conservation, while the developed world continues unabated its own drive to secure a disproportionate share of the world's goods in order to supplement a standard of living of which we do not even dream. We are sorry if our National Parks policies do not please those who have already destroyed their own wildlife, and indeed who continue to endanger what little remains. But although we are anxious to learn from the failures of the developed world, we do not intend to allow it to sacrifice our people in an orgy of expiation . . . . If, as a result of our policies, some people try, and succeed, to get the Tanzanian National Parks struck off the United Nations List of National Parks and Equivalent Reserves, I can assure you that our preservation policy will not change as a result.[245]

Nyerere reaffirmed his decision to allow the grazing, no matter what the "international community" thought about his decision. Despite an obsequious mea culpa from Bernhard a few weeks later, the Lamai Wedge decision drove a chasm between Nyerere and the green network that was never repaired during his presidency.[246] Around this same time, Grzimek and the expat British community who had been "Africanized out" found that Nyerere had grown cold to their entreaties.[247] To them, Nyerere had deliberately "set a fox in the coop to guard the chickens" by putting Bryceson in charge of the parks system.[248]

Amid these crises over hotel construction and local land use, the Tanzanian tourism industry continued to show signs of stagnation, further weakening Grzimek and the green network's bargaining position. According to the government's statistics, the number of visitors in the Serengeti dipped from 81,000 in 1971 to 75,000 in 1972. The numbers recovered to 90,000 in 1974, just after the OPEC crisis had hit Tanzania hard, but by 1977 that number had plummeted by almost two-thirds, to just under 33,000.[249] Tanzania had already begun to turn away from tourist-led development in 1973—the year that Operation Vijiji began—when the government decided to suddenly ban all hunting safaris. The government seized and impounded foreign-registered land cruisers, supply trucks, minibuses, and other equipment. Of course, Tanzania had a lot on its mind in 1971–1972; a bungled invasion of Uganda across the Kagera River in an attempt to topple Amin's government had led to bombings of the countryside by the dictator's air force.[250] In 1976, the East African Community had dissolved amid trade disputes and tensions over the collapse of East African Airways.[251]

In 1977 Nyerere sealed off the border with Kenya altogether. The decision had multiple aims, but one was to gain a fair share of the tourist traffic by stopping the Serengeti from remaining a mere "day trip" from Kenya.[252] As the ecologist Anthony Sinclair describes it: "Hapless tourists, waking up that fateful day in the Serengeti and expecting to be taken on a game drive, instead found themselves effectively captives of the Tanzanian immigration authorities." Tanzania's minister of tourism, ole Saibull, lectured the visitors on Kenya's many wrongdoings and the injustice of a tourist trade that benefited capitalist Kenya over socialist Tanzania. Ole Saibull then forced the tourists to pay for a chartered plane back to Nairobi.[253] The government's move was supposed to teach tourists to start and finish their safaris in Tanzania, but the entire plan backfired: "roughing up" the tourists only convinced Western travel agents and tour companies that their guests were not welcome in Tanzania. Indeed, tourism experts estimated that the number of visitors in Tanzania plummeted from 165,000 in 1976 to just 54,000 in 1983.[254]

With so few tourists coming to the parks, the revenue from entrance fees also suffered a downward spiral, leaving little money for the newly minted African trainees from Mweka to maintain existing facilities or mount effective anti-poaching patrols.[255] Tanzanian officials insisted that this was the best course for their country: "Fewer tourists, landing in Tanzania and spending the whole of their time here, are of greater financial benefit to the country" than the previous system of quick trips with drivers "paid outside the country."[256] Yet border controls and permits made it exceedingly difficult to visit Tanzania after 1972. As Myles Turner lamented, "In the last ten years under John Owen, they've built these magnificent parks and hotels—and now they aren't going to welcome tourists!" The danger was obvious—when the politicians in places such as Lamai could no longer point to the revenue from tourists to stop land-hungry interlopers, "that literally is the end."[257] The border remained closed from 1977 to 1986, a time when only the most intrepid West German tourists visited Tanzania. As one writer noted, "Even the game wardens have no shoes."[258]

———

Though scholars have seen Nyerere's border closure primarily as an ideological about-face against a capitalist rival, the underperformance of tourism clearly played a role. Having the best wildlife and scenery in East Africa offered no guarantee that Tanzania could "catch up" to Kenya and divert its golden hordes southward for longer stays—a point that paeans to Grzimek's pioneering efforts in nature tourism often overlook. As Nyerere and his ministers learned during this period, the bundle of roads, railways, hotels, and airports that each territory received at independence created path dependencies that were difficult to overcome, irrespective of the country's ideological orientation. Given these stark choices facing Tanzania by 1972, Nyerere chose to pursue a path of greater self-reliance, even if that cost him international recognition, donations, and visitors. Development theorists' insistence that Tanzania "mismanaged" its parks and tourist facilities has usually missed the deep resentments inherited from the first postcolonial decade, a time when Grzimek and Owen had worked tirelessly to "make wildlife pay for themselves"—but fell short.

The border closure came on the heels of disenchantment with the green network over the goals and outcomes of technical assistance and the amount and timing of international aid. Grzimek and Owen knew they needed to prove animals' worth before the wildlife sector came under African control but tried to hang on to the administrative strings for as long as they could. Nyerere granted the national parks a large degree of latitude, especially with the United Kingdom offering indirect support and Owen's string of successes in raising scientific funds and subsidizing the parks. Nyerere also found that wildlife greased the wheels of diplomacy and gave the country access to prestige and other kinds of foreign investment. Many of his West German interlocutors, such as Eugen Gerstenmaier, were big game hunters, and Nyerere skillfully indulged their romantic and, at times, brazenly paternalist remembrances of the German colonial period to curry favor. Once Nyerere ran into diplomatic troubles with West Germany and the United Kingdom, however, the Arusha Bargain had less appeal, as it seemed to constrain the country's exercise of environmental sovereignty without offering enough tangible benefits in return.

Nyerere's ministers, such as Tewa and Fundikira, saw emotional affinities between African cultures and wildlife but insisted that the West's environmental redemption came at a price. They soon learned that Europeans were not willing to mount an emergency infusion of aid, despite all of the talk about planetary heritage at the Arusha Conference. As the sustained yields and donation pledges faltered, Tanzanians found themselves saddled with an underfinanced national park system that they had to subsidize, again and again, in the ever-receding hopes for massive numbers of tourists. Not surprisingly, Grzimek found his room for maneuver increasingly constrained by the early 1970s, a time when his correspondence with the president was formal, distanced, often contrite—quite a contrast from the chumminess that characterized their early years. Whatever its economic fallout and misguided assumptions, Nyerere's border closure did not stem solely from ideological prerogatives, nor did it destroy a tourist sector that was meeting its targets. Instead, at the point of Africanization, Tanzania absorbed a sector already languishing due to modest visitation and competition with Kenya.[259] As Harold T. P. Hayes has noted, Grzimek and his allies had become mere onlookers over a Tanzanian man's (not "mankind's") decision about the fate of the Serengeti. "Only a few years ago they had been the quarreling carpenters of the last ark," he wrote, "now that task lay to others."[260]

Epilogue

A Visit to Seronera

Six decades after the Grzimeks first arrived in the Serengeti, their quest still shapes the way that tourists, scientists, park staff, and locals are invited to understand the park's origins and its significance for global conservation. Before my first visit to the Serengeti in 2011, the late Lazaro Moringe Parkipuny, a long-time advocate for pastoral land rights in Tanzania, told me that he considered Seronera, the headquarters of the park and the Serengeti Wildlife Research Center, the "last bastion of the German Empire in East Africa." I had met Mr. Parkipuny quite by chance, after being contacted by a European environmental justice advocate who had come across my article, "Serengeti Shall Not Die," online. She wanted me to know much more about the imperiled state of Maasai livelihoods in Loliondo, on the eastern borderlands of the park, and suggested that I meet with Mr. Parkipuny during my stay in Arusha. Parkipuny decried a fortress conservation model that he believed had deprived the Maasai and other pastoralists of their ability to graze cattle extensively and keep their traditional culture intact.[1]

The Tanzania National Parks Authority (TANAPA) maintains an office at Seronera, as does the Frankfurt Zoological Society (FZS), whose Help for Threatened Wildlife follows in Grzimek's footsteps by supplying and maintaining patrol vehicles, supporting monitoring and research on animal populations, and offering technical support for park management. There I met briefly with Markus Borner, a one-time colleague of Grzimek's and the now-retired head of the society's Africa Programme. Mr. Borner underscored that the Serengeti and other national parks were a product of African tradition, not European imposition, and reminded me that the Maasai were recent arrivals to the savannas— having come barely fifty years before the first wave of German colonialists in the 1880s. Mr. Borner was insistent that the Maasai were not, in this sense, "indigenous" to the savannas as so many human rights organizations had argued.[2] His comments were a reminder of the UN's fraught understanding of "indigeneity,"

Our Gigantic Zoo. Thomas M. Lekan, Oxford University Press (2020). © Oxford University Press.
DOI: 10.1093/oso/9780199843671.001.0001

but his leap into this discussion and wariness about my visit short circuited the conversation I really wanted to have with him about the troubled relationship between Grzimek, Nyerere, and Bryceson in the 1970s that had emerged in the archives.

In retrospect, I realize that kind of conversation was quite impossible. My visit to Seronera had come just a few months after Tanzania's then-president Jakaya Kikwete had given the green light for building a hard-packed road through the heart of the northern Serengeti, and no Western NGO working in Tanzania was interested in what my conservation biology colleagues call "problem histories."[3] The rationale was to connect Musoma to Arusha, thereby linking up isolated areas of the country—the populous district east of Lake Victoria, the Serengeti, and Loliondo—to the national road network. Grzimek, it may be recalled, had worried about the Lake Victoria region and his beloved Rubondo already in the 1970s, recommending that West German donors support a connection from Mwanza to Arusha with a highway running well south of the Serengeti. Much like the 1956 plan to divide the Serengeti, the 1968 proposal to allow range management in the NCA, or the 1972 occupation of the Lamai Wedge, the road project, the FZS and other global conservation organizations insisted, would doom the wildebeest migration, destroy the tourism industry, and set a bad precedent for development in a wilderness area that Grzimek and others had hoped would remain an "animal state" for all time. The clash of perspectives evident in Seronera in 2011 made it clear that memories of the Serengeti's 1959 division are ongoing and raw: an unmasterable conservation past.

The unresolved conflicts between international NGOs, the Tanzanian state, and local and indigenous African communities over the meaning and significance of conservation are on display in Seronera at the Serengeti Visitor Center, where an FZS and EU-funded "House of Conservation" exhibit places the Grzimeks' Flying Zebra at the center of interpretation. Cut-out figures of "good friends," Grzimek and Nyerere, can be viewed here; even after rescaling the figure of the six-foot-four Grzimek, he still seems to loom over the former president.

The figures announce a story of global conservation and world heritage in a timeless paradise that tourists can now appreciate—yet the panels reveal a deep ambivalence about who is responsible for and benefits from conserving the Serengeti. Grzimek, as one panel announces, was the "man with the vision" who conducted the research for establishing the Serengeti's borders, offered "persistence and guidance" for expanding its park system (eleven new parks since independence, with over 25 percent of the territory in protected areas), and, most important, raised the funds for the administration of the parks. A panel affixed to one of the building's posts summarizes one of the Grzimeks' best-known quotations about global heritage from the book *Serengeti Shall Not Die*. As lions walk into "the red dawn" fifty years hence, they argued, it would meaningful to all people and "quicken their hearts whether they are Bolsheviks or democrats, or whether they speak English, German, Russian or Swahili."⁴

Such wildlife panoramas and the income they generate appear in the House of Conservation as the outcome of the Grzimeks' otherworldly vision, one that glimpsed beyond the intractable conflicts between the colonial state and rural peoples in 1958 by documenting the precarious state of wildlife and their habitat and making the world care about the fate of animals. Without the Grzimeks' mission to save the Serengeti, *millions* of migrating wildebeest, zebra, and gazelle in this 5,700-square-mile wilderness might have gone the way of the threatened American buffalo: inbred, dispersed, and isolated into small cluster herds. Visitors learn that Grzimek parlayed the success of *Serengeti Shall Not Die* into donations from television viewers that funneled millions of Deutsche marks into Tanzania to help "manage" the vast wilderness by conducting scientific research, arming anti-poaching brigades, training African wildlife rangers, developing tourist facilities, and aiding search and rescue operations.

Come to the Serengeti at the right time, perhaps just after the short autumn rains in December or in the weeks following the spring rains in early May, and the savannas are filled with these salvaged animals as far as the eye can see. One cannot help being captivated by this breathtaking spectacle that has finally paid off for Tanzania, with more than a hundred thousand visiting the Serengeti each year, contributing to a tourism industry worth about $2 billion in 2010.⁵ Putting up with the vanloads of other nature tourists further down the park's main trunk road seems a small price to pay for such a glimpse of paradise. That is, until we consider that such tourists have replaced the pastoralists and livestock who roamed these plains in the early 1950s. When he visited the Moru Kopjes in 1952, Myles Turner lamented that the area would soon become a dustbowl due to the removal of trees, overgrazing, and Maasai dogs that scared off wildlife. Yet one can't help feeling that tourists are loving Serengeti nature to death as they descend upon the few rhino left in the crater or watch as a lioness goes hungry after giving up on stalking a juvenile zebra, even as the cameras start to roll. Who poses the greater threat to the ecosystem today?

The Frankfurt Zoo's Grzimek House contains a similar set of panels documenting and honoring the Grzimeks' Serengeti research, fundraising, and tourism promotion. The panels make more sense in the Frankfurt Zoo, where the zookeeper is still much loved and remembered and where fundraising targets the affluent generations who came of age from the 1960s to the 1980s, when Grzimek's celebrity was at its height. Perusing the displays at the Grzimek House, European visitors can recall the first time they saw *Serengeti Shall Not Die*, the famous television bluff, the audacious accusation that high-density poultry farms produced "concentration camps eggs." Such panels are part of repertoire of images and memories that have made Germans proud of partaking in

Figure E.1: The great wildebeest migration in the wet season. Wildebeest numbers rebounded fivefold between 1961 and 1977, after a long drought in the savannas that had accompanied the division of the Serengeti in 1959. Such numbers confounded ecologists' expectations, until Anthony Sinclair and others drew attention to the role of rinderpest in keeping the pre-1961 numbers below historical norms. Photograph by the author.

international conservation campaigns and supporting the FZS mission abroad. But the replication of this exhibit in Tanzania, right in the heart of East Africa's savannas, raises the specter of a not-yet-resolved colonial past. The exhibit lauds German colonial governor Hermann von Wissmann for passing the first laws to protect wildlife for "future generations" and then touts the "British Way" of using wildlife management for crop protection as a stepping stone to modern conservation.

Opening up a discussion of conservation's colonial origins and the banning of African hunting also invites uncomfortable questions about a Global Nature supposedly set aside for both Europeans and Africans, leading the exhibition leaders to compensate with another panel on "Precolonial Nature Conservation" that is reminiscent of Grzimek's 1970s view. Here we learn that nature and wildlife were key elements of Africans' "tribal traditions" and "folklore" and that "nature conservation was practiced by the indigenous people long before Europeans came to Africa" with "hunting . . . . permitted only at certain times." This panel comes amid others discussing colonial resettlement campaigns and the evacuation of tsetse-infested areas—actions that historians and geographers have shown were neither socially just nor ecologically beneficial. We are left with the disquieting suggestion that Africans have somehow grown accustomed to exclusion and displacement—maybe even welcoming it. Indeed, the exhibition echoes Grzimek's ujamaa-era insistence on the "sacrifices" that Africans were making on behalf of wildlife. "These people are proud of their heritage," he wrote in 1977, having once created "taboo regions" that reflected Africans' "mysterious bonds with the animal soul."[6] It is no wonder that Elizabeth Garland has called the colonial character of wildlife conservation the "elephant in the room" and has called on the FZS, the AWF, the WWF, and the National Geographic Society to "exercise restraint in glorifying the accomplishments and personas of individual charismatic conservationists" in their outreach efforts.[7]

Garland worries, too, about how such colonial imaginaries have structured tourists' expectations of African landscapes in such a way that they forget the hard work of thousands of Africans whose "conservation labor" makes their odyssey possible: game wardens, tour operators, hotel and lodge managers, park staff, maintenance workers.[8] More than most of the "charismatic megabiologists" that Garland has studied, Grzimek did write about this growing constituency in his call for donations, admonishing his viewers not to forget the "black people" who, as curators and gamekeepers, "defend such a paradise." But tourism has meanwhile produced a new generation of conservation laborers for whom the Serengeti is a day job or a stepping stone to a career. Indeed, outside the entrance to the Visitor Center were a number of tour leaders in training, eager to test out their knowledge of flora and fauna and earn a few tips—including Samwel, a self-described "Metro Maasai" who led one group I accompanied.

The visit to Seronera revealed that tourists do not always unthinkingly accept colonialist images and heroic stories of white heroes. Tourists from the United States, the United Kingdom, and Australia that I encountered seemed baffled by an exhibition focused on a German television star they had never heard of. "Did he create the park, then?," I overheard someone ask. "Wasn't this a British colony?," inquired another. They were puzzled, too, by the presentation of Grzimek as the savior of the Serengeti when, as the panels demonstrated, the park was divided against his and Michael's wishes in 1958. Most tourists I spoke to had also visited Ngorongoro on their way to Serengeti and delighted in the presence of cattle herds right next to giraffe —a mix of the wild and the domesticated that the Grzimeks had seen as catastrophic. They also enjoyed seeing Ngorongoro Maasai draped in *shuka* cloth, which many had purchased at one of the bomas specially outfitted for tourists. Their confusion made them eager to exit the House of Conservation and head outside for the nature-centered displays where they could learn about "Life on the Move," the "Spectacle of Birth," or the "Poisoned Milk" of the candelabra tree, which was known to cause blindness for those unlucky enough to come into contact with it. Samwel boldly snapped off a segment of the candelabra, running its thick sap between his fingers to the worried looks of visitors. In this spectacle of nature's dangers and fragility, Grzimek had achieved his greatest influence: Serengeti Shall Not Die had left its mark by transforming an ecosystem into a resilient protagonist—and potent commodity—that remained vibrant despite fires, downpours, diseases, and human encroachment.

One senses that Grzimek himself would be uneasy with the hagiography on display at the House of Conservation. After all, unlike most "charismatic megascientists," Grzimek had always insisted that John Owen had done the hard work expanding the park system and lauded Nyerere's Arusha Manifesto as the true watershed in African and global conservation. Grzimek's "unwavering friendship" with the country's great Mwalimu allowed the president to see the light on conservation, so the panel texts go, implementing an enlightened environmental policy. At the core of that policy is Nyerere's stirring statement about trusteeship over wildlife, which remains, as one panel notes, "the fundamental principle" of the government's policy toward wildlife conservation. Nyerere stands side-by-side with the zookeeper in the House of Conservation, a symbol of Euro-African partnership. Yet Nyerere's own understanding of conservation and its role in national life remain elusive. Grzimek is the "man with a vision." Nyerere merely adopts this philosophy and brings it to the masses. Or so it seems.

A better exhibit script, one more attuned to a Tanzanian national context, would dispense with the rhetoric of ancient hunting taboos and focus squarely on the hopes and aspirations of political modernizers in the early 1960s who embraced conservation as a tool of socialist development. As we have seen, Grzimek found it especially heroic that Nyerere had made the unpopular decision to "evacuate whole villages" during the Lamai controversies, something that Grzimek claimed "was never proposed under European colonial rule, let alone done: to be willing to evacuate people to make room for animals." This was willful forgetting: the German and British governments did not just contemplate evacuating villages for conservation but resettled thousands of Africans in dubious disease- and wildlife-control regimes. Nyerere shared Grzimek's hopes for a robust tourist industry and saw wildlife as a gateway for other kinds of development aid, trade, and goodwill. This bargain accepted a degree of direction and interference from the Industrial North in Tanzanian affairs—at least for a time.

Nyerere, Tewa, Mahinda, and Fundikira wanted to adopt the mode of biopolitical power that conservation offered and use it to "manage" human and animal populations.[9] They knew that game reserves and national parks had served the colonial state's needs of stabilizing the workforce by cutting off access to wild areas where farmers and pastoralists could hunt, gather honey, graze animals, or start a farm. They wanted to adapt these spaces to their socialist goals so as to modernize those rural populations deemed especially "backward" or recalcitrant. The notion of Grzimek and Nyerere as "good friends" also overlooks the rifts that emerged between two different understandings of environmental sovereignty: did national parks and rhinoceroses really "belong to everybody," as Grzimek insisted? Or were the Tanzanian parks a national heritage, established by and for Africans to make profits and serve the population? As the 1960s wore on, the scale tipped toward the latter view, encouraged by faltering donations, lackluster tourism performance, and deep misgivings about the compatibility of self-reliant socialism and foreign-backed tourism.

Nyerere's decision to side with international conservationists against the interests of pastoralists or other rural citizens was fully in line with the socialist government's plans to modernize agriculture, shift traditional pastoralism toward beef production, and, especially, sedentarize the population in villages.[10] Early on in the independence era, his government began to see the national parks as a tool for concentrating African settlement.[11] In 1963 and 1964, over two hundred "scattered African huts" began "springing up" in the Ikorongo area along the western corridor boundary. Nyerere promised the government's full support in evacuating the settlers outside the pathway of the wildebeest migration to protect the "security of the Serengeti herds." Here conservation rhetoric merged with spatial planning, as such "sporadic settlement" ran counter to the country's long-term villagization goals.[12] Indeed, the national parks, supported by the FZS and the WWF, provided funding for the salary and expenses of a village resettlement expert, who coordinated government and national park field forces to remove the settlers and destroy their huts. Neither Grzimek nor Owen thought about the impact of such relocations on local people's attitudes toward the park or their struggles with an increasingly disciplinary, one-party state.[13] Wildlife conservation, after all, was "apolitical"—above local squabbles and parochial concerns.

After John Owen had stepped down from leadership, at a time when Grzimek was still vying for the favor of the "enigmatic and ascetic" Nyerere, Bryceson was working quietly to strengthen this link between national parks and villagization. "Previously the parks tended to be a foreign organization within Tanzania," he told Harold T.P. Hayes in 1976. John Owen could not speak Swahili—a symbol of the "colonial culture" that Tanzanians had sought to escape. As tourist revenues dried up, Bryceson began to justify the parks' existence as an extension of Operation Vijiji, serving as the lynchpin for rational "land utilization" and concentrated settlement. National parks, in this view, served not just as buffers for animals against human encroachment but also restrained the "unplanned diffusion" of the population beyond designated village centers.[14]

The synergy between international conservation and African nation building helps to explain why the exhibit struggles to incorporate the stories of the Ikoma, Iraqw, Arusha, and Maasai who have lived in these regions of northern

Tanzania near the park (never, in the exhibit script, the territory *within* the park boundaries). These groups appear at the very end of the displays, on the bottom floor, as "friends of conservation" who are still learning to see wildlife as an income source with the help of white interlocutors through community conservation projects. Such projects, visitors are assured, have replaced the "fines and fences" approach of the colonial and early postcolonial years with a notion of conservation "by the people and for the people." Such integrated conservation and development projects (ICDPs) became an important part of the democratizing side of the neoliberal era that gained steam in the 1990s. As Tanzania sold off its tourist parastatals and opened its doors to foreign investors, the proponents of sustainable development believed these village-centered projects offered grassroots, non-statist alternatives that would ensure monetary benefits for local communities.

Such projects have expanded in the wildlife management areas bordering the Serengeti and other national parks. Yet it remains difficult to create private incentives for game lodges in Tanzania because the government still "owns" the animals that roam through customary lands and many rural denizens still do not

Figure E.2: Managing the Serengeti is a Huge Task. An installation at the Serengeti Visitor Center depicts the constant mobilization of resources necessary to keep out poachers and herders, school Tanzanians in the benefits of wildlife, and rescue tourists. Once gazetted and set outside the working lands of the region, the Serengeti never stops needing a savior. Photograph by the author.

have secure land tenure. And those foreign companies promising a "magical," ecotourism experience—most notably the US-based Thomson Safaris—hold long-term leases and stand accused of violence against Maasai who trespass with their herds in the Loliondo region.[15] Such private "land grabs" have resulted in numerous human rights cases—a tragic codicil to the trend toward ecotourism and sustainable development that were supposed to redefine liberal and socialist modernization strategies and increase participation and environmental auton-omy. Part of the problem with the ICDPs and the foreign ecotourism projects is that outsiders, not locals, have more power than ever to define what "ought to be seen" in and how to value the assets of the Tanzanian savannas. Such notions of development—sustainable or otherwise—still assume that Africans do not already know how to value their wildlife as heritage or commodity. As such, market- and community-based approaches have not really changed the power dynamic from the 1960s—Africans have become "stakeholders" in community and environmental development, but they do not help to create the conservation norms used to define and assess the outcomes of such projects. Indeed, as the graphic of "managing the Serengeti" makes clear, they remain largely intruders, as game wardens chase them away from animals, admonish them for building fires, or instruct them in animal biology. Managing the Serengeti remains a "huge task" from which they remain largely excluded, as outsiders provide TANAPA with the requisite "technical equipment, assistance, infrastructure development, and funding for research." In this sense, contested memories of 1959, when for-tress conservation competed with mixed-use models and the Maasai and others hoped for both political emancipation and environmental sovereignty, remain unresolved. The Serengeti thus remains under constant "threat" from people it should also serve—and will never stop needing to be saved.

NOTES

Introduction

1. This story is recounted in Grzimek's "Wie steht es jetzt um die Nationalparke Afrikas," *Schweizer Monatshefte* (July 1961): 481 and Jens Ivo Engels, "Von der Sorge um Tiere zur Sorge um die Umwelt: Tiersendungen als Umweltpolitik in Westdeutschland zwischen 1950 und 1980," *Archiv für Sozialgeschichte* 43 (March 2003): 305.

2. On package tours and the "massification" of travel, see James Buzard, *The Beaten Track: European Tourism, Literature, and the Ways of Culture, 1800–1918* (Oxford: Clarendon, 1993); Lynn Withey, *Grand Tours and Cook's Tours: A History of Leisure Travel, 1750–1915* (New York: William Morrow and Co., 1997); and Hartmut Berghoff, "From Privilege to Commodity? Modern Tourism and the Rise of Consumer Society," in *The Making of Modern Tourism: The Cultural History of the British Experience, 1600–2000*, ed. Hartmut Berghoff, et al. (New York: Palgrave, 2002), 159–180. On German mass travel cultures, see Hasso Spode, *Goldstrand und Teutonengrill: Kultur- und Sozialgeschichte des Tourismus in Deutschland 1945 bis 1989* (Berlin: W. Moser: Verlag für universitäre Kommunikation, 1996) and Hasso Spode, *Wie die Deutschen "Reiseweltmeister" wurden: Eine Einführung in die Tourismusgeschichte* (Erfurt: Landeszentrale für politische Bildung Thüringen, 2003); Christina Keitz, *Reisen als Leitbild: die Entstehung des modernen Massentourismus in Deutschland* (Munich: DTV, 1997); Rudy Koshar, "'What Ought to Be Seen': Tourists' Guidebooks and National Identities in Modern Germany and Europe," *Journal of Contemporary History* 33, no. 3 (1998): 323–340 and Shelley Baranowski, *Strength Through Joy: Consumerism and Mass Tourism in the Third Reich* (Cambridge, UK: Cambridge University Press, 2007), 118–161.

3. Shirley Brooks, "Images of 'Wild Africa': Nature Tourism and the (Re)Creation of Hluhluwe Game Reserve, 1930–1945," *Journal of Historical Geography* 31, no. 2 (April 2005): 220–240.

4. The sense that decolonization was a crisis that "other" Europeans faced left West Germans free to become "globetrotters" unencumbered by the imperial past. On this point, see Sara Friedrichsmeyer, Sara Lennox and Susanne Zantop, eds., *German Colonialism and Its Legacy: The Imperialist Imagination* (Amherst: University of Massachusetts Press, 1999) and Eric Ames, Marcia Klotz, and Lora Wildenthal, eds., *Germany's Colonial Pasts* (Lincoln: University of Nebraska Press, 2005); Bradley Naranch and Geoff Eley, *German Colonialism in a Global Age* (Durham, NC: Duke University Press, 2014). On decolonization in German Studies see Thomas Moser, *Europäische Integration, Dekolonisation, Eurafrika: Eine historische Analyse über die Entstehungsbedingungen der Eurafrikanischen Gemeinschaft von der Weltwirtschaftskrise bis zum Jaunde-Vertrag, 1929–1963* (Baden-Baden, Germany: Nomos, 2000) and Volker M. Langbehn, ed., *German Colonialism, Visual Culture, and Modern Memory* (New York: Routledge), 165–301.

5. On the redemptive themes in Grzimek's work, see Franziska Torma, *Eine Naturschutzkampagne in der Ära Adenauer: Bernhard Grzimeks Afrikafilme in den Medien der 50er Jahre*

(Munich: Martin Meidenbauer, 2004), 127–164 and Michael Flitner, "Vom 'Platz in der Sonne' zur 'Platz für Tiere,'" in *Der Deutsche Tropenwald: Bilder, Mythen, Politik*, ed. Michael Flitner (Frankfurt: Campus, 2000), 244–262.

6. It was also, in many ways, an "impossible" one with long-standing precursors in German cultural history. See Nina Berman, *Impossible Missions? German Economic, Military, and Humanitarian Efforts in Africa* (Lincoln: University of Nebraska Press, 2004), 99–138.

7. The literature of Tanganyikan independence is extensive and cannot be cited here in detail. For the overall political framework, see John Iliffe, *A Modern History of Tanganyika* (Cambridge, UK: Cambridge University Press, 1979), 507–567; Susan Geiger, *TANU Women: Gender and Culture in the Making of Tanganyikan Nationalism, 1955–1965* (Portsmouth, NH: Heinemann, 1997); Andreas Eckert, *Herrschen und Verwalten: Afrikanische Bürokraten, Staatliche Ordnung und Politik in Tanzania, 1920–1970* (Munich: Oldenbourg, 2007); Chambi Chachage and Annar Cassam, eds., *Africa's Liberation: The Legacy of Nyerere* (Kampala: Fountain Publishers, 2010); Ronald Aminzade, "The Dialectic of Nation Building in Postcolonial Tanzania," *The Sociological Quarterly* 54, no. 3 (2013): 335–366; Paul Bjerk, *Building a Peaceful Nation: Julius Nyerere and the Establishment of Sovereignty in Tanzania, 1960–1964* (Rochester: University of Rochester Press, 2015). On independence struggles and land rights, see Steven Feierman, *Peasant Intellectuals: History and Anthropology in Tanzania* (Madison: University of Wisconsin Press, 1990), 167–180; Thaddeus Sunseri, *Wielding the Ax: State Forestry and Social Conflict in Tanzania, 1820–2000* (Athens: Ohio University Press, 2009), 117–142; and Pamela Maack, "'We Don't Want Terraces!': Protest and Identity under the Uluguru Land Usage Scheme," in *Custodians of the Land: Ecology and Culture in the History of Tanzania*, ed. Gregory H. Maddox (London: Currey, 2006), 152–169.

8. The classic account of Tanzania's development as a wilderness "exporter" is found in Roderick Nash, *Wilderness and the American Mind*, 4th ed. (New Haven, CT: Yale University Press, 2001), 365–367. Many development economists remained optimistic about the possibilities of using wildlife tourism as a form of export substitution until, in the 1990s, social scientists became more critical about the social and cultural impacts of tourism. See Klaus Frentrup, *Die Ökonomische Bedeutung des Internationalen Tourismus für die Entwicklungsländer* (Hamburg: Deutsches Übersee-Institut, 1969); Vojislav Popović, *Tourism in Eastern Africa* (Munich: Weltforum Verlag, 1972); John R. Watkin, *The Evolution of Ecotourism in East Africa: From an Idea to an Industry* (London: International Institute for Environment and Development, 2003). For critical perspectives see Chilla Bulbeck, *Facing the Wild: Ecotourism, Conservation and Animal Encounters* (London: Earthscan, 2005); Martha Honey, *Ecotourism and Sustainable Development: Who Owns Paradise?* 2nd ed. (Washington, DC: Island Press, 2008).

9. Bernhard Grzimek, *Auch Nashörner Gehören allen Menschen: Kämpfe um die Tierwelt Afrikas* (Frankfurt: Ullstein, 1962), 140.

10. Harold T.P. Hayes, *The Last Place on Earth* (New York: Stein and Day, 1977), 16.

11. The literature on the Serengeti division and human rights struggles of the 1950s is quite extensive and cannot be cited here in full. Some of the best accounts include Myles Turner, *My Serengeti Years: The Memoirs of an African Game Warden* (New York: W.W. Norton, 1988), 39–54; Jonathan S. Adams and Thomas O. McShane, *The Myth of Wild Africa: Conservation without Illusion* (New York: W.W. Norton, 1992), 50–51; Roderick P. Neumann, *Imposing Wilderness: Struggles over Livelihood and Nature Preservation in Africa* (Berkeley: University of California Press, 1998), 129–139 and "Ways of Seeing Africa: Colonial Recasting of African Society and Landscape in Serengeti National Park," *Ecumene* 2, no. 2 (1995): 149–169; Jan Bender Shetler, *Imagining Serengeti: A History of Landscape Memory in Tanzania from Earliest Times to the Present* (Athens: Ohio University Press, 2007), 201–217.

12. Bernhard Grzimek, *No Room for Wild Animals* (London: Thames and Hudson, 1956), 22. On the Grzimeks' filmic quest, see Tobias Boes, "Political Animals: *Serengeti Shall Not Die* and the Cultural Heritage of Mankind," *German Studies Review* 36, no. 1 (2013): 41–59.

13. On Michael Grzimek's death, see Bernhard Grzimek and Michael Grzimek, *Serengeti darf nicht Sterben: 367,000 Suchen einen Staat* (Berlin: Ullstein, 1959), 328. Citations come from the 1961 English version unless otherwise specified: *Serengeti Shall Not Die*, trans. E.L. Rewald and D. Rewald (New York: E.P. Dutton, 1961), 328; and Franziska Torma,

Naturschutzkampagne, 130–132. Torma's well-researched master's thesis is the best source of information about Grzimek's films.

14. Bernhard and Michael Grzimek, *Serengeti darf nicht Sterben*, 245.

15. Numerous Africanist scholars have critiqued Grzimek's impact on Tanzania and other African nations. Here I try to connect the dots between this flourishing political-ecological literature and the situated German origins of his brand of environmental globalism. See, among many others, Adams and McShane, *Myth of Wild Africa*, 50–53; Shetler, *Imagining Serengeti*, 4–5; 15; 25; 35; 165; and Mark Dowie, *Conservation Refugees: The Hundred-Year Conflict between Global Conservation and Native Peoples* (Cambridge, MA: MIT Press, 2009), 12–13, 23–26.

16. On the "projection screen," see Torma, *Naturschutzkampagne*, 22–29. On fears of Americanization in particular, see Victoria de Grazia, *Irresistible Empire: America's Advance through Twentieth-Century Europe* (Cambridge, MA: Harvard University Press, 2005) and Alexander Stephan, *The Americanization of Europe: Culture, Diplomacy, and Anti-Americanism after 1945* (New York: Berghahn, 2006). On race after Hitler, see Heide Fehrenbach, *Race after Hitler: Black Occupation Children in Postwar Germany and America* (Princeton, NJ: Princeton University Press, 2005) and Rita Chin, *After the Nazi Racial State: Difference and Democracy in Germany and Europe* (Ann Arbor: University of Michigan Press, 2009).

17. Grzimek's many domestic and international animal protection campaigns are documented in Claudia Sewig, *Der Mann, der die Tiere liebte: Bernhard Grzimek: Biografie* (Bergisch Gladbach: Lübbe, 2009) and Jens-Ivo Engels, *Naturpolitik in der Bundesrepublik. Ideenwelt und politische Verhaltensstile in Naturschutz und Umweltbewegung, 1950–1980* (Paderborn: Schöningh, 2006), 214–274.

18. Sewig, *Der Mann, der die Tiere liebte*, 263–425; Jens Ivo Engels, "Tiersendungen," 297–323.

19. William Beinart, "The Renaturing of African Animals: Film and Literature in the 1950s and 1960s, *Kronos: Journal of Cape History* 27 (November 2001): 201–226. Grzimek's *Platz für Tiere* resembled in content and format Marlin Perkins's *Wild Kingdom*, whose environmental implications are discussed in Gregg Mitman, *Reel Nature: America's Romance with Wildlife on Film* (Cambridge, UK: Cambridge University Press, 1999), 132–156 and Cynthia Chris, *Watching Wildlife* (Minneapolis: University of Minnesota Press, 2006), 52–70, 79, 87.

20. Engels, "Tiersendungen," 303.

21. Engels, *Naturpolitik in der Bundesrepublik*, 214–274; Sewig, *Der Mann, der die Tiere liebte*, 373; and Sandra Chaney, *Nature of the Miracle Years: Conservation in West Germany, 1945–1975* (New York: Berghahn, 2008), 178–185; 219–226; 232–236.

22. On this point, see Engels, "Tiersendungen" and Stephen Milder, *Greening Democracy: The Anti-Nuclear Movement and Political Environmentalism in West Germany and Beyond, 1968–1983* (Cambridge, UK: Cambridge University Press, 2017).

23. Hayes, *Last Place on Earth*, 29.

24. Grzimek borrowed ideas from Fairfield Osborn in this context. See Mitman, *Reel Nature*, 180–202. On "environmental sovereignty" and indigenous rights, see Karen Litfin, *The Greening of Sovereignty in World Politics* (Cambridge, MA: MIT Press, 1998) and Bradley Condon, *Environmental Sovereignty and the WTO: Trade Sanctions and International Law* (Leiden: Brill, 2006).

25. Hayes, *Last Place on Earth*, 32–33.

26. Adams and McShane, *Myth of Wild* Africa, 50.

27. Hayes, *Last Place on Earth*, 29; Sewig, *Der Mann, der die Tiere liebte*, 343.

28. My conception of the "green network" is in this sense broader and more dynamic than the IUCN and its affiliates, for it encompasses German and other bilateral aid for wildlife as well as African conservationists. See, for example, *The Green Web: A Union for Would Conservation* (London: Earthscan/ IUCN, 1999); Raymond Bonner, *At the Hand of Man: Peril and Hope for Africa's Wildlife* (New York: Vintage, 1993); William M. Adams, *Against Extinction: The Story of Conservation* (London: Earthscan, 2004), 67–69; 124; 128. On the British colonial linkages of such green networks, see Roderick P. Neumann, "The Postwar Conservation Boom in British Colonial Africa," *Environmental History* 7, no. 1 (January 2002): 22–47; Joseph M. Hodge, *Triumph of the Expert: Agrarian Doctrines of Development and the Legacies of British Colonialism* (Athens: Ohio University Press, 2007); and Mark Cioc, *The Game of Conservation: International Treaties to Protect the World's Migratory Animals* (Athens: Ohio University Press, 2009).

29. Gerald G. Watterson, UNESCO, and FAO, *Conservation of Nature and Natural Resources in Modern African States: Report of a Symposium Organized by CCTA and IUCN and Held under the Auspices of FAO and UNESCO at Arusha, Tanganyika, September 1961* (Morges, Switzerland: IUCN, 1963).

30. Grzimek especially elided Germany's former "green imperial" ambitions. See William H. Rollins, "Imperial Shades of Green: Conservation and Environmental Chauvinism in the German Colonial Project," *German Studies Review* 22, no. 2 (1999): 187–214; Johannes Paulmann, *Deutscher Kolonialismus und Natur vom Kaiserreich bis zur Bundesrepublik* (Berlin: Metropol-Verl., 2008); and Thomas Lekan, "'Serengeti Shall Not Die': Bernhard Grzimek, Wildlife Film, and the Making of a Tourist Landscape in East Africa," *German History* 29, no. 2 (June 2011): 224–264.

31. Grzimek, *Auf den Mensch gekommen: Erfahrungen mit Leuten* (Munich: C. Bertelsmann, 1974), 43.

32. Anthony R. E. Sinclair, *Serengeti Story: Life and Science in the World's Greatest Wildlife Region* (Oxford: Oxford University Press, 2012), xiv.

33. Elizabeth Garland, "State of Nature: Colonial Power, Neoliberal Capital, and Wildlife Management in Tanzania" (PhD diss., University of Chicago, 2006), 121–172.

34. On the conflicts between conservation and indigenous rights, see Jim Igoe, *Conservation and Globalization: A Study of the National Parks and Indigenous Communities from East Africa to South Dakota* (Belmont, CA: Thomson/Wadsworth, 2004) and William M. Adams and Martin Mulligan, *Decolonizing Nature: Strategies for Conservation in a Postcolonial Era* (Sterling, VA: Earthscan Publications, 2002). On the peculiarities of Tanzania's "environmental-conservation complex" see Adams and McShane, *Myth of Wild Africa,* 37–58; Dan Brockington, "The Politics and Ethnography of Environmentalisms in Tanzania," *African Affairs* 105 (2006): 102 and *Fortress Conservation: The Preservation of Mkomazi Game Reserve, Tanzania* (Oxford: Oxford University Press, 2002). See also Brockington, Hassan Sachedina, and Katherine Scholfield, "Preserving the New Tanzania: Conservation and Land Use Change," *International Journal of African Historical Studies* 41, no. 3 (2008): 557–580 and Benedicto Kazuzuru "History, Performance, and Challenges of the Tourism Industry in Tanzania," *International Journal of Business and Social Science* 5, no. 11 (October 2014): 123.

35. This is a twist on a slogan of the 1970s environmental movement that highlights the situatedness of global ecological knowledge. On the politics of the God's eye view, see Donna Haraway, "Situated Knowledges: The Science Question in Feminism and the Privilege of Partial Perspective," *Feminist Studies* 14, no. 3 (1988): 579–599. I develop this further in "Fractal Eaarth: Visualizing the Global Environment in the Anthropocene," *Environmental Humanities* 5 (2014): 171–201.

36. On this theme, see Elizabeth Garland, "The Elephant in the Room: Confronting the Colonial Character of Wildlife Conservation in Africa," *African Studies Review* 51, no. 3 (December, 2008): 51–74 and Dan Brockington, *Celebrity and the Environment: Fame, Wealth and Power in Conservation* (London: Zed, 2009).

37. Noël Sturgeon, *Environmentalism in Popular Culture: Gender, Race, Sexuality, and the Politics of the Natural* (Tucson: University of Arizona Press, 2009), 80–102.

38. Denis Cosgrove, "Contested Global Visions: One-World, Whole-Earth, and the Apollo Space Photographs," *Annals of the Association of American Geographers* 84, no. 2 (1994): 270–294 and Sheila Jasanoff, "Image and Imagination: The Formation of Global Environmental Consciousness," in *Changing the Atmosphere: Expert Knowledge and Environmental Governance,* ed. Clark A. Miller and Paul N. Edwards (Cambridge, MA: MIT Press, 2001), 310–311.

39. Ursula K. Heise, *Sense of Place and Sense of Planet: The Environmental Imagination of the Global* (Oxford: Oxford University Press, 2008), 3–13.

40. Here I suggest a more dialogic approach than the "ecological imperialism" pioneered by Alfred Crosby in *Ecological Imperialism: The Biological Expansion of Europe, 900–1900* (Cambridge, UK: Cambridge University Press, 1986) and as suggested in Richard Grove, *Green Imperialism: Colonial Expansion, Tropical Island Edens, and the Origins of Environmentalism, 1600–1860* (Cambridge, UK: Cambridge University Press, 1995), 1–15; 73–94.

41. Anna L. Tsing, *Friction: An Ethnography of Global Connection* (Princeton, NJ: Princeton University Press, 2005), 57–59; 63–65 .

42. Tsing, *Friction*, 1.
43. Tsing, *Friction*, 3; 88–112.
44. Such an approach engages what Nina Berman has pioneered as a form of global studies from a German base in her recent work on German tourists' informal development aid on the Kenya coast. Nina Berman, *Germans on the Kenyan Coast: Land, Charity, and Romance* (Bloomington: Indiana University Press, 2017), 1–21.
45. Thomas Lekan, "A Natural History of Modernity: Bernhard Grzimek and the Globalization of Environmental *Kulturkritik*," *New German Critique* 2 (August 2016): 55–82.
46. Gisela Bonn, *Afrika verlässt den Busch. Kontinent der Kontraste* (Düsseldorf: Econ-Verlag, 1965).
47. James Ferguson, *Expectations of Modernity: Myths and Meanings of Urban Life on the Zambian Copperbelt* (Berkeley: University of California Press, 1999), 1–37.
48. Matthew Connelly, *Fatal Misconception: The Struggle to Control World Population* (Cambridge, MA: Belknap Press of Harvard University Press, 2008).
49. Mark Spence, "Dispossessing the Wilderness: Yosemite Indians and the National Park Ideal, 1864–1930," *Pacific Historical Review* 65, no. 1 (1996): 27–59.
50. On the racialization of "tribe" and territory, see Dorothy Louise Hodgson, *Once Intrepid Warriors: Gender, Ethnicity, and the Cultural Politics of Maasai Development* (Bloomington: Indiana University Press, 2001), 1–7. Grzimek drew on a long-standing racialization of landscape "purity" in German environmental culture as well. See Paul Schultze-Naumburg, *Die Gestaltung der Landschaft durch den Menschen* (Munich: G. D. W. Callwey, 1922) and *Kunst und Rasse* (Munich: Lehmann, 1928).
51. Thomas Spear and Richard Waller, eds., *Being Maasai: Ethnicity and Identity in East Africa* (Athens: Ohio University Press, 1993), 1–9.
52. Ferguson, *Expectations of Modernity*, 38–81.
53. Depictions of impurity also made it more difficult to claim indigenous belonging—and hence to translate customary landholding into secure rights of occupancy. See Issa G. Shivji, Wilbert B. L. Kapinga, and Drylands Programme, *Maasai Rights in Ngorongoro, Tanzania* (Dar es Salaam: Hakiardhi, 1998).
54. Robin S. Reid, *Savannas of Our Birth: People, Wildlife, and Change in East Africa* (Berkeley: University of California Press, 2012).
55. Henry Fosbrooke, *Ngorongoro: The Eighth Wonder* (London: Deutsch, 1972), 155–218.
56. Kaj Århem, *Pastoral Man in the Garden of Eden: The Maasai of the Ngorongoro Conservation Area, Tanzania* (Uppsala: Scandinavian Institute of African Studies, 1985); Katherine Homewood and W. A. Rodgers, *Maasailand Ecology: Pastoralist Development and Wildlife Conservation in Ngorongoro, Tanzania* (Cambridge, UK: Cambridge University Press, 1991); and Katherine Homewood, *Staying Maasai? Livelihoods, Conservation and Development in East African Rangelands* (New York: Springer, 2009).
57. See Grzimek's assessment in Bernhard Grzimek, Reinhold Messner, and Herbert Tichy, *Paradiese* (Munich: Saphir, 1978). With 31 percent of its land mass in national parks or controlled game reserves and the largest conservation estate in sub-Saharan Africa, Tanzania has in many ways realized Grzimek's vision. On this point, see Brockington et al., "Preserving the New Tanzania," 557–579.
58. The literature on development failures is enormous and cannot be cited here in detail. Three works I found useful are William Easterly, *The White Man's Burden: Why the West's Efforts to Aid the Rest Have Done so Much Ill and so Little Good* (New York: Penguin Press, 2006); James Ferguson, *The Anti-Politics Machine: "Development," Depoliticization, and Bureaucratic Power in Lesotho* (Minneapolis: University of Minnesota Press, 2007); and Hubertus Büschel, *Entwicklungswelten: Globalgeschichte der Entwicklungszusammenarbeit* (Frankfurt: Campus, 2009).
59. Julie M. Weiskopf, "Socialism on Safari: Wildlife and Nation-Building in Postcolonial Tanzania, 1966–77," *The Journal of African History* 56, no. 3 (2015): 429–447. Weiskopf shows that animals served as critical media of exchange for "wildlife diplomacy" between Tanzania and its allies in this period.
60. Sara Berry, "Hegemony on a Shoestring: Indirect Rule and Access to Agricultural Land," *Africa: Journal of the International African Institute* 62, No. 3 (1992): 327–355.
61. Hubert Job and Daniel Metzler, "Tourismusentwicklung und Tourismuspolitik in Ostafrika," *Geographische Rundschau* 55 (2003): 10–17.

62. Susan Charnley, "From Nature Tourism to Ecotourism? The Case of the Ngorongoro Conservation Area, Tanzania," *Human Organization* 64, no. 1 (2005): 65–88; Ben Gardner, *Selling the Serengeti: The Cultural Politics of Safari Tourism* (Athens: University of Georgia Press, 2016).

63. Neumann, "Postwar Conservation Boom," 22–47 and Christopher Conte, "Creating Wild Places from Domesticated Landscapes: The Internationalization of the American Wilderness Concept," in *American Wilderness: A New History,* ed. Michael Lewis (Oxford, 2007), 223–242.

64. Recent work has qualified these assumptions about the globalization of Yellowstone. See Bernhard Gissibl, Sabine Höhler, and Patrick Kupper, eds. *Civilizing Nature: National Parks in Global Historical Perspective* (New York: Berghahn, 2012).

65. Young-Sun Hong, *Cold War Germany, the Third World, and the Global Humanitarian Regime* (New York: Cambridge University Press, 2015).

66. William Glenn Gray, *Germany's Cold War: The Global Campaign to Isolate East Germany, 1949–1969* (Chapel Hill: University of North Carolina Press, 2003).

67. John R. McNeill and Corinna R. Unger, eds., *Environmental Histories of the Cold War* (Cambridge, UK: Cambridge University Press, 2013).

68. On this point, see Clark C. Gibson, *Politicians and Poachers: The Political Economy of Wildlife Policy in Africa* (Cambridge, UK: Cambridge University Press, 1999).

69. Mary Louise Pratt, *Imperial Eyes: Travel Writing and Transculturation.* 2nd ed. (London: Routledge, 2008).

70. Here I draw on Bernhard Gissibl, "Grzimeks 'Bayerische Serengeti': Zur transnationalen politischen Ökologie des Nationalparks Bayerischer Wald," in *"Wenn sich alle in der Natur erholen, wo erholt sich dann die Natur?": Naturschutz, Freizeitnutzung, Erholungsvorsorge und Sport— gestern, heute, morgen,* ed. Hans-Werner Frohn, Jürgen Rosebrock, Friedemann Schmoll (Bonn-Bad Godesberg: Bundesamt für Naturschutz, 2009), 229–263.

71. Neumann, "Ways of Seeing Africa," 149–169.

72. Institute of Current World Affairs, "Letter from Ian Michael Wright to Richard Nolte," September 22, 1961, available in the ICWA online archive.

73. See, on Tanzania's high-modernist planners, James C. Scott, *Seeing Like a State: How Certain Schemes to Improve the Human Condition Have Failed* (New Haven, CT: Yale University Press, 1998), 223–261.

74. Anthony R. Sinclair, "The Eruption of the Ruminants," in *Serengeti: Dynamics of an Ecosystem,* ed. Sinclair and M. Norton-Griffiths (Chicago: University of Chicago Press, 1979), 82–103.

75. In this sense the international organizations that inherited the Serengeti controversy and spoke for Global Nature were unfortunately replaying the same tropes of underdevelopment as the late British Empire. See Mark Mazower, *No Enchanted Palace: The End of Empire and the Ideological Origins of the United Nations* (Princeton, NJ: Princeton University Press, 2009).

Chapter 1

1. Bernhard Grzimek, Moritz Pathé, and R. H. Stevens, *Doctor Jimek, I Presume* (New York: Norton, 1956), 1–2. This is the English translation of *Flug ins Schimpansenland. Reise durch ein Stück Afrika von heute* (Stuttgart: Franckh'sche Verlagshandlung, 1952). I have used the English translation in this chapter unless otherwise indicated.

2. On the popularity of such explorers, see Matthew Unangst, "Men of Science and Action: The Celebrity of Explorers and German National Identity, 1870–1895," *Central European History* 50, no. 2 (September 2017): 305–327.

3. Despite Germany's short colonial history, postcolonial fantasies of reoccupation, often centered on Africa's tropical forests, permeated interwar popular culture. On interwar travel writing, see Jared Poley, *Decolonization in Germany: Weimar Narratives of Colonial Loss and Foreign Occupation* (Oxford: Peter Lang, 2005); Christian Rogowski, "The 'Colonial Idea' in Weimar Cinema" in *German Colonialism, Visual Culture, and Modern Memory,* ed. Volker M. Langbehn (New York: Routledge, 2010), 220–238; Luke Springman, "Exotic Attractions and Imperialist Fantasies in Weimar Youth Literature," in *Weimar Culture Revisited,* ed. John Williams (New York: Palgrave Macmillan, 2011), 96–116; and Bernhard Gissibl, *The*

Nature of German Imperialism: Conservation and the Politics of Wildlife in Colonial East Africa (New York: Berghahn, 2016), 299–304.

4. Colin Ross, *Mit Kamera, Kind, und Kegel durch Africa* (Leipzig: Brockhaus, 1934) and Hans Schomburgk, *Mein Afrika: Erlebtes und Erlauschtes aus dem Innern Afrikas* (Leipzig: Deutsche Buchwerkstätten, 1928). On popular film, see Jörg Schöning, ed., *Triviale Tropen: Exotische Reise- und Abenteuerfilme aus Deutschland, 1919–1939* (Munich: Text + Kritik, 1997), particularly Bodo-Michael Baumunk, "Ein Pfadfinder der Geopolitik: Colin Ross und seine Reisefilme," 85–94 and Gerlinde Waz, "Auf der Suche nach dem letzten Paradies: Der Afrika Forscher und Regisseur Hans Schomburgk," 95–110. On film and tropicality, see also Michael Flitner, ed., *Der Deutsche Tropenwald: Bilder, Mythen, Politik* (Frankfurt: Campus, 2000), particularly the essays by Wolfgang Strück, "Erzählter Traum: Der Tropenwald in der deutschen Kolonialliteratur," 61–78 and Jörg Schöning, "Die Dschungelfantasien des Filmproduzenten John Hagenbeck," 79–93.

5. Bernhard Grzimek, *Auf den Mensch gekommen: Erfahrungen mit Leuten* (Munich: C. Bertelsmann, 1974), 250.

6. Grzimek, *Dr. Jimek*, 2–3.

7. Schomburgk, *Mein Afrika*, 12–13; Grzimek, *Dr. Jimek*, 10–11.

8. Grzimek, *Dr. Jimek*, 1.

9. On the distinction between "traveler" and "tourist," see James Buzard, *The Beaten Track: European Tourism, Literature, and the Ways to Culture, 1800–1918* (Oxford: Oxford University Press, 1992) and Jeremy Boissevain, *Coping with Tourists: European Reactions to Mass Tourism* (Providence, RI: Berghahn, 1996). For overviews of cultural responses to mass tourism, see Rudy Koshar, "'What Ought to Be Seen': Tourists' Guidebooks and National Identities in Modern Germany and Europe," *Journal of Contemporary History* 33 (1998): 323–340 and *German Travel Cultures* (Oxford: Berg, 2000), 1–18; and Shelley Baranowski and Ellen Furlough, eds. *Being Elsewhere: Tourism, Consumer Culture, and Identity in Modern Europe and North America* (Ann Arbor: University of Michigan Press, 2001), 1–14.

10. Grzimek's ruminations on human-animal relations invite comparisons to recent "posthumanist" perspectives, but I have elsewhere cautioned against such an ahistorical rendering of his context. See Kristin Asdal, Tone Druglitrø, and Steve Hinchliffe, *Humans, Animals and Biopolitics: The More-than-Human Condition* (New York: Routledge, 2017) and Thomas Lekan, "A Natural History of Modernity: Bernhard Grzimek and the Globalization of Environmental *Kulturkritik*," *New German Critique* 43, no. 2 (2016): 55–82.

11. Bernhard Grzimek, *Auf den Mensch gekommen*, 9–10; Sandra Chaney, *Nature of the Miracle Years: Conservation in West Germany, 1945–1975* (New York: Berghahn, 2008), 182–199; 219–236 and Bernhard Gissibl, "A 'Bavarian Serengeti': Space, Race, and Time in the Entangled History of Nature Conservation in East Africa and Germany," in *Civilizing Nature: National Parks in Global Historical Perspective*, ed. Bernhard Gissibl, Sabine Höhler, and Patrick Kupper (New York: Berghahn, 2012), 102–122.

12. On the dubious universalisms of European anthropologies of the self, see Andrew Zimmermann, *Anthropology and Antihumanism in Imperial Germany* (Chicago: University of Chicago Press, 2001), 1–37.

13. Heini Hediger, *Mensch und Tier im Zoo: Tiergarten-Biologie* (Rüschlikon-Zürich: A. Müller, 1965); *Wild Animals in Captivity* (New York: Dover, 1964); and *The Psychology and Behaviour of Animals in Zoos and Circuses* (New York: Dover, 1968). For a biography of Hediger, see Thomas A. Sebeok, *The Swiss Pioneer in Nonverbal Communication Studies, Heini Hediger (1908–1992)* (New York: Legas, 2001). Many thanks to Nigel Rothfels for alerting me to the importance of Hediger for Grzimek and to Veronika Hofer for sharing her work on Hediger's zoo biology with me.

14. David Blackbourn, *The Conquest of Nature: Water, Landscape, and the Making of Modern Germany* (London: Jonathan Cape, 2006), 315; Jens-Ivo Engels, "'Hohe Zeit' und 'dicker Strich': Vergangenheitsdeutung und Bewahrung im westdeutschen Naturschutz nach dem Zweiten Weltkrieg," in *Naturschutz und Nationalsozialismus*, ed. Joachim Radkau and Frank Uekötter (Frankfurt: Campus, 2003), 262–304; and Harold T. P. Hayes, *The Last Place on Earth* (New York: Stein and Day), 165. In his book *Nature and Power: A Global History of the Environment* (Cambridge, UK: Cambridge University Press, 2008), 265, Joachim Radkau counts

Grzimek among the "grandfather generation" of the German environmental movement compromised by their affinity with Nazism. On the continuities between Nazi landscape representation and Grzimek's work, see Michael Flitner, "Vom 'Platz in der Sonne' zur 'Platz für Tiere,'" in *Der deutsche Tropenwald: Bilder, Mythen, Politik*, ed. Flitner (Frankfurt: Campus, 2000), 244–262.

15. On Grzimek's relationship to Nazism, see the detailed discussion in Claudia Sewig, *Der Mann, der die Tiere liebte: Bernhard Grzimek: Biografie* (Bergisch Gladbach: Lübbe, 2009), 55–78, 88–90, 178, 196.

16. Several scholars have argued that West Germans' obsession with "occupation children" reveals a transference of postwar racial fears from Jews to persons of African descent. See Tina Campt, *Other Germans: Black Germans and the Politics of Race, Gender, and Memory in the Third Reich* (Ann Arbor: University of Michigan Press, 2005); Heide Fehrenbach, *Race after Hitler: Black Occupation Children in Postwar Germany and America* (Princeton, NJ: Princeton University Press, 2005); Rita Chin, ed., *After the Nazi Racial State: Difference and Democracy in Germany and Europe* (Ann Arbor: University of Michigan Press, 2009).

17. Grzimek, *Dr. Jimek*, 6.

18. On this theme, see the growing literature on Afro-German history, particularly Robbie Aitken and Eve Rosenhaft's meticulous study *Black Germany: The Making and Unmaking of a Diaspora Community* (Cambridge, UK: Cambridge University Press, 2013).

19. On the legacies of Social Darwinist evolutionism within 1950s histories of Africa, see Kairn A. Klieman, *"The Pygmies Were Our Compass": Bantu and Batwa in the History of West Central Africa, Early Times to C. 1900 C.E.* (Portsmouth, NH: Heinemann, 2003), 20–27.

20. The scholarly literature on modernity and "degeneration" is too vast to cite here in detail. For a good introduction, see Sander L. Gilman and J. Edward Chamberlin, *Degeneration: The Dark Side of Progress* (New York: Columbia University Press, 1985), particularly Nancy Stepan's essay "Biological Degeneration: Races and Proper Places," 97–120. On race and German visual culture, see David Ciarlo, *Advertising Empire: Race and Visual Culture in Imperial Germany* (Cambridge, MA: Harvard University Press, 2011).

21. Grzimek, *Auf den Mensch gekommen*, 37–38; 54–55.

22. Grzimek, *Auf den Mensch gekommen*, 54.

23. The literature on regionalism and *Heimat* in German culture is extensive. See, for example, Celia Applegate, *A Nation of Provincials: The German Idea of Heimat* (Berkeley: University of California Press, 1990).

24. Bernhard Grzimek, et al. *Visions of Paradise* (London: Hodder and Stoughton, 1981), 97.

25. John A. Williams, *Turning to Nature in Germany: Hiking, Nudism, and Conservation, 1900–1940* (Stanford, CA: Stanford University Press, 2007).

26. Konrad Guenther, *Der Naturschutz* (Freiburg: Friedrich Ernst Fehlenfeld, 1912), iii, 5, 13.

27. Works that detail the aesthetic, nationalist, and cultural foundations of prewar German nature conservation include William Rollins, *A Greener Vision of Home: Cultural Politics and Environmental Reform in the German Heimatschutz Movement* (Ann Arbor: University of Michigan Press, 1997); Thomas M. Lekan, *Imagining the Nation in Nature: Landscape Preservation and German Identity* (Cambridge, MA: Harvard University Press, 2004); and Willi Oberkrome, *"Deutsche Heimat": Nationale Konzeption und Regionale Praxis von Naturschutz, Landschaftsgestaltung und Kulturpolitik in Westfalen-Lippe und Thüringen, 1900–1960* (Paderborn: F. Schöningh, 2004).

28. Hugo Conwentz, *Die Gefährdung der Naturdenkmäler und Vorschläge zu ihrer Erhaltung* (Berlin: Gebrüder Bornträger, 1904). On the creation of the State Office, see Michael Wettengel, "Staat und Naturschutz, 1906–1945: Zur Geschichte der Staatlichen Stelle für Naturdenkmalpflege in Preussen und der Reichsstelle für Naturschutz," *Historische Zeitschrift* 257, no. 2 (October 1993): 355–399 and Raymond Dominick, *The Environmental Movement in Germany: Prophets and Pioneers, 1871–1971* (Bloomington: Indiana University Press, 1992), 51–53.

29. Bernhard Grzimek, *Wir Tiere sind ja gar nicht so!: Plaudereien, Beobachtungen und Versuche aus dem Tierreich* (1941; Stuttgart: Franckh, 1952), 7.

30. Grzimek, *Auf den Mensch gekommen*, 77–79.

31. Grzimek, *Auf den Mensch gekommen*, 77–82.

32. Grzimek, *Auf den Mensch gekommen*, 81; on German fascination with the American West, see H. Glenn Penny, *Kindred by Choice: Germans and American Indians since 1800* (Chapel Hill: University of North Carolina Press, 2013).

33. Grzimek, *Dr. Jimek*, 108–109.

34. Sewig, *Der Mann, der die Tiere liebte*, 55–64.

35. Bernhard Grzimek, "Rundlauf am Tischbein spielt Ulla jetzt am liebsten," *Das illustrierte Blatt*, no. 4, January 27, 1940.

36. Sewig, *Der Mann, der die Tiere liebte*, 69–70; 164.

37. Sewig, *Der Mann, der die Tiere liebte*, 114–116.

38. Grzimek, *Auf den Mensch gekommen*, 140–166; 193–195; Sewig, *Der Mann, der die Tiere liebte*, 110–111.

39. Bernhard Grzimek, *Such Agreeable Friends* (New York: Hill and Wang, 1964), 117–149.

40. For an introduction to Lorenz's work on degeneration and aggression, see *Über tierisches und menschliches Verhalten: gesammelte Abhandlungen* (Munich: Piper, 1965) and Boria Sax, *Animals in the Third Reich: Pets, Scapegoats, and the Holocaust* (New York: Continuum, 2000), 124–136.

41. Lorenz, "Durch Domestikation verursachte Störungen arteignen Verhaltens," *Zeitschrift für angewandte Psychologie und Charakterkunde* 59 (1940), 2–81. Cited in Sax, *Animals in the Third Reich*, 128.

42. On Lorenz's ties to Nazism, see Boria Sax, "What is a 'Jewish Dog?': Konrad Lorenz and the Cult of Wildness," *Society and Animals* 1, no. 5 (1997): 3–21.

43. Grzimek, *Wir Tiere sind ja gar nicht so!*, 59–66.

44. Bernhard Grzimek, *Wolf Dschingis: Neue Erlebnisse, Erkenntnisse und Versuche mit Tieren* (1943; reprint Stuttgart: Franckh, 1955).

45. Sabine Nessel, "Grzimek, Zoo und Kino," in *Zoo und Kino: mit Beiträgen zu Bernhard und Michael Grzimeks Film- und Fernseharbeit*, ed. Sabine Nessel and Heide Schlüpmann (Frankfurt: Stroemfeld-Verlag, 2012), 138.

46. Grzimek, *Wolf Dschingis*, 31.

47. Grzimek, *Wolf Dschingis*, 79.

48. Nessel, "Grzimek, Zoo und Kino," 158.

49. Nessel, "Grzimek, Zoo und Kino," 140–142.

50. Riefenstahl, who was already notorious for her Nazi propaganda films, claimed that the extras had survived Nazi incarceration, a statement she later retracted under pressure from a Sinti-Roma human rights organization. See "Die Causa Leni Riefenstahl zum Hundersten: Staatsanwalt ermittelt gegen die umstrittene Kuenstlerin/Die Schicksale nach *Tiefland*," *Frankfurter Allgemeine Zeitung*, August 23, 2002.

51. Grzimek, *Wolf Dschingis*, 41; recounted also in *Auf den Mensch gekommen*, 128–129.

52. Grzimek, *Wolf Dschingis*, 31–55; *Such Agreeable Friends*, 162–202. On Dschingis and *Tiefland*, see Nessel, "Grzimek, Zoo und Kino," 137–142. On the controversies surrounding the film, see Christopher Morris, *Modernism and the Cult of Mountains: Music, Opera, Cinema* (London: Taylor and Francis, 2016).

53. Boria Sax, *Animals in the Third Reich*, 123.

54. Sax, *Animals in the Third Reich*, 111–112.

55. Cited in Sax, *Animals in the Third Reich*, 111.

56. Sax, *Animals in the Third Reich*, 111.

57. Wettengel, "Staat und Naturschutz," 383. On the history and provisions of the *Reichsnaturschutzgesetz*, see also Walter Mrass, *Die Organisation des staatlichen Naturschutzes und der Landschaftspflege im deutschen Reich und der Bundesrepublik Deutschland seit 1935* (Stuttgart: Eugen Ulmer, 1970). For an overview of Nazi environmental policy, see Frank Uekötter, *The Green and the Brown: A History of Conservation in Nazi Germany* (Cambridge, UK: Cambridge University Press, 2006).

58. See Charles Clossmann, "Legalizing a Volksgemeinschaft: Nazi Germany's Reich Nature Protection Law of 1935," in Franz-Josef Brüggemeier, Mark Cioc, and Thomas Zeller, eds., *How Green Were the Nazis?: Nature, Environment, and Nation in the Third Reich* (Athens: Ohio University Press, 2005), 18–42.

59. Thomas M. Lekan, "'It Shall Be the Whole Landscape!': The Reich Nature Protection Law and Regional Planning in the Third Reich," in *How Green Were the Nazis?*, ed. Brüggemeier, et al., 73–100.

60. Sax, *Animals in the Third Reich*, 112–113.

61. Grzimek, *Auf den Mensch gekommen*, 190.

62. Clemens Driessen and Jamie Lorimer, "Back Breeding the Aurochs: The Heck Brothers, National Socialism, and Imagined Geographies for Non-Human *Lebensraum*," in *Hitler's Geographies: The Spatialities of the Third Reich*, ed. Paolo Giaccaria and Claudio Minca (Chicago: University of Chicago Press, 2016), 138–160.

63. Frank Fox, "Endangered Species: Jews and Buffaloes, Victims of Nazi Pseudo-Science," *East European Jewish Affairs* 31, no. 2 (2001): 82–84.

64. Ueköter, *The Green and the Brown*, 99–109.

65. Fox, "Endangered Species," 87–90; Driessen and Lorimer, "Back Breeding the Aurochs."

66. Bernhard Grzimek, *Kein Platz für Wilde Tiere* (Munich: Kindler, 1954), 4–5.

67. Grzimek, *Auf den Mensch gekommen*, 190.

68. Grzimek, *Auf den Mensch gekommen*, 190.

69. Mark Dowie, *Conservation Refugees: The Hundred-Year Conflict Between Global Conservation and Native Peoples* (Cambridge, MA: MIT Press, 2009), 24.

70. Sewig, *Der Mann, der die Tiere liebte*, 56–60.

71. Grzimek, *Auf den Mensch gekommen*, 215–235; Sewig, *Der Mann, der die Tiere liebte*, 148–154.

72. Sewig, *Der Mann, der die Tiere liebte*, 178. On Grzimek's reinstatement as zoo director, see the personnel file at the Frankfurt City Archive (Frankfurter Stadtarchiv, hereafter FSA. The archive is housed within the Institut für Stadtgeschichte, or Institute for the History of Frankfurt), Nr. 48.

73. On German narratives of postwar victimhood, see Robert G. Moeller, *War Stories: The Search for a Usable Past in the Federal Republic of Germany* (Berkeley: University of California Press, 2001); Konrad Jarausch and Michael Geyer, eds., *Shattered Past: Reconstructing German Histories* (Princeton, NJ: Princeton University Press, 2009), 317–341; and David F. Crew, *Bodies and Ruins: Imagining the Bombing of Germany, 1945 to the Present* (Ann Arbor: University of Michigan Press, 2017).

74. Grzimek, *Auf den Mensch gekommen*, 130–131.

75. Grzimek, *Auf den Mensch gekommen*, 126.

76. Grzimek, *Auf den Mensch gekommen*, 151.

77. Grzimek, *Auf den Mensch gekommen*, 150–152. Interestingly, Silesia's special status under the Versailles Treaty also meant that citizens with Jewish ancestry were not initially subject to Nazi anti-Semitic laws, leading some Nazi leaders to grumble that it had become a "Jewish National Park": see Brendan Karch, "A Jewish Nature Preserve: League of Nations Minority Protections in Nazi Upper Silesia, 1933–1937," *Central European History* 46, no. 1 (2013): 124–160.

78. Grzimek, *Auf den Mensch gekommen*, 131–133; Sewig, *Der Mann, der die Tiere liebte*, 88–90.

79. Grzimek, *Auf den Mensch gekommen*, 133.

80. Grzimek, *Auf den Mensch gekommen*, 194. See also Iris Wigger, *Black Horror on the Rhine: Intersections of Race, Nation, Gender and Class in 1920s Germany* (New York: Palgrave Macmillan, 2016).

81. Grzimek, *Auf den Mensch gekommen*, 203.

82. On this topic, see Lisa Gates, "Of Seeing and Otherness: Leni Riefenstahl's Africa Photographs," in *The Imperialist Imagination: German Colonialism and Its Legacy*, ed. Sara Friedrichsmeyer, Sara Lennox, and Susanne Zantop (Ann Arbor: University of Michigan Press, 1998), 163–188.

83. See Warwick Anderson, *Colonial Pathologies: American Tropical Medicine, Race, and Hygiene in the Philippines* (Durham, NC: Duke University Press, 2006) and John Collins, "'But What if I Should Need to Defecate in Your Neighborhood, Madame?': Empire, Redemption, and the 'Tradition of the Oppressed' in a Brazilian World Heritage Site," *CUAN Cultural Anthropology* 23, no. 2 (2008): 279–328.

84. Grzimek, *Auf den Mensch gekommen*, 194.

85. Fehrenbach, *Race after Hitler*, 74–168. For a broader discussion of race relations after the Third Reich, see Chin, et al., *After the Nazi Racial State*, 1–54. See also David McBride, Leroy Hopkins, and Carol Blackshire-Belay, *Crosscurrents: African Americans, Africa, and Germany in the Modern World* (Columbia, SC: Camden House, 1998) and Patricia M. Mazón and Reinhild Steingröver, *Not So Plain as Black and White: Afro-German Culture and History, 1890-2000* (Rochester, NY: University of Rochester Press, 2005).

86. Fehrenbach, *Race After Hitler*, 132–168; Chin, et al., *After the Nazi Racial State*, 30–54.

87. Fehrenbach, *Race After Hitler*, 107–131; Angelica Fenner, *Race under Reconstruction in German Cinema: Robert Stemmle's Toxi* (Toronto: University of Toronto Press, 2011).

88. Sewig, *Der Mann, der die Tiere liebte*, 199–201.

89. Grzimek, *Auf den Mensch gekommen*, 314.

90. Grzimek, *Visions of Paradise*, 78.

91. Grzimek, *Auf den Mensch gekommen*, 320–321.

92. Johannes von Moltke, *No Place like Home: Locations of Heimat in German Cinema* (Berkeley: University of California Press, 2005).

93. Hayes, *Last Place on Earth*, 130.

94. Grzimek, *Auf den Mensch gekommen*, 179–235; Sewig, *Der Mann, der die Tiere liebte*, 119–150; 162–169.

95. For a useful introduction to the history of ecology in Germany, see Eugene Cittadino, *Nature as the Laboratory: Darwinian Plant Ecology in the German Empire, 1880-1900* (Cambridge, UK: Cambridge University Press, 1990) and Robert J. Richards, *The Tragic Sense of Life: Ernst Haeckel and the Struggle Over Evolutionary Thought* (Chicago: University of Chicago Press, 2008).

96. Donald Worster, *Nature's Economy: A History of Ecological Ideas* (Cambridge, UK: Cambridge University Press, 1991), 133–138; Malcolm Nicolson, "Humboldtian Plant Geography after Humboldt: The Link to Ecology," *British Journal of the History of Science* 29 (1996): 289–310.

97. Lynn K. Nyhart, *Modern Nature: The Rise of the Biological Perspective in Germany* (Chicago: University of Chicago Press, 2009).

98. Grzimek, *Auf den Mensch gekommen*, 191.

99. Johannes Paulmann, "Jenseits von Eden: Kolonialismus, Zeitkritik und Wissenschaftlicher Naturschutz in Bernhard Grzimeks Tierfilmen der 1950er-Jahre," *Zeitschrift für Geschichtswissenschaft* 56, no. 6 (2008): 547; Heini Hediger, *Bedeutung und Aufgabe der zoologischen Gärten für den Naturschutz* (Basel: Schweizerischer Bund für Naturschutz, 1955).

100. Grzimek, *Auf den Mensch gekommen*, 240–241.

101. Grzimek, *Auf den Mensch gekommen*, 242; Heini Hediger, *Wild Animals in Captivity* (London: Butterworths, 1950).

102. Eric Ames, *Carl Hagenbeck's Empire of Entertainments* (Seattle: University of Washington Press, 2008).

103. Herman Reichenbach, "Carl Hagenbeck's Tierpark and Modern Zoological Gardens," *Journal of the Society for the Bibliography of Natural History* 9 (1980): 573–585.

104. Reichenbach, "Carl Hagenbeck's Tierpark," 577–579.

105. Grzimek, *Auf den Mensch gekommen*, 241.

106. Grzimek, *Auf den Mensch gekommen*, 238–240; *Dr. Jimek*, 70–71.

107. Grzimek, *Auf den Mensch gekommen*, 241–242.

108. William Beinart, "The Renaturing of African Animals: Film and Literature in the 1950s and 1960s," *Kronos: Journal of Cape History* 27 (November 2001): 203; Nigel Rothfels, *Savages and Beasts: The Birth of the Modern Zoo* (Baltimore: Johns Hopkins University Press, 2002), 44–80.

109. Beinart, "Renaturing of African Animals," 211.

110. Grzimek, *Dr. Jimek*, 2–3.

111. Hediger, *Wild Animals in Captivity*, 4–26.

112. Grzimek, *Dr. Jimek*, 58.

113. Hayes, *Last Place on Earth*, 132.

114. Kalevi Kull, *Jakob von Uexküll: A Paradigm for Biology and Semiotics* (Berlin: Mouton de Gruyter, 2001).

115. Heini Hediger and Adolf Portmann, *Wildtiere in Gefangenschaft* (Basel: Schwabe, 1942), 20–24.
116. Grzimek, *Dr. Jimek*, 5.
117. Grzimek, *Kein Platz für Wilde Tiere*, 250.
118. Sewig, *Der Mann, der die Tiere liebte*, 166–169.
119. Grzimek, *Auf den Mensch gekommen*, 250.
120. Grzimek, *Auf den Mensch gekommen*, 250–251.
121. Grzimek, *Flug ins Schimpansenland*, 12–13.
122. Grzimek, *Dr. Jimek*, 27–39.
123. Grzimek, *Auf den Mensch gekommen*, 250–254.
124. Grzimek, *Dr. Jimek*, 58.
125. Grzimek, *Dr. Jimek*, 59.
126. Grzimek, *Dr. Jimek*, 4.
127. Grzimek, *Dr. Jimek*, 68.
128. Grzimek, *Flug ins Schimpansenland*, 73–74.
129. Grzimek, *Dr. Jimek*, 4.
130. Grzimek, *Flug ins Schimpansenland*, 74.
131. Grzimek, *Dr. Jimek*, 3–4.
132. Paulmann, "Jenseits von Eden," 541–560.
133. Grzimek, *Dr. Jimek*, 29.
134. Grzimek, *Dr. Jimek*, 150.
135. Grzimek, *Dr. Jimek*, 43.
136. Charles Burdett and Derek Duncan, *Cultural Encounters: European Travel Writing in the 1930s* (New York: Berghahn, 2002).
137. On this theme, see Zimmermann, *Anthropology and Antihumanism in Imperial Germany*; Johannes Fabian, *Time and the Other: How Anthropology Makes Its Object* (New York: Columbia University Press, 2002). On review of *Flug ins Schimpansenland*, see *Der Tag*, "Flug ins Schimpansenland: Der Direktor des Frankfurter Zoo, Bernhard Grzimek, Fuhr nach Afrika," January 18, 1953.
138. Grzimek, *Dr. Jimek*, 31.
139. Grzimek, *Dr. Jimek*, 34; 151.
140. Victoria de Grazia, *Irresistible Empire: America's Advance through Twentieth-Century Europe* (Cambridge, MA: Harvard University Press, 2005).
141. Stepan, "Biological Degeneration," 115.
142. Grzimek, *Dr. Jimek*, 99.
143. Grzimek, *Dr. Jimek*, 51.
144. Hayes, *Last Place on Earth*, 132–133.
145. There is a large literature on the relationship between demography and colonialism, but three I have found useful for this chapter are Alison Bashford, *Imperial Hygiene: A Critical History of Colonialism, Nationalism and Public Health* (New York: Palgrave Macmillan, 2004); Chloe Campbell, *Race and Empire: Eugenics in Colonial Kenya* (Manchester, UK: Manchester University Press, 2007) and Nancy Rose Hunt, *A Nervous State: Violence, Remedies, and Reverie in Colonial Congo* (Durham, NC: Duke University Press, 2016), 167–205.
146. On this theme, see Thomas Robertson, *Malthusian Moment: Global Population Growth and the Birth of American Environmentalism* (New Brunswick, NJ: Rutgers University Press, 2012), 13–35.
147. Grzimek, *Dr. Jimek*, 108.
148. Grzimek, *Dr. Jimek*, 4; On Malthusian fears, see Connelly, *Fatal Misconception*, 115–154.
149. Fairfield Osborn, *Our Plundered Planet* (Boston: Little, Brown, 1948). On the shift from eugenics to family planning, see also Jacqueline R. Kasun, *The War Against Population: The Economics and Ideology of World Population Control* (San Francisco: Ignatius Press, 1988); Matthew Connelly, "Seeing Beyond the State: The Population Control Movement and the Problem of Sovereignty," *Past & Present*, no. 193 (2006): 197–233.
150. Osborn, *Our Plundered Planet*, ix.
151. Osborn, *Our Plundered Planet*, 50.

152. Connelly, *Fatal Misconception*, 155–194; Robertson, *Malthusian Moment*, 10–11; 36–60. See also Robert C. Cook, *Human Fertility: The Modern Dilemma* (New York: W. Sloane Associates, 1951); Erich Hornsmann, . . . *sonst Untergang; die Antwort der Erde auf die Missachtung ihrer Gesetze* (Rheinhausen: Verlagsanstalt Rheinhausen, 1951).

153. Frederick Cooper, *Citizenship Between Empire and Nation: Remaking France and French Africa, 1945–1960* (Princeton, NJ: Princeton University Press, 2014).

154. I take this idea of Africans as "junior brothers" from Chinua Achebe's comment on the dangers of Albert Schweitzer's humanitarian legacy in "Africa's Tarnished Name," in *Multiculturalism and Hybridity in African Literatures*, ed. Hal Wylie and Bernth Lindfors (Trenton, NJ: Africa World Press, 2000), 15.

155. Gissibl, *Nature of German Imperialism*, 304.

156. Gisela Bonn, *Afrika verlässt den Busch: Kontinent der Kontraste* (Düsseldorf: Econ-Verlag, 1965).

157. Lutz Heck, *Grosswild Im Etoschaland: Erlebnisse Mit Tieren Südwestafrika* (Berlin: Ullstein, 1955); *Fahrt Zum Weissen Nashorn: Im Auto Durch Südafrika und Seine Wildschutzgebiete* (Stuttgart: Engelhornverlag, 1957).

158. Gates, "Of Seeing and Otherness"; Leni Riefenstahl, *The Last of the Nuba* (New York: Harper & Row, 1974); *The People of Kau* (New York: Harper & Row, 1976).

159. Sewig, *Der Mann, der die Tiere liebte*, 88–89, 196.

Chapter 2

1. Bernhard Grzimek, *Kein Platz für Wilde Tiere* (Munich: Kindler, 1954), 3; Bernhard Grzimek, *No Room for Wild Animals*, trans. R. H. Stevens (London: Thames & Hudson, 1956), 1.

2. Scholars have identified such desertification narratives with colonialist efforts to justify land grabs in the name of conservation. See, for example, Jeremy Swift, "Desertification: Narratives, Winners, and Losers," in *The Lie of the Land: Challenging Received Wisdom on the African Environment*, ed. Melissa Leach and Robin Mearns. International African Institute (Oxford: James Currey, 1996), 73–90; James C. McCann, "The Plow and the Forest: Narratives of Deforestation in Ethiopia, 1840–1992," *Environmental History* 2, no. 2 (April 1997): 138–159; Diana K. Davis, *Resurrecting the Granary of Rome: Environmental History and French Colonial Expansion in North Africa* (Athens: Ohio University Press, 2007).

3. Donald Worster, *Dust Bowl: The Southern Plains in the 1930s* (New York: Oxford University Press, 1979).

4. Grzimek, *No Room*, 7. Grzimek's use of "locusts" has disturbing eliminationist connotations in a colonialist context. See Clapperton C. Mavhunga, "Vermin Beings: On Pestiferous Animals and Human Game," *Social Text* 106 (2011): 151–176.

5. Bernhard Grzimek and Michael Grzimek, *Kein Platz für Wilde Tiere*. Original release Okapia Films, GmBH 1956. (DVD version: Berlin: Universal Music Family Entertainment, 2004)

6. In a German film context, the traffic light has long served as a symbol of both the emancipatory possibilities and homogenizing terrors of modernity. On the symbolism of the recreated 1924 traffic light at Potsdamer Platz, for example, see Claire Colomb, *Staging the New Berlin: Place Marketing and the Politics of Urban Reinvention Post-1989* (London: Routledge, 2012), 155–157.

7. Raf de Bont, "A World Laboratory: Framing the Albert National Park," *Environmental History* 22, no. 3 (2017): 404–432.

8. Franziska Torma, *Eine Naturschutzkampagne in der Ära Adenauer: Bernhard Grzimeks Afrikafilme in den Medien der 50er Jahre* (Munich: Martin Meidenbauer, 2004), 129–130. Grzimek was one of many zoo directors at this time who began to refashion zoological gardens' mission to accommodate scientific conservation. See, for example, Gerald Durrell, *The New Noah* (New York: Viking, 1954); R. J. Prickett, *The African Ark* (New York: Drake, 1974). According to Dan Brockington, such "mediagenic" portrayals sidestepped local participation in conservation and failed to challenge viewers' environmental actions at home. See *Celebrity and the Environment: Fame, Wealth, and Power in Conservation* (London: Zed, 2009).

9. Torma, *Naturschutzkampagne*, 43 and Michael Flitner, "Vom 'Platz an der Sonne,' zum 'Platz für Tiere' " in *Der Deutsche Tropenwald: Bilder, Mythen, Politik*, ed. Michael Flitner (Frankfurt: Campus, 2000), 244–262.

10. *Kein Platz für Wilde Tiere*, Heft zum Film, cited in Torma, *Naturschutzkampagne*, 59.

11. On this point, see Thomas Robertson, *The Malthusian Moment: Global Population Growth and the Birth of American Environmentalism* (New Brunswick, NJ: Rutgers University Press, 2012) and Ursula K. Heise, *Sense of Place and Sense of Planet: The Environmental Imagination of the Global* (Oxford: Oxford University Press, 2008), especially chapter 2.

12. On this point, see especially Nwachukwu Frank Ukadike, *Black African Cinema* (Berkeley: University of California Press, 1994), 35–58 and Vivian Bickford-Smith and Richard Mendelsohn, *Black and White in Colour: African History on Screen* (Athens: Ohio University Press, 2007).

13. Grzimek, *No Room*, 28.

14. Dirk van Laak, *Über Alles in der Welt: Deutscher Imperialismus im 19. und 20. Jahrhundert* (Munich: C.H. Beck, 2005); Shelley Baranowski, *Nazi Empire: German Colonialism and Imperialism from Bismarck to Hitler* (New York: Cambridge University Press, 2011), 172–232. On the connections between homeland and empire, see Claus-Christian W. Szejnmann and Maiken Umbach, *Heimat, Region and Empire: Spatial Identities under National Socialism* (New York: Palgrave Macmillan, 2012).

15. See Gisela Bonn, *Afrika verlässt den Busch. Kontinent der Kontraste* (Düsseldorf: Econ-Verlag, 1965) and Kasimir Edschmid, *Afrika: Nackt und Angezogen* (Munich: Desch, 1952).

16. Young-Sun Hong, *Cold War Germany, the Third World, and the Global Humanitarian Regime* (New York: Cambridge University Press, 2015), 231.

17. Letter from Hans Erich Freudenberg to West German Foreign Minister Heinrich von Brentano, "The Problem of European Overseas Territories in Africa," February 15, 1957 in Politisches Archiv des Auswärtigen Amts (PAAA) B1 64.

18. Report to Brentano about the "Visit of Herzog Alfred Friedrich zu Mecklenburg to West Africa," August 1, 1956 in PAAA B1 64.

19. Hong, *Cold War Germany*, 216.

20. Torma, *Naturschutzkampagne*, 117–118.

21. Katherine Pence, "Showcasing Cold War Germany in Cairo: 1954 and 1957 Industrial Exhibitions and the Competition for Arab Partners," *Journal of Contemporary History* 47, no. 1 (2012): 69–95. On the trade exhibitions the FRG sponsored in Tanganyika, see files and commentary on the "German Mobile Exhibition" of 1963 in PAAA B1 439.

22. Thomas Moser, *Europäische Integration, Dekolonisation, Eurafrika: Eine historische Analyse über die Entstehungsbedingungen der Eurafrikanischen Gemeinschaft von der Weltwirtschaftskrise bis zum Jaunde-Vertrag, 1929–1963* (Baden-Baden, Germany: Nomos Verlagsgesellschaft, 2000).

23. Dirk van Laak, *Imperiale Infrastruktur: Deutsche Planungen für eine Erschliessung Afrikas 1880 Bis 1960* (Paderborn: Schöningh, 2004). Van Laak notes that 1950s vision of Euro-Africa revived plans for a vast "Mittelafrika" colony. On this point see Emil Zimmermann, *The German Empire of Central Africa as the Basis of a New German World Policy* (New York: George H. Doran, 1918).

24. Torma, *Naturschutzkampagne*, 180–183.

25. Thaddeus Sunseri, "Exploiting the Urwald: German Post-Colonial Forestry in Poland and Central Africa, 1900–1960," *Past and Present* 214, no. 1 (2012): 337–340.

26. Torma, *Naturschutzkampagne*, 183.

27. Anton Zischka, "Kongo Ya Sika—Der Neue Kongo," *Atlantis* 25, no. 8 (August 1954): 349.

28. Kevin C. Dunn, *Imagining the Congo: The International Relations of Identity* (New York: Palgrave Macmillan, 2003), 66–74. Jean Tilmont and J. Baurin, *Notre Congo* (Brussels: Institut Géographique Militaire, 1948).

29. Werner G. Krug, "Der Neger und die Neue Zeit," *Atlantis* 25, no. 8 (August 1954): 361.

30. R. F. Holland, *European Decolonization, 1918–1981: An Introductory Survey* (New York: St. Martin's Press, 1985), 176; Samuel Henry Nelson, *Colonialism in the Congo Basin, 1880–1940* (Athens: Ohio University Center for International Studies, 1994), 178–193.

31. Zischka, "Der Neue Kongo," 350–351. On Congo cities, see J. S. Fontaine, *City Politics: A Study of Léopoldville, 1962–63* (Cambridge, UK: Cambridge University Press, 1970) and Bill Freund, *The African City: A History* (New York: Cambridge University Press, 2007).

32. Zischka, "Der Neue Kongo," 350.

33. James Ferguson, *Expectations of Modernity: Myths and Meanings of Urban Life on the Zambian Copperbelt* (Berkeley: University of California Press, 1999), 5–6.

34. Joseph Morgan Hodge, *Triumph of the Expert: Agrarian Doctrines of Development and the Legacies of British Colonialism* (Athens: Ohio University Press, 2007), 207–253; Andrew Wigley, "Against the Wind: The Role of Belgian Colonial Tourism Marketing in Resisting Pressure to Decolonise from Africa," *Journal of Tourism History* 7, no. 3 (2015): 194–198; Bekeh Utietiang Ukelina, *The Second Colonial Occupation: Development Planning, Agriculture, and the Legacies of British Colonial Rule in Nigeria* (Lanham, MD: Lexington Books, 2017).

35. Grant S. McClellan, *Colonial Progress in Central Africa—Belgian Congo and French Equatorial Africa* (New York: Foreign Policy Association, Inc., 1944).

36. Wigley, "Against the Wind," 195–196; Belgium. Ministère des affaires africaines, *Plan Décennal pour le Développement Économique et Social du Congo Belge* (Brussels: De Visscher, 1949).

37. Adam Hochschild, *King Leopold's Ghost: A Story of Greed, Terror, and Heroism in Colonial Africa* (Boston: Houghton Mifflin, 1998); Marie-Bénédicte Dembour, *Recalling the Belgian Congo: Conversations and Introspection* (New York: Berghahn, 2000); Osumaka Likaka, *Naming Colonialism: History and Collective Memory in the Congo, 1870–1960* (Madison: University of Wisconsin Press, 2009).

38. Arthur Conan Doyle, *The Crime of the Congo* (New York: Doubleday, 1909); Dunn, *Imagining the Congo*, 21–59.

39. Nancy Rose Hunt, *A Nervous State: Violence, Remedies, and Reverie in Colonial Congo* (Durham, NC: Duke University Press, 2016), 3–11; 95–133.

40. Holland, *European Decolonization*, 175–177.

41. Zischka, "Der Neue Kongo," 354.

42. Grzimek, *No Room*, 2.

43. Grzimek, *No Room*, 3.

44. Grzimek, *No Room*, 15.

45. Nicholas Luard and World Wildlife Fund, *The Wildlife Parks of Africa* (Salem, NH: Salem House, 1986).

46. Donna Haraway, "Teddy Bear Patriarchy: Taxidermy in the Garden of Eden, New York City, 1908–1936," *Social Text*, No. 11 (Winter, 1984–1985): 20–64; Mary L. Jobe Akeley, *Congo Eden: A Comprehensive Portrayal of the Historical Background and Scientific Aspects of the Great Game Sanctuaries of the Belgian Congo with the Story of a Six Months Pilgrimage throughout That Most Primitive Region in the Heart of the African Continent* (New York: Dodd, Mead & Co., 1950).

47. Luard, *The Wildlife Parks of Africa*, 51.

48. De Bont, "World Laboratory," 409–411.

49. Manfred Behr and Hans Otto Meissner, *Keine Angst um wilde Tiere: Fünf Kontinente geben ihnen Heimat* (Munich: Bayerischer Landwirtschaftsverlag, 1959), 124.

50. On the transition from Sabi Game Reserve to Kruger, see Jane Carruthers, *The Kruger National Park: A Social and Political History* (Pietermaritzburg: University of Natal Press, 1995), 29–88. On the relationship between conservation and white settler nationalism, see William Beinart, *The Rise of Conservation in South Africa: Settlers, Livestock, and the Environment, 1770–1950* (Oxford: Oxford University Press, 2003).

51. William M. Adams, *Against Extinction: The Story of Conservation* (London: Earthscan, 2004), 22–41; Bernhard Gissibl, "German Colonialism and the Beginning of International Wildlife Conservation in Africa," *German Historical Institute Washington, DC, Bulletin*, Supplement 3 (2006): 121–144.

52. Behr and Meissner, *Keine Angst um wilde Tiere*, 69.

53. Jonathan S. Adams and Thomas O. McShane, *The Myth of Wild Africa: Conservation without Illusion* (New York: W.W. Norton, 1992), 46–47; Mark Cioc, *The Game of Conservation: International Treaties to Protect the World's Migratory Animals* (Athens: Ohio University Press, 2009), 40–41.

54. Bernhard Gissibl, *The Nature of German Imperialism: Conservation and the Politics of Wildlife in Colonial East Africa* (New York: Berghahn, 2016), 245–253.

55. Caroline Ford, "Imperial Preservation and Landscape Reclamation: National Parks and Nature Reserves in French Colonial Africa," in *Civilizing Nature: National Parks in Global Historical*

Perspective, ed. Bernhard Gissibl, Sabine Höhler, and Patrick Kupper (New York: Berghahn, 2012), 68–83. Ford and others in this volume argue convincingly that Yellowstone was not the global benchmark for national parks across the Global South that many environmental historians have assumed.

56. Luard, *The Wildlife Parks of Africa*, 56.
57. Institut des parcs nationaux du Congo belge, Heini Hediger, and Jacques Verschuren, *Exploration des parcs nationaux du Congo belge* (Brussels: Institut des parcs nationaux, 1951). Thanks to Veronika Hofer for this reference.
58. De Bont, "World Laboratory," 410–411.
59. Cited in De Bont, "World Laboratory," 413.
60. Bernhard Grzimek, "Rinderherden vernichten die Berggorillas," *Das Tier* (November 1960): 19.
61. De Bont, "World Laboratory," 417–418.
62. De Bont, "World Laboratory," 417.
63. Nelson, *Colonialism in the Congo Basin*, 1; Torma, *Naturschutzkampagne*, 22–30; Adams and McShane, *Myth of Wild Africa*, 3–23; Kairn A. Klieman, "*The Pygmies Were Our Compass*": *Bantu and Batwa in the History of West Central Africa, Early Times to C. 1900 C.E.* (Portsmouth, NH: Heinemann, 2003), 1–3; Michael J. Sheridan and Celia Nyamweru, eds., *African Sacred Groves: Ecological Dynamics and Social Change* (Oxford: James Currey, 2008).
64. Dunn, *Imagining the Congo*, 23–24; Ian Watt, *Conrad in the Nineteenth Century* (Berkeley: University of California Press, 1981), 139.
65. Nelson, *Colonialism in the Congo Basin*, 14–26.
66. Jean-François Bayart, *The State in Africa: The Politics of the Belly* (New York: Longman, 1993), particularly his comments on the "paradigm of the yoke," 1–37. Klieman uses "forest specialist" versus "hunter-gatherer" to dispense with a "Pygmy Paradigm" that has straitjacketed Batwa history based on Western myths. See *Pygmies Were Our Compass*, 3–20.
67. Tamara Giles-Vernick uses the term *doli* to describe a body and process of environmental knowledge in her study of the Mpiemu in the Sangha River basin of the Central African Republic. See *Cutting the Vines of the Past: Environmental Histories of the Central African Rain Forest* (Charlottesville: University Press of Virginia, 2002), 193–194.
68. Bayart, *The State in Africa*.
69. Klieman, *Pygmies Were Our Compass*, 169–218. On the political history of the region before European contact, see Jan Vansina, *How Societies Are Born: Governance in West Central Africa before 1600* (Charlottesville: University of Virginia Press, 2012), 107–159 and *Paths in the Rainforest: Toward a History of Political Tradition in Equatorial Africa* (London: James Currey, 1990).
70. Nelson, *Colonialism in the Congo Basin*, 42–78.
71. Bernhard Grzimek, *Auf den Mensch gekommen: Erfahrungen mit Leuten* (Munich: C. Bertelsmann, 1974), 262–263. Johannes Paulmann "Jenseits von Eden: Kolonialismus, Zeitkritik und Wissenschaftlicher Naturschutz in Bernhard Grzimeks Tierfilmen der 1950er-Jahre," *Zeitschrift für Geschichtswissenschaft* 56, no. 6 (2008): 543.
72. Claudia Sewig, *Der Mann, der die Tiere liebte: Bernhard Grzimek: Biografie* (Bergisch Gladbach: Lübbe, 2009), 262.
73. Grzimek, *No Room*, 197–203.
74. Grzimek, *No Room*, 204–209.
75. Grzimek, *No Room*, 205.
76. Torma, *Naturschutzkampagne*, 42–43. "Primitive" Africans had long been part of German and European imperial fantasies, a tradition that Grzimek's sober perspective sought to upend. See Wolfram Hartmann, *The Colonising Camera: Photographs in the Making of Namibian History* (Athens: Ohio University Press, 1999) and Assenka Oksiloff, *Picturing the Primitive: Visual Culture, Ethnography, and Early German Cinema* (New York: Palgrave, 2001).
77. Grzimek, *No Room*, 120.
78. As Cornelia Essner has observed, being an "Africa researcher" had long been seen as a "calling" rather than a career. See *Deutsche Afrikareisende im neunzehnten Jahrhundert: Zur Sozialgeschichte des Reisens* (Stuttgart: Steiner Verlag, 1985).
79. Grzimek, *No Room*, 22. Emphasis in the original.

80. Grzimek, *No Room*, 22.

81. On the rituals of the Hunt, see John M. Mackenzie, "Chivalry, Social Darwinism and Ritualised Killing: The Hunting Ethos in Central Africa up to 1914," in *Conservation in Africa: People, Policies, and Practice*, ed. David Anderson and Richard Grove (New York: Cambridge University Press, 1987), 41–62.

82. Grzimek, *Kein Platz*, 29–50.

83. There is an extensive literature on German expeditions to Central Africa, the focus of much scientific and geographic "exploration" before colonial acquisition shifted sponsorship to East, Southwest, and West Africa. See for example Emin Pasha et al., *Emin Pasha in Central Africa: Being a Collection of His Letters and Journals* (London: G. Philip & Son, 1888); Arthur J. Knoll and Lewis H. Gann, *Germans in the Tropics: Essays in German Colonial History* (New York: Greenwood Press, 1987); Brigitte Hoppe, "Naturwissenschaftliche und zoologische Forschungen in Afrika während der deutschen Kolonialbewegung bis 1914," *Berichte zur Wissenschafts-Geschichte* 13, no. 4 (December 1990): 193–206; Matthias Fiedler, *Zwischen Abenteuer, Wissenschaft und Kolonialismus: Der deutsche Afrikadiskurs im 18. und 19. Jahrhundert* (Cologne: Böhlau, 2005).

84. Franz-Josef Schulte-Althoff, "Geographische Forschung und Imperialismus: Zentralafrika und die deutsche geographische Forschung in den Anfängen des imperialistischen Zeitalters," *Saeculum: Jahrbuch für Universalgeschichte* 24, no. 1/2 (January 1973): 79–93; Adekeye Adebajo, *The Curse of Berlin: Africa After the Cold War* (New York: Columbia University Press, 2010).

85. Grzimek, *No Room*, 88–90; Michelle R. Moyd, *Violent Intermediaries: African Soldiers, Conquest, and Everyday Colonialism in German East Africa* (Athens: Ohio University Press, 2014).

86. Oksiloff, *Picturing the Primitive*, 43–70; Volker M. Langbehn, *German Colonialism, Visual Culture, and Modern Memory* (New York: Routledge, 2010); David Ciarlo, *Advertising Empire: Race and Visual Culture in Imperial Germany* (Cambridge, MA: Harvard University Press, 2011).

87. Kathrin Fritsch, "You Have Everything Confused and Mixed Up . . .! Georg Schweinfurth, Knowledge and Cartography of Africa in the 19th Century," *History in Africa* 36 (2009): 87–101.

88. Georg August Schweinfurth, *Im Herzen von Afrika: Reisen und Entdeckungen im Zentralen Aquatorial-Afrika während der Jahre 1868–1871* (Leipzig: F.A. Brockhaus, 1878).

89. Sewig, *Der Mann, der die Tiere liebte*, 189–190.

90. Gissibl, *Nature of German Imperialism*, 44–46.

91. Grzimek, *No Room*, 42–45.

92. Grzimek, *No Room*, 120.

93. Klieman, *Pygmies Were Our Compass*, 66–132.

94. Grzimek, *No Room*, 179.

95. Reinhold Wagnleitner, *Coca-colonization and the Cold War: The Cultural Mission of the United States in Austria after the Second World War*, trans. Diana M. Wolf (Chapel Hill: University of North Carolina Press, 1994).

96. Grzimek, *No Room*, 187.

97. Grzimek, *No Room*, 181–183; 189–191.

98. Grzimek, *No Room*, 185. On the assertion of power through parodies of Africans in European dress, see Dunn, *Imagining the Congo*, 32–34.

99. Grzimek, *No Room*, 196.

100. Grzimek, *No Room*, 4–10.

101. Grzimek, *No Room*, 17–19; Davis, *Resurrecting the Granary of Rome*, 16–44.

102. Grzimek, *No Room*, 19–20.

103. On the challenges of narrating extinction at different scales and temporalities, see Heise, *Sense of Place*, 17–67 and "Lost Dogs, Last Birds, and Listed Species: Cultures of Extinction," *Configurations* 18 (2010): 49–72; Thom van Dooren, *Flight Ways: Life and Loss at the Edge of Extinction* (New York: Columbia University Press, 2014), 1–20; Elizabeth Kolbert, *The Sixth Extinction: An Unnatural History* (London: Bloomsbury, 2014), 4–22.

104. The exact causes of the late Quaternary extinctions remain contested. See Alfred W. Crosby, *Ecological Imperialism: The Biological Expansion of Europe, 900–1900*. 2nd ed. (Cambridge,

UK: Cambridge University Press, 2009), 269–293 and Paul L. Koch and Anthony D. Barnosky, "Late Quaternary Extinctions: State of the Debate," *Annual Review of Ecology, Evolution, and Systematics* 37 (2006): 215–250.

105. Adams and McShane, *Myth of Wild Africa*, 4–5.

106. Errol Fuller, *Dodo: A Brief History* (New York: St. Martin's Press, 2002).

107. Grzimek, *No Room*, 11.

108. On so-called forest remnants, see James Fairhead, Melissa Leach, and Dominique Millimouno, *Misreading the African Landscape: Society and Ecology in a Forest-Savanna Mosaic* (Cambridge, UK: Cambridge University Press, 2011); Emmanuel Kreike, *Deforestation and Reforestation in Namibia: The Global Consequences of Local Contradictions* (Princeton, NJ: Markus Wiener Publishers, 2012).

109. Grzimek, *No Room*, 11.

110. David D. Smits, "The Frontier Army and the Destruction of the Buffalo: 1865–1883," *The Western Historical Quarterly* 25, no. 3 (Autumn, 1994): 312–338; Andrew C. Isenberg, *The Destruction of the Bison: An Environmental History, 1750–1920* (New York: Cambridge University Press, 2000), 123–163.

111. William Beinart, "Empire, Hunting and Ecological Change in Southern and Central Africa," *Past & Present*, no. 128 (1990): 173.

112. Clark C. Gibson, *Politicians and Poachers : The Political Economy of Wildlife Policy in Africa* (Cambridge, UK: Cambridge University Press, 1999); Rob Nixon, *Slow Violence and the Environmentalism of the Poor* (Cambridge, MA: Harvard University Press, 2011).

113. Grzimek, *No Room*, 189.

114. On *Nagana* as protector of the wilderness, see Grzimek, *Flug ins Schimpansenland*, 120–125.

115. Grzimek, *No Room*, 122.

116. Grzimek, *No Room*, 130–134.

117. Matteo Rizzo, "What Was Left of the Groundnut Scheme? Development Disaster and Labour Market in Southern Tanganyika 1946–1952," *Journal of Agrarian Change* 6, no. 2 (2006): 205–238.

118. Grzimek, *No Room*, 78–79.

119. Hunt, *A Nervous State*, 47–48, 82–85, 138–166, 177–205.

120. Sewig, *Der Mann, der die Tiere liebte*, 191–201.

121. Grzimek, *No Room*, 249–250.

122. Torma, *Naturschutzkampagne*; 57–63; Sewig, *Der Mann, der die Tiere liebte*, 201–203; Grzimek, *Auf den Mensch gekommen*, 268, 273–274.

123. Grzimek and Grzimek, *Serengeti Shall Not Die*, 18.

124. On film and conservation, see Gregg Mitman, *Reel Nature: America's Romance with Wildlife on Film* (Cambridge, MA: Harvard University Press, 1999), 85–108.

125. Sewig, *Der Mann, der die Tiere liebte*, 204–205.

126. Torma, *Naturschutzkampagne*, 8, 61–62.

127. Grzimek, *Auf den Mensch gekommen*, 303; Mitman, *Reel Nature*, 109–131; Cynthia Chris, *Watching Wildlife* (Minneapolis: University of Minnesota Press, 2006), 28–44.

128. Mitman, *Reel Nature*, 5–25; Arthur Lindgens, *Afrika aufs Korn genommen: mit Büchse und Kamera durch Ostafrika* (Hamburg: P. Parey, 1953). See also Klaus Kreimeier, "Mechanik, Waffen und Haudegen Überall. Expeditionsfilme: das bewaffnete Auge des Ethnografen," in *Triviale Tropen: Exotische Reise- und Abenteuerfilme aus Deutschland, 1919–1939*, ed. Jörg Schöning (Munich: Text + Kritik, 1997), 47–61.

129. William Beinart, "The Renaturing of African Animals: Film and Literature in the 1950s and 1960s," *Kronos: Journal of Cape History* 27 (November 2001): 203.

130. Mitman, *Reel Nature*, 26–58.

131. Chris, *Watching Wildlife*, 20–23.

132. Mitman, *Reel Nature*, 109–112.

133. Torma, *Naturschutzkampagne*, 31–41; Ariane Heimbach, "Die Inszenierte Wildniss," in *Triviale Tropen: Exotische Reise und Abenteurfilme aus Deutschland 1919–1939*, ed. Schöning, 158–166; and Jörg Schöning, "'Kleines Urwaldreich gedeiht': Die Dschungelfantasien des Filmproduzenten John Hagenbeck," in *Der Deutsche Tropenwald*, ed. Flitner, 79–93.

134. Torma, *Naturschutzkampagne*, 31–35; Sabine Hake, "Mapping the Native Body: On Africa and the Colonial Film in the Third Reich," in *The Imperialist Imagination: German Colonialism and Its Legacy* (Ann Arbor: University of Michigan Press, 1998), ed. Sara Friedrichsmeyer, Sara Lennox, and Susanne Zantop, 163–188.

135. Gissibl, "Jagd und Herrschaft," 510–520.

136. Gerlinde Waz, "Auf der Suche nach dem letzten Paradies: Der Afrika Forscher und Regisseur Hans Schomburgk," in *Triviale Tropen*, ed. Schöningh, 95–110; see also Lutz Heck, *Aus der Wildnis in den Zoo: Auf Tierfang in Ostafrika* (Berlin: Ullstein, 1930), 57.

137. Cited in Torma, *Naturschutzkampagne*, 34. Typical of this genre are Senta Dinglreiter, *Wann Kommen die Deutschen Endlich Wieder? Eine Reise Durch Unsere Kolonien in Afrika* (Leipzig: Koehler & Amelang, 1935) and Louise Diel, *Die Kolonien Warten! Afrika im Umbruch* (Leipzig: Paul List, 1939).

138. Mitman, *Reel Nature*, 59–84.

139. Beinart, "Renaturing of African Animals," 220–221.

140. Mitman, *Reel Nature*, 109–131.

141. Grzimek, *Auf den Mensch gekommen*, 303.

142. Heise, *Sense of Place and Sense of Planet*, 68–90.

143. De Bont, "World Laboratory," 417–420.

144. Grzimek appeared unaware of the other meaning of *Kiboko*: a rhino hide whip used by colonial authorities to discipline African subjects. See Paul Ocobock, "Spare the Rod, Spoil the Colony: Corporal Punishment, Colonial Violence, and Generational Authority in Kenya, 1897—1952," *The International Journal of African Historical Studies* 45, no. 1 (2012): 29–56.

145. Torma argues that such scenes reveal Grzimek's interest in Raymond Dart's emerging anthropological theories about the unique bloodlust of *Homo sapiens*. See Torma, *Naturschutzkampagne*, 77–78. Raymond Dart, "The Predatory Transition from Ape to Man," *International Anthropological and Linguistic Review* 1 (1953): 201–217.

146. Dan Brockington sees such distanced viewing as part of late capitalism's "spectacular conservation" producing ineffective virtual environmentalisms. See *Celebrity and the Environment*, 126–141.

147. Mitman, *Reel Nature*, 132–156.

148. Heini Hediger and Adolf Portmann, *Wildtiere in Gefangenschaft* (Basel: Schwabe, 1942).

149. See Grzimek, *Kein Platz*, 177–196 and the film sequence: 35:54–54:59.

150. De Bont, "World Laboratory," 414.

151. Torma, *Naturschutzkampagne*, 71–72; Dunn, *Imagining the Congo*, 31–33.

152. See Sewig, *Der Mann, der die Tiere liebte*, 230.

153. Grzimek, *No Room*, 190.

154. On the pygmy "race" as a social construction and the fluid genetic and glottochronological connections between Batwa and Bantu, see Klieman, *Pygmies Were Our Compass*, 18. The equation of racial degeneration with a Western-dressed African is striking in a German filmic context because of the long history of anti-Semitic imagery that accused European Jews of "mere imitation" of Germanic cultures. See Valerie Weinstein, "Dissolving Boundaries: Assimilation and Allosemitism in E.A. Dupont's *Das Alte Gesetz* (1923) and Veit Harlan's *Jud Süss* (1940)," *German Quarterly* 78, no. 4 (2005): 496–516.

155. Klieman, *Pygmies Were Our Compass*, 20–34, 66–94. On the interethnic world of the forest, see also Christopher Conte, *Highland Sanctuary: Environmental History in Tanzania's Usambara Mountains* (Athens: Ohio University Press, 2004), 17–31.

156. James Buzard, *The Beaten Track: European Tourism, Literature, and the Ways of Culture, 1800–1918* (Oxford: Clarendon, 1993).

157. Victoria de Grazia, *Irresistible Empire: America's Advance through Twentieth-Century Europe* (Cambridge, MA: Harvard University Press, 2005), 226–283; Bernhard Grzimek, *Rhinos Belong to Everybody* (New York: Hill and Wang, 1965), 187.

158. Grzimek and Grzimek, *Serengeti Shall Not Die*, 232–233. On the Grzimeks' critique of the hunting industry, see Torma, *Naturschutzkampagne*, 121–137.

159. Grzimek, *Kein Platz*, 64.

160. John S. Akama, "Neocolonialism, Dependency and External Control of Africa's Tourism Industry: A Case Study of Wildlife Safari Tourism in Kenya," in *Tourism and Postcolonialism: Contested Discourses, Identities and Representations*, ed. C. Michael Hall and Hazel Tucker (London: Routledge, 2004), 142.

161. Grzimek, *No Room*, 68.

162. Grzimek and Grzimek, *Serengeti Shall Not Die*, 242.

163. Bernhard Grzimek and Michael Grzimek, *Serengeti darf nicht Sterben: 367,000 Tiere Suchen einen Staat* (Berlin: Ullstein, 1959), 12.

164. See Mitman, *Reel Nature*, 187.

165. Torma, *Naturschutzkampagne*, 81-82.

Chapter 3

1. Franziska Torma, *Eine Naturschutzkampagne in der Ära Adenauer: Bernhard Grzimeks Afrikafilme in den Medien der 50er Jahre* (Munich: Martin Meidenbauer, 2004), 127-132; Johannes Paulmann, "Jenseits von Eden: Kolonialismus, Zeitkritik und Wissenschaftlicher Naturschutz in Bernhard Grzimeks Tierfilmen der 1950er-Jahre," *Zeitschrift für Geschichtswissenschaft* 56, no. 6 (2008): 543. On redemption and anti-politics in West German political culture, see Konrad Jarausch, *After Hitler: Recivilizing Germans, 1945-1995* (Oxford: Oxford University Press, 2006).

2. Monika Bergmeier, *Umweltgeschichte der Boomjahre, 1949-1973* (Münster: Waxmann, 2002). Such reflections revealed an interplay between metropolis and empire in conservation. See Richard Grove, *Green Imperialism: Colonial Expansion, Tropical Island Edens, and the Origins of Environmentalism, 1600-1860* (Cambridge, UK: Cambridge University Press, 1995) and Bernhard Gissibl, "Grzimeks 'Bayerische Serengeti': Zur transnationalen politischen Ökologie des Nationalparks Bayerischer Wald," in *"Wenn sich alle in der Natur erholen, wo erholt sich dann die Natur?": Naturschutz, Freizeitnutzung, Erholungsvorsorge und Sport—gestern, heute, morgen*, ed. Hans-Werner Frohn, Jürgen Rosebrock, Friedemann Schmoll (Bonn-Bad Godesberg: Bundesamt für Naturschutz, 2009), 229-263.

3. On colonialist continuities and the "anti-politics" of saving Africa, see James Ferguson, *The Anti-Politics Machine: "Development," Depoliticization, and Bureaucratic Power in Lesotho* (Minneapolis: University of Minnesota Press, 2007).

4. Jens-Ivo Engels, *Naturpolitik in der Bundesrepublik: Ideenwelt und Politische Verhaltenstile in Naturschutz und Umweltbewegung, 1950-1980* (Paderborn: Schöningh, 2006), 214-221.

5. William Beinart, "The Renaturing of African Animals: Film and Literature in the 1950s and 1960s, *Kronos: Journal of Cape History* 27 (November 2001): 203

6. On the media, class, and leisure in the Federal Republic, see Axel Schildt, *Moderne Zeiten: Freizeit, Massenmedien und "Zeitgeist" in der Bundesrepublik der 50er Jahre* (Hamburg: Christians, 1995); *Medialisierung und Konsumgesellschaften in der zweiten Hälfte des 20. Jahrhunderts* (Essen: Klartext-Verl., 2004); and "Mach mal Pause! Freie Zeit, Freizeitverhalten und Freizeit Diskurse in der Westdeutschen Wiederaufbau-Gesellschaft der 1950er Jahre," *Archiv für Sozialgeschichte* 33 (January 1993): 357-406.

7. Torma, *Naturschutzkampagne*, 54-55.

8. Bernhard Grzimek, *No Room for Wild Animals* (London: Thames and Hudson, 1956), 10.

9. On the new apocalyptic environmentalism of the 1950s, see Raymond H. Dominick, *The Environmental Movement in Germany: Prophets and Pioneers, 1871-1971* (Bloomington: Indiana University Press, 1992), 148-181.

10. Sandra Chaney, *Nature of the Miracle Years: Conservation in West Germany, 1945-1975* (New York: Berghahn, 2008), 114-147.

11. Bernhard Gissibl, "A 'Bavarian Serengeti': Space, Race, and Time in the Entangled History of Nature Conservation of Germany and East Africa," in *Civilizing Nature: National Parks in Global Historical Perspective*, ed. Bernhard Gissibl, Sabine Höhler, and Patrick Kupper, (New York: Berghahn Books, 2012), 102-122.

12. Torma, *Naturschutzkampagne*, 59.

13. Sara Friedrichsmeyer, Sara Lennox, and Susanne . Zantop, eds. *The Imperialist Imagination: German Colonialism and Its Legacy* (Ann Arbor: University of Michigan Press,

1998), 1–32; Kai Nowak, "Der Schock der Authentizität. Der Filmskandal um *Africa Addio* (1966) und antikolonialer Protest in der Bundesrepublik," *Werkstatt-Geschichte* 69 (2015): 37–53.

14. Claudia Sewig, *Der Mann, der die Tiere liebte: Bernhard Grzimek: Biografie* (Bergisch Gladbach: Lübbe, 2009), 196–197.
15. Torma, *Naturschutzkampagne*, 63.
16. *Süddeutsche Zeitung*, 20 July 1956. Cited in Torma, *Naturschutzkampagne*, 63.
17. Torma, *Naturschutzkampagne*, 130.
18. Torma, *Naturschutzkampagne*, 109–120.
19. Sewig, *Der Mann, der die Tiere liebte*, 194–198.
20. Grzimek, *Auf den Mensch gekommen*, 287–288.
21. Hayes, *Last Place on Earth*, 130.
22. Sewig, *Der Mann, der die Tiere liebte*, 197–198; 221–222.
23. Grzimek, *Auf den Mensch gekommen*, 286–287.
24. Sewig, *Der Mann, der die Tiere liebte*, 166–167.
25. Sewig, *Der Mann, der die Tiere liebte*, 209–216.
26. Grzimek, *Auf den Mensch gekommen*, 295–296.
27. Hayes, *Last Place on Earth*, 49.
28. The shift from the studio "pet" to the live-action film was part of a broader trend in wildlife television that shaped Perkins's *Mutual of Omaha's Wild Kingdom* and *National Geographic Specials* as well. See Gregg Mitman, *Reel Nature: America's Romance with Wildlife on Film* (Cambridge, MA: Harvard University Press, 1999), 132–156; Cynthia Chris, *Watching Wildlife* (Minneapolis: University of Minnesota Press, 2006), 45–69.
29. Jens-Ivo Engels, "Von der Sorge um Tiere zur Sorge um die Umwelt: Tiersendungen als Umweltpolitik in Westdeutschland zwischen 1950 and 1980," *Archiv für Sozialgeschichte* 43 (March 2003): 297–323.
30. See *Auf den Mensch gekommen*, 294–297.
31. Engels, *Naturpolitik*, 242–246.
32. Hayes, *Last Place on Earth*, 48–49.
33. Engels, "Tiersendungen," 304.
34. On this point, see Sewig, *Der Mann, der die Tiere liebte*, 211–213. Television was critical also to the growth of environmentalism. See Engels, "Tiersendungen," 297–301.
35. Grzimek, *Auf den Mensch gekommen*, 241. On this theme, see also Chris, *Watching Wildlife*, ix–xxii and John Berger, *Why Look at Animals?* (London: Penguin, 2009).
36. Grzimek, *Auf den Mensch gekommen*, 240.
37. Grzimek, *Auf den Mensch gekommen*, 243.
38. Grzimek, *Auf den Mensch gekommen*, 259–262; Sewig, *Der Mann, der die Tiere liebte*, 195–196.
39. Grzimek, *Auf den Mensch gekommen*, 297.
40. Grzimek, *Auf den Mensch gekommen*, 53; 399.
41. Andrew Lees, *Cities, Sin, and Social Reform in Imperial Germany* (Ann Arbor: University of Michigan Press, 2002); Dorothy Rowe, *Representing Berlin: Sexuality and the City in Imperial and Weimar Germany* (London: Taylor and Francis, 2017).
42. Torma, *Naturschutzkampagne*, 109–120; Schildt, *Moderne Zeiten*, 301–321.
43. Bergmeier, *Umweltgeschichte der Boomjahre*, Chap. 1; Chaney, *Nature of the Miracle Years*, 3–11; 46–48; 114–118.
44. Hanna Schissler, ed., *The Miracle Years: A Cultural History of West Germany, 1949–1968* (Princeton, NJ: Princeton University Press, 2001); Uta Poiger, *Jazz, Rock, and Rebels: Cold War Politics and American Culture in a Divided Germany* (Berkeley: University of California Press, 2002); David F. Crew, ed., *Consuming Germany and the Cold War* (New York: Berg, 2003).
45. Shelley Baranowski, *Strength through Joy: Consumerism and Mass Tourism in the Third Reich* (Cambridge, UK: Cambridge University Press, 2004), 1–39.
46. Robert G. Moeller, ed., *West Germany Under Construction: Politics, Society, and Culture in the Adenauer Era* (Ann Arbor: University of Michigan Press, 1997); Axel Schildt, *Konservatismus in Deutschland: Von den Anfängen im 18. Jahrhundert bis zur Gegenwart* (Munich: C.H. Beck, 1998) and *Zwischen Abendland und Amerika: Studien zur Westdeutschen Ideenlandschaft der 50er Jahre* (Munich: R. Oldenbourg, 1999); Anson Rabinbach, "Restoring the

German Spirit: Humanism and Guilt in Post-War Germany," in *German Ideologies since 1945: Studies in the Political Thought and Culture of the Bonn Republic*, ed. Jan-Werner Müller (New York: Palgrave Macmillan, 2003), 23–39.

47. See Reinhold Wagnleitner, *Coca-colonization and the Cold War: The Cultural Mission of the United States in Austria after the Second World War*, trans. Diana M. Wolf (Chapel Hill: University of North Carolina Press, 1994).

48. Grzimek, *Auf den Mensch gekommen*, 281–286; Jeffry M. Diefendorf, *In the Wake of War: The Reconstruction of German Cities after World War II* (New York: Oxford University Press, 1993), 67–106.

49. Torma, *Naturschutzkampagne*, 9.

50. Ulrike Lindner, *Hybrid Cultures, Nervous States: Britain and Germany in a (Post)Colonial World* (Amsterdam: Rodopi, 2010).

51. Werner G. Krug, "Der Neger und die Neue Zeit," *Atlantis* 25, no. 8 (August 1954): 361. Note that Africans being labeled as "primitive" under the surface was a denial, too, that they were ready for self-rule. Elazar Barkan and Ronald Bush, *Prehistories of the Future: The Primitivist Project and the Culture of Modernism* (Stanford, CA: Stanford University Press, 1995), 2.

52. Krug, "Der Neger und die Neue Zeit," 362–363.

53. Robert Nye, "Savage Crowds, Modernism, and Modern Politics," in *Prehistories of the Future*, ed. Barkan and Bush, 42–55.

54. Reinhard Demoll, *Heimat: Wandern und Schauen in Berg und Tal*, Vol. 2 (Munich: Faunus, 1959), 400.

55. José Ortega y Gasset, *The Revolt of the Masses* (New York: W.W. Norton, 1932).

56. Krug, "Der Neger und die neue Zeit," 365.

57. Engels, *Naturpolitik*, 272–273.

58. Thomas Lekan, "Saving the Rhine: Ecology, Culture, and *Heimat* in Post-World War II Germany," in *Rivers in History: Perspectives on Waterways in Europe and North America*, ed. Christof Mauch and Thomas Zeller (Pittsburgh: University of Pittsburgh Press, 2008), 110–136.

59. Engels, *Naturpolitik*, 226–231.

60. Grzimek, *No Room* , 10.

61. Lekan, "Saving the Rhine," 123.

62. See Dominick, *Environmental Movement in Germany*, 141–143; Lekan, "Saving the Rhine," 114–123; Erich Hornsmann, *Hätten wir das Wasser nicht* (Frankfurt: Vereinigung Deutscher Gewässerschutz, 1957).

63. Alwin Seifert, "Die Versteppung Deutschlands," in *Im Zeitalter des Lebendigen. Natur – Heimat – Technik* (Munich: Müllersche Verlagshandlung, 1943), 24–51.

64. *Der Spiegel*, "Wasser: Alarm in der Leitung," 47, no. 13 (November 18, 1959): 36–47.

65. Dominick, *Environmental Movement in Germany*, 141.

66. "Kampf für die Tiere: Rinderherden vernichten die Berggorillas" and "Mission fängt geschützte Tiere," in *Das Tier* 2 (November 1960): 19.

67. Konrad Lorenz, "Uns treibt die Sehnsucht nach dem Paradies," *Das Tier* 1 (October 1960): 4.

68. Wilhelm Hochgreve, "Wilde Hirsche zaum wie Haustiere," *Das Tier* 2 (November 1960): 48–50.

69. "Die Störche sterben bei uns aus," *Das Tier* 2 (November 1960): 8–11.

70. Dominick, *Environmental Movement in Germany*, 148–158.

71. Günther Schwab, *Der Tanz mit dem Teufel: Ein abenteuerliches Interview* (Hannover: Adolf Sponholtz Verlag, 1958).

72. "Warum wir *Das Tier* geschaffen haben?," *Das Tier* 1 (October 1960): 3.

73. Manfred Behr and Hans Otto Meissner, *Keine Angst um Wilde Tiere. Fünf Kontinente Geben Ihnen Heimat* (Munich: Verlagsgesellschaft, 1959), 37.

74. Behr and Meissner, *Keine Angst um Wilde Tiere. Fünf Kontinente Geben Ihnen Heimat*, 35–37.

75. Cited in Josef Zimmermann, "Die Entwicklung des Naturschutzes, insbesondere in den rheinischen Gebieten, und Gedanken über eine allgemeine Geschichte des Naturschutzes," *Eifeljahrbuch* (1995): 40. On Wetekamp's efforts see Lekan, *Imagining the Nation*, 49–52.

76. Hugo Conwentz, *Die Gefährdung der Naturdenkmäler und Vorschläge zu ihrer Erhaltung* (Berlin: Gebrüder Bornträger, 1904). On the creation of the State Office, see Michael

Wettengel, "Staat und Naturschutz, 1906–1945: Zur Geschichte der Staatlichen Stelle für Naturdenkmalpflege in Preussen und der Reichsstelle für Naturschutz," *Historische Zeitschrift* 257, no. 2 (October 1993): 355–399.

77. Dominick, *Environmental Movement in Germany*, 54–55; Engels, *Naturpolitik*, 95–96. See also Verein Naturschutzpark e.V. *Naturschutzparke. Fünfzig Jahre Verein Naturschutzpark* (Stuttgart: Verlag des Vereins Naturschutzparke, 1959) and Andrea Kiendl, *Die Lüneburger Heide: Fremdenverkehr und Literatur* (Hamburg: Reimer, 1993).

78. Jeffrey K. Wilson, *The German Forest: Nature, Identity, and the Contestation of a National Symbol, 1871–1914* (Toronto: University of Toronto Press, 2012), 49–85.

79. See Chaney, *Nature of the Miracle Years*, 215–218. On the regionalist tradition, see Thomas Lekan, "The Nature of Home: Landscape Preservation and Local Identity," in *Localism, Landscape, and the Ambiguities of Place: German-Speaking Central Europe 1860–1933*, ed. David Blackbourn and James Retallack (Toronto: University of Toronto Press, 2007), 165–194.

80. Chaney, *Nature of the Miracle Years*, 217; Behr and Meissner, *Keine Angst um Wilde Tiere*, 35.

81. Engels, *Naturpolitik*, 93–110.

82. Chaney, *Nature of the Miracle Years*, 117–118.

83. Alfred Toepfer, "Der Tätigkeitsbericht des Vorsitzenden für die Zeit von Dezember 1955 bis Anfang April 1956," *Naturschutzparke* (May 1956): 136–138; "Naturpark—Idee und Verwirklichung," *Naturschutzparke* (Jan. 1962): 3–6.

84. Chaney, *Nature of the Miracle Years*, 118–126.

85. Engels, *Naturpolitik*, 103–108 and "'Rückenwind oder Hemmschuh?' Tourismus und politische Optionen des Vereinnaturschutzes am Beispiel des Vereins Naturschutzpark in den 1950er- und 1960er-Jahren," in *"Wenn sich alle in der Natur erholen,"* ed. Frohn et al., 126–146.

86. Dieter Langewiesche, "Freizeit und 'Massenbildung.' Zur Ideologie und Praxis der Volksbildung in der Weimarer Republik," 223–248 and Hasso Spode, "'Der deutsche Arbeiter reist': Massentourismus im Dritten Reich," in *Sozialgeschichte der Freizeit: Untersuchungen zum Wandel der Alltagskultur in Deutschland*, ed. Gerhard Huck (Wuppertal: Peter Hammer, 1980), 281–306; Hasso Spode, ed., *Goldstrand und Teutonengrill. Kultur- und Sozialgeschichte des Tourismus in Deutschland, 1945 bis 1989* (Berlin: W. Moser: Verlag für universitäre Kommunikation, 1996); Christina Keitz, *Reisen als Leitbild: die Entstehung des modernen Massentourismus in Deutschland* (Munich: DTV, 1997).

87. *Frankfurter Allgemeine Zeitung*, February 1, 1953; reprinted in Christoph Kleßmann and Georg Wagner, eds., *Das gespaltene Land. Leben in Deutschland 1945–1990. Texte und Dokumente zur Sozialgeschichte* (Munich: C.H. Beck, 1993), 335–366. Found at the German Historical Institute "German History in Documents and Images," http://germanhistory-docs.ghi-dc.org/index.cfm. Accessed August 15, 2018.

88. Chaney, *Nature of the Miracle Years*, 120–121.

89. Chaney, *Nature of the Miracle Years*, 121.

90. Chaney, *Nature of the Miracle Years*, 122; Engels, *Naturpolitik*, 94–131.

91. Chaney, *Nature of the Miracle Years*, 122–123; Engels, *Naturpolitik*, 108–110.

92. Behr and Meissner, *Keine Angst um Wilde Tiere*, 14.

93. Sewig, *Der Mann, der die Tiere liebte*, 206–207.

94. Grzimek, *Auf den Mensch gekommen*, 367–371.

95. See the planning documents for the "Die Weilburger Tier-Freiheit" in FSA Zoo 32.

96. See Günther Grzimek, "Tierfreiheit," Gutachtliche Stellungnahme, June 3, 1964 in FSA Zoo 32.

97. Gissibl, "'Bavarian Serengeti,'" 102–103.

98. Sewig, *Der Mann, der die Tiere liebte*, 207.

99. Chaney, *Nature of the Miracle Years*, 139; 195–196.

100. Chaney, *Nature of the Miracle Years*, 219–236.

101. Chaney, *Nature of the Miracle Years*, 221; Gissibl, "'Bavarian Serengeti,'" 114–116.

102. Grzimek, *Auf den Mensch gekommen*, 456.

103. Grzimek, *Auf den Mensch gekommen*, 455–457.

104. Grzimek, *Auf den Mensch gekommen*, 455.

105. Grzimek, *No Room*, 68.

106. Sewig, *Der Mann, der die Tiere liebte*, 204.
107. Georg von Opel, "Müssen die Tiere hungern? Anmerkungen zum Jagdgesetz," *Frankfurter Allgemeine Zeitung*, May 12, 1961.
108. Behr and Meissner, *Keine Angst um Wilde Tiere*, 65–66.
109. Gissibl, *Nature of German Imperialism*, 159–168.
110. Gissibl, *Nature of German Imperialism*, 85–105.
111. Bernhard Gissibl, "German Colonialism and the Beginning of International Wildlife Conservation in Africa," *German Historical Institute Washington, DC, Bulletin*, Supplement 3 (2006): 121–144.
112. Gissibl, *Nature of German Imperialism*, 146–147; 156–159. There is an extensive literature on the relationship between empire, hunting, and conservation that cannot be cited in detail here. For a good introduction, see John M. Mackenzie, "Chivalry, Social Darwinism and Ritualised Killing: The Hunting Ethos in Central Africa up to 1914," in *Conservation in Africa*, ed. Anderson and Grove, 41–62 and William Beinart, "Empire, Hunting, and Ecological Change in Southern and Central Africa," *Past and Present* 128, no. 1 (1990): 162–186.
113. Bernhard Gissibl, "Jagd und Herrschaft – Zur politischen Okologie des deutschen Kolonialismus in Ostafrika," *Zeitschrift für Geschichtswissenschaft* 56, no. 6 (2008): 501–520 and "The Conservation of Luxury: Safari Hunting and the Consumption of Wildlife in Twentieth-Century East Africa," in *Luxury in Global Perspective: Objects and Practices, 1600–2000*, ed. Bernd-Stefan Grewe and Karin Hofmeester (New York: Cambridge University Press, 2016), 263–300.
114. Grzimek, *No Room*, 57; 61.
115. Grzimek and Grzimek, *Serengeti darf nicht Sterben*, 232; Bernhard Grzimek, "Zeitvertrieb für schwache Männer: Löwenjagd," in *Die Welt*, June 6, 1959.
116. Grzimek, *No Room*, 63.
117. Torma, *Naturschutzkampagne*, 121–137.
118. Grzimek, *Auf den Mensch gekommen*, 316–317.
119. Torma, *Naturschutzkampagne*, 139.
120. Behr and Meissner, *Keine Angst um Wilde Tiere*, 7.
121. Grzimek, *Auf den Mensch gekommen*, 315–316.
122. Sewig, *Der Mann, der die Tiere liebte*, 241–242; Grzimek, *Auf den Mensch gekommen*, 315–316.
123. Grzimek, *No Room*, 68.
124. Behr and Meissner, *Keine Angst um Wilde Tiere*, 232.
125. Behr and Meissner, *Keine Angst um Wilde Tiere*, 224, see photos 50–51.
126. Cited in Behr and Meissner, *Keine Angst um Wilde Tiere*, 184.
127. Torma, *Naturschutzkampagne*, 141.
128. Behr and Meissner, *Keine Angst um Wilde Tiere*, 59–66.
129. Like so many European conservationists, Behr and Meissner ignored the Yellowstone legacy altogether—a stark contrast to conservation histories focused on the globalization of the US model. See Behr and Meissner, *Keine Angst um Wilde Tiere*, 67–71 vs. Roderick Nash, *Wilderness and the American Mind*, 4th ed. (New Haven, CT: Yale University Press, 2001), 342–378.
130. Cited in Behr and Meissner, *Keine Angst um Wilde Tiere*, 67.
131. Behr and Meissner, *Keine Angst um Wilde Tiere*, 67–69.
132. Adams and McShane, *Myth of Wild Africa*, 47.
133. Nicholas Luard and World Wildlife Fund, *The Wildlife Parks of Africa* (Salem, NH: Salem House, 1986), 50–51.
134. "Letter from Hans Otto Meissner to Safariland in Nairobi," March 9, 1958, in PAAA Michael Grzimek Memorial Laboratory.
135. Grzimek, *Auf den Mensch gekommen*, 317; Torma, *Naturschutzkampagne*, 139–142.
136. A. Mankowski, "Ein Aüsserst Seltsames Buch," March 9, 1958. Translated from *Esser du Congo*, February 1, 1960 in PAAA Michael Grzimek Memorial Lab.
137. Otto Koehler, "Besprechung: Keine Angst um Wilde Tiere," *Zeitschrift für Tierpsychologie*, 17, no. 1 (1960): 131–132.
138. *Der Spiegel*, September 14, 1960, described in Torma, *Naturschutzkampagne*, 81–83.
139. Torma, *Naturschutzkampagne*, 139; 146–159.

140. Hans Otto Meissner, *Ich Ging Allein . . . Auf Grosswildjagd in Afrika* (Giessen: Bruhlscher, 1955).

141. Torma, *Naturschutzkampagne*, 151–159.

142. Torma, *Naturschutzkampagne*, 141.

143. Grzimek, *Auf den Mensch gekommen*, 326–328.

144. Jan Bender Shetler, *Imagining Serengeti: A History of Landscape Memory in Tanzania from Earliest Times to the Present* (Athens: Ohio University Press, 2007), 180–181; Juhani Koponen, *Development for Exploitation: German Colonial Policies in Mainland Tanzania, 1884–1914* (Helsinki: Tiedekirja, 1994), 590–595.

145. Robin S. Reid, *Savannas of Our Birth: People, Wildlife, and Change in East Africa* (Berkeley: University of California Press, 2012), 114.

146. Gissibl, *Nature of German Imperialism*, 252.

147. Ben Gardner, *Selling the Serengeti: The Cultural Politics of Safari Tourism* (Athens: University of Georgia Press, 2016), 39.

148. On the relationship between conservation and labor policy see Thaddeus Sunseri, *Wielding the Ax: State Forestry and Social Conflict in Tanzania, 1820–2000* (Athens: Ohio University Press, 2009), 97–116; Neumann, *Imposing Wilderness*, 97–121.

149. Young-Sun Hong, *Cold War Germany, the Third World, and the Global Humanitarian Regime* (New York: Cambridge University Press, 2015), 233–235; John Iliffe, *Modern History of Tanganyika* (Cambridge, UK: Cambridge University Press, 1979), 558–572.

150. Bernhard Grzimek, *Auch Nashörner gehören allen Menschen: Kämpfe um die Tierwelt Afrikas* (Berlin: Ullstein), 62.

151. Grzimek, "Wie steht es jetzt um die Nationalparke Afrikas," *Schweizer Monatshefte* (July 1961): 471–474.

152. Grzimek, *Serengeti Shall Not Die*, 240.

153. Grzimek, *Serengeti Shall Not Die*, 241.

154. Grzimek, "Wie steht es jetzt," 471–474.

155. Grzimek, *Auf den Mensch gekommen*, 335–336.

156. Grzimek, *Auf den Mensch gekommen*, 314–315.

157. Grzimek, *Serengeti Shall Not Die*, 242.

158. Torma, *Naturschutzkampagne*, 10.

159. Hans Grimm, *Volk ohne Raum* (Munich: A. Langen, 1926).

160. Michael Flitner, "Vom 'Platz an der Sonne,' zum 'Platz für Tiere,'" in *Der Deutsche Tropenwald: Bilder, Mythen, Politik*, ed. Michael Flitner (Frankfurt: Campus, 2000), 244–262.

161. Grzimek, *No Room*, 250.

162. Grzimek, *No Room*, 68; Glenda Sluga, "UNESCO and the (One) World of Julian Huxley," *Journal of World History* 21, no. 3 (2010): 393–418.

163. Anna-Katharina Wöbse, "Framing the Heritage of Mankind: National Parks on the International Agenda," in *Civilizing Nature: National Parks in Global Historical Perspective*, ed. Gissibl et al., 140–156 and "'The World After All Was One': The International Environmental Network of UNESCO and IUPN, 1945–1950," *Contemporary European History* 20, no. 3 (2011): 331–348.

164. Sluga, "UNESCO and the (One)World of Julian Huxley," 393.

165. Wöbse, "'The World After All Was One,'" 341; William M. Adams, *Against Extinction: The Story of Conservation* (London: Earthscan, 2004), 49–51; 169–174.

166. Grzimek et al., *Paradiese*, 100; Huxley, *UNESCO: Its Purpose and its Philosophy*, 8. Cited in Wöbse, "'The World After All Was One,'" 339.

167. Anna-Katharina Wöbse, "Tourismus und Naturschutz—die international Dimension einer schwierigen Beziehung," in *"Wenn sich alle in der Natur erholen,"* ed. Frohn et al., 195.

Chapter 4

1. Bernhard and Michael Grzimek, *Serengeti darf nicht Sterben*, postscript (Berlin: Ullstein, 1959). On Michael Grzimek's death, see Myles Turner, *My Serengeti Years: The Memoirs of an African Game Warden* (New York: W.W. Norton, 1988), 21 and Franziska Torma, *Eine Naturschutzkampagne in der Ära Adenauer: Bernhard Grzimeks Afrikafilme in den Medien der 50er Jahre* (Munich: Martin Meidenbauer, 2004), 130–132.

2. See Hermann Gimbel, "Obituary: Michael Grzimek, 1934–1959," *The Journal of Wildlife Management* 23, no. 3 (July 1959): 368–369.
3. The scholarly literature on the Serengeti debates of the 1950s is quite extensive and cannot be cited here in full. Some of the best accounts include Turner, *My Serengeti Years*, 39–54; Roderick P. Neumann, "Ways of Seeing Africa: Colonial Recasting of African Society and Landscape in Serengeti National Park," *Ecumene* 2, no. 2 (1995): 149–169; Jan Bender Shetler, *Imagining Serengeti: A History of Landscape Memory in Tanzania from Earliest Times to the Present* (Athens: Ohio University Press, 2007), 201–217.
4. Roderick P. Neumann, *Imposing Wilderness: Struggles over Livelihood and Nature Preservation in Africa* (Berkeley: University of California Press, 1998), 129–139 and Prakash Kashwan, *Democracy in the Woods: Environmental Conservation and Social Justice in India, Tanzania, and Mexico* (Oxford: Oxford University Press, 2017), 146–173.
5. Bernhard Grzimek and Michael Grzimek, *Serengeti Shall Not Die*, trans. E.L. Rewald and D. Rewald (New York: E.P. Dutton, 1961), 225. The notion that pastoralism, rather than long-term climate change, was causing desiccation of mid-century savannas was under debate already in the 1960s. See, for example, Henry Fosbrooke, *Ngorongoro: The Eighth Wonder* (London: Deutsch, 1972), 49–72. The desertification hypothesis subsequently came under extensive scientific critique. See, for example, Kaj Århem, *Pastoral Man in the Garden of Eden: The Maasai of the Ngorongoro Conservation Area, Tanzania* (Uppsala: Scandinavian Institute of African Studies, 1985) and Katherine Homewood and W. A. Rodgers, "Pastoralism, Conservation, and the Overgrazing Controversy," in *Conservation in Africa: People, Policies, and Practice* (New York: Cambridge University Press, 1987) ed. David Anderson and Richard Grove, 111–128.
6. Grzimek and Grzimek, *Serengeti Shall Not Die*, 245.
7. Jonathan S. Adams and Thomas O. McShane, *The Myth of Wild Africa: Conservation Without Illusion* (New York: W.W. Norton, 1992), 51–54. On the evolution of the Serengeti from game reserve to national park, see Fosbrooke, "Serengeti and Ngorongoro Diamond Jubilee, 1921–1981: The Serengeti Ecosystem" 2–3, in Henry A. Fosbrooke Collection (HFC), University of Dar es Salaam Library, East Africana collection.
8. Claudia Sewig, *Der Mann, der die Tiere liebte. Bernhard Grzimek: Biografie* (Bergisch Gladbach: Lübbe, 2009), 225.
9. I borrow this term from Ellen Wohl, "Wilderness Is Dead: Whither Critical Zone Studies and Geomorphology in the Anthropocene?," *Anthropocene* 2 (2013): 4–5.
10. On colonialism and ecological memory, see Hans G. Schabel, "Tanganyika Forestry under German Colonial Administration, 1891–1919," *Forest and Conservation History* 34, no. 3 (1990): 130–141; Thaddeus Sunseri, "Forestry and the German Imperial Imagination: Conflicts over Forest Use in German East Africa," in *Germany's Nature: Cultural Landscapes and Environmental History*, ed. Thomas Lekan and Thomas Zeller (New Brunswick, NJ: Rutgers University Press, 2005), 81–107, and Thomas Lekan, "'Serengeti Shall Not Die': Bernhard Grzimek, Wildlife Film, and the Making of a Tourist Landscape in East Africa," *German History* 29, no. 2 (June 2011): 224–264.
11. Shetler, *Imagining Serengeti*, 135–199; Bernhard Gissibl, *The Nature of German Imperialism: Conservation and the Politics of Wildlife in Colonial East Africa* (New York: Berghahn, 2016), 35–198.
12. On historical erasures and rewilding in national parks see Amalia Tholen Baldwin, *Becoming Wilderness: Nature, History, and the Making of Isle Royale National Park* (Houghton, MI: Isle Royale & Keweenaw Parks Association, 2011) and James W. Feldman and William Cronon, *Storied Wilderness: Rewilding the Apostle Islands* (Seattle: University of Washington Press, 2013).
13. On such technological mediations, see Etienne Benson, *Wired Wilderness: Technologies of Tracking and the Making of Modern Wildlife* (Baltimore: Johns Hopkins University Press, 2010).
14. Critical to this chapter is Tobias Boes's reading of key scenes in the film that draw connections to the crisis of humanism and the search for a global heritage after World War II. See "Political Animals: *Serengeti Shall Not Die* and the Cultural Heritage of Mankind," *German Studies Review* 36, no. 1 (2013): 41–59.

15. The Serengeti they presented was made possible through a disembodied, masculine gaze that feminist critic Donna Haraway has rightly called the "god trick." See "Situated Knowledges: The Science Question in Feminism and the Privilege of Partial Perspective," *Feminist Studies* 14, no. 3 (1988): 583.

16. Boes notes the subtle but important differences between the English-dubbed and German versions of the film (see endnote 2), one of which is the use in English versions of "cultural heritage of all mankind" versus the German "ideeller Gemeinbesitz der ganzen Menschheit," or "common property of humanity," a phrasing with rich nineteenth-century associations in German environmental culture over access to forests. On this point, see Jeffrey K. Wilson, *The German Forest: Culture, Identity, and the Contestation of a National Symbol, 1871–1914* (Toronto: University of Toronto Press, 2012).

17. W. H. Pearsall, *Report on an Ecological Survey of the Serengeti National Park, Tanganyika* (London: Fauna Preservation Society, 1957), 5–9.

18. On the theories behind division, see Bernhard Grzimek and Michael Grzimek, "A Study of the Game of the Serengeti Plains," *Zeitschrift für Säugetierkunde* 25 (1960): 14–15.

19. Grzimek and Grzimek, "Study of the Game," 14.

20. Sewig, *Der Mann, der die Tiere liebte*, 225; Gerd Lettow-Vorbeck, *Am Fusse des Meru: Das Leben von Margarete Trappe, Afrikas Grosser Jägerin*, 2nd ed. (Hamburg: P. Parey, 1957).

21. Sewig, *Der Mann, der die Tiere liebte*, 225.

22. Grzimek and Grzimek, *Serengeti Shall Not Die*, 20–21.

23. Roderick P. Neumann, "The Postwar Conservation Boom in British Colonial Africa," *Environmental History* 7, no. 1 (January 2002): 22–47.

24. George Petrides, *Report: Kenya's Wild-Life Resources and the National Parks* (Nairobi: Trustees of the Royal National Parks of Kenya, 1955) in HFC. Petrides's recommendations followed the broader shift in US national park priorities from management for recreation to management for ecological integrity. Richard Sellars, *Preserving Nature in the National Parks: A History*. 2nd ed. (New Haven, CT: Yale University Press, 2009), 91–148; 214–216.

25. Raymond Dasmann, *Environmental Conservation* (New York: John Wiley & Sons, 1959), 194, 219–220.

26. Bernhard Grzimek, *Grzimek unter Afrikas Tieren: Erlebnisse, Beobachtungen, Forschungsergebnisse* (Frankfurt: Ullstein, 1974), 270–329.

27. Petrides, *Kenya's Wild-Life Resources*, 12–22.

28. On the potential for wildlife to be commoditized as a "resource" for future development, see E. B. Worthington, *The Wild Resources of East and Central Africa* (London: Her Majesty's Stationery Office, 1961).

29. Pearsall, *Ecological Survey of the Serengeti National Park*, 1.

30. Grzimek and Grzimek, "Study of the Game," 3–4.

31. Turner, *My Serengeti Years*, 25.

32. Siegfried Passarge, *Die Inselsberglandschaften im tropischen Afrika* (Jena, 1904).

33. Cited in Harold T.P. Hayes, *The Last Place on Earth* (New York: Stein and Day, 1977), 15.

34. Anthony Sinclair, *Serengeti Story: Life and Science in the World's Greatest Wildlife Region* (Oxford: Oxford University Press), 10.

35. Grzimek and Grzimek, "Study of the Game," 4.

36. Turner, *My Serengeti Years*, 27.

37. Sinclair, *Serengeti Story*, 10.

38. Pearsall, *Ecological Survey of the Serengeti National Park*, 7.

39. Grzimek and Grzimek, "Study of the Game," 4–9.

40. Among those cited were Fritz Jaeger, *Das Hochland der Riesenkrater und die umliegenden Hochländer Deutch-Ostafrikas* (Berlin: Mittler, 1911) and Moritz Merker, *Die Masai* (Berlin: D. Reimer, 1910).

41. Oscar Baumann, *Durch Massailand zur Nilquelle* (Berlin: D. Reimer, 1894).

42. Sinclair, *Serengeti Story*, 42–44.

43. Anthony Sinclair et al., "Shaping the Serengeti Ecosystem," in *Serengeti IV: Sustaining Biodiversity in a Coupled Human-Natural System* (Chicago: University of Chicago Press, 2015), ed. Sinclair, Kristine L. Metzger, Simon A. R. Mduma, and John M. Fryxell, 16.

44. Gissibl, *Nature of German Imperialism*, 35–66; 95–96.
45. Robin S. Reid, *Savannas of Our Birth: People, Wildlife, and Change in East Africa* (Berkeley: University of California Press, 2012), 103–105.
46. Sinclair et al., "Shaping the Serengeti Ecosystem," 15.
47. Sinclair, *Serengeti Story*, 39–41.
48. Thomas Spear and Richard Waller, eds., *Being Maasai: Ethnicity and Identity in East Africa* (Athens: Ohio University Press, 1993), 5; Benjamin Gardner, *Selling the Serengeti: The Cultural Politics of Safari Tourism* (Athens: University of Georgia Press, 2016), 32–33.
49. Cited in Turner, *My Serengeti Years*, 25.
50. Sinclair, *Serengeti Story*, 47.
51. Quoted in Grzimek and Grzimek, *Serengeti Shall Not Die*, 55.
52. Grzimek and Grzimek, *Serengeti Shall Not Die*, 54–55.
53. Grzimek and Grzimek, *Serengeti Shall Not Die*, 54–56.
54. Sinclair et al., "Shaping the Serengeti Ecosystem," 15; Thaddeus Sunseri, "The African Rinderpest Panzootic," in Oxford Research Encyclopedia of African History, online publication date April 2018. doi: 10.1093/acrefore/9780190277734.013.375.
55. Richard Waller, "Emutai: Crisis and Response in Maasailand, 1883–1902," in *The Ecology of Survival: Case Studies from Northeast African History*, ed. Douglas H. Johnson and David Anderson (London: L. Crook, 1988), 73–112.
56. Shetler, *Imagining Serengeti*, 34–35; 135–166.
57. John Ford, *The Role of the Trypanosomiases in African Ecology: A Study of the Tsetse Fly Problem* (Oxford: Clarendon Press, 1971); Holly Dublin, "Dynamics of Serengeti-Mara Woodlands: An Historical Perspective," in *Forest and Conservation History* 35, no. 4 (1991): 169–178; Helge Kjekshus, *Ecology Control and Economic Development in East African History: The Case of Tanganyika 1850–1950* (Athens: Ohio University Press, 1996), 126–160.
58. Sinclair et al., "Shaping the Serengeti Ecosystem," 16–17.
59. Sinclair, *Serengeti Story*, 48–49.
60. Peter Rogers, "History and Governance in the Ngorongoro Conservation Area, Tanzania, 1959–1966," *Global Environment* 2, no. 4 (2009): 78–117.
61. George Steer, *Judgment on German Africa* (London: Hodder and Stoughton, 1939), 305–306; On German-British continuities, see Christopher A. Conte, *Highland Sanctuary: Environmental History in Tanzanias Usambara Mountains* (Athens: Ohio University Press, 2004), 11–14, 76–95.
62. Bernhard Gissibl, *Nature of German Imperialism*, 232–267 and "German Colonialism and the Beginning of International Wildlife Conservation in Africa," *German Historical Institute Washington, DC, Bulletin*, Supplement 3 (2006): 121–122; 132–144.
63. Steer, *Judgment on German Africa*, 305.
64. Shetler, *Imagining Serengeti*, 181.
65. Shetler, *Imagining Serengeti*, 181.
66. Sinclair et al., "Shaping the Serengeti Ecosystem," 21–22. For a detailed review of the Serengeti reserve's borders and ordinances, see Fosbrooke, "The Serengeti Ecosystem," 2–3 and "Short History of the Serengeti and Ngorongoro," 10–11 (1981) in HFC.
67. Fosbrooke, "The Serengeti Ecosystem," 2–3; Sinclair et al., "Shaping the Serengeti Ecosystem," 22–23.
68. Juhani Koponen, *Development for Exploitation: German Colonial Policies in Mainland Tanzania, 1884–1914* (Helsinki: Finnish Historical Society, 1995); Johannes Paulmann, *Deutscher Kolonialismus und Natur vom Kaiserreich bis zur Bundesrepublik* (Berlin: Metropol-Verlag, 2008).
69. Shelter, *Imagining Serengeti*, 169–173.
70. Shelter, *Imagining Serengeti*, 205–206.
71. Sinclair et al., "Shaping the Serengeti Ecosystem," 22.
72. Elizabeth Garland, "State of Nature: Colonial Power, Neoliberal Capital, and Wildlife Management in Tanzania" (PhD diss., University of Chicago, 2006), 84–106.
73. Thaddeus Sunseri, *Wielding the Ax: State Forestry and Social Conflict in Tanzania, 1820–2000* (Athens: Ohio University Press, 2009), 97–116.
74. Shelter, *Imagining Serengeti*, 177–178.

75. Shetler, *Imagining Serengeti*, 181–182.
76. Mark Cioc, *The Game of Conservation: International Treaties to Protect the World's Migratory Animals* (Athens: Ohio University Press, 2009), 1; John M. MacKenzie, *The Empire of Nature: Hunting, Conservation, and British Imperialism* (Manchester, UK: Manchester University Press, 1988).
77. Neumann, *Imposing Wilderness*, 129–139 and "Ways of Seeing Africa," 153–169.
78. Neumann, *Imposing Wilderness*, 106–111; 122–148; John S. Akama, "Neocolonialism, Dependency and External Control of Africa's Tourism Industry: A Case Study of Wildlife Safari Tourism in Kenya," in *Tourism and Postcolonialism: Contested Discourses, Identities and Representations*, ed. C. Michael Hall and Hazel Tucker (London: Routledge, 2004), 140–150.
79. Sinclair et al., "The Shaping of the Serengeti Ecosystem," 22.
80. On Mau Mau, see E.S. Atieno Odhuambo and John Lonsdale, eds., *Mau Mau and Nationhood: Aims, Authority and Narration* (Athens: Ohio University Press, 2003) and Wunyarabi O. Maloba, *Mau Mau and Kenya: An Analysis of a Peasant Revolt* (Bloomington: Indiana University Press, 1993).
81. Neumann, "Ways of Seeing Africa," 159–163.
82. Neumann, *Imposing Wilderness*, 68–77.
83. Grzimek and Grzimek, "Study of the Game," 13.
84. Grzimek and Grzimek, *Serengeti Shall Not Die*, 245–246.
85. Michael Grzimek and Bernhard Grzimek, "Census of Plains Animals in the Serengeti National Park, Tanganyika," *The Journal of Wildlife Management* 24, no. 1 (1960): 27–28. See also the German Museum of Technology in Berlin's permanent exhibition on the Dornier DO 27 and the Grzimeks' survey: *Serengeti Shall Not Die*.
86. Sewig, *Der Mann, der die Tiere liebte*, 226–227; Sabine Nessel, "Grzimek, Zoo, und Kino," in *Zoo und Kino: Mit Beiträgen zu Bernhard und Michael Grzimeks Film- und Fernseharbeit*, ed. Sabine Nessel and Heide Schlüpmann (Frankfurt: Strömfeld-Verlag, 2012), 151–154.
87. Sewig, *Der Mann, der die Tiere liebte*, 227–228.
88. Root would become famous for the *Survival* series on BBC television. See Sewig, *Der Mann, der die Tiere liebte*, 232.
89. Bernhard Grzimek, *Serengeti Darf Nicht Sterben* (Frankfurt: Okapia Productions, 1959). The film has been redistributed by Family Entertainment (Berlin, 2004). Citations and clips in this chapter come from the DVD version, which according to Okapia contains the original film cut.
90. Grzimek and Grzimek, "Census of Plains Animals," 28–30.
91. Boes, "Political Animals," 47.
92. William Beinart, "The Renaturing of African Animals: Film and Literature in the 1950s and 1960s, *Kronos: Journal of Cape History* 27 (November 2001): 203.
93. Turner, *My Serengeti Years*, 21.
94. Grzimek, *Auf den Mensch gekommen*, 70.
95. Russell A. Berman, *Enlightenment or Empire: Colonial Discourse in German Culture* (Lincoln: University of Nebraska Press, 1998); Matthias Fiedler, *Zwischen Abenteuer, Wissenschaft und Kolonialismus: Der deutsche Afrikadiskurs im 18. und 19. Jahrhundert* (Cologne: Böhlau, 2005); Tracey Reimann-Dawe, "The British Other on African Soil: The Rise of Nationalism in Colonial German Travel Writing on Africa," *Patterns of Prejudice* 45, no. 5 (2011): 417–433.
96. Cornelia Essner, *Deutsche Afrikareisende im neunzehnten Jahrhundert: Zur Sozialgeschichte des Reisens* (Stuttgart: Steiner, 1985), 10; Brigitte Hoppe, "Naturwissenschaftliche und zoologische Forschungen in Afrika während der deutschen Kolonialbewegung bis 1914," *Berichte zur Wissenschafts-Geschichte* 13, no. 4 (December 1990): 193–206.
97. Grzimek and Grzimek, *Serengeti Shall Not Die*, 14–15.
98. Grzimek and Grzimek, *Serengeti Shall Not Die*, 13.
99. On Harthoorn, see Beinart, "Renaturing of African Animals," 211. On the Grzimeks' use of projectile syringes to narcotize and tag wildlife, see Grzimek and Grzimek, "Study of the Game," 19–24 and H. K. Buechner, A. M. Harthoorn, and J. A. Lock, "Using Drugs to Control Game," *Wildlife (Nairobi)* 1, no. 4 (1959): 49–52.

100. Grzimek and Grzimek, "Study of the Game," 24–25.
101. Grzimek and Grzimek, "Study of the Game," 26–28. On animal tracking, see Etienne Benson, "Trackable Life: Data, Sequence, and Organism in Movement Ecology," *Studies in History and Philosophy of Biological and Biomedical Sciences* 57 (2016): 137–147.
102. Grzimek and Grzimek, "Study of the Game," 36–40.
103. Hayes, *Last Place on Earth*, 38.
104. Grzimek and Grzimek, "Study of the Game," 29–55.
105. Grzimek and Grzimek, "Study of the Game," 56–57.
106. Grzimek and Grzimek, *Serengeti Shall Not Die*, 49.
107. Grzimek and Grzimek, *Serengeti Shall Not Die*, 314 (italics in original).
108. Gissibl, *Nature of German Imperialism*, 3–8.
109. Daniel Steinbach, "Carved out of Nature: Identity and Environment in German Colonial Africa," in *Cultivating the Colonies: Colonial States and Their Environmental Legacies*, ed. Christina Folke Ax, Niels Brimnes, Niklas Thode Jensen, and Karen Oslund (Athens: Ohio University Press, 2011), 47–77.
110. Grzimek and Grzimek, *Serengeti Shall Not Die*, 82.
111. Torma, *Naturschutzkampagne*, 184–189.
112. Heide Fehrenbach, "The Fight for the Christian West: German Film Control, the Churches, and the Reconstruction of Civil Society in the Early Bonn Republic," in *West Germany under Construction: Politics, Society, and Culture in the Adenauer Era*, ed. Robert Moeller (Ann Arbor: University of Michigan Press, 1997), 321–346.
113. Grzimek, *Auf den Mensch gekommen*, 304–305.
114. Fosbrooke, *Eighth Wonder*, 152–154; Dorothy L. Hodgson, *Once Intrepid Warriors: Gender, Ethnicity, and the Cultural Politics of Maasai Development* (Bloomington: Indiana University Press, 2001), 24–26.
115. Shetler, *Imagining Serengeti*, 33–37.
116. See Dublin, "Dynamics of Serengeti-Mara Woodlands" and Kjekshus, *Ecology Control and Economic Development*, 9–26, 126–160.
117. Boes, "Political Animals," 46–47. On aerial photography and environmental knowledge, see David A. Biggs, "Aerial Photography and its Role in Shifting Colonial Discourse on Peasants and Land Management in Late-Colonial Indochina, 1930–1945," in *Cultivating the Colonies*, ed. Christina Folke Ax, et al., 109–132 and Matthew Dyce, "Canada between the Photograph and the Map: Aerial Photography, Geographical Vision and the State," *Journal of Historical Geography* 39 (January 2013): 69–84.
118. Michael Grzimek and Bernhard Grzimek, "Flamingoes Censused in East Africa by Aerial Photography," *The Journal of Wildlife Management* 24, no. 2 (1960): 215–217.
119. Dyce, "Canada Between the Photograph and the Map," 73–75.
120. Grzimek and Grzimek, "Flamingoes Censused in East Africa," 215–217.
121. Grzimek and Grzimek, "Census of Plains Animals," 31.
122. Grzimek and Grzimek, "Study of the Game," 11.
123. The Grzimeks seemed unaware here that references to pastoralists' inability to create a permanent "homeland" had uncomfortable affinities with anti-Semitic discourses about European Jews as "nomadic" agents of environmental destruction. See Thomas M. Lekan, *Imagining the Nation in Nature: Landscape Preservation and German Identity, 1885–1945* (Cambridge, MA: Harvard University Press, 2004), 141–152.
124. Sewig, *Der Mann, der die Tiere liebte*, 256–257. As Fatima Tobing Rony explains, "goona-goona," was Hollywood slang for scenes of bare-breasted women that censors allowed in ethnographic films of non-Western racial "others": *The Third Eye: Race, Cinema, and Ethnographic Spectacle* (Durham, NC: Duke University Press, 1996), 47–53.
125. Boes, "Political Animals," 47–48; Mary Louise Pratt, *Imperial Eyes: Travel Writing and Transculturation*, 2nd ed. (London: Routledge, 2008).
126. Boes, "Political Animals," 46.
127. Denis Cosgrove, "Contested Global Visions: One-World, Whole-Earth, and the Apollo Space Photographs," *Annals of the Association of American Geographers* 84, no. 2 (1994): 279. On German aerial missions in Africa, see Nina Berman, *Impossible Missions?: German*

Economic, Military, and Humanitarian Efforts in Africa (Lincoln: University of Nebraska Press, 2004), 99–138.

128. Boes, "Political Animals," 50.
129. Boes, "Political Animals," 46.
130. Grzimek and Grzimek, *Serengeti Shall Not Die*, 169.
131. Grzimek and Grzimek, *Serengeti Shall Not Die*, 169.
132. Boes, "Political Animals," 48.
133. Grzimek and Grzimek, *Serengeti Shall Not Die*, 224–225.
134. Grzimek and Grzimek, *Serengeti Shall Not Die*, 224.
135. Shelter, *Imagining Serengeti*, 198–199, 212–217.
136. Feldman and Cronon, *Storied Wilderness*, 149–190.
137. On the visual culture of environmentalism, see Gisela Park, "Our Only World—An American Vision," in *Eco-Images: Historical Views and Political Strategies*, ed. Gisela Parak and Rachel Carson Center (Munich: Rachel Carson Center for Environment and Society), 53–60 and Noël Sturgeon, *Environmentalism in Popular Culture: Gender, Race, Sexuality, and the Politics of the Natural* (Tucson: University of Arizona Press, 2009), 80–102.
138. Grzimek and Grzimek, *Serengeti Shall Not Die*, 37–38.
139. Sinclair, *Serengeti Story*, 52.
140. Grzimek and Grzimek, *Serengeti Shall Not Die*, 89; Turner, *My Serengeti Years*, 32–33.
141. Grzimek and Grzimek, *Serengeti Shall Not Die*, 89.
142. Turner, *My Serengeti Years*, 33.
143. Grzimek and Grzimek, *Serengeti Shall Not Die*, 90–110.
144. Small wonder: the Grzimeks knew about George Steer's indictment of German colonial policies from *Judgment on German Africa* (1939), published during the height of fears that the Hitler regime would try to reclaim African territory but relied on Richard Wichterich's notoriously revisionist *Dr. Carl Peters, der Weg eines Patrioten* (Berlin: Keil, 1934) for their account.
145. Grzimek and Grzimek, *Serengeti Shall Not Die*, 107.
146. Shetler, *Imagining Serengeti*, 31–40, 101–237.
147. Turner, *My Serengeti Years*, 27.
148. Grzimek and Grzimek, *Serengeti Shall Not Die*, 56–57. On the Siedentopfs and the German colonial period, see Fosbrooke, *Eighth Wonder*, 25–28 and Gissibl, *Nature of German Imperialism*, 3–8.
149. Neumann, *Imposing Wilderness*, 133.
150. Kjekshus, *Ecology Control and Economic Development*, 74–75.
151. Gissibl, *Nature of German Imperialism*, 5–6.
152. Gissibl, *Nature of German Imperialism*, 141–177; 278–285.
153. Kjekshus, *Ecology Control and Economic Development*, 75.
154. Grzimek and Grzimek, *Serengeti Shall Not Die*, 13.
155. Jens Ivo Engels, "'Hohe Zeit' und 'dicker Strich': Vergangenheitsdeutung und Bewahrung im westdeutschen Naturschutz nach dem Zweiten Weltkrieg," 262–304 and Stefan Körner, "Kontinuum und Bruch: Die Transformation des naturschützerischen Aufgabenverständnisses nach dem Zweiten Weltkrieg," 405–434, in *Naturschutz und Nationalsozialismus*, ed. Joachim Radkau and Frank Uekötter (Frankfurt: Campus, 2003).
156. Grzimek and Grzimek, *Serengeti Shall Not Die*, 240.
157. On this beautiful scene, see Boes, "Political Animals," 51–53.
158. Boes, "Political Animals," 52.
159. Cosgrove, "Contested Global Visions," 271.
160. UNESCO has good online documentation of its efforts in the Abu Simbel campaign, which lasted from 1960 to 1980. See "Abu Simbel: The campaign that revolutionized the international approach to safeguarding heritage," at http://en.unesco.org/70years/abu_simbel_safeguarding_heritage. Accessed July 1, 2017.
161. Boes, "Political Animals," 54–55. Later, as Bernhard flew regularly to Africa, his glances out the window at Aswan served as a reminder of the need for Africans to avoid large dam-building projects. See Grzimek, *Auf den Mensch gekommen*, 365.

162. Grzimek, *Auf den Mensch gekommen,* 366–367.

163. Grzimek and Grzimek, *Serengeti Shall Not Die,* 170.

164. Grzimek and Grzimek, *Serengeti Shall Not Die,* 173.

165. Grzimek and Grzimek, *Serengeti Shall Not Die,* 172–173, emphasis in the original.

166. Cited in Grzimek and Grzimek, *Serengeti Shall Not Die,* 173.

167. Hayes, *Last Place on Earth,* 101.

168. Grzimek and Grzimek, *Serengeti Shall Not Die,* 240.

169. Bernhard Grzimek, "Wie steht es jetzt um die Nationalparke Afrikas," *Schweizer Monatshefte* (July 1961): 472.

170. On this point, see Mitman, *Reel Nature,* 207–208; Beinart, "Renaturing of African Animals," 147–167; Kenneth M. Cameron, *Africa on Film: Beyond Black and White* (New York: Continuum, 1994).

171. Grzimek and Grzimek, *Serengeti Shall Not Die,* 234.

172. Louis Turner, *The Golden Hordes: International Tourism and the Pleasure Periphery* (New York: St. Martin's Press, 1976).

173. Rudy Koshar, "'What Ought to Be Seen': Tourists' Guidebooks and National Identities in Modern Germany and Europe," *Journal of Contemporary History* 33, no. 3 (1998): 323–340; Ben Gardner, *Selling the Serengeti,* 101–123.

174. Sewig, *Der Mann, der die Tiere liebte,* 260 and Lee M. Talbot and D. R. M. Stewart, "First Wildlife Census of the Entire Serengeti-Mara Region, East Africa," *The Journal of Wildlife Management* 28, no. 4 (1964): 815–827.

175. Sinclair, *Serengeti Story,* 4.

Chapter 5

1. Bernhard Grzimek and Michael Grzimek, *Serengeti Shall Not Die,* trans. E. L. Rewald and D. Rewald (New York: E. P. Dutton, 1961), 251–253.

2. On Maasai stereotypes, see Dorothy Louise Hodgson, *Once Intrepid Warriors: Gender, Ethnicity, and the Cultural Politics of Maasai Development* (Bloomington: Indiana University Press, 2001), 1–7 and Thomas Spear and Richard Waller, eds., *Being Maasai: Ethnicity and Identity in East Africa* (Athens: Ohio University Press, 1993), 1–9.

3. Grzimek and Grzimek, *Serengeti Shall Not Die,* 254.

4. Grzimek and Grzimek, *Serengeti Shall Not Die,* 255.

5. Harold T. P. Hayes, *The Last Place on Earth* (New York: Stein and Day, 1977), 25–26.

6. W. H. Pearsall, *Report on an Ecological Survey of the Serengeti National Park, Tanganyika: November and December 1956* (London: The Fauna Preservation Society, 1957), 13.

7. Grzimek and Grzimek, *Serengeti Shall Not Die,* 246.

8. Grzimek and Grzimek, *Serengeti Shall Not Die,* 246.

9. Robin S. Reid, *Savannas of Our Birth: People, Wildlife, and Change in East Africa* (Berkeley: University of California Press, 2012), 50–61.

10. Chris Conte has described this dichotomy in terms of "insiders" who receive their knowledge of landscapes from ancestors via complex processes of social memory and "outsiders"— bureaucrats, settlers and scientists—who understand it in abstract terms. See Christopher A. Conte, *Highland Sanctuary: Environmental History in Tanzania's Usambara Mountains* (Athens: Ohio University Press, 2004), 10–14.

11. Roderick P. Neumann, "Ways of Seeing Africa: Colonial Recasting of African Society and Landscape in Serengeti National Park," *Ecumene* 2, no. 2 (1995): 159–160.

12. The Serengeti controversies are well documented in the scholarly literature, but the Grzimeks' participation in both the late colonial and postcolonial stories of the region has not received extensive attention thus far. For the British colonial history, see Myles Turner, *My Serengeti Years: The Memoirs of an African Game Warden* (New York: W.W. Norton, 1988), 39–45; Jonathan S. Adams and Thomas O. McShane, *The Myth of Wild Africa: Conservation without Illusion* (New York: W.W. Norton, 1992), 51–54; Roderick P. Neumann, *Imposing Wilderness: Struggles over Livelihood and Nature Preservation in Africa* (Berkeley: University of California Press, 1998), 129–139; Jan Bender Shetler, *Imagining Serengeti: A History of Landscape Memory in Tanzania from Earliest Times to the Present* (Athens: Ohio University Press, 2007), 201–217.

13. The relationship between indirect rule and the evolution of local authority in Tanganyika is extensive and cannot be cited here in detail. Historiographical debates center on the authority of "chiefs" in various regions, the extent to which such authorities operated as or competed with other colonial district administration, and in the wake of Mahmood Mamdani's work, the long-term effect of indirect rule on Tanganyikan and other state building projects. My goal in this chapter is more modest: to follow Sara Berry's insights about how notions of customary tenure intersected with ethnographic imaginaries that linked land use to particular understanding of rural African lifeways. On indirect rule and its migration from British West Africa to East Africa, see Frederick Lugard, *The Dual Mandate in British Tropical Africa*, a 1922 essay reprinted by Routledge in 2014 and *Representative Forms of Government and "Indirect Rule" in British Africa* (Edinburgh: Blackwood, 1928); Sara Berry, *No Condition Is Permanent: The Social Dynamics of Agrarian Change in Sub-Saharan Africa* (Madison, WI: University of Wisconsin Press, 1993); Mahmood Mamdani, *Citizen and Subject: Contemporary Africa and the Legacy of Late Colonialism* (Princeton, NJ: Princeton University Press, 1996); Andreas Eckert, *Herrschen und Verwalten: Afrikanische Bürokraten, Staatliche Ordnung und Politik in Tanzania, 1920–1970* (Munich: Oldenbourg, 2007).
14. Historical Section of the Foreign Office, *German African Possessions* (New York: Greenwood Press, 1920), 34–36; Sara Berry, "Debating the Land Question in Africa," *Comparative Studies in Society and History* 44, No. 4 (October 2002): 638–668.
15. I emphasize "customary land tenure" here because the 1928 Land Ordinance for Tanganyika did not provide fixed title, leaving rural Africans vulnerable to alienation without legal recourse. See Shetler, *Imagining Serengeti*, 220.
16. Hayes, *Last Place on Earth*, 26.
17. On the application of Horst Rittel's formulation to the topics in this chapter, see *Wicked Environmental Problems: Managing Uncertainty and Conflict* (Washington, DC: Island Press, 2011). This chapter underscores the robust and unexpected material agencies of non-human factors in shaping the Serengeti controversy. On such an approach, see Timothy Mitchell, *Rule of Experts: Egypt, Techno-Politics, Modernity* (Berkeley: University of California Press, 2009), especially 19–54.
18. Narrated in Ben Gardner, *Selling the Serengeti: The Cultural Politics of Safari Tourism* (Athens: University of Georgia Press, 2016), 37–38; Shetler, *Imagining Serengeti*, 185–199.
19. Barclay Leechman, Chairman of the Serengeti Board of Trustees, "Human Problems of the Serengeti," *Tanganyika Standard*, March 16, 1954; *Report of the Serengeti Committee of Enquiry* (Dar es Salaam: Government Printer, 1957), 5–7 in Henry A. Fosbrooke Collection (HFC), University of Dar es Salaam Library, East Africana collection.
20. United Nations Visiting Mission to Trust Territories, 1960, *Report on Tanganyika*, Supplement no. 2 (New York: Trusteeship Council, 1960), 23–24.
21. Grzimek and Grzimek, "A Study of the Game of the Serengeti Plains," *Zeitschrift für Säugetierkunde*, 25 (1960): 10.
22. *Report of the Serengeti Committee of Enquiry*, 6.
23. Grzimek and Grzimek, "Study of the Game," 10–11. Even the Hingston report indicated that the Maasai could "live amicably amongst the game." See Raymond Bonner, *At the Hand of Man: Peril and Hope for Africa's Wildlife* (New York: Vintage, 1993), 170.
24. Shetler, *Imagining the Serengeti*, 208.
25. Cited in Turner, *My Serengeti Years*, 40.
26. Cited in Henry Fosbrooke, *Ngorongoro: The Eighth Wonder* (London: Deutsch, 1972), 196.
27. Pearsall, *Ecological Survey of the Serengeti National Park*, 11–12.
28. See Memorandum of Board of Trustees from Meeting at Ngorongoro, February 16 to 20, 1954, p. 3 in Tanzania National Archives (TNA) H15: 270/B18/Part I: Serengeti Board of Trustees; Tanganyika and Kenya Wild Life Societies, "Comments on the Tanganyika Government's White Paper Entitled 'Serengeti Park' (1957)" in HFC.
29. Neumann, "Ways of Seeing Africa," 161.
30. Pearsall, *Ecological Survey of the Serengeti National Park*, 10; Shetler, *Imagining Serengeti* 207.
31. Shetler, *Imagining Serengeti*, 182–183.
32. Elizabeth Garland, "State of Nature: Colonial Power, Neoliberal Capital, and Wildlife Management in Tanzania" (PhD diss., University of Chicago, 2006), 109–116.
33. Neumann, *Imposing Wilderness*, 132.

34. Shetler, *Imagining Serengeti*, 182.
35. "Letter from Game Warden in Arusha to Chief Secretary in Dar es Salaam regarding Issuance of Free Game Licences to Native Hunters," May 17, 1932, in TNA H15/273/Tanganyika Secretariat.
36. Cited in Neumann, "Ways of Seeing Africa," 156.
37. Roderick P. Neumann, "The Postwar Conservation Boom in British Colonial Africa," *Environmental History* 7, no. 2 (January 2002): 25–28, 30.
38. Shelter, *Imagining Serengeti*, 207; George Petrides, *Report: Kenya's Wild-Life Resources and the National Parks* (Nairobi: Trustees of the Royal National Parks of Kenya, 1955), 21–23.
39. Grzimek and Grzimek, "Study of the Game," 10.
40. Turner, *My Serengeti Years*, 41–42.
41. Grzimek and Grzimek, *Serengeti Shall Not Die*, 246.
42. Neumann, "Ways of Seeing Africa," 160.
43. Pearsall, *Ecological Survey of the Serengeti National Park*, 12.
44. Grzimek and Grzimek, "Study of the Game," 9.
45. Neumann, *Imposing Wilderness*, 131.
46. On the composition of the board, see "Tanganyika National Park Appointment of Trustees," in TNA H15: 273/MLSW.575; Thaddeus Sunseri, "'Every African a Nationalist': Scientific Forestry and Forest Nationalism in Colonial Tanzania," *Comparative Studies in Society and History* 49, no. 4 (October 2007): 888.
47. Barclay Leechman, Chairman of the Serengeti Board of Trustees, "The Administration of the Serengeti," *Tanganyika Standard*, March 17, 1954.
48. Fosbrooke, *Eighth Wonder*, 49–72.
49. Shetler, *Imagining Serengeti*, 35.
50. Fosbrooke, *Eighth Wonder*, 174–218; Turner, *My Serengeti Years*, 42–43.
51. Grzimek and Grzimek, "Study of the Game," 5. See I. Masih et al., "A Review of Droughts on the African Continent: A Geospatial and Long-Term Perspective," *Hydrology and Earth System Sciences* 18, no. 9 (2014): 3635–3649.
52. Grzimek and Grzimek, "Study of the Game," 11.
53. Reid, *Savannas of our Birth*, 56; J. T. Mwaikusa, "Community Rights and Land Use Policies in Tanzania: The Case of Pastoral Communities," *Journal of African Law* 37, no. 2 (1993): 144–147.
54. On the transference of dustbowl fears to East Africa, see Daniel Brockington and Katherine Homewood, "Wildlife, Pastoralists and Science: Debates Concerning Mkomazi Game Reserve in Tanzania," in *The Lie of the Land: Challenging Received Wisdom on the African Environment*, ed. Melissa Leach and Robin Mearns (Portsmouth, NH: Heinemann, 1996), 91–104.
55. Grzimek and Grzimek, "Study of the Game," 11; See, for example, "Letter from J.S. Groome, Chief Conservator of Forests, to Secretariat for Agriculture and Natural Resources," January 29, 1954, in TNA H15: 270/B18/1.
56. Grzimek and Grzimek, "Study of the Game," 12.
57. Grzimek and Grzimek, "Study of the Game," 11.
58. Neumann, *Imposing Wilderness*, 133.
59. Cited in Grzimek and Grzimek, *Serengeti Shall Not Die*, 256.
60. Neumann, *Imposing Wilderness*, 131.
61. Leechman, "The Administration of the Serengeti;" "Memorandum: Joint Discussion of Board of Management held at Ngorongoro, February 16, 1954," in TNA H15: 270/B18/Part I: Serengeti Board of Trustees.
62. Pearsall, *Ecological Survey of the Serengeti National Park*, 47.
63. Barclay Leechman, "What Is the Serengeti?," *Tanganyika Standard*, March 15, 1954.
64. Grzimek and Grzimek, "Study of the Game," 4.
65. Pearsall, *Ecological Survey of the Serengeti National Park*, 4; "Report of the Chairman of the Board of Management of Serengeti National Park" for 1952 in TNA H15: 270/B18/Part I: Serengeti Board of Trustees.
66. Pearsall, *Ecological Survey of the Serengeti National Park*, 52.

67. See Petrides, *Report: Kenya's Wild-Life Resources*, 1–5. On the EATTA, see Joseph Ouma, *Evolution of Tourism in East Africa (1900–2000)* (Nairobi: East African Literature Bureau, 1970), 9–10.

68. Neumann, "Postwar Conservation Boom," 35–36. On the South African experience, see Shirley Brooks, "Images of 'Wild Africa': Nature Tourism and the (Re)Creation of Hluhluwe Game Reserve, 1930–1945," *Journal of Historical Geography* 31, no. 2 (April 2005): 220–240

69. On tourism and empire, see John M. Mackenzie, "Empires of Travel: British Guidebooks and Cultural Imperialism in the Nineteenth and Twentieth Centuries," in *Histories of Tourism: Representation, Identity, and Conflict*, ed. John K. Walton (Clevedon, UK: Channel View Publications, 2005), 19–39. See also the roundtable on "Tourism and Empire" in the *Journal of Tourism History*, August 2015.

70. William Denis Battershill, *The Tanganyika Guide* (Letchworth, UK: Garden City Press, 1948).

71. Neumann, "Postwar Conservation Boom," 36.

72. Neumann, "Postwar Conservation Boom," 37.

73. Cited in Shetler, *Imagining Serengeti*, 208.

74. Reid, *Savannas of Our Birth*, 23–24.

75. Leechman, "Human Problems of the Serengeti," *Tanganyika Standard*, March 16, 1954.

76. John G. Galaty, "Maasai Expansion and the New East African Pastoralism," in *Being Maasai*, ed. Spear and Waller, 61–86.

77. Leechman, "Human Problems of the Serengeti."

78. Turner, *My Serengeti Years*, 40–42.

79. Hodgson, *Once Intrepid Warriors*, 36; David Collett, "Pastoralists and Wildlife: Image and Reality in Kenya Maasailand," in *Conservation in Africa: People, Policies, and Practice*, ed. David Anderson and Richard Grove (New York: Cambridge University Press, 1987), 138–139.

80. Pearsall, *Ecological Survey of the Serengeti National Park*, 10–11.

81. See "Letter from Henry Fosbrooke to Provincial Commissioner in Arusha," April 24, 1956 in TNA: 544/G1/II Game, 1956–1960, Mara Regime, Tarime or North Mara. Fosbrooke developed this perspective further in numerous reports and memorandum, where he decried the tendency to blame Maasai for long-term changes that stemmed from colonial land alienations and climate changes that had little to do with pastoralism. See Fosbrooke, *Eighth Wonder*, 156–173.

82. Fosbrooke, *Eighth Wonder*, 195; Brockington and Homewood, "Wildlife, Pastoralists, and Science," 96.

83. Berry, "Debating the Land Question in Africa," 644–645; Peter Rogers, "History and Governance in the Ngorongoro Conservation Area, Tanzania, 1959–1966," *Global Environment* 2, no. 4 (2009): 86.

84. Grzimek and Grzimek, *Serengeti Shall Not Die*, 263.

85. Grzimek and Grzimek, "Study of the Game," 10–11.

86. Such stereotypes came from Lugard, Joseph Thomson and Karl Peters, see Neumann, "Ways of Seeing Africa," 159.

87. Mwaikusa, "Community Rights," 144–147; Reid, *Savannas of our Birth*, 111.

88. G. L. Steer, *Judgment on German Africa* (London: Hodder and Stoughton, 1939), 239–240; Reid, *Savannas of Our Birth*, 110–111.

89. Hodgson, *Once Intrepid Warriors*, 11–16, 50–67. On the contours of and contestations over "Maasailand," see J. E. G. Sutton, "Becoming Maasailand," 38–60, and John G. Galaty, "Maasai Expansion and the New East African Pastoralism," in *Being Maasai*, ed. Spear and Waller, 61–86.

90. Grzimek and Grzimek, *Serengeti Shall Not Die*, 251; David Collett, "Pastoralists and Wildlife: Image and Reality in Kenya Maasailand," in *Conservation in Africa*, eds. Anderson and Grove, 129–148

91. Spear, "Being 'Maasai,' but not 'People of the Cattle': Arusha Agricultural Maasai in the Nineteenth Century," in *Being Maasai*, ed. Spear and Waller, 120–136. See also Thomas Spear, *Mountain Farmers: Moral Economies of Land and Agricultural Development in Arusha and Meru* (Oxford: James Curry, 1997).

92. Hodgson, *Once Intrepid Warriors*, 50–52. My depiction here only scratches the surface of Hodgson's intricate depiction of the complexities of a social organization based on age-class sets and gender roles.

93. Hodgson, *Once Intrepid Warriors*, 57–58.

94. Hodgson, *Once Intrepid Warriors*, 51–55. There are myriad examples of British officials restricting rural Africans' trade under the assumption that their economies were strictly localized, crushing the very market capacities they believed Africans lacked. See James L. Giblin, *The Politics of Environmental Control in Northeastern Tanzania: 1840–1940* (Philadelphia: University of Pennsylvania Press, 1992).

95. Reid, *Savannas of Our Birth People*, 111–112; David Campbell, "Land as Ours, Land as Mine: Economic, Political, and Ecological Marginalization in Kajiado District," in *Being Maasai*, ed. Spear and Waller, 260.

96. Mwaikusa, "Community Rights," 145.

97. Hodgson, *Once Intrepid Warriors*, 91; Brockington and Homewood, "Wildlife, Pastoralists and Science," 94. On Maasai "modernization," see also Peter Rigby, *Cattle, Capitalism, and Class: Ilparakuyo Maasai Transformations* (Philadelphia: Temple University Press, 1992).

98. Reid, *Savannas of our Birth*, 127–128. The classical statement of this so-called cattle complex was Melville Herskovits, *The Cattle Complex in East Africa* (New York: Cambridge University Press, 1927). For a contrasting view see Mwaikusa, "Community Rights," 144–163.

99. Hodgson, *Once Intrepid Warriors*, 100–126. Hodgson emphasizes that Maasai welcomed development schemes that provided water and health benefits—but not the draconian quarantine measures demanded by colonial veterinary experts: see 74–87. See also Elliot Fratkin, "Pastoralism: Governance and Development Issues," *Annual Review of Anthropology*, 26 (1997): 235–261 and Lotte Hughes, "Rough Time in Paradise: Claims, Blames and Memory Making around Some Protected Areas in Kenya," *Conservation and Society* 5, no. 3 (2007): 307–330. Such selective adoption of "modern" economic practices contrasts with Marxist theories of underdevelopment. See, for example, Göran Hydén, *Beyond Ujamaa in Tanzania: Underdevelopment and an Uncaptured Peasantry* (London: Heinemann, 1985).

100. Brockington and Homewood, "Wildlife, Pastoralists and Science," 95–96.

101. Grzimek and Grzimek, *Serengeti Shall Not Die*, 252.

102. Grzimek and Grzimek, *Serengeti Shall Not Die*, 267.

103. Daniel R. Smith, "Independence for Tanganyika: An Analysis of the Political Developments Which Led to the Emancipation of the Trust Territory, 1946–1961" (PhD diss., St. John's University, 1974), 45–54; Ullrich Lohrmann, *Voices from Tanganyika: Great Britain, the United Nations and the Decolonization of a Trust Territory, 1946–1961* (Berlin: Global Book Marketing, 2007).

104. Neumann, "Postwar Conservation Boom," 28–29; Sunseri, "'Every African a Nationalist'," 896–897; Garland, "State of Nature," 106–108.

105. Hodgson, *Once Intrepid Warriors*, 72–92, 100–138.

106. Hayes, *Last Place on Earth*, 23.

107. Adams and McShane, *Myth of Wild Africa*, 49.

108. Fosbrooke, *Eighth Wonder*, 65–70; Adams and McShane, *Myth of Wild Africa*, 44. More recent literature assumes that a variety of vernacular "management" schemes are compatible with the sustainability of rangeland environments. See Katherine Homewood and W. A. Rodgers, "Pastoralism, Conservation and the Overgrazing Controversy," in *Conservation in Africa*, ed. Anderson and Grove, 111–128 and *Maasailand Ecologies: Pastoralist Development and Wildlife Conservation in Ngorongoro, Tanzania* (Cambridge, UK: Cambridge University Press, 1991), 35–55.

109. Neumann, *Imposing Wilderness*, 135–139.

110. Spear, *Mountain Farmers*, 89; 209–235; Simeon Mesaki, "Recapping the Meru Land Case, Tanzania," *Global Journal of Human Social Sciences Economics*, 13. no. 1 (2013): 19–22.

111. Nkura Kirilo Japhet and Earle Edward Seaton, *The Meru Land Case* (Nairobi: East African Pub. House, 1967).

112. Detailed in Spear, *Mountain Farmers*, 226–230.

113. United Nations and General Assembly, *Report of the Trusteeship Council A/2342* (New York: General Assembly, United Nations, 1952); Steven Feierman, *Peasant*

Intellectuals: History and Anthropology in Tanzania (Madison: University of Wisconsin Press, 1990), 167–180; Pamela Maack, "'We Don't Want Terraces!': Protest and Identity under the Uluguru Land Usage Scheme," in *Custodians of the Land: Ecology and Culture in the History of Tanzania*, ed. Gregory H. Maddox (London: Currey, 2006), 152–169.

114. Mesaki, "Recapping the Meru Land Case," 19–22; Illiffe, *Modern History of Tanganyika*, 507–520.

115. Cited in Neumann, "Ways of Seeing Africa," 162.

116. Garland, "State of Nature," 116–117.

117. Neumann, "Ways of Seeing Africa," 161–163; Garland, "State of Nature," 113.

118. On forests and everyday acts of resistance, see Sunseri, "'Every African a Nationalist,'" 889–890, 905–910.

119. See, for example, "Letter from J.S. Groome, Chief Conservator of Forests, to Secretariat for Agriculture and Natural Resources," January 29, 1954 and "Letter from F.W. Champion, Provincial Forestry Officer in Northern Province in Moshi, to Chief Conservator Groome," October 21, 1953, in TNA H15: 270/B18/Part I: Serengeti Board of Trustees.

120. Turner, *My Serengeti Years*, 40.

121. Pearsall, *Ecological Survey of the Serengeti National Park*, 45.

122. Fosbrooke, *Eighth Wonder*, 55–57; Neumann, "Ways of Seeing Africa," 160–161.

123. Adams and McShane, *Myth of Wild Africa*, 48.

124. Fosbrooke, *Eighth Wonder*, 68.

125. Reid, *Savannas of our Birth*, 137–138.

126. Pearsall, *Ecological Survey of the Serengeti National Park*, 12.

127. See Pearsall, *Ecological Survey of the Serengeti National Park*, 11–12; Brockington and Homewood, "Wildlife, Pastoralists and Science," 97.

128. Mwaikusa, "Community Rights," 145–146.

129. Pearsall, *Ecological Survey of the Serengeti National Park*, 13.

130. Historical Section of the Foreign Office, *German African Possessions*, 73; Mwaikusa, "Community Rights," 145–147, 157–161. See also Ernest Chiwanga, "Indigenous Knowledge Systems in Environmental Management and Sustainable Development: The Case of the Maasai," in *Sustainable Development and the Environment in Tanzania: Issues, Experiences and Policy Responses*, ed. Adalgot A. Komba (Dar es Salaam: Organisation for Social Science Research in Eastern and Southern Africa, Tanzania Chapter, 2006), 143–152.

131. Peter D. Little and David W. Brokensha, "Local Institutions, Tenure, and Resource Management in East Africa," in *Conservation in Africa*, ed. Anderson and Grove, 193–209.

132. Brockington and Homewood, "Wildlife, Pastoralists and Science," 96; Reid, *Savannas of Our Birth*, 146–152.

133. Recent ecological research has confirmed that Serengeti resilience depends on regular disturbances fostered by mixed wild-domesticate ecologies. See Anthony R. E. Sinclair et al., *Serengeti IV: Sustaining Biodiversity in a Coupled Human-Natural System* (Chicago: University of Chicago Press, 2015).

134. "Extracts from a Diary Report Submitted by C.L. Bancroft, Assistant Conservator of Forests," based on a 1951 visit to Ngorongoro area in TNA 270/B18/Part I: Serengeti Board of Trustees.

135. "Extracts from a Diary Report Submitted by C.L. Bancroft," TNA 270/B18/Part I: Serengeti Board of Trustees.

136. "Letter from F.W. Champion, Provincial Forestry Officer in Northern Province in Moshi, to Chief Conservator Groome," October 21, 1953, in TNA H 15: 270/B18/Part I: Serengeti Board of Trustees, 3.

137. "Letter from J.E.F. Wilkins to the Board of Trustees," February 16, 1954, 1 in TNA H15: 270/B18/Part I: Serengeti Board of Trustees, 1.

138. "Letter from J.E.F. Wilkins to the Board of Trustees," February 16, 1954, 1 and "Memorandum of Board of Trustees from Meeting at Ngorongoro," February 16–20, 1954.

139. "Letter from F.W. Champion, Provincial Forestry Officer to Chief Conservator Groome," November 5, 1952, in TNA H 15: 270/B18/Part I: Serengeti Board of Trustees.

140. "Letter from E.F. Twinning in Government House to Chairman of the National Parks in Tanganyika," November 25, 1953, in TNA H 15: 270/B18/Part I: Serengeti Board of Trustees.

141. Legislative Council of Tanganyika, Sessional Paper No. 1 and "Proposals for Reconstituting the Serengeti National Park," Government Paper No. 5 (Dar es Salaam: Government Printer, 1956), in HFC.

142. *Report of the Serengeti Committee of Enquiry*, 7.

143. "Letter from J.E.F. Wilkins to the Board of Trustees," February 16, 1954, 2. Government ethnographers and sociologists such as Philip H. Guliver supported the notion that non-customary inter-marriage and cultural exchange between the Maasai and Arusha had led to the presence of cultivators in the park. See his 1957 report "A History of Relations between the Arusha and the Masai," in HFC.

144. "Joint Discussion Board of Management Held at Ngorongoro," February 19, 1954 in TNA H15: 270/B18/Part I: Serengeti Board of Trustees.

145. Historical Section of the Foreign Office, *German African Possessions*, 16–17.

146. Leechman, "Human Problems of the Serengeti."

147. Guliver, "History of Relations," 3–9.

148. Spear, *Mountain Farmers*, 39–59. Such patterns of exchange, intermarriage, and economic dependency between farmers and pastoralists also characterized the Usambara mountain cultures southeast of the Serengeti region. See Conte, *Highland Sanctuary*, 17–31.

149. Spear, *Being Maasai*, 6.

150. Spear, "Being 'Maasai,' but not 'People of the Cattle,'" 120–136 and *Mountain Farmers*, chaps. 2–3.

151. Turner, *My Serengeti Years*, 42; Shetler, *Imagining Serengeti*, 208.

152. Leechman, "Human Problems of the Serengeti;" H. S. Grant, *Report on the Human Habitation of the Serengeti National Park, 1954*, Tanganyika National Parks (typewritten), in HFC.

153. "Letter from J.E.F. Wilkins to the Board of Trustees," February 16, 1954, 1.

154. Neumann, *Imposing Wilderness*, 53–96.

155. Spear, *Mountain Farmers*, 87–91.

156. Steer, *Judgment on German Africa*, 255–256.

157. Cited in Mesaki, "Recapping the Meru Land Case," 18–19. On the movement onto the plains and into the Ngorongoro highlands, see Spear, *Mountain Farmers*, 146–157.

158. "Minutes of the Sixth Meeting of the Board of Trustees," September 29, 1953, in TNA H15: 270/B18/Part I: Serengeti Board of Trustees.

159. Turner, *My Serengeti Years*, 42.

160. Leechman, "The National Park and the Public," *Tanganyika Standard*, March 18, 1954.

161. Shetler, *Imagining Serengeti*, 207–210.

162. Turner, *My Serengeti Years*, 42.

163. "Letter from H.S.L. Grant, District Officer in Ngorongoro to W. J. Eggeline, Conservator of Forests for Morogoro," March 2, 1954, in TNA H15: 270/B18/Part I: Serengeti Board of Trustees.

164. "Letter from H.S.L. Grant to W.J. Eggeline," March 2, 1954.

165. Neumann, "Ways of Seeing Africa," 159.

166. Neumann, *Imposing Wilderness*, 134.

167. Grzimek and Grzimek, *Serengeti Shall Not Die*, 248.

168. Grzimek and Grzimek, "Study of the Game," 11.

169. Grzimek and Grzimek, *Serengeti Shall Not Die*, 261.

170. Grzimek and Grzimek, *Serengeti Shall Not Die*, 256.

171. Bonner, *At the Hand of Man*, 172–173: Legislative Council of Tanganyika, Sessional Paper No. 1 and "Proposals for Reconstituting the Serengeti National Park," Government paper No. 5.

172. Quoted in Turner, *My Serengeti Years*, 43.

173. Legislative Council of Tanganyika, Sessional Paper No. 1.

174. Shetler, *Imagining Serengeti*, 208.

175. There is unfortunately no detailed map of this proposed division, only rough sketches found in the Tanganyika and Kenya Wildlife Societies' letter and in Hayes, *Last Place on Earth*, 26–27.

176. Grzimek and Grzimek, "Study of the Game," 13. Tanganyika and Kenya Wild Life Societies, "Comments on the Tanganyika Government's White Paper Entitled 'Serengeti Park,'" 1.

177. Turner, *My Serengeti Years*, 43–44.
178. Shelter, *Imagining Serengeti*, 209.
179. Tanganyika and Kenya Wild Life Societies, "Comments on the Tanganyika Government's White Paper," 2.
180. Tanganyika and Kenya Wild Life Societies, "Comments on the Tanganyika Government's White Paper," 3.
181. Shetler, *Imagining Serengeti*, 209.
182. Russell Arundel, "Petition in Behalf of the American Nature Conservancy, the National Parks Association, the Wilderness Society, among others," in FPS Box Af/X1/NP. Many thanks to Roderick Neumann for sharing this source.
183. Arundel, "Petition in Behalf of the American Nature Conservancy," 1–2.
184. Arundel, "Petition in Behalf of the American Nature Conservancy," 5.
185. Arundel, "Petition in Behalf of the American Nature Conservancy," 5–7.
186. Arundel, "Petition in Behalf of the American Nature Conservancy," 2–7.
187. Arundel, "Petition in Behalf of the American Nature Conservancy," 2–7.
188. Arundel, "Petition in Behalf of the American Nature Conservancy," 7.
189. Turner, *My Serengeti Years*, 47.
190. Arundel, "Petition in Behalf of the American Nature Conservancy," 2–3.
191. Garland, "State of Nature," 119–120.
192. Pearsall, *Ecological Survey of the Serengeti National Park*, 3–4, 24–25, 42–46.
193. Pearsall, *Ecological Survey of the Serengeti National Park*, 24–25.
194. *Report of the Serengeti Committee of Enquiry*, 16–37 .
195. Anthony Sinclair, *Serengeti Story: Life and Science in the World's Greatest Wildlife Region* (Oxford: Oxford University Press), 63.
196. Turner, *My Serengeti Years*, 47.
197. Turner, *My Serengeti Years*, 50.
198. Cited in Bonner, *At the Hand of Man*, 178 and "Agreement by the Maasai to Vacate the Western Serengeti, 21 April 1958," cited in Rogers, "History and Governance in the Ngorongoro Conservation Area," 89.
199. Cited in Bonner, *At the Hand of Man*, 179.
200. Grzimek and Grzimek, *Serengeti Shall Not Die*, 256.
201. Cited in Gardner, *Selling the Serengeti*, 41.
202. "New Game Park will be Empty," *Tanganyika Standard*, October 24, 1958.
203. Grzimek, *Serengeti Shall Not Die*, 225.
204. Jeremy Swift, "Desertification: Narratives, Winners, and Losers," in *Lie of the Land*, ed. Leach and Mearns, 75, 82–83.
205. Grzimek's global narrative of desertification had striking continuities with American conservationist George Perkins Marsh; see Karl Jacoby, *Crimes against Nature: Squatters, Poachers, Thieves, and the Hidden History of American Conservation* (New York: Cambridge University Press, 2001), 14–15.
206. Shetler, *Imagining Serengeti*, 205–211.
207. Homewood and Rodgers, *Maasailand Ecology*, 111.
208. On the "trickster" quality of nature, see Donna Haraway, "Situated Knowledges: The Science Question in Feminism and the Privilege of Partial Perspective," *Feminist Studies* 14, no. 3 (1988): 579–580.

Chapter 6

1. Bernhard Grzimek, *Auch Nashörner Gehören Allen Menschen: Kämpfe um die Tierwelt Afrikas* (Berlin: Ullstein, 1962), 139–140; Claudia Sewig, *Der Mann, der die Tiere liebte: Bernhard Grzimek: Biografie* (Bergisch Gladbach: Lübbe, 2009), 263–264.
2. Bernhard Grzimek, *Rhinos Belong to Everybody*, trans. Oliver Coburn (New York: Hill and Wang, 1962), 173–175. Grzimek reported this meeting to the West German Consul General in Nairobi, Herbert von Stackelberg, February 15, 1961, in Politisches Archiv des Auswärtigen Amts (PAAA): Michael Grzimek Memorial Laboratory.
3. Grzimek, *Rhinos Belong to Everybody*, 174.

4. The notion of the Decade of Development comes from a 1961 United Nations speech by US President John F. Kennedy. Since then an enormous literature in the social sciences has criticized the Eurocentric hubris and uneven outcomes of such projects. See Frederick Cooper, *Colonialism in Question: Theory, Knowledge, History* (Berkeley: University of California Press, 2010) and Arturo Escobar, *Encountering Development: The Making and Unmaking of the Third World* (Princeton, NJ: Princeton University Press, 1995).

5. Gregg Mitman, *Reel Nature: America's Romance with Wildlife on Film*. 2nd ed. (Seattle: University of Washington Press, 2009), 191–195.

6. Harold T. P. Hayes, *The Last Place on Earth* (New York: Stein and Day, 1977), 101. On the hope for a tourist-led take off in East Africa, see Klaus Frentrup, *Die Ökonomische Bedeutung des Internationalen Tourismus für die Entwicklungsländer* (Hamburg: Deutsches Übersee-Institut, 1969). On wilderness and tourism, see Roderick Nash, *Wilderness and the American Mind*, 4th ed. (New Haven, CT: Yale University Press, 2001), 343–347 and Anna-Katharina Wöbse, "Tourismus und Naturschutz—die international Dimension einer schwierigen Beziehung," in *"Wenn sich alle in der Natur erholen, wo erholt sich dann die Natur?": Naturschutz, Freizeitnutzung, Erholungsvorsorge und Sport—gestern, heute, morgen*, ed. Hans-Werner Frohn, Jürgen Rosebrock, Friedemann Schmoll (Bonn-Bad Godesberg: Bundesamt für Naturschutz, 2009), 185–206.

7. "Letter from Herbert von Stackelberg to Grzimek," February 12, 1960, in PAAA: Michael Grzimek Memorial Lab.

8. Cited in Grzimek, *Rhinos Belong to Everybody*, 174.

9. Bernhard Grzimek, *Auf den Mensch gekommen: Erfahrungen mit Leuten* (Munich: C. Bertelsmann, 1974), 332.

10. Sewig, *Der Mann, der die Tiere liebte*, 264.

11. Gerald G. Watterson, UNESCO, and FAO, *Conservation of Nature and Natural Resources in Modern African States: Report of a Symposium Organized by CCTA and IUCN and Held under the Auspices of FAO and UNESCO at Arusha, Tanganyika, September* (Morges, Switzerland: IUCN, 1963). Many observers do not believe that Nyerere wrote the speech but rather an ad agency hired by the World Wildlife Fund. See Raymond Bonner, *At the Hand of Man: Peril and Hope for Africa's Wildlife* (New York: Vintage, 1993), 64–65.

12. Helmut K. Buechner, "Review: Conservation of African Wildlife," *Ecology* 45, no. 2 (April 1964): 420–421.

13. Ian Michael Wright, IMW 6-Arusha Conference, "Letter to Richard H. Nolte, Institute of Current World Affairs," September 22, 1961, at ICWA Archives online [https://www.icwa.org/ian-michael-wright-newsletters/]. Accessed October 15, 2018. See Nyerere's signed copy of the original manifesto in Frankfurt Stadtarchiv (FSA) Zoo 194.

14. Elizabeth Garland, "State of Nature: Colonial Power, Neoliberal Capital, and Wildlife Management in Tanzania" (PhD diss., University of Chicago, 2006), 121–123.

15. The Arusha Manifesto is not to be confused with the "Arusha Declaration" of 1967 declaring Tanzania's intention to follow a socialist path to development. On the significance of the event, William M. Adams, *Against Extinction: The Story of Conservation* (London: Earthscan, 2005), 195–196.

16. On expert knowledge in the transition from colony to postcolony, see Joseph Hodge, *Triumph of the Expert: Agrarian Doctrines of Development and the Legacies of British Colonialism* (Athens: Ohio University Press, 2007) and "Colonial Experts, Developmental and Environmental Doctrines and the Legacies of Late British Colonialism," in *Cultivating the Colony: Colonial States and Their Environmental Legacies*, ed. Christina Folke Ax, Niels Brimnes, Niklas Thode Jensen, and Karen Oslund (Athens: Ohio University Press, 2011), 300–326.

17. Nash, *Wilderness and the American Mind*, 358–372, sees Arusha as the culmination of the efforts by Paul Sarasin and others to realize the goals of a "world conservation" movement. On Sarasin, see Anna-Katharina Wöbse, *Weltnaturschutz: Umweltdiplomatie in Völkerbund und Vereinten Nationen 1920–1950* (Frankfurt: Campus, 2011), 35–64 and Patrick Kupper, *Creating Wilderness: A Transnational History of the Swiss National Park* (New York: Berghahn, 2014).

18. Hayes, *Last Place on Earth*, 61; John Hillaby, "Conservation in Africa: A Crucial Conference," *New Scientist* 250 (August 1961): 54–57.

19. On this point, see especially Roderick P. Neumann, *Imposing Wilderness: Struggles over Livelihood and Nature Preservation in Africa* (Berkeley: University of California Press, 1998), 139–143; Jim Igoe, *Conservation and Globalization: A Study of the National Parks and Indigenous Communities from East Africa to South Dakota* (Belmont, CA: Thomson/Wadsworth, 2004), 97–99; Jan Bender Shetler, *Imagining Serengeti: A History of Landscape Memory in Tanzania from Earliest Times to the Present* (Athens: Ohio University Press, 2007), 212–213.

20. Mark Cioc, *The Game of Conservation: International Treaties to Protect the World's Migratory Animals* (Athens: Ohio University Press, 2009), 56; Christopher Bonneuil, "Development as Experiment: Science and State Building in Late Colonial and Postcolonial Africa, 1930–1970," *Osiris* 15 (2000): 258–281.

21. Hayes, *Last Place on Earth*, 43.

22. On Tanganyika as the "poor sister," see Susan Geiger, *TANU Women: Gender and Culture in the Making of Tanganyikan Nationalism, 1955–1965* (Portsmouth, NH: Heinemann, 1997), 6.

23. On the relationship between natural resource management and state building, see Elizabeth Garland, "State of Nature," 128 and Mark Whitehead, Rhys Jones, and Martin Jones, *The Nature of the State: Excavating the Political Ecologies of the Modern State* (Oxford: Oxford University Press, 2007). Jean-François Bayart would likely argue here that the presence of Western NGOs led Tanganyikan leaders to "extravert" the cost of resources necessary to maintain hegemony at home. See his "Africa in the World: A History of Extraversion," *African Affairs* 99, no. 395 (2000): 217–267 and *The State in Africa: The Politics of the Belly* (London: Longman, 1993), 20–32.

24. See Bruce Kinloch, *The Shamba Raiders: Memories of a Game Warden* (Kinloss: Librario, 2003). On the slowness and unevenness of Africanization see Rodger Yeager, *Tanzania, An African Experiment* (Boulder, CO: Gower, 1982), 29–32 and Paul Bjerk, *Building a Peaceful Nation: Julius Nyerere and the Establishment of Sovereignty in Tanzania, 1960–1964* (Rochester: University of Rochester Press, 2015), 71–73.

25. Almost all of these parks required eviction of human inhabitants for their establishment. See Dan Brockington, "The Politics and Ethnography of Environmentalisms in Tanzania," *African Affairs* 105 (2006): 102 and *Fortress Conservation: The Preservation of Mkomazi Game Reserve, Tanzania* (Oxford: Oxford University Press, 2002).

26. See Julie M. Weiskopf, "Socialism on Safari: Wildlife and Nation-Building in Postcolonial Tanzania, 1966–77," *The Journal of African History* 56, no. 3 (2015): 429–447.

27. Shetler, *Imagining Serengeti*, 212. On wildlife and development, see "Socialism and Rural Development," in Julius K. Nyerere, *Freedom and Socialism. Uhuru Na Ujamaa: A Selection from Writings and Speeches, 1965–1967* (Dar es Salaam: Oxford University Press, 1968), 122–123.

28. Garland, "State of Nature", 138.

29. On continuities between colonial and postcolonial images of rural Africans, see Shetler, *Imagining Serengeti*, 217–223; Dorothy L. Hodgson, *Once Intrepid Warriors: Gender, Ethnicity, and the Cultural Politics of Maasai Development* (Bloomington: Indiana University Press, 2001), 148–240.

30. On independence leaders' adoption of the late imperial developmentalist program to justify postcolonial state-building, see Frederick Cooper, "Modernizing Bureaucrats, Backward Africans, and the Development Concept in International Development and the Social Sciences," *Essays on the History and Politics of Knowledge*, ed. Frederick Cooper and Randall Packard (Berkeley: University of California Press, 1997), 64–92 and Sara Berry, "Debating the Land Question in Africa," *Comparative Studies in Society and History* 44, no. 4 (October 2002): 645–652. Much has been written about the coercive potential of Nyerere's vision of rural socialism, which became especially apparent in the "Operation Dress Up" campaign that outlawed Maasai adornment of their bodies and the wearing of the traditional *lugeba*. For a good summary, see Leander Schneider, *Government of Development: Peasants and Politicians in Postcolonial Tanzania* (Bloomington: Indiana University Press, 2014), 95–98.

31. Leander Schneider, "Colonial Legacies and Postcolonial Authoritarianism in Tanzania: Connects and Disconnects," *African Studies Review* 49, no. 1 (2006): 93–118.

32. On the fluidity of definitions and meanings of citizenship in this transition, see Frederick Cooper, *Citizenship Between Empire and Nation: Remaking France and French Africa, 1945–1960* (Princeton, NJ: Princeton University Press, 2014).

33. Grzimek, *Auch Nashörner Gehören Allen Menschen,* 42.
34. Grzimek, "Wie steht es jetzt um die Nationalparke Afrikas," in *Schweizer Monatshefte für Politik, Wirtschaft, Kultur* (July 1961): 469–470; see also his essay "Was wird jetzt aus den Wildtieren Afrikas?: Die Probleme der Nationalparks," special printing from *Die Zeit,* no. 39–40 (September 1960), 23, 30.
35. Grzimek, *Rhinos Belong to Everybody,* 7–8.
36. Grzimek, *Rhinos Belong to Everybody,* 42.
37. See, for example, "Plane hit vulture in mid-air: Arusha inquest on survey pilot," *East African Standard,* February 10, 1959.
38. Grzimek, *Auf den Mensch gekommen,* 330; Sewig, *Der Mann, der die Tiere liebte,* 250–257.
39. Grzimek, "Wie steht es jetzt?," 469.
40. Grzimek, *Rhinos Belong to Everybody,* 7.
41. The main venue for the debate was a series of 1959 articles and op-eds in the *Süddeusche Zeitung,* particularly August 25, 1959. Torma has analyzed this debate in detail in *Eine Naturschutzkampagne in der Ära Adenauer: Bernhard Grzimeks Afrikafilme in den Medien der 50er Jahre* (Munich: Martin Meidenbauer, 2004), 165–189.
42. Tobias Boes, "Political Animals: *Serengeti Shall Not Die* and the Cultural Heritage of Mankind," *German Studies Review* 36, no. 1 (2013): 42. The FBW's recommendations were not, it should be emphasized, part of an evaluation system equivalent to the American Motion Picture Association's ratings system based on violence or sexual content.
43. Grzimek, *Auf den Mensch gekommen,* 307–308.
44. Torma, *Naturschutzkampagne,* 165–189.
45. Torma, *Naturschutzkampagne,* 178–189.
46. Nachrichtendienst der *Welt,* Zürich, September 2, 1959 in: *Die Welt,* September 3, 1959.
47. Grzimek, *Auf den Mensch gekommen,* 308.
48. Torma, *Naturschutzkampagne,* 171.
49. Grzimek, *Auf den Mensch gekommen,* 308.
50. Grzimek, *Auf den Mensch gekommen,* 304–308; Sewig, *Der Mann, der die Tiere liebte,* 276–277.
51. Grzimek, "Wie steht es jetzt?," 478.
52. See Grzimek's references to George Petrides and W. G. Swank in particular in "Wie steht es jetzt?," 470.
53. Watterson, et al., *Conservation of Nature and Natural Resources,* 10 and Igoe, *Conservation and Globalization,* 98–99.
54. Wöbse, "Tourismus und Naturschutz," 196–197.
55. Watterson et al., *Conservation of Nature and Natural Resources,* 9.
56. Watterson et al., *Conservation of Nature and Natural Resources,* 52–53.
57. Grzimek, Wie steht es jetzt?," 470.
58. Huxley, "Wild Fauna and Flora of Africa as a Cultural and Economic Asset, and the World Interest Therein," in *Conservation of Nature and Natural Resources,* ed. Watterson et al., 206.
59. On the IUCN assessments, see Watterson et al., *Conservation of Nature and Natural Resources,* 8–10; Bonner, *At the Hand of Man,* 61.
60. Igoe, *Conservation and Globalization,* 86–91.
61. Julian Huxley, *The Conservation of Wildlife and Natural Habitats* (Paris: UNESCO, 1961), 94.
62. Juliette Huxley, *Wild Lives in Africa* (London: Collins, 1964), 43–44.
63. Watterson et al., *Conservation of Nature and Natural Resources,* 207.
64. The history of the WWF's founding is well documented and beyond the scope of this chapter. See Adams, *Against Extinction,* 54–57.
65. Sewig, *Der Mann, der die Tiere liebte,* 297.
66. Huxley, "Wild Fauna and Flora of Africa," 206–207. On the limited fundraising, see Bonner, *At the Hand of Man,* 67–81.
67. Lt-Col P. G. Molloy, Director of Tanganyika National Parks, "Michael Grzimek Memorial Fund," *Tanganyika Standard,* February 19, 1959.
68. Grzimek, "Wie steht es jetzt?," 477; "Letter from Von Stackelberg, Consul General in Nairobi, to Molloy, Director of Tanganyika National Parks," May 13, 1959 and "Letter from Molloy to von Stackelberg," May 6, 1960 in PAAA: Michael Grzimek Memorial Lab.
69. *Tanganyika Standard,* "German Gift to National Parks," March 30, 1960.

70. "Letter from Molloy, Director of the Tanganyika National Parks, to Herbert von Stackelberg, the Consul General for the Federal Republic of Germany," August 19, 1959, in PAAA: Michael Grzimek Memorial Laboratory.

71. John Owen, "Draft Appeal for Funds by the Trustees of the Tanganyikan National Parks" (1963?), in FSA Zoo 193.

72. Grzimek, "Wie steht es jetzt?," 476; See John Owen, "The Serengeti Research Project: The Future Programme of Wildlife and Ecological Research," January 13, 1965 in FSA Zoo 196.

73. "Memorandum from Von Stackelberg, General Consul in Nairobi to AA in Bonn," February 12, 1960 in PAAA, Michael Grzimek Lab; List of equipment requested by Grzimek from the Deutsche Forschungsgemeinschaft, August 22, 1960, in FSA Zoo 193. See also "Game Study Laboratory Opened in Serengeti," *Tanganyika Standard*, 1962. Gerstenmaier lauded leaders in Dar es Salaam for supporting the protection of wildlife. "Serengeti darf nicht Sterben: Michael Grzimek Gedächtnis Laboratorium für zoologische Forschung," *Bulletin of the Foreign Office*, February 28, 1962.

74. Sewig, *Der Mann, der die Tiere liebte*, 286–287.

75. Henry Fosbrooke, *Ngorongoro: The Eighth Wonder* (London: Andre Deutsch, 1972), 89–90; Lee M. Talbot and D. R. M. Stewart, "First Wildlife Census of the Entire Serengeti-Mara Region, East Africa," *The Journal of Wildlife Management* 28, no. 4 (1964): 815–827. On Grzimek's anger, see "Letter from Owen to Grzimek," January 18, 1962, in FSA Zoo 193.

76. See Grzimek's correspondence with Oskar Splett of the German-Africa Society on the "Working Group for Landscape Preservation and Nature Conservation in Africa," August 18, 1961, in Zoo 193. On this theme, see Helen Tilley, *Africa as a Living Laboratory: Empire, Development, and the Problem of Scientific Knowledge, 1870–1950* (Chicago: University of Chicago Press, 2013).

77. The violent decolonization of the Congo has an extensive literature too detailed to cite here. See Jeanne M. Haskin, *The Tragic State of the Congo: From Decolonization to Dictatorship* (New York: Algora, 2007); Lise A. Namikas, *Battleground Africa: Cold War in the Congo, 1960–1965* (Stanford, CA: Stanford University Press, 2013). Despite conservationists' sense that Tanganyika could replace the Congo as the model conservation state, Nyerere saw the events there as a sure sign of the dangers of a Second Scramble for Africa. See Bjerk, *Building a Peaceful Nation*, 1–19.

78. Grzimek, *Rhinos Belong to Everybody*, 63; Grzimek, *Auf den Mensch gekommen*, 348–350.

79. Grzimek, "Wie steht es jetzt?," 482.

80. "Schwarze Wildhüter geben Ihr Leben für Verteidigung der Tiere im Kongo," *Das Tier*, 1 February 1961, 44.

81. Sewig, *Der Mann, der die Tiere liebte*, 275; 279.

82. Grzimek, *Rhinos Belong to Everybody*, 93–94.

83. Grzimek's efforts to recognize Africans stand in contrast to ongoing neglect of their efforts, see Jonathan S. Adams and Thomas O. McShane, *The Myth of Wild Africa: Conservation without Illusion* (New York: W.W. Norton, 1992), 229–230.

84. Grzimek, *Rhinos Belong to Everybody*, 88–124; Raf De Bont, "A World Laboratory: Framing the Albert National Park," *Environmental History* 22, no. 3 (2017): 421.

85. "Letter from Legation Councilor Werz in AA to Grzimek," acknowledging transfer of Congo funds, October 19, 1961 in PAAA B34 278.

86. Grzimek, *Rhinos Belong to Everybody*, 123.

87. Grzimek, *Rhinos Belong to Everybody*, 123-124.

88. On UNESCO funds for the park wardens, see "Letter from Harold Coolidge, Chairman of the IUCN International Commission on National Parks, to Grzimek," December 11, 1961 in FSA Zoo 193. On von Brentano's support, see "Letter from Grzimek to von Brentano," September 4, 1961, in PAAA B34 278.

89. Grzimek, *Rhinos Belong to Everybody*, 124; Organizers of the Arusha conference expressed congratulations to the Republic of Congo in Leopoldville for its "exemplary attitude toward its National Parks." See Watterson, et al., *Conservation of Nature and Natural Resources*, 15–16.

90. Hayes, *Last Place on Earth*, 161.

91. Hayes, *Last Place on Earth*, 50.

92. See "Letter from Friends of Africa to Grzimek," January 23, 1963, and "Letter from Grzimek to Fairfield Osborn New York Zoological Society," October 4, 1962, in FSA Zoo 194.

93. Grzimek, "Wie steht es jetzt?," 478.

94. On debates over Africanization, see Gwendolen Margaret Carter and Charles F. Gallagher, *African One-Party States* (Ithaca, NY: Cornell University Press, 1964), 462–463 and Schoeller, "Die innenpolitische Lage Tanganyikas vor der Unabhängigkeit," October 27, 1961, in PAAA B34 276.

95. Ronald Aminzade, "The Dialectic of Nation Building in Postcolonial Tanzania," *The Sociological Quarterly* 54, no. 3 (2013): 335–366.

96. See Turner, *My Serengeti Years*, 172–198.

97. Hayes, *Last Place on Earth*, 187–188.

98. Hayes, *Last Place on Earth*, 67.

99. Grzimek, *Auf den Mensch gekommen*, 332–334.

100. On Tanganyika as a "classical" example of an underdeveloped territory, see Carter and Gallagher, *One Party States*, 441.

101. Owen, "Draft Appeal by the Trustees," 1, 5.

102. Owen, "Draft Appeal by the Trustees," 2, 5; On Mkumi, see "Game Park Near Dar," *Tanganyika Standard*, December 15, 1958.

103. Grzimek, *Auf den Mensch gekommen*, 332–333.

104. Grzimek, "Wie steht es jetzt?," 477. On the use of the airplane, see Turner, *My Serengeti Years*, 55–78.

105. Owen, "Draft Appeal by the Trustees," 6–7.

106. Tanganyika National Parks, *Reports and Accounts of the Board of Trustees for the Period 1st July, 1962 to 30th June 1964*, 27. In Henry A. Fosbrooke Collection (HFC), University of Dar es Salaam Library, East Africana collection.

107. Tanganyika National Parks, *Reports and Accounts of the Board of Trustees*, 12.

108. Sewig, *Der Mann, der die Tiere liebte*, 289.

109. Tanganyika National Parks, *Reports and Accounts of the Board of Trustees*, 9.

110. Garland, "State of Nature," 173–221.

111. Garland, "State of Nature," 125–132.

112. Tanganyika National Parks, *Reports and Accounts of the Board of Trustees*, 9.

113. Letter from Grzimek to the Foreign Office, concerning the "Beschaffung von zwei Auto-Projektoren für biologische Erziehungsarbiet in Tanganyika," August 23, 1961, PAAA B34 278. See also "Parks Poster Campaign," in *Tanganyika Standard*, January 15, 1963.

114. Tanganyika National Parks, *Reports and Accounts of the Board of Trustees*, 20.

115. "Letter from John Owen to Grzimek," April 18, 1961, in Zoo 193; "Letter from Grzimek to Legationsrat Werz in AA," November 29, 1961, and "Letter from Grzimek to Heinrich von Brentano," September 4, 1961, in PAAA B34 278, which resulted in DM 9000 to support poster campaign. Owen formally unveiled the Tanganyikan efforts at the conference itself: see "Awakening Public Opinion to the Value of the Tanganyikan National Parks," in *Conservation of Nature and Natural Resources*, ed. Watterson et al., 261–264.

116. Tanganyika National Parks, *Reports and Accounts of the Board of Trustees*, 19–20.

117. "Application from Frankfurt Zoological Society to AA, concerning youth hostel accommodations for black schoolchildren," August 23, 1961, in PAAA B34 278.

118. Tanganyika National Parks, *Reports and Accounts of the Board of Trustees*, 21.

119. "Letter from Grzimek to Legationsrat Stelzer in AA," August 23, 1961, in PAAA B34 278; Sewig, *Der Mann, der die Tiere liebte*, 283–284.

120. See Letter from Grzimek to von Brentano asking to transfer funds from the "saving of the eastern Congo national parks" to the youth hostel project, September 4, 1961, and "Letter from Werz in AA to Grzimek," October 19, 1961, In PAAA B34 278.

121. Weiskopf, "Socialism on Safari," 430.

122. See "Letter from Grzimek to Director von Etzdorff in the AA," May 26, 1961, and the call for donations "Hilfe für Tanganyikas Tierwelt," in PAAA B34 278.

123. Owen, "Draft Appeal by the Trustees," 10–11.

124. Owen, "Draft Appeal by the Trustees," 10–11.

125. On such hybrids, see Bayart, "Africa in the World," 217–267.

126. The book was also a commercial success: it was translated into twenty-two languages and eight hundred thousand were sold in West Germany alone by 1973. See "Game film praised in London," January 9, 1959, and "Pilot of game survey dies in crash: Serengeti work praised," *East African Standard,* January 13, 1959.

127. Grzimek collated the reviews for von Stackelberg to show his growing influence and to prepare the ground for additional donations: "London Newspapers about the film *Serengeti Shall Not Die*," in PAAA Michael Grzimek Memorial Laboratory.

128. Edward Hindle, Review of *Serengeti Shall Not Die, The Geographical Journal,* 127, no. 3 (September 1961): 363.

129. Grzimek, *Auf den Mensch gekommen,* 308–310.

130. "Letter from Von Stackelberg to Vortr. Legationsrat von Gehlen in the AA," November 30, 1959, in PAAA Michael Grzimek Lab.

131. "Game expert gives talk to Nairobi film audience," *East African Standard,* January 22, 1960.

132. Von Stackelberg, "Augenmerke bei dem Filmabend 'Serengeti Shall Not Die,'" in PAAA Michael Grzimek Lab.

133. "Letter from Holzer in AA in Bonn to von Stackelberg ," April 30, 1959, in PAAA Michael Grzimek Memorial Lab.

134. Sewig, *Der Mann, der die Tiere liebte,* 274.

135. "Letter from Grzimek to Tom Lithgow, 'Shangri-La' Estate," April 12, 1961, in FSA Zoo 193.

136. On the evolution from animals in the studio to outdoor settings, see Cynthia Chris, *Watching Wildlife* (Minneapolis: University of Minnesota Press, 2006), 46.

137. This was part of an international trend as Gregg Mitman noted in *Reel Nature,* 132–156.

138. Grzimek, *Auf den Mensch gekommen,* 299.

139. On this point, see Engels, *Naturpolitik in der Bundesrepublik,* 239–251.

140. Sewig, *Der Mann, der die Tiere liebte,* 274.

141. Sewig, *Der Mann, der die Tiere liebte,* 273–275, 290.

142. Grzimek, *Auf den Mensch gekommen,* 347-348; Sewig, *Der Mann, der die Tiere liebte,* 274.

143. Grzimek, *Rhinos Belong to Everybody,* 175.

144. Grzimek, *Auf den Mensch gekommen,* 341. On average FRG families made only DM 527, or $126, before taxes.

145. Grzimek, *Rhinos Belong to Everybody,* 189-190.

146. Grzimek, *Rhinos Belong to Everybody,* 175, 189; Sewig, *Der Mann, der die Tiere liebte,* 272-273.

147. Mitman, *Reel Nature,* 191–202.

148. Joseph Ouma, *Evolution of Tourism in East Africa (1900–2000)* (Nairobi: East African Literature Bureau, 1970), 9–12. See also "Move to Cut Formalities for Tourists," in *Tanganyika Standard,* October 23, 1958.

149. "Letter from Chief Fundikira of East African Airways to Grzimek," April 10, 1965; "Letter from Grzimek to Fundikira, East African Airways," September 23, 1965, in FSA Zoo 195.

150. "Letter from EATTA to Grzimek," May 15, 1962, in FSA Zoo 194.

151. Grzimek, "Value of the Tourist Industry," in *Conservation of Nature and Natural Resources,* ed. Watterson et al., 191.

152. Sewig, *Der Mann, der die Tiere liebte,* 272–279.

153. See Letter from Harold Coolidge congratulating Grzimek on the tours on behalf of the IUCN: February 15, 1962; "Letter from Grzimek to Henry Collings, Commonwealth Office of High Commissioner," January 11, 1962 in FSA Zoo 193.

154. *FZS Mitteilungen* 6, 1971. Cited in Engels, *Naturpolitik,* 6.

155. "Letter from Grzimek to Fairfield Osborn," October 29, 1962, in Zoo 194.

156. "Letter from Owen to Grzimek," October 28, 1961, in FSA Zoo 193.

157. McShane and Adams, *Myth of Wild Africa,* 53–54. Many conservationists saw the NCA as a "far sighted policy" on the part of Tanzania to reconcile competing interests. For example, see the Foreword by Prince Bernhard of the Netherlands to Fosbrooke's *Eighth Wonder.*

158. Cited in Bonner, *At the Hand of Man,* 179.

159. Peter J. Rogers, "History and Governance in the Ngorongoro Conservation Area, Tanzania, 1959–1966," in *Global Environment* 4 (2009): 79–117.

160. See "Letter from D.D. Younge, Permanent Secretary of the Ministry of Lands, Surveys, and Water," inviting Grzimek to be a part of the advisory board for the NCA, August 12, 1961, in FSA Zoo 193.

161. Rogers, "History and Governance in the Ngorongoro," 90.

162. Fosbrooke was more sympathetic to a wise-use approach and to Maasai interests, though Peter Rogers has rightly argued that, in many ways, Fosbrooke followed national parks forms of environmental governance: Rogers, "History and Governance in the Ngorongoro," 94–95.

163. Cited in Rogers, "History and Governance in the Ngorongoro," 91–93.

164. Rogers, "History and Governance in the Ngorongoro," 99–100.

165. See Owen's letter about the "unhappy atmosphere" at NCA, January 18, 1962 in FSA Zoo 193.

166. Owen, "Draft Appeal by the Trustees," 5.

167. "German Gift to National Parks," *Tanganyika Standard*, March 30, 1960.

168. Owen, "Draft Appeal by the Trustees," 5.

169. See Sewig, *Der Mann, der die Tiere liebte*, 286.

170. Grzimek, *Rhinos Belong to Everybody*, 152, 186.

171. Grzimek, *Rhinos Belong to Everybody*, 187.

172. Grzimek, *Rhinos Belong to Everybody*, 152; 188–189.

173. Grzimek, *Auf den Mensch gekommen*, 341.

174. Grzimek and Grzimek, *Serengeti Shall Not Die*, 264–267.

175. Fosbrooke, *Eighth Wonder*, 93–105.

176. Grzimek, "Wie steht es jetzt?," 469.

177. Juliette Huxley, *Wild Lives in Africa*, 131.

178. Rogers, "History and Governance in the Ngorongoro," 91.

179. Cited in Rogers, "History and Governance in the Ngorongoro," 91; Fosbrooke later pinned the trade in rhino horn instead on desperation due to the drought: Fosbrooke, *Eighth Wonder*, 93.

180. Rogers, "History and Governance in the Ngorongoro," 93.

181. Rogers, "History and Governance in the Ngorongoro," 91.

182. Sewig, *Der Mann, der die Tiere liebte*, 279.

183. Grzimek, *Rhinos Belong to Everybody*, 191.

184. Grzimek, *Rhinos Belong to Everybody*, 191.

185. Grzimek, "Das Schicksal der Nashörner im Ngorongoro-Krater," *Das Tier*, February 1, 1961, 3.

186. "Masai 'Waste Talents' in Rhino Attacks," *Tanganyika Standard*, January 21, 1961.

187. Bjerk, *Building a Peaceful Nation*, 46–57.

188. Grzimek, *Rhinos Belong to Everybody*, 186–188.

189. "Masai 'Waste' Talents in Rhino Attacks," January 21, 1961.

190. See "Letter from Lithgowto Grzimek," April 5, 1961, and Grzimek's reply from April 12, 1961, in FSA Zoo 193.

191. Grzimek, *Rhinos Belong to Everybody*, 186.

192. Grzimek, *Rhinos Belong to Everybody*, 187.

193. Such a plan still does not exist. See Susan Charnley, "From Nature Tourism to Ecotourism? The Case of the Ngorongoro Conservation Area, Tanzania," *Human Organization* 64, no. 1 (2005): 65–88

194. Ben Gardner, *Selling the Serengeti: The Cultural Politics of Safari Tourism* (Athens: University of Georgia Press, 2016), xx.

195. Memorandum from Jürgen Kalkbrenner, German Consulate in Nairobi to AA, "Allgemeine politische Lage in Tanganyika," October 26, 1960, 1–2 in PAAA B34 180. On *Uhuru Na Kazi*, see also Ben Wattenberg and Ralph Lee Smith, *The New Nations of Africa* (New York: Hart, 1963), 390–391.

196. See Nyerere, "Ujamaa—The Basis of African Socialism," in *Freedom and Socialism*, 4.

197. Helge Kjekshus, "The Tanzanian Villagization Policy: Implementational Lessons and Ecological Dimensions," *Canadian Journal of African Studies* 11, no. 2 (1977): 274.

198. Shetler, *Imagining Serengeti*, 212–223; Weiskopf, "Socialism on Safari," 442–443. On the nationalization of land, animals, and parks, see Nyerere, "Ujamaa—The Basis of African

Socialism," 7–9 and "The Varied Paths to Socialism," 84–85 in *Freedom and Socialism* along with the correspondence in *Parliamentary Debates (Hansard): National Assembly: Official Report*, sittings from June 5, 1961, to July 3, 1962, 214–216.

199. On this theme, see Thaddeus Sunseri, *Wielding the Ax: State Forestry and Social Conflict in Tanzania, 1820–2000* (Athens: Ohio University Press, 2009), 143–163.
200. See Hodgson, *Once Intrepid Warriors*, 149.
201. Cited in William Edgett Smith, *Nyerere of Tanzania: The First Decade, 1961–1971* (Harare: African Publishing Group, 2011), 12.
202. Grzimek, *Auf den Mensch gekommen*, 330.
203. Sunseri, *Wielding the Ax*, 143–163; Andrew Hurst, "State Forestry and Spatial Scale in the Development Discourses of Post-Colonial Tanzania: 1961–1971," *The Geographical Journal* 169, no. 4 (December 2003): 358–369.
204. Garland, "State of Nature," 27–37.

Chapter 7

1. Claudia Sewig, *Der Mann, der die Tiere liebte: Bernhard Grzimek: Biografie* (Bergisch Gladbach: Lübbe, 2009), 334–335.
2. "Tanzania 'Yes' to Plan for a Rival Treetops," *Zambia News*, November 12, 1968.
3. Bernhard Grzimek, *Auf den Mensch gekommen: Erfahrungen mit Leuten* (Munich: C. Bertelsmann, 1974), 429–430.
4. "Letter from A. Starker Leopold to H. Macame, Minister for Information and Tourism," June 12, 1968, in Frankfurt Stadtarchiv (FSA) Zoo 197.
5. Sewig, *Der Mann, der die Tiere liebte*, 334; "Letter from Joan E. Wicken, Personal Assistant of the President, to Bernhard Grzimek," June 8, 1968, at FSA Zoo 197.
6. Grzimek, *Auf den Mensch gekommen*, 430.
7. Sewig, *Der Mann, der die Tiere liebte*, 343–344; "Grzimek Hits at Ngorongoro Crater Plan," *The Standard*, September 6, 1969; Michael Parry, "Serengeti May Have to Die," *East African Standard*, August 29, 1969 and "Angry Reaction to Ngorongoro Plan," *East African Standard*, September 1, 1969.
8. Sewig, *Der Mann, der die Tiere liebte*, 344. Among the dozens of rebukes to Grzimek, see "Tanzania Rebuffs Critics," *East African Standard*, September 19, 1969.
9. Harold T. P. Hayes, *The Last Place on Earth* (New York: Stein and Day, 1977), 19.
10. Jan Bender Shetler, *Imagining Serengeti: A History of Landscape Memory in Tanzania from Earliest Times to the Present* (Athens: Ohio University Press, 2007), 211–212.
11. Bernhard Grzimek et al., *Visions of Paradise* (London: Hodder & Stoughton, 1981), 100–101.
12. Myles Turner, *My Serengeti Years: The Memoirs of an African Game Warden* (New York: W.W. Norton, 1988), 180.
13. See Anthony Rweyemamu, "Managing Planned Development: Tanzania's Experience," in *The Journal of Modern African Studies*, no. 4, 1 (1966): 1–16. As recent research has shown, Tanzania's elites moved quickly from channeling local protest against the colonial state's conservation measures to wresting control over natural resources from the same populations. See, for example, Clark C. Gibson, *Politicians and Poachers: The Political Economy of Wildlife Policy in Africa* (Cambridge, UK: Cambridge University Press, 1999), especially chap. 1; Andrew Hurst, "State Forestry and Spatial Scale in the Development Discourses of Post-Colonial Tanzania: 1961–1971," *The Geographical Journal* 169, no. 4 (December 2003): 362; Thaddeus Sunseri, "'Every African a Nationalist': Scientific Forestry and Forest Nationalism in Colonial Tanzania," *Comparative Studies in Society and History* 49, no. 4 (October 2007): 883–913; Leander Schneider, *Government of Development: Peasants and Politicians in Postcolonial Tanzania* (Bloomington: Indiana University Press, 2014), 19–45; Daniel Speich, "Der Entwicklungsautomatismus: Ökonomisches Wissen als Heilsversprechen in der ostafrikanischen Dekolonisation," in *Dekolonisation: Prozesse und Verflechtungen 1945–1990*, ed. Anja Kruke (Bonn: Dietz, 2009), 183–212.
14. Julian Huxley, "Wildlife as a Resource," *The North American Review* 249, no. 1 (March 1964): 41.
15. Huxley, "Wildlife as a Resource," 58.

16. On the overall aims of the project, see "Afrika-Wild zur Volksernährung? Tanganjika Universität soll Wildtiere erforschen," in *Kiel Morgen Zeitung*, September 14, 1962; "Research into the Utilisation of the Game Animals of the Serengeti: The Problem," (1962) in Politsches Archiv des Auswärtigen Amts (PAAA): Momella; and Raymond F. Dasmann, "Game Ranching in African Land-Use Planning," in *Conservation of Nature and Natural Resources in Modern African States: Report of a Symposium Organized by CCTA and IUCN and Held under the Auspices of FAO and UNESCO at Arusha, Tanganyika, September 1961* (Morges, Switzerland: IUCN, 1963), ed. Gerald G. Watterson, UNESCO, and FAO, 133–136.

17. Hubertus Büschel, "In Afrika Helfen: Akteure westdeutscher 'Entwicklungshilfe' und ostdeutscher 'Solidarität,' 1955–1975," in *Dekolonisation*, ed. Kruke, 333–366; Young-Sun Hong, *Cold War Germany, the Third World, and the Global Humanitarian Regime* (New York: Cambridge University Press, 2015), 215–218, 233–249.

18. Such penury linked the colonial and postcolonial eras. See Sara Berry, "Hegemony on a Shoestring: Indirect Rule and Access to Agricultural Land," *Africa: Journal of the International African Institute* 62, no. 3 (1992): 327–355. Development reports from this period touted Tanzania's national parks as engines of economic development: Klaus Frentrup, *Die Ökonomische Bedeutung des Internationalen Tourismus für die Entwicklungsländer* (Hamburg: Deutsches Übersee-Institut, 1969). Yet scholars have grown more skeptical about the promises of eco-tourism to stimulate sustainable development. See Che Hamis Chenjah, "Promotion of Tourism in Tanzania: A Critical Approach" (MA thesis, University of Dar es Salaam, 1998) and Ben Gardner, *Selling the Serengeti: The Cultural Politics of Safari Tourism* (Athens: University of Georgia Press, 2016).

19. See John Owen, "Es steht uns Europäern schlecht an ...," *Das Tier* 3 (May 5, 1963): 3.

20. Roderick P. Neumann, *Imposing Wilderness: Struggles over Livelihood and Nature Preservation in Africa* (Berkeley: University of California Press, 1998), 144.

21. See Fosbrooke, "Serengeti and Ngorongoro Diamond Jubilee, 1921–1981: The Serengeti Ecosystem," (1981), 14–15, in Henry A. Fosbrooke Collection (HFC), University of Dar es Salaam Library, East Africana collection.

22. Cited in Elizabeth Garland, "State of Nature: Colonial Power, Neoliberal Capital, and Wildlife Management in Tanzania" (PhD diss., University of Chicago, 2006), 162–163. On Tanzania's failed "take-off" see Hubert Job and Daniel Metzler, "Tourismusentwicklung und Tourismuspolitik in Ostafrika," *Geographische Rundschau* 55 (2003): 10–17.

23. Helge Kjekshus, "The Tanzanian Villagization Policy: Implementational Lessons and Ecological Dimensions," *Canadian Journal of African Studies* 11, no. 2 (1977): 269–282; Yusufu Qwaray Lawi, "Tanzania's Operation 'Vijiji' and Local Ecological Consciousness: The Case of Eastern Iraqwland, 1974–1976," *Journal of African History* 48, no. 1 (2007): 69–93.

24. Garland, "State of Nature," 65–66, 158–162.

25. The literature on structural adjustment and neoliberalism in Tanzania is far too extensive to cite here. For a good introduction to the topic, see Shetler, *Imagining Serengeti*, 223–226; Katherine Homewood et al., "Long-Term Changes in Serengeti-Mara Wildebeest and Land Cover: Pastoralism, Population, or Policies?," *Proceedings of the National Academy of Sciences* 98, no. 222 (October 2001): 12544–12549. See also Sara Berry's observation that "it is worth remembering that the development plans of the 1960s were written by the same international institutions and experts who since 1980 have insisted that excessive state interference is the primary cause of Africa's economic failures" in "Debating the Land Question in Africa," *Comparative Studies in Society and History* 44, no. 4 (October 2002): FN 9, 648.

26. See the title page of *Das Tier* 2, no. 5 (May 1962): 3. On Nyerere's image abroad, see Shetler, *Imagining Serengeti*, 212; Andreas Eckert, *Herrschen und Verwalten: Afrikanische Bürokraten, staatliche Ordnung und Politik in Tanzania, 1920–1970* (Munich: R. Oldenbourg, 2007), 194–200; and Paul Bjerk, *Building a Peaceful Nation: Julius Nyerere and the Establishment of Sovereignty in Tanzania, 1960–1964* (Rochester: University of Rochester Press, 2015), 61–96.

27. *Das Tier*, 2, no. 5 (May 1962): 3.

28. Ronald Aminzade, "The Dialectic of Nation Building in Postcolonial Tanzania," *The Sociological Quarterly* 54, no. 3 (2013): 344. Debates about Africanization reached a

crescendo in January 1962 when Nyerere resigned as prime minister in favor of Kawawa after only forty-four days in office, partly to shift the political system toward a republic centered on a strong president.

29. See Memorandum from Jürgen Kalkbrenner, German Consulate in Nairobi to AA, "Allgemeine politische Lage in Tanganyika," October 26, 1960, in PAAA B34 180.

30. Hans Jenny, "Julius Nyerere: Tanganyikas demokratischer Staatschef und Freund der Weissen," in *Christ und Welt*, January 27, 1961.

31. Memorandum from Herbert von Stackelberg to AA in Bonn, "Rechtzeitige Einbeziehung Tanganyikas in die deutsche Entwicklungshilfe," September 15, 1960 in PAAA B34 277.

32. William Edgett Smith, *Nyerere of Tanzania: The First Decade, 1961-1971* (Harare: African Publishing Group, 2011), 138.

33. "Germans Stop Parliament for Nyerere," *Tanganyika Standard*, January 1, 1961, and "Nyerere in Bonn for Aid Talks," *Uganda Argus*, January 24, 1961.

34. Dirk van Laak, *Imperiale Infrastruktur: deutsche Planungen für eine Erschliessung Afrikas 1880 bis 1960* (Paderborn: Schöningh, 2004), 338-342; Karen Hagen, "Internationalism in Cold War Germany" (PhD diss., University of Washington, 2008), 1-42.

35. Kalkbrenner, "Allgemeine politische Lage in Tanganyika," 6.

36. Nyerere, "Tanganyika and the Problems of its Future," a lecture to the German Society for Foreign Policy and German-Africa Society in PAAA B34 276.

37. Andrew Coulson, *Tanzania, 1800-1980: A Political Economy* (Oxford: Clarendon Press, 1982), 50-59; Edmund W. Clark, *Socialist Development and Public Investment in Tanzania, 1964-73* (Toronto: University of Toronto Press, 1978), 42-43.

38. "Tanganjika wünscht Hilfe Bonns: Chiefminister Nyerere unterrichtet FR über Pläne seines Landes," *Frankfurter Rundschau*, January 27, 1961 and "Tanganyika Welcomes German Interest," *East African Standard*, January 25, 1961.

39. "More Aid from West Germany: Technical Advisors and Cash from Six Projects," *Tanganyika Standard*, December 8, 1962. See also Steltzer, "Auszug aus dem Informationserlass über den Verlauf des Nyerere-Besuchs vom 24.-26. Januar 1961," August 31, 1963, in PAAA B1 439 and "Germany to Send Team to Survey Territory," *East African Standard*, January 27, 1961.

40. On the German-German rivalry, see Hagen, "Internationalism in Cold War Germany," 47-110; Hong, *Cold War Germany*, 215-249; Fritz Schatten, *Afrika, schwarz oder rot? Revolution eines Kontinents* (Munich: Piper, 1961).

41. Massimiliano Trentin, "Modernization as State Building: The Two Germanys in Syria, 1963-1972," in *Diplomatic History* 33, no. 3 (June 2009): 487-505.

42. William Glenn Gray, *Germany's Cold War: The Global Campaign to Isolate East Germany, 1949-1969* (Chapel Hill: University of North Carolina Press, 2003), 2.

43. Gray, *Germany's Cold War*, 3.

44. Gray, *Germany's Cold War*, 10-13.

45. Katherine Pence, "Showcasing Cold War Germany in Cairo: 1954 and 1957 Industrial Exhibitions and the Competition for Arab Partners," in *Journal of Contemporary History* 47, no. 1 (2011): 72; Quinn Slobodian, ed. *Comrades of Color: East Germany in the Cold War World* (New York: Berghahn, 2017).

46. Nyerere's comments came at the third annual meeting of the Afro-Asian Solidarity Conference in Moshi: "Nyerere on New Imperialism: Unity Can Beat this 'Second Scramble,'" *Tanganyika Standard*, February 5, 1963. On Afro-Asia, see Hong, *Cold War Germany*, 35-36. On the FRG's growing fears about GDR influence in East Africa, see "Das Bundnis Bonn-Pretoria: Denkschrift des Afro-Asiatischen Solidaritätskomitees der DDR" (1964) and the FRG response to this "fantasy-filled thought paper" in "Sonderdienst: Bundesrepublik Deutschland: Partner der Freiheit: Deutsche Militärhilfe für Afrika" (1965) in PAAA B57 491.

47. See Memorandum from Werz in AA to West German Embassy in Dar es Salaam, "Danktelegramm des Premierministers Kawawa an Grotewohl," February 22, 1962, and Schoeller, "Memorandum on 'Antikommunistische Öffentlichtkeitsarbeit in Tanganyika,'" September 29, 1962, in PAAA B34 366.

48. Bernhard Grzimek and Michael Grzimek, *Serengeti Shall Not Die*, trans. E. L. Rewald and D. Rewald (New York: E. P. Dutton, 1961), 42.

49. Grzimek, et al., *Visions of Paradise*, 100.

50. Hayes, *Last Place on Earth*, 46.

51. Letter from Grzimek to Owen concerning "Six Things to Report," May 26, 1961.

52. "Letter from Owen to Grzimek," January 18, 1962 in FSA Zoo 193.

53. "Letter from Von Stackelberg to Grzimek," February 12, 1960, in PAAA Michael Grzimek Memorial Lab.

54. Julie M. Weiskopf, "Socialism on Safari: Wildlife and Nation-Building in Postcolonial Tanzania, 1966–77," *The Journal of African History* 56, no. 3 (2015): 433.

55. Weiskopf, "Socialism on Safari," 435–436.

56. Sunseri, "'Every African a Nationalist,'" 884–890.

57. Peter J. Rogers, "History and Governance in the Ngorongoro Conservation Area, Tanzania, 1959–1966," in *Global Environment* 4, no. 2(2009): 98, 106.

58. Garland, "State of Nature," 135–165; Weiskopf, "Socialism on Safari," 439.

59. H. S. Mahinda, "An Experiment in Spreading Propaganda among Indigenous People as to the Value of Wild Life, and the Need for its Conservation," in *Conservation of Nature and Natural Resources*, ed. Watterson et al., 235.

60. T.S. Tewa, "The Value of the Tourist Industry in the Conservation of Natural Resources in Tanganyika," in *Conservation of Nature and Natural Resources*, ed. Watterson et al., 336–337.

61. Tewa, "The Value of the Tourist Industry," 337.

62. "Tanganyikas neuer Minister für Wildleben," in *Das Tier* 3, no. 1 (January 1963): 3

63. Mahinda, "An Experiment in Spreading Propaganda," 235–237.

64. "Public Urged to Help Save Wild Life," *Tanganyika Standard*, March 12, 1963.

65. "Wanyama ni wetu: Msituhangaishe," *Uhuru*, April 28, 1962. Cited in Weiskopf, "Socialism on Safari," 438.

66. Weiskopf, "Socialism on Safari," 440.

67. David P. S. Wasawo, "Wild Fauna and Flora of Africa as a Cultural and Economic Asset and the World Interest Therein," in *Conservation of Nature and Natural Resources*, ed. Watterson et al., 352.

68. Wasawo, "Wild Fauna and Flora of Africa as a Cultural and Economic Asset," 354.

69. "More Aid from West Germany," *Tanganyika Standard*, December 8, 1962.

70. For good overviews of the Serengeti Research Project (1962–1965) and the evolution of the Serengeti Research Institute (1966–1978), see Hayes, *Last Place on Earth*, 18–19, 42–43; Anthony R. E. Sinclair, *Serengeti Story: Life and Science in the World's Greatest Wildlife Region* (Oxford: Oxford University Press, 2012) and Wolfgang Wickler, *Wissenschaft auf Safari: Verhaltensforschung als Beruf und Hobby* (Berlin: Springer, 2017), 93–100, 119–124.

71. Tanganyika National Parks, *Reports and Accounts of the Board of Trustees for the Period 1st July, 1962 to 30th June 1964*, 22–27 in HFC. "Letter from Grzimek to John Owen concerning funding of Serengeti Research Project," October 27, 1965, in FSA Zoo 197.

72. Tanganyika National Parks, *Reports and Accounts of the Board of Trustees*, 22–23.

73. On the SRI, see Hayes, *Last Place on Earth*, 192; Jonathan S. Adams and Thomas O. McShane, *The Myth of Wild Africa: Conservation without Illusion* (New York: W.W. Norton, 1992), 85–102. See Grzimek's letter to Nyerere on the "large amounts of donations from the Fritz Thyssen Foundation" in "Letter from Grzimek to Nyerere," April 13, 1966, and Nyerere's reply, April 23, 1966, in FSA Zoo 197.

74. Hayes, *Last Place on Earth*, 20–21. Critics of the SRP and SRI have argued that the research there has yielded few data that help with management, with "boffins in the bush" endangering the animals by killing too many specimens for research. See Adams and McShane, *Myth of Wild Africa*, 85–102; Turner, *My Serengeti Years*, 156–163.

75. Tanganyika National Parks, *Reports and Accounts of the Board of Trustees*, 22–23; Hayes, *Last Place on Earth*, 78–79.

76. See Sewig, *Der Mann, der die Tiere liebte*, 284–288, and Draft Lecture "Biophylaxis," in FSA Zoo 195.

77. "Letter from Grzimek to Kai-Uwe Hassel, Minister-President of Schleswig-Holstein," February 1, 1962, in FSA Zoo 194. Grzimek hoped to create alliances with Hassel's proposal for a satellite campus of the University of Kiel's veterinary school in Tanganyika. See "The Serengeti Research Project: The Future Programme of Wildlife and Ecological Research," in FSA Zoo 196.

78. Anthony R. E. Sinclair, "The Eruption of the Ruminants," in *Serengeti: Dynamics of an Ecosystem*, ed. Sinclair and M. Norton-Griffiths (Chicago: University of Chicago Press, 1979), 82–103.

79. Shetler, *Imagining Serengeti*, 212.

80. Sinclair, *Serengeti Story*, 88–91.

81. "Tanganyikas neuer Minister für Wildleben," in *Das Tier* 1 (January 1963): 3.

82. Sewig, *Der Mann, der die Tiere liebte*, 293–295. Beyond the scope here is Grzimek's growing uneasiness with the culling of hippos, which he saw as an unnecessary intrusion of American modes of park management into Africa's Belgian model of wildlife conservation. See "Letter from C.D. Trimmer to Grzimek," February 18, 1963 in FSA Zoo 194.

83. See Grzimek's comments on his background as veterinarian in "Letter to the Editor in Chief of the *East African Standard*," March 15, 1965, in FSA Zoo 195.

84. The Federal Republic's negotiations of the project are extensively documented in PAAA Momella especially "Letter from FRG Ambassador Herbert Schroeder to Ministry of Lands, Forest and Wildlife in Tanganyika," November 28, 1963 as well as "Letter from Grzimek to Aloys P. Achieng, Ministry of Natural Resources in Kenya," March 16, 1965, in FSA Zoo 196, in PAAA Momella.

85. For a summary of the German team's activities, see the Nuffield Foundation's "Report on the German Game Utilization Scheme in the Grumeti Controlled Area of the Serengeti-Mara Region for the Period September 1964 to December 1965," in PAAA Momella.

86. Raymond Dasmann, "Game Ranching in African Land Use Planning," in *Conservation of Nature and Natural Resources*, ed. Watterson et al., 133–136.

87. Raymond Dasmann, *African Game Ranching* (Oxford: Pergamon Press, 1964), 36–39.

88. Grzimek, "Biophylaxis," 15 in FSA Zoo 195.

89. Dasmann, "Game Ranching in African Land Use Planning," 135.

90. Rüdiger Sachs, "Bericht aus dem Michael Grzimek Memorial Laboratory: Serengeti Research Project: FE 428 Wildgehege, Wildnutzung und Wildbretverwertung Tanganyika, September/Oktober 1964," in PAAA Momella.

91. See Letter from Schroeder to AA, "Technische Hilfe für Tanganyika: Wildnutzung und Wildbretverwertung," October 9, 1963 in PAAA Momella.

92. Quoted in Grzimek, "Biophylaxis," 14.

93. Aaron Segal, "Can Game Be Made to Pay?," *East African Standard*, February 26, 1965. See also Grzimek's angry response in a "Letter to the Editor," March 15, 1965, in FSA Zoo 195.

94. Dorothy L. Hodgson, *Once Intrepid Warriors: Gender, Ethnicity, and the Cultural Politics of Maasai Development* (Bloomington: Indiana University Press, 2001), 50–59.

95. See "Zwischenbericht: Wildgehege, Wildnutzung and Wildbretverwertung: Starker Finnenbefall der Serengeti-Antilopen" (1964) in PAAA Momella; "Letter from Grzimek to Achieng at Muguga," March 16, 1965, in FSA Zoo 196.

96. See Nuffield Foundation, "Report on the German Game Utilization Scheme," 4.

97. Nuffield Foundation, "Report on the German Game Utilization Scheme," 2–3; "Letter from GAWI to Sachs," January 20, 1965 in PAAA Momella.

98. Sachs, "Technische Hilfe für Tanganyika: Wildnutzung und Wildbretverwertung: Bericht August/September/Oktober 1964," 1–9 in PAAA Momella.

99. Sachs, "Technische Hilfe für Tanganyika: Wildnutzung und Wildbretverwertung: Bericht August/September/Oktober 1965," 1–3 in PAAA Momella.

100. Sachs, "Zwischenbericht: Fleischkonservierungsversuche durch Rindosen," November 1966 in FSA Zoo 196.

101. "Preliminary Meeting of the Serengeti Research Institute," July 1, 1966, in FSA Zoo 196.

102. See "Letter of Tanzanian Minister of Agriculture to Sachs about the Game Utilization Project," November 15, 1966, and "Letter from the AA to the Tanzania Ministry of Agriculture, Forestry and Wildlife," December 13, 1966, in PAAA Momella.

103. Bjerk, *Building a Peaceful Nation*, 131–154.

104. Smith, *Nyerere of Tanzania*, 137–138.

105. Garth A. Myers, "Making the Socialist City of Zanzibar," *Geographical Review* 84, no. 4 (October 1994): 451–464.

106. Bjerk, *Building a Peaceful Nation*, 2–19.
107. Eckert, *Herrschen und Verwalten*, 220; Hong, *Cold War Germany*, 295–316.
108. Smith, *Nyerere of Tanzania*, 164–166.
109. On the Sudan incident, see Sewig, *Der Mann, der die Tiere liebte*, 314. On Grzimek's efforts to smooth relations between Tanzania and the FRG, see "Letter from Grzimek to Foreign Minister Schroeder," May 13, 1966; "Letter from Grzimek to Nyerere about his conservation efforts on behalf of Tanzania," March 8, 1966, and Nyerere's hope that Grzimek's meeting with the Foreign Office might help in "clarifying some of the problems between our two countries," April 23, 1966, in FSA Zoo 197.
110. Grzimek, *Auf den Mensch gekommen*, 401–402.
111. Grzimek, *Auf den Mensch gekommen*, 415.
112. John Owen, "Draft Appeal for Funds by the Trustees of the Tanganyika National Parks," 9, in FSA Zoo 193.
113. Tanganyika National Parks, *Reports and Accounts of the Board of Trustees*, 5–6.
114. Ministry of Lands, Forests, and Wildlife, "Game Policy in Tanganyika," February 28, 1963 in FSA Zoo 194.
115. Tanganyika National Parks, *Reports and Accounts of the Board of Trustees*, 6.
116. See John Owen, "Draft Appeal by the Trustees," 2, in FSA Zoo 193.
117. Owen, "Draft Appeal by the Trustees," 2.
118. John Owen, "A Letter Sent to a Few Friends with Influence in the United Kingdom," August 23, 1968, in FSA Zoo 197.
119. Hayes, *Last Place on Earth*, 67.
120. John Owen, "An Appeal to the British Government for the Continuation of H.M.G's Support of the British Officers of the Tanzania National Parks," June 26, 1968, in FSA Zoo 197.
121. Tanganyika National Parks, *Reports and Accounts of the Board of Trustees*, 4.
122. Garland, "State of Nature," 158. In 1971, Owens stepped aside in favor of Ole Saibull and, a year later, David Babu replaced John Stephenson as Chief Warden.
123. Watterson et al. *Conservation of Nature and Natural Resources*, 22–23.
124. D. O. Matthews, "The Value of the Tourist Industry," in *Conservation of Nature and Natural Resources*, ed. Watterson et al., 238–241.
125. Matthews, "The Value of the Tourist Industry," 239.
126. Huxley, "Wildlife as a Resource," 40.
127. Watterson et al., *Conservation of Nature and Natural Resources*, 58.
128. Tanganyika National Parks, *Reports and Accounts of the Board of Trustees*, 6.
129. Garland, "State of Nature," 150–158.
130. Tanganyika National Parks, *Reports and Accounts of the Board of Trustees*, 35.
131. Tanganyika National Parks, *Reports and Accounts of the Board of Trustees*, 8–16. "Letter from Owen to Grzimek," October 31, 1964 in FSA Zoo 194.
132. Tanganyika National Parks, *Reports and Accounts of the Board of Trustees*, 13.
133. See "Road Plans in Three Parks," *Tanganyika Standard*, March 10, 1961; J. M. Hunter "Development Plan for the Ngurdoto Crater National Park," February 25, 1963 in FSA Zoo 194.
134. "Letter from Owen to Grzimek on Ngurdoto plan," March 25, 1963, in FSA Zoo 194.
135. On the relinquishment of mortgage claims, see "Letter from Lithgow to Grzimek," April 5, 1961, and from "Grzimek to Fürst zu Wied," January 17, 1962, in FSA Zoo 193. On the final acquisition of the lands, see "Letter from Owen to Grzimek," January 18, 1962, in FSA Zoo 193.
136. "Letter from Grzimek and Georg von Opel, Chairman of the FZS, concerning Development Plan for the Ngurdoto Crater National Park," February 25, 1963, in PAAA Michael Grzimek Lab.
137. Hayes, *Last Place on Earth*, 50; Sultan Jessa, "Crater Park for Mount Meru," *East African Standard*, May 24, 1967.
138. Tanganyika National Parks, *Reports and Accounts of the Board of Trustees*, 13; Joseph Ouma, *Evolution of Tourism in East Africa (1900–2000)* (Nairobi: East African Literature Bureau, 1970), 87.
139. Tanganyika National Parks, *Reports and Accounts of the Board of Trustees*, 8.

140. Ouma, *Evolution of Tourism in East Africa*, 87.
141. Hayes, *Last Place on Earth*, 63.
142. Tanganyika National Parks, *Reports and Accounts of the Board of Trustees*, 29–38.
143. Turner, *My Serengeti Years*, 180.
144. Hayes, *Last Place on Earth*, 121; Garland, "State of Nature," 148.
145. Turner, *My Serengeti Years*, 79–107.
146. Tanganyika National Parks, *Reports and Accounts of the Board of Trustees*, 33.
147. Hayes, *Last Place on Earth*, 51.
148. Grzimek, *Auf den Mensch gekommen*, 412.
149. Garland, "State of Nature," 148.
150. Tanganyika National Parks, *Reports and Accounts of the Board of Trustees*, 13.
151. Tanganyika National Parks, *Reports and Accounts of the Board of Trustees*, 13. On fines and fees see also Hansard, National Parks Ordinance (Amendment) Bill, 1962, 24–26.
152. Tanganyika National Parks, *Reports and Accounts of the Board of Trustees*, 14.
153. "Cable from Owen to Grzimek," June 4, 1963, in FSA Zoo 194.
154. "Letter from John Owen to Fairfield Osborn," June 3, 1963, 3 in FSA Zoo 194.
155. John Owen, "Who Cares for Africa's Game," *Daily Telegraph*, October 27, 1963.
156. Owen, "Who Cares for Africa's Game"; on the colonial record, see Hayes, *Last Place on Earth*, 100.
157. Owen, "Es steht uns Europäern schlecht an," 1. On West German nostalgia for the colonial past in the 1960s, see also Grzimek, *Auf den Mensch gekommen*, 400–401 and Eckard Michels, "Geschichtspolitik im Fernsehen: Die WDR-Dokumentation *Heia Safari* von 1966/67 über Deutschlands Kolonialvergangenheit," *Vierteljahresheft für Zeitgeschichte* 56, no. 3 (2008): 467–494.
158. Owen, "A Letter Sent to a Few Friends with Influence in the United Kingdom," 2.
159. Owen, "An Appeal to the British Government for the Continuation of H.M.G.'s Support," 2.
160. Owen, "Tanzanian National Parks," November 1966 in FSA Zoo 197.
161. Owen, "Draft Appeal by the Trustees," 9.
162. "Letter from Grzimek to Nyerere," May 27, 1968 in Zoo 32.
163. Owen, "Draft Appeal by the Trustees," 9.
164. Tanganyika National Parks, *Reports and Accounts of the Board of Trustees*, 6–7.
165. See Bernhard Gissibl, *Nature of German Imperialism: Conservation and the Politics of Wildlife in Colonial East Africa* (New York: Berghahn, 2016), 191–193. See also "Letter from D.O. Matthews, General Manager of the EATTA to Grzimek," May 15, 1962, disputing Grzimek's presentation of Tanganyika as a "shining example" in FSA Zoo 194.
166. Clark, *Socialist Development and Public Investment in Tanzania*, 30–33.
167. See also "Kenya Plans for Influx of Middle-Class Tourists," *Tanganyika Standard*, October 8, 1958, and "Kenya Can Have a Great Tourist Future," *Tanganyika Standard*, January 21, 1963.
168. Job and Metzler, "Tourismusentwicklung und Tourismuspolitik in Ostafrika," 10.
169. Grzimek, "The Value of the Tourist Industry," 191.
170. "Tourist Association Urged to Pep Up Their Work," *Tanganyika Standard*, February 4, 1963.
171. See "Minister of Information, Broadcast and Tourism," *Kenia Safari* (1967) and EATTA, "Paradies für wilde Tiere," 1963, in the brochure collection of the Historisches Archiv zum Tourismus (HAT). See also Nina Berman, *Germans on the Kenyan Coast: Land, Charity, and Romance* (Bloomington: Indiana University Press, 2017), 38–67.
172. Ouma, *Evolution of Tourism in East Africa*, 10, 22–31.
173. Grzimek, "Letter to the Editor of the *East African Standard*," April 15, 1969, in Zoo 198.
174. Ouma, *Evolution of Tourism in East Africa*, 16.
175. United Nations Visiting Mission to Trust Territories, 1960, *Report on Tanganyika*, Supplement no. 2 (New York: Trusteeship Council, 1960), 23–24.
176. "Pangani Could be a Holiday Playground," *Tanganyika Standard*, October 23, 1958.
177. "Dar is Losing Tourists to the Kenyan Coast," *Tanganyika Standard*, April 9, 1960.
178. Grzimek, "The Value of the Tourist Industry," 191.
179. Hayes, *Last Place on Earth*, 63.
180. Job and Metzler, "Tourismusentwicklung und Tourismuspolitik in Ostafrika," 13; Sinclair, *Serengeti Story*, 97.

181. Grzimek, "The Value of the Tourist Industry," 192.

182. "Letter from Grzimek to Tom Lithgow, 'Shangri-La Estate,' " April 12, 1961, in FSA Zoo 193.

183. "Letter from D.O. Matthews to Grzimek," May 15, 1962, 2.

184. Nyerere, "Socialism and Rural Development," 122–123.

185. Clark, *Socialist Development and Public Investment in Tanzania*, 106–107; Weiskopf, "Socialism on Safari," 443–444.

186. Job and Metzler, "Tourismusentwicklung und Tourismuspolitik in Ostafrika," 15.

187. Vojislav Popović, *Tourism in Eastern Africa* (Munich: Weltforum Verlag, 1972), 169; Frank Mitchell, "The Value of Tourism in East Africa." University College, Nairobi. Discussion paper no. 82 (July 1969) in HFC.

188. Popović, *Tourism in Eastern Africa*, 151–152.

189. Grzimek, *Auf den Mensch gekommen*, 447–448; Benedicto Kazuzuru, "History, Performance, and Challenges of the Tourism Industry in Tanzania," *International Journal of Business and Social Science* 5, no. 11 (October 2014): 123.

190. Grzimek, *Auf den Mensch gekommen*, 403–404; Sewig, *Der Mann, der die Tiere liebte*, 316–318.

191. Bernhard Grzimek, *Grzimek unter Afrikas Tieren: Erlebnisse, Beobachtungen, Forschungsergebnisse* (Berlin: Ullstein, 1975), 11–38.

192. Nyerere, "Socialism and Rural Development," 122–123.

193. Letter from D.N.M. Mkloma in Ministry of Information and Tourism to John Owen, "Poaching in the National Parks," January 9, 1970, in FSA Zoo 198 and Fosbrooke, "The Serengeti Ecosystem," 14–17.

194. Popović, *Tourism in Eastern Africa*, 18.

195. Popović, *Tourism in Eastern Africa*, 151–152; Job and Metzler, "Tourismusentwicklung und Tourismuspolitik in Ostafrika," 13.

196. "Letter from Grzimek to Norbert Hebich, Ambassador to Tanzania," April 14, 1970, in FSA 198.

197. Willy Brandt, "Deutsche Afrikapolitik," in *Afrika Heute*, June 15, 1968, 161–163.

198. Volker Sengbusch, "Afrikanische Länder als Ziele des internationalen Tourismus," *Afrika Heute*, May 15, 1967, 149.

199. "Letter from Grzimek to Hebich" April 14, 1970.

200. Popović, *Tourism in Eastern Africa*, 155; Job and Metzler, "Tourismusentwicklung und Tourismuspolitik in Ostafrika," 11–12.

201. Haug von Künheim, "In den Klauen Afrikas: Baden im Indischen Ozean und Jagd auf Elefantenhaar," *Die Zeit*, nr. 46, November 17, 1972.

202. Ermano Höpner, "Ein Hauch von Wildniss," *Modernes Reisen*, nr. 19, May 9, 1971, 41.

203. Von V. Kipke, "An 600 Meilen Strand 800 Betten: Studienreise nach Ostafrika," *Touristik Aktuell* 2, no. 7 (February 15, 1972): 8.

204. Höpner, "Ein Hauch von Wildniss."

205. Künheim, "In den Klauen Afrikas."

206. Clark, *Socialist Development and Public Investment in Tanzania*, 146.

207. Clark, *Socialist Development and Public Investment in Tanzania*, 145–149.

208. Clark, *Socialist Development and Public Investment in Tanzania*, 146–147.

209. Heinz Bischoff, "Ostafrika—mit und ohne Safari," *Die Welt*, February 6, 1967. On the popularity of Kenya as a West German tourism destination, see also Memorandum from West German Embassy to AA "Kenia als deutsche Ferienkolonie," September 22, 1966, in PAAA B57 494.

210. Popović, *Tourism in Eastern Africa*, 152–160.

211. See West German Embassy in Dar es Salaam, "Tourismus-Förderung in Tansania," October 26, 1966, in PAAA B57 494.

212. Hebich, "Tourismus in Tansania: Gesetzgebung über Fremdenverkehr," February 13, 1969, in PAAA B57 494.

213. Memorandum of Embassy in Dar es Salaam, "Deutsche Kontake zu den drei ostafrikanischen Staaten im Bereich Fremdenverkehr," July 21, 1969, in PAAA B57 494.

214. West German Embassy, "Tourismus-Förderung in Tansania," October 26, 1966, 2–3.

215. Hayes, *Last Place on Earth*, 86.

216. Hayes, *Last Place on Earth*, 275.
217. "Letter from Grzimek to Nyerere," May 27, 1968, 2, in FSA Zoo 32.
218. Grzimek, *Auf den Mensch gekommen*, 429–432.
219. "Letter from Grzimek to Nyerere," May 27, 1968, 2–3.
220. Hayes, *Last Place on Earth*, 121.
221. "Tanzania 'Yes' to Plan for a Rival Treetops," *Zambia News*, November 12, 1968.
222. Letter from Grzimek to Nyerere, May 27, 1968, 1.
223. "Letter from Joan E. Wicken to Grzimek," June 8, 1968.
224. Sewig, *Der Mann, der die Tiere liebte*, 283, 334–335; "Letter from Hebich to Grzimek," June 28, 1968, in FSA 197.
225. "Letter from Hebich to Grzimek," June 28, 1968.
226. Hayes, *Last Place on Earth*, 86–89; Sewig, *Der Mann, der die Tiere liebte*, 343–344; Michael Parry, "Why Ngorongoro Wildlife is in Danger," *East African Standard*, September 5, 1969; "Serikali Yazipuuza Lawama: Ngorongoro sio jumba la makumbusho," *Uhuru*, May 28, 1968.
227. Rogers, "History and Governance in the Ngorongoro," 103–109.
228. Hodgson, *Once Intrepid Warriors*, 158–162, 202–219.
229. "Grzimek Hits at Ngorongoro Crater Plan," September 6, 1969.
230. "Masai Burning Land around Ngorongoro," *East African Standard*, September 2, 1969
231. Hayes, *Last Place on Earth*, 87.
232. "Bryceson Hits at Plan Critics," *East African Standard*, September 1, 1969.
233. Cited in Sewig, *Der Mann, der die Tiere liebte*, 344.
234. Hayes, *Last Place on Earth*, 202–204.
235. Turner, *My Serengeti Years*, 51–52.
236. Grzimek, *Visions of Paradise*, 100; Hayes, *Last Place on Earth*, 209–211.
237. Turner, *My Serengeti Years*, 52–53.
238. See "Letter from Fritz Vollmar, Director-General of the WWF, to Bernhard Grzimek," April 27, 1972, in FSA Zoo 198; "Serengeti Land for Grazing," *Daily Nation*, March 16, 1972; "Muss Serengeti nun doch sterben? Afrikanische Farmer roden im Norden des Tierreservats das Land," *Mindener Tageblatt*, March 16, 1972.
239. "Letter from Michaela Denis to Grzimek," March 7, 1972, in FSA Zoo 198.
240. Letter from Grzimek to Prince Bernhard et al., "Situation in Tanzania National Parks," FSA Zoo 198.
241. Letter from Prince Bernhard to Nyerere, "Reported 'Hand Over' of Part of the SNP to Settlers," March 15, 1972, in FSA Zoo 198.
242. "Letter from Nyerere to Prince Bernhard," April 14, 1972, in Zoo 198.
243. "Letter from Prince Bernhard to Nyerere," May 2, 1972, in Zoo 198.
244. "Letter from Nyerere to Prince Bernhard," April 14, 1972.
245. "Letter from Nyerere to Prince Bernhard," May 29, 1972, in FSA Zoo 198.
246. See the handwritten note from Prince Bernhard to "Mr. President, 'My Dear Friend," June 4, 1972, in FSA Zoo 198.
247. "Letter from Owen to Grzimek," May 31, 1972, and "Letter from John J. Kambona, Ministry of Natural Resources and Tourism to Grzimek," September 5, 1972, in FSA Zoo 198.
248. Hayes, *Last Place on Earth*, 89–90.
249. Fosbrooke, "*The Serengeti Ecosystem*," 20.
250. Sinclair, *Serengeti Story*, 81.
251. Michael T. Kaufman, "Kenyan-Tanzania Frontier Remains Shut, and Some Say Nyerere Had Barricaded the Road to Socialism," *New York Times*, May 18, 1977.
252. Weiskopf, "Socialism on Safari," 430, 445–447.
253. Sinclair, *Serengeti Story*, 96–97.
254. Job and Metzler, "Tourismusentwicklung und Tourismuspolitik in Ostafrika," 15.
255. Shetler, *Imagining Serengeti*, 224; Gardner, *Selling the Serengeti*, 159–162.
256. Fosbrooke, "Serengeti and Ngorongoro Diamond Jubilee, 1921–1981: A Short History of Serengeti and Ngorongoro," 16 in HFC.
257. Cited in Hayes, *Last Place on Earth*, 226.
258. Brigitte Scherer, "Ein Rückfall in die Pionierzeit: Tansania und die Touristen: Wenn die Wildhüter erst keine Schuhe mehr haben," *Frankfurter Allgemeine Zeitung* 160, July 16, 1982.

259. "Letter from Grzimek to Mwalimu," May 18, 1972, in FSA Zoo 198.
260. Hayes, *Last Place on Earth*, 107.

Epilogue

1. On Parkipuny, Loliondo, and the long-term tensions over fortress conservation and neo-liberalism in the Serengeti, there is no better source than Benjamin Gardner, *Selling the Serengeti: The Cultural Politics of Safari Tourism* (Athens: University of Georgia Press, 2016).
2. Stephen Allen and Alexandra Xanthaki, eds., *Reflections on the UN Declaration on the Rights of Indigenous Peoples* (Oxford: Hart, 2011).
3. Frankfurt Zoological Society, "Statement on the Proposed Serengeti Commercial Road," June 15, 2010. https://fzs.org/en/news/press-releases/fzs-statement-proposed-serengeti-commercial-road/. Jeffrey Gettleman, "Serengeti Road Plan Offers Prospects and Fears," *New York Times*, October 30, 2010.
4. Bernhard Grzimek and Michael Grzimek, *Serengeti Shall Not Die*, trans. E. L. Rewald and D. Rewald (New York: E. P. Dutton, 1961), 13.
5. Gettleman, "Serengeti Road," October 30, 2010.
6. Bernhard Grzimek, Reinhold Messner, and Herbert Tichy, *Paradiese* (Munich: Saphir, 1978), 100.
7. Elizabeth Garland, "The Elephant in the Room: Confronting the Colonial Character of Wildlife Conservation in Africa," *African Studies Review* 51, no. 3 (December 17, 2008): 70.
8. Elizabeth Garland, "State of Nature: Colonial Power, Neoliberal Capital, and Wildlife Management in Tanzania" (PhD diss., University of Chicago, 2006), 222–272.
9. Roderick P. Neumann, *Imposing Wilderness: Struggles over Livelihood and Nature Preservation in Africa* (Berkeley: University of California Press, 1998), 97–122.
10. Julie M. Weiskopf, "Socialism on Safari: Wildlife and Nation-Building in Postcolonial Tanzania, 1966–77," *The Journal of African History* 56, no. 3 (2015): 431.
11. Sunseri, "'Every African a Nationalist': Scientific Forestry and Forest Nationalism in Colonial Tanzania," *Comparative Studies in Society and History* 49, No. 4 (October 2007): 884.
12. Tanganyika National Parks, *Reports and Accounts of the Board of Trustees for the Period 1st July, 1962 to 30th June 1964*, 33–34, in Henry A. Fosbrooke Collection (HFC), University of Dar es Salaam Library, East Africana collection.
13. Leander Schneider, "Colonial Legacies and Postcolonial Authoritarianism in Tanzania: Connects and Disconnects," *African Studies Review* 49, no. 1 (2006): 93–118; Paul Bjerk, *Building a Peaceful Nation: Julius Nyerere and the Establishment of Sovereignty in Tanzania, 1960–1964* (Rochester: University of Rochester Press, 2015), 28–57.
14. Harold T. P. Hayes, *Last Place on Earth* (New York: Stein and Day, 1977), 279–280.
15. Alex Renton, "'Tourism is a Curse to Us,'" *The Guardian*, September 5, 2009.

INDEX

For the benefit of digital users, indexed terms that span two pages (e.g., 52–53) may, on occasion, appear on only one of those pages.